THRIVING ON VAGUE OBJECTIVES

OBJECTIVES

DILBERT THRIVING ON VAGUE OBJECTIVES

A DILBERT BOOK
BY SCOTT ADAMS

Andrews McMeel
Publishing

Kansas City

05 06 07 08 09 BBG 10 9 8 7 6 5 4 3 2 1

ISBN-13: 978-0-7407-5533-0
ISBN-10: 0-7407-5533-1

Library of Congress Control Number: 2005929262

www.andrewsmcmeel.com

www.dilbert.com

ATTENTION: SCHOOLS AND BUSINESSES

Other DILBERT books from Andrews McMeel Publishing

The Fluorescent Light Glistens Off Your Head
ISBN: 0-7407-5113-1

It's Not Funny If I Have to Explain It
ISBN: 0-7407-4658-8

Don't Stand Where the Comet Is Assumed to Strike Oil
ISBN: 0-7407-4539-5

Words You Don't Want to Hear During Your Annual Performance Review
ISBN: 0-7407-3805-4

When Body Language Goes Bad
ISBN: 0-7407-3298-6

What Do You Call a Sociopath in a Cubicle? Answer: A Coworker
ISBN: 0-7407-2663-3

Another Day in Cubicle Paradise
ISBN: 0-7407-2194-1

When Did Ignorance Become a Point of View?
ISBN: 0-7407-1839-8

Excuse Me While I Wag
ISBN: 0-7407-1390-6

Dilbert—A Treasury of Sunday Strips: Version 00
ISBN: 0-7407-0531-8

Random Acts of Management
ISBN: 0-7407-0453-2

Dilbert Gives You the Business
ISBN: 0-7407-0338-2 hardcover
ISBN: 0-7407-0003-0 paperback

Don't Step in the Leadership
ISBN: 0-8362-7844-5

Journey to Cubeville
ISBN: 0-8362-7175-0 hardcover
ISBN: 0-8362-6745-1 paperback

I'm Not Anti-Business, I'm Anti-Idiot
ISBN: 0-8362-5182-2

Seven Years of Highly Defective People
ISBN: 0-8362-5129-6 hardcover
ISBN: 0-8362-3668-8 paperback

Casual Day Has Gone Too Far
ISBN: 0-8362-2899-5

Fugitive from the Cubicle Police
ISBN: 0-8362-2119-2

Still Pumped from Using the Mouse
ISBN: 0-8362-1026-3

It's Obvious You Won't Survive by Your Wits Alone
ISBN: 0-8362-0415-8

Bring Me the Head of Willy the Mailboy!
ISBN: 0-8362-1779-9

Shave the Whales
ISBN: 0-8362-1740-3

Dogbert's Clues for the Clueless
ISBN: 0-8362-1737-3

Build a Better Life by Stealing Office Supplies
ISBN: 0-8362-1757-8

Always Postpone Meetings with Time-Wasting Morons
ISBN: 0-8362-1758-6

For ordering information, call 1-800-223-2336.

Introduction

My publisher just informed me that I should finish writing the introduction to my book *Thriving on Vague Objectives*, "sooner." This guidance is based on the theory that sooner is better, and all things being equal, it's better to be better, especially if it's sooner.

My first impulse was to get literal and argue that everything is sooner than something else. Therefore, there's no real rush. But I can't do that because one of my other personality defects involves compulsive earliness. I don't mean that I'm merely punctual—generally considered a good trait. I mean I'm early to the point of being spectacularly annoying.

I'm the guy who shows up at your 7 p.m. party at 6:45 p.m., when the host and hostess are still unwashed and staring into their closets wishing they had shopped more. I've become quite the expert at making conversation with the appetizers until other humans arrive. It usually goes something like this:

> Me:
> "Hello, bean dip. The traffic wasn't bad. I guess I got here too early."
>
> Bean dip:
> (creepy silence)
>
> Me:
> "You look very brown. Have you been getting some sun?"
>
> Bean dip:
> (more creepy silence)
>
> Me:
> "Okay, be that way. Let's see how you like having this chip rammed into your torso.
> BUWHAHAHA!!! MMMPHPH! Gulp!"

That, in a nutshell, is everything you need to know about why I don't get invited to many parties.

So now I have this vague objective of writing the introduction "sooner." Ever since I received this logically unjustifiable objective ten minutes ago, I find it impossible to do anything else. I wish I could be tardy like normal people, but I just don't know how. I can't take a break until I am done. My bladder is the size of a small ottoman—damn you, delicious Diet Coke! — but I must finish this task before all the others that are not due "sooner." I worry that my body will get all backed up and poison my brain with urine. When you are semifamous like me, you hope that you won't die in a way that the newspapers find both humorous and easy to pun. Here's one to avoid: PEE-BRAINED CARTOONIST DIES!

I prefer to die from a pulmonary thrombosis, or anything else that makes a lousy headline. I don't even know what a pulmonary thrombosis is, but it sounds bad. Oh God, the urine poisoning has begun. I'm not making any sense. How many words have I written? Wait, I don't recall that my editor mentioned a specific word-count objective for the introduction. Ha ha! More vagueness! But this time it works in my favor! I am done!

Speaking of done, our civilization is obviously about to self-destruct. And when it does, Dogbert will be there to take his rightful position as supreme overlord. If you would like to rule by his side, sign up for the free *Dilbert Newsletter* and automatically become part of Dogbert's New Ruling Class. The newsletter comes out approximately whenever I feel like it (if not "sooner"), which is about four times a year. To sign up, go to www.dilbert.com and follow the subscription instructions. If that doesn't work for some reason, send e-mail to newsletter@unitedmedia.com.

S.Adams

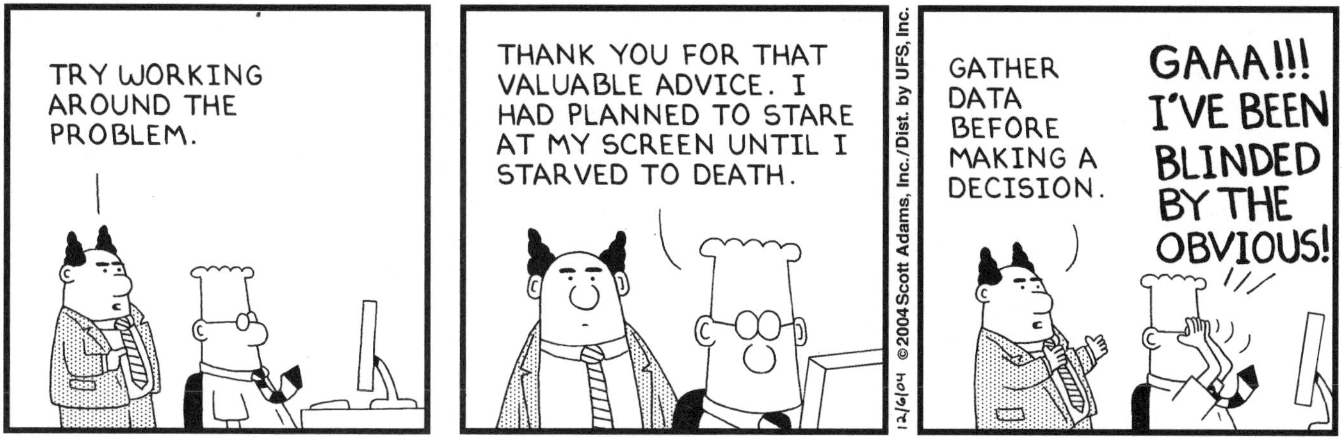
TRY WORKING AROUND THE PROBLEM.
THANK YOU FOR THAT VALUABLE ADVICE. I HAD PLANNED TO STARE AT MY SCREEN UNTIL I STARVED TO DEATH.
12/6/04 © 2004 Scott Adams, Inc./Dist. by UFS, Inc.
GATHER DATA BEFORE MAKING A DECISION.
GAAA!!! I'VE BEEN BLINDED BY THE OBVIOUS!

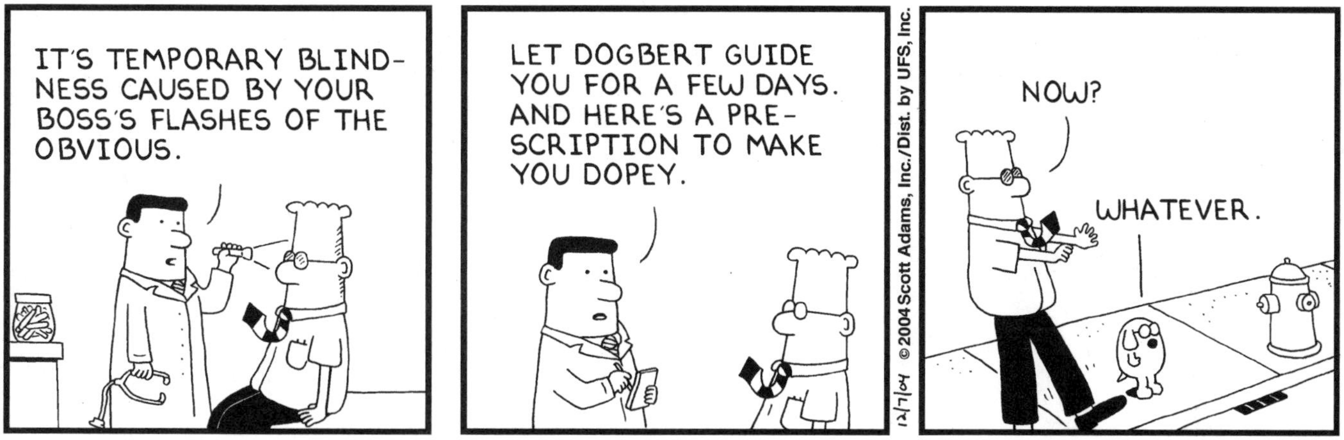
IT'S TEMPORARY BLIND-NESS CAUSED BY YOUR BOSS'S FLASHES OF THE OBVIOUS.
LET DOGBERT GUIDE YOU FOR A FEW DAYS. AND HERE'S A PRE-SCRIPTION TO MAKE YOU DOPEY.
12/7/04 © 2004 Scott Adams, Inc./Dist. by UFS, Inc.
NOW?
WHATEVER.

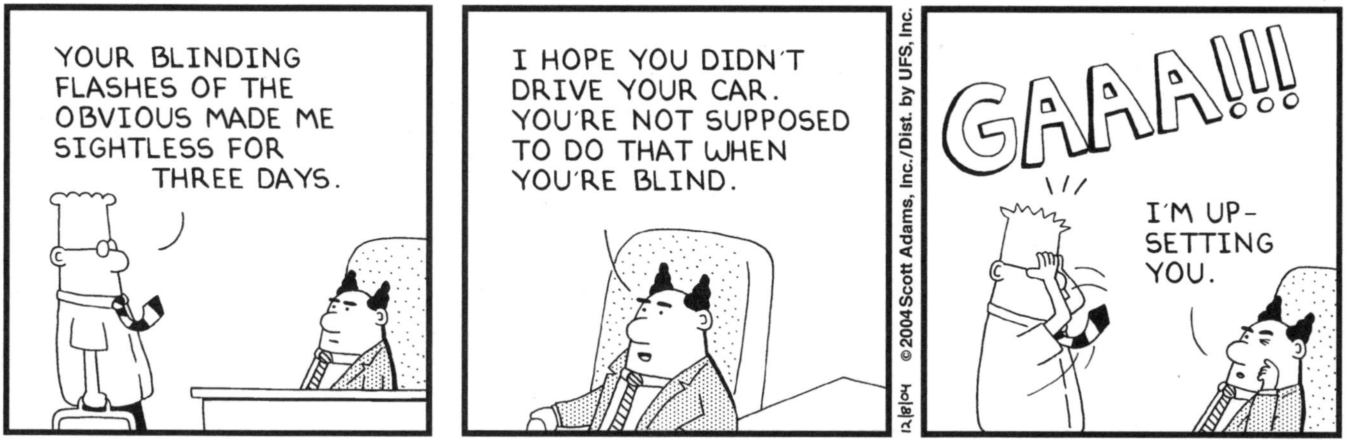
YOUR BLINDING FLASHES OF THE OBVIOUS MADE ME SIGHTLESS FOR THREE DAYS.
I HOPE YOU DIDN'T DRIVE YOUR CAR. YOU'RE NOT SUPPOSED TO DO THAT WHEN YOU'RE BLIND.
12/8/04 © 2004 Scott Adams, Inc./Dist. by UFS, Inc.
GAAA!!!
I'M UP-SETTING YOU.

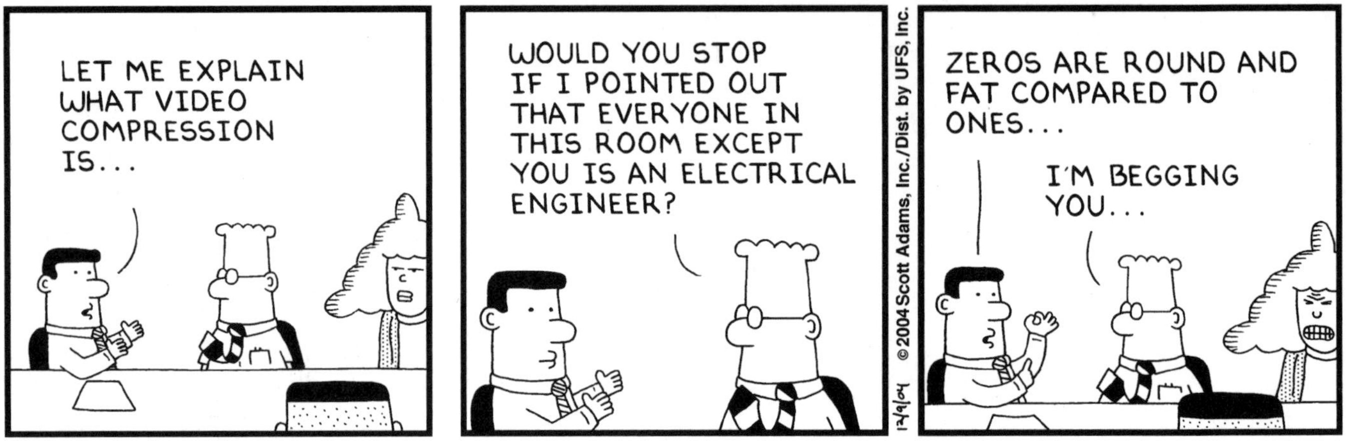
LET ME EXPLAIN WHAT VIDEO COMPRESSION IS...
WOULD YOU STOP IF I POINTED OUT THAT EVERYONE IN THIS ROOM EXCEPT YOU IS AN ELECTRICAL ENGINEER?
12/9/04 ©2004 Scott Adams, Inc./Dist. by UFS, Inc.
ZEROS ARE ROUND AND FAT COMPARED TO ONES...
I'M BEGGING YOU...

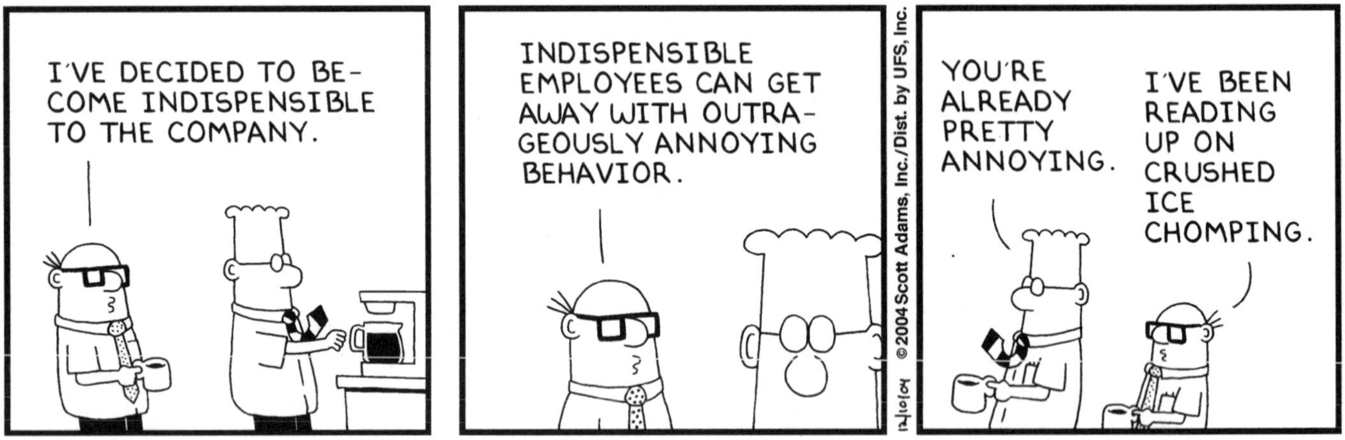
I'VE DECIDED TO BE-COME INDISPENSIBLE TO THE COMPANY.
INDISPENSIBLE EMPLOYEES CAN GET AWAY WITH OUTRA-GEOUSLY ANNOYING BEHAVIOR.
12/10/04 ©2004 Scott Adams, Inc./Dist. by UFS, Inc.
YOU'RE ALREADY PRETTY ANNOYING.
I'VE BEEN READING UP ON CRUSHED ICE CHOMPING.

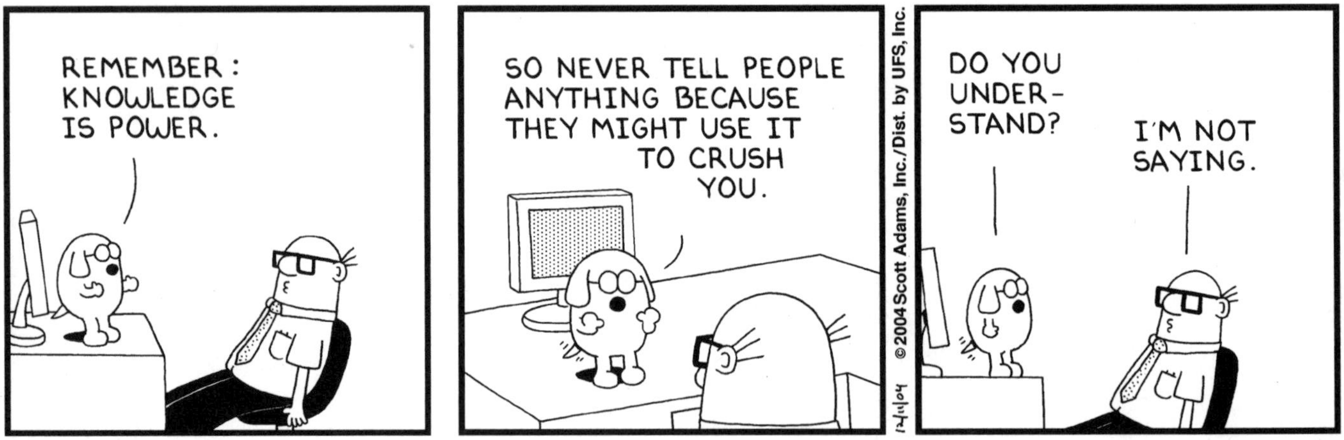
REMEMBER: KNOWLEDGE IS POWER.
SO NEVER TELL PEOPLE ANYTHING BECAUSE THEY MIGHT USE IT TO CRUSH YOU.
12/11/04 ©2004 Scott Adams, Inc./Dist. by UFS, Inc.
DO YOU UNDER-STAND?
I'M NOT SAYING.

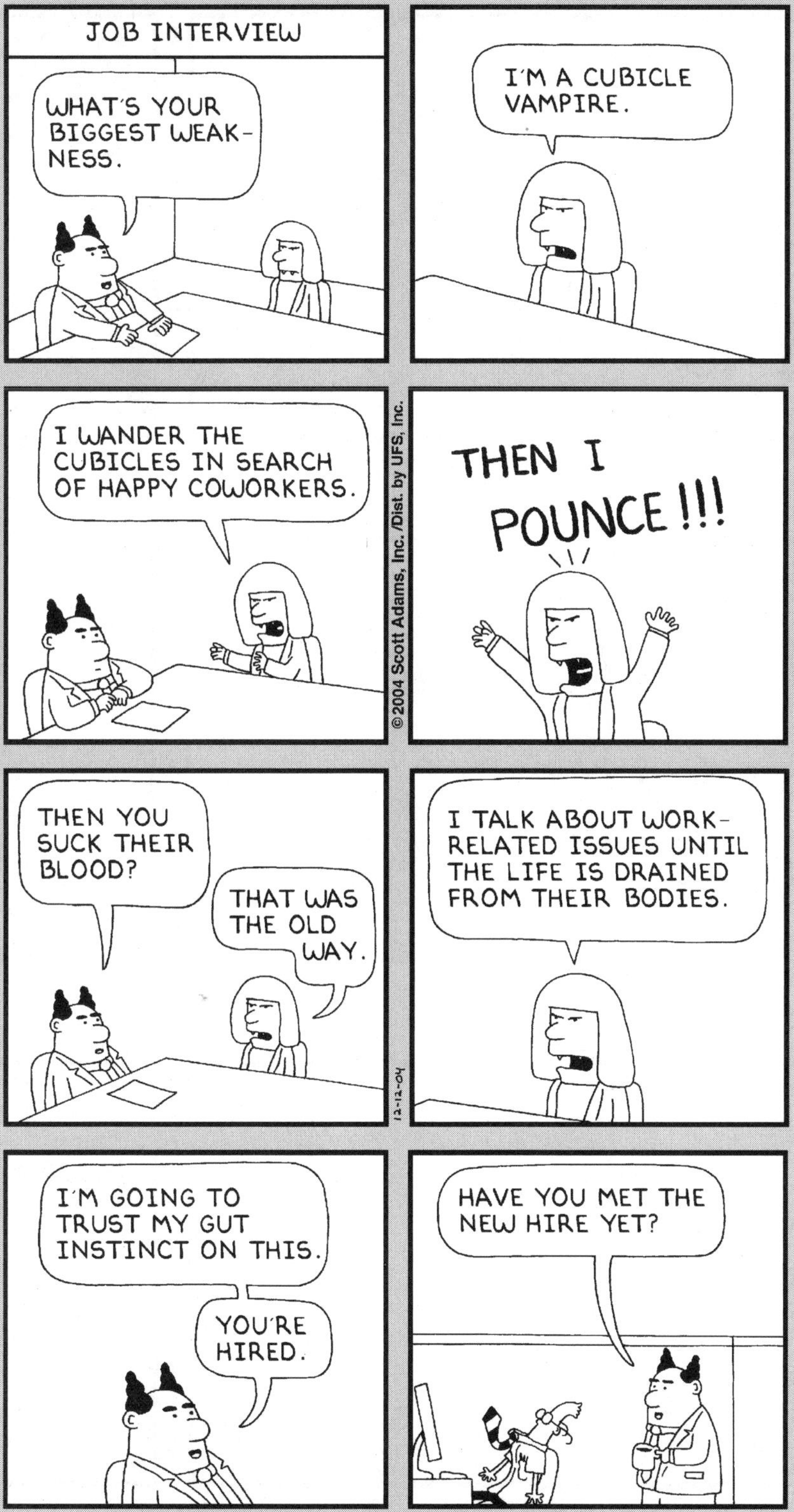
JOB INTERVIEW
WHAT'S YOUR BIGGEST WEAK-NESS.
I'M A CUBICLE VAMPIRE.
I WANDER THE CUBICLES IN SEARCH OF HAPPY COWORKERS.
© 2004 Scott Adams, Inc./Dist. by UFS, Inc.
THEN I POUNCE!!!
THEN YOU SUCK THEIR BLOOD?
THAT WAS THE OLD WAY.
12-12-04
I TALK ABOUT WORK-RELATED ISSUES UNTIL THE LIFE IS DRAINED FROM THEIR BODIES.
I'M GOING TO TRUST MY GUT INSTINCT ON THIS.
YOU'RE HIRED.
HAVE YOU MET THE NEW HIRE YET?

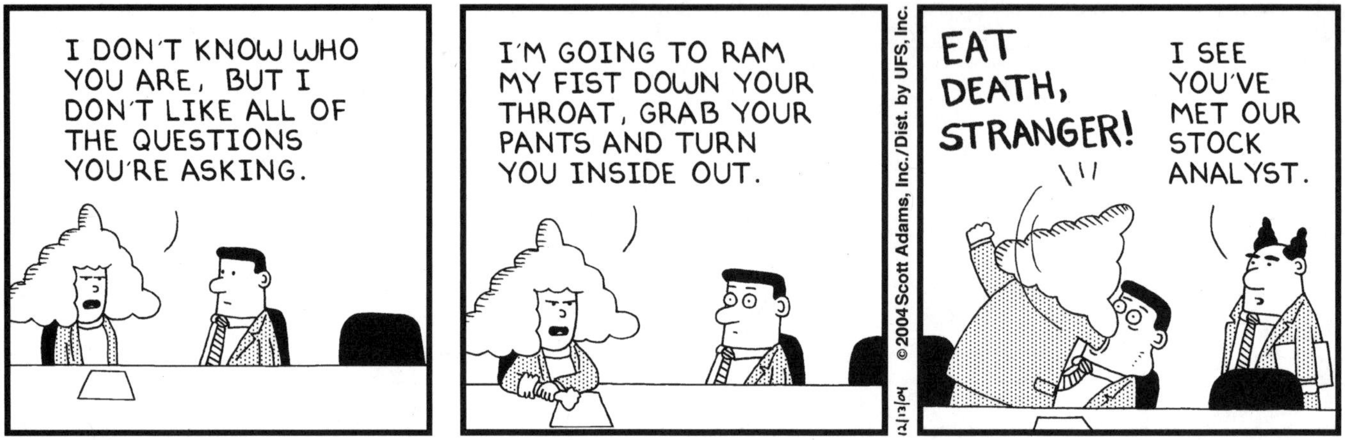
I DON'T KNOW WHO YOU ARE, BUT I DON'T LIKE ALL OF THE QUESTIONS YOU'RE ASKING.
I'M GOING TO RAM MY FIST DOWN YOUR THROAT, GRAB YOUR PANTS AND TURN YOU INSIDE OUT.
12/13/04 © 2004 Scott Adams, Inc./Dist. by UFS, Inc.
EAT DEATH, STRANGER!
I SEE YOU'VE MET OUR STOCK ANALYST.

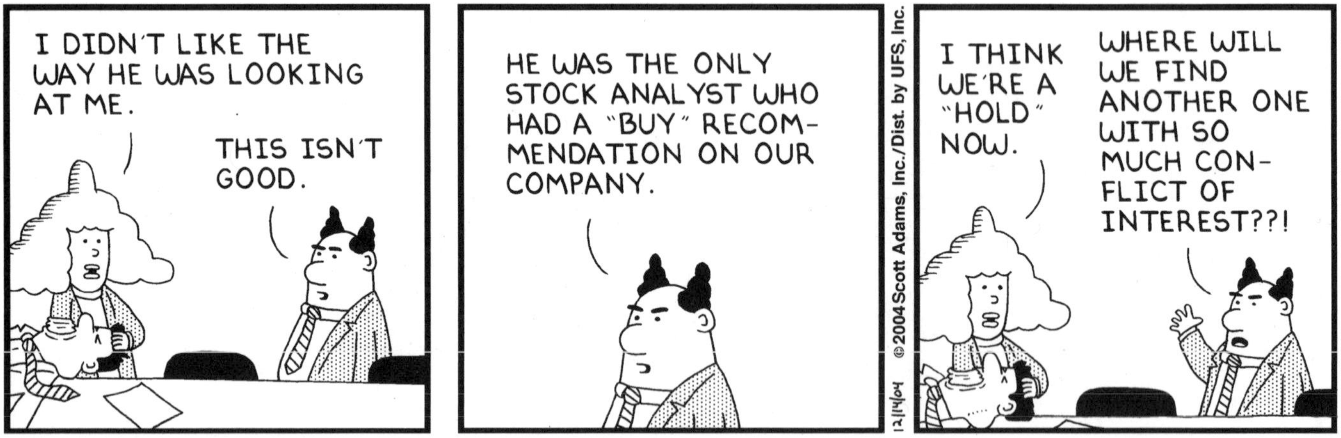
I DIDN'T LIKE THE WAY HE WAS LOOKING AT ME.
THIS ISN'T GOOD.
HE WAS THE ONLY STOCK ANALYST WHO HAD A "BUY" RECOMMENDATION ON OUR COMPANY.
12/14/04 © 2004 Scott Adams, Inc./Dist. by UFS, Inc.
I THINK WE'RE A "HOLD" NOW.
WHERE WILL WE FIND ANOTHER ONE WITH SO MUCH CONFLICT OF INTEREST??!

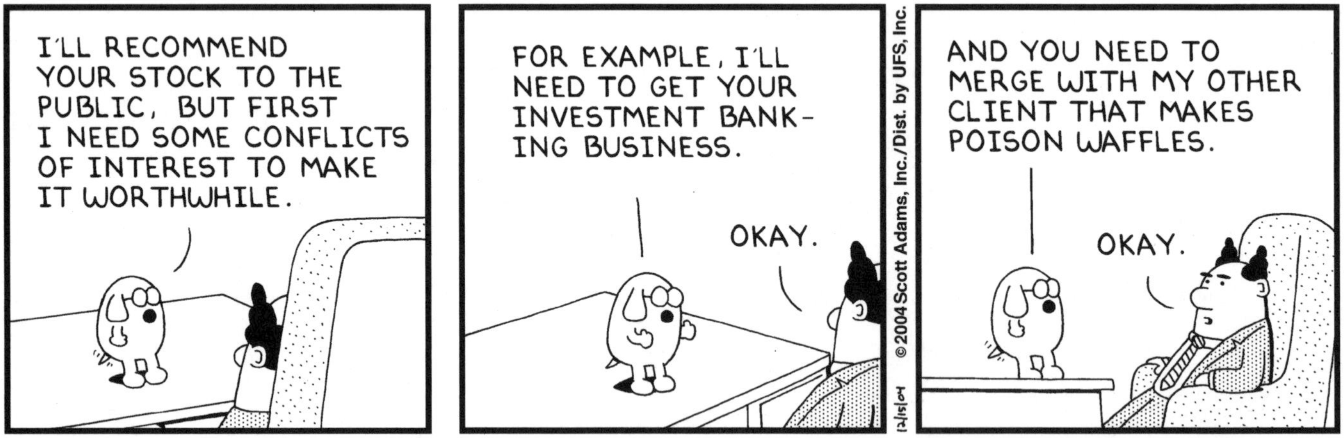
I'LL RECOMMEND YOUR STOCK TO THE PUBLIC, BUT FIRST I NEED SOME CONFLICTS OF INTEREST TO MAKE IT WORTHWHILE.
FOR EXAMPLE, I'LL NEED TO GET YOUR INVESTMENT BANKING BUSINESS.
OKAY.
12/15/04 © 2004 Scott Adams, Inc./Dist. by UFS, Inc.
AND YOU NEED TO MERGE WITH MY OTHER CLIENT THAT MAKES POISON WAFFLES.
OKAY.

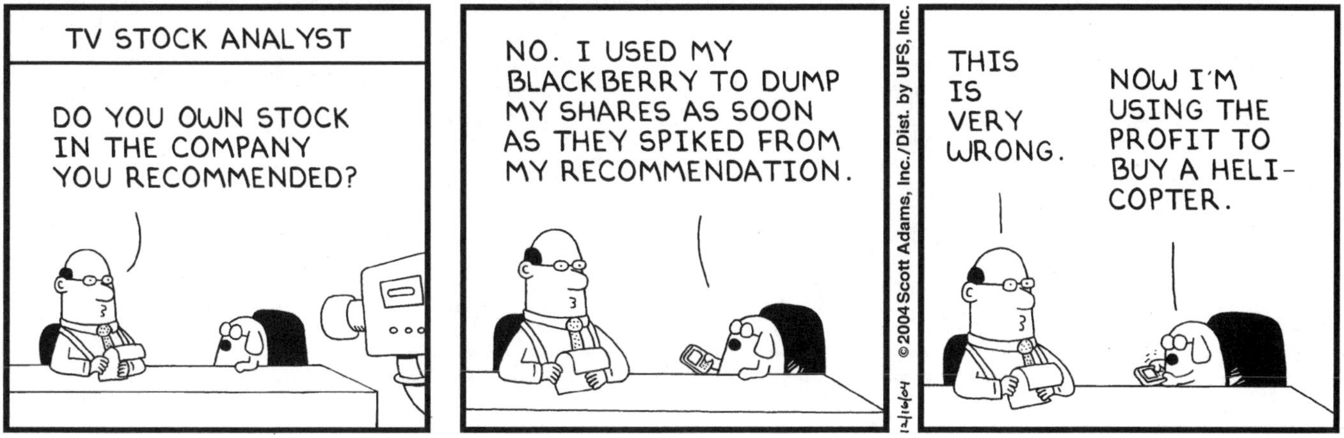
TV STOCK ANALYST
DO YOU OWN STOCK IN THE COMPANY YOU RECOMMENDED?
NO. I USED MY BLACKBERRY TO DUMP MY SHARES AS SOON AS THEY SPIKED FROM MY RECOMMENDATION.
© 2004 Scott Adams, Inc./Dist. by UFS, Inc.
THIS IS VERY WRONG.
NOW I'M USING THE PROFIT TO BUY A HELI-COPTER.

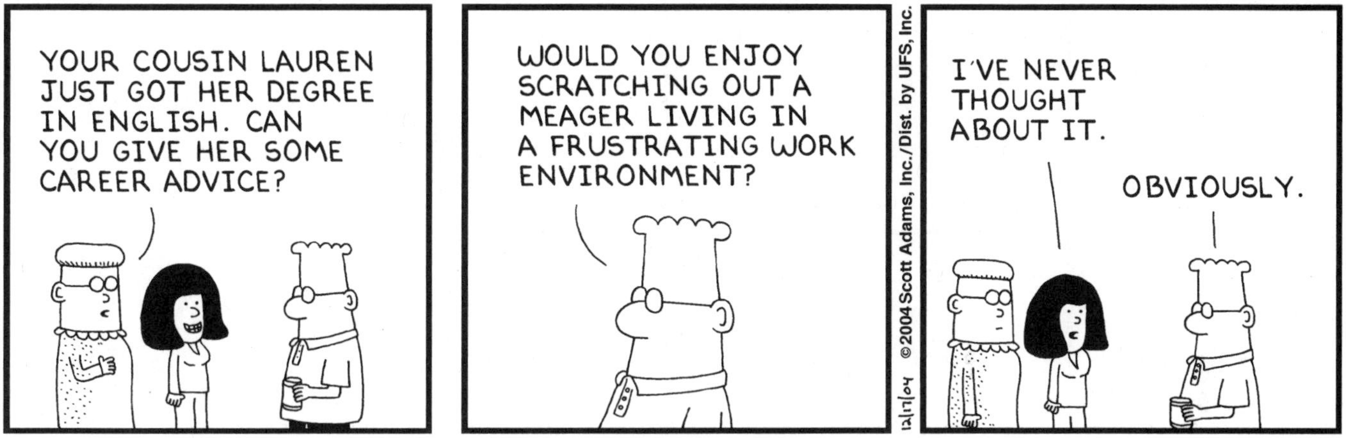
YOUR COUSIN LAUREN JUST GOT HER DEGREE IN ENGLISH. CAN YOU GIVE HER SOME CAREER ADVICE?
WOULD YOU ENJOY SCRATCHING OUT A MEAGER LIVING IN A FRUSTRATING WORK ENVIRONMENT?
© 2004 Scott Adams, Inc./Dist. by UFS, Inc.
I'VE NEVER THOUGHT ABOUT IT.
OBVIOUSLY.

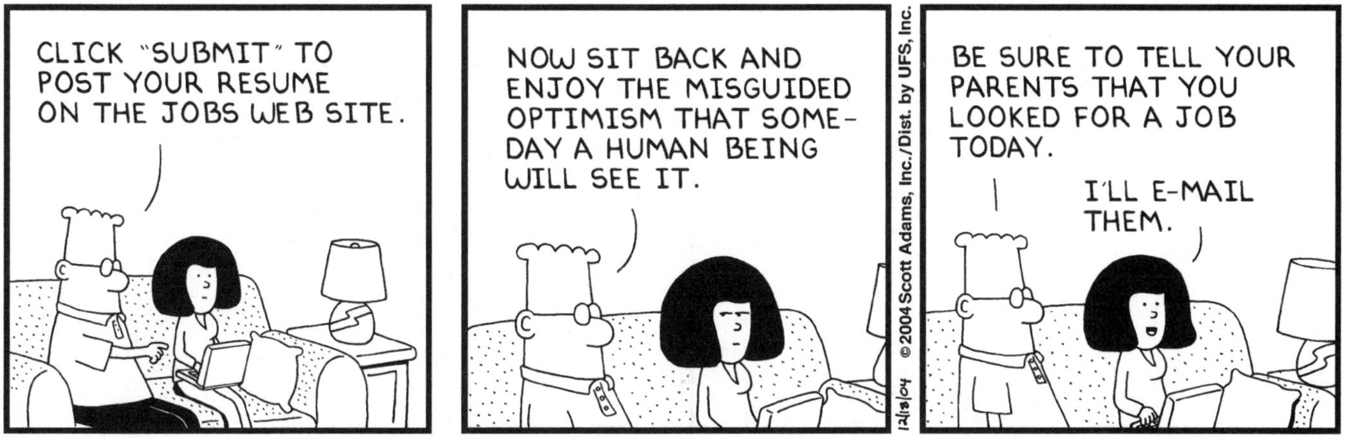
CLICK "SUBMIT" TO POST YOUR RESUME ON THE JOBS WEB SITE.
NOW SIT BACK AND ENJOY THE MISGUIDED OPTIMISM THAT SOME-DAY A HUMAN BEING WILL SEE IT.
© 2004 Scott Adams, Inc./Dist. by UFS, Inc.
BE SURE TO TELL YOUR PARENTS THAT YOU LOOKED FOR A JOB TODAY.
I'LL E-MAIL THEM.

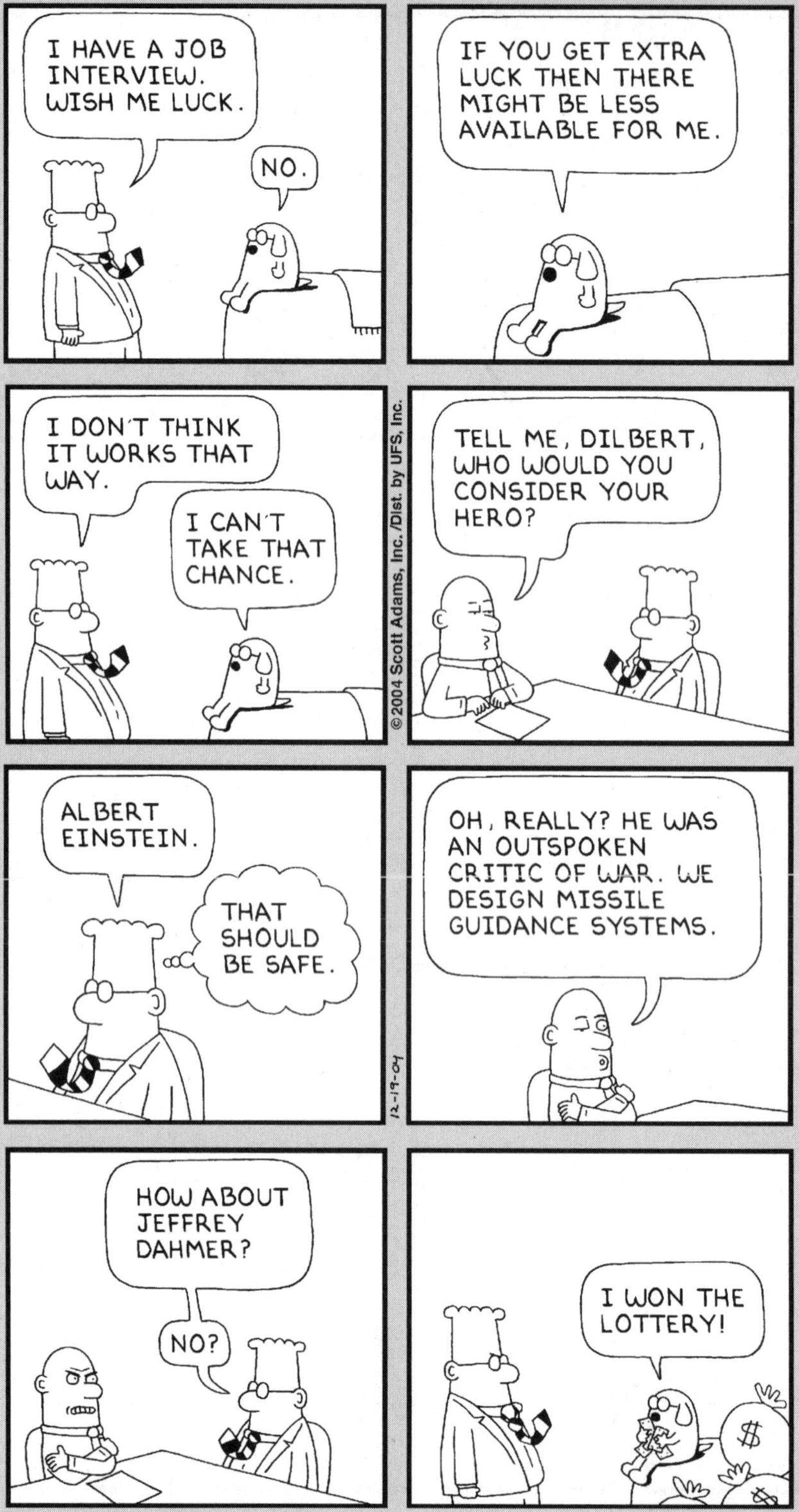
I HAVE A JOB INTERVIEW. WISH ME LUCK.
NO.
IF YOU GET EXTRA LUCK THEN THERE MIGHT BE LESS AVAILABLE FOR ME.
I DON'T THINK IT WORKS THAT WAY.
I CAN'T TAKE THAT CHANCE.
©2004 Scott Adams, Inc. /Dist. by UFS, Inc.
TELL ME, DILBERT, WHO WOULD YOU CONSIDER YOUR HERO?
ALBERT EINSTEIN.
THAT SHOULD BE SAFE.
OH, REALLY? HE WAS AN OUTSPOKEN CRITIC OF WAR. WE DESIGN MISSILE GUIDANCE SYSTEMS.
12-19-04
HOW ABOUT JEFFREY DAHMER?
NO?
I WON THE LOTTERY!

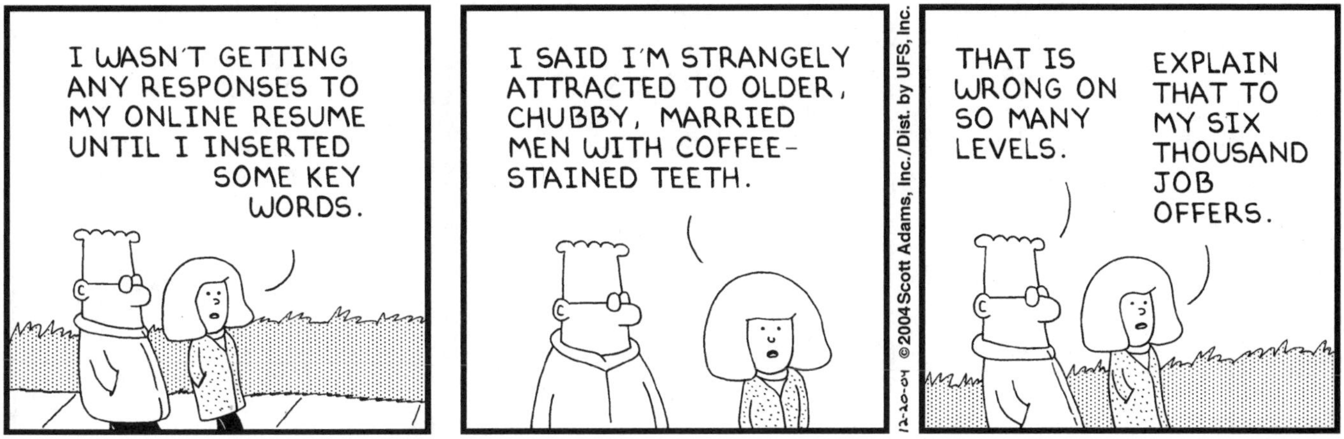
I WASN'T GETTING ANY RESPONSES TO MY ONLINE RESUME UNTIL I INSERTED SOME KEY WORDS.
I SAID I'M STRANGELY ATTRACTED TO OLDER, CHUBBY, MARRIED MEN WITH COFFEE-STAINED TEETH.
12-20-04 © 2004 Scott Adams, Inc./Dist. by UFS, Inc.
THAT IS WRONG ON SO MANY LEVELS.
EXPLAIN THAT TO MY SIX THOUSAND JOB OFFERS.

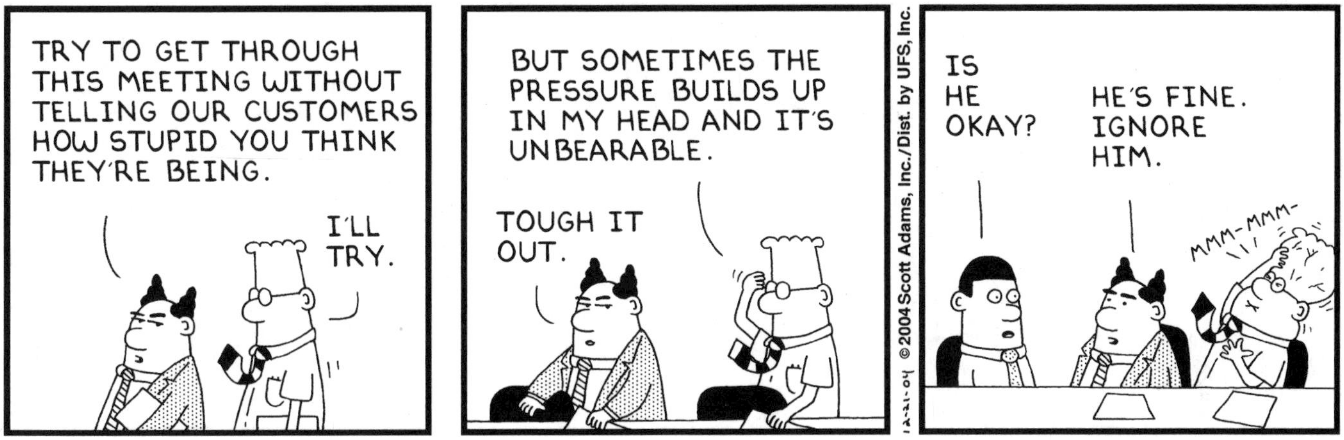
TRY TO GET THROUGH THIS MEETING WITHOUT TELLING OUR CUSTOMERS HOW STUPID YOU THINK THEY'RE BEING.
I'LL TRY.
BUT SOMETIMES THE PRESSURE BUILDS UP IN MY HEAD AND IT'S UNBEARABLE.
TOUGH IT OUT.
12-21-04 © 2004 Scott Adams, Inc./Dist. by UFS, Inc.
IS HE OKAY?
HE'S FINE. IGNORE HIM.
MMM-MMM-

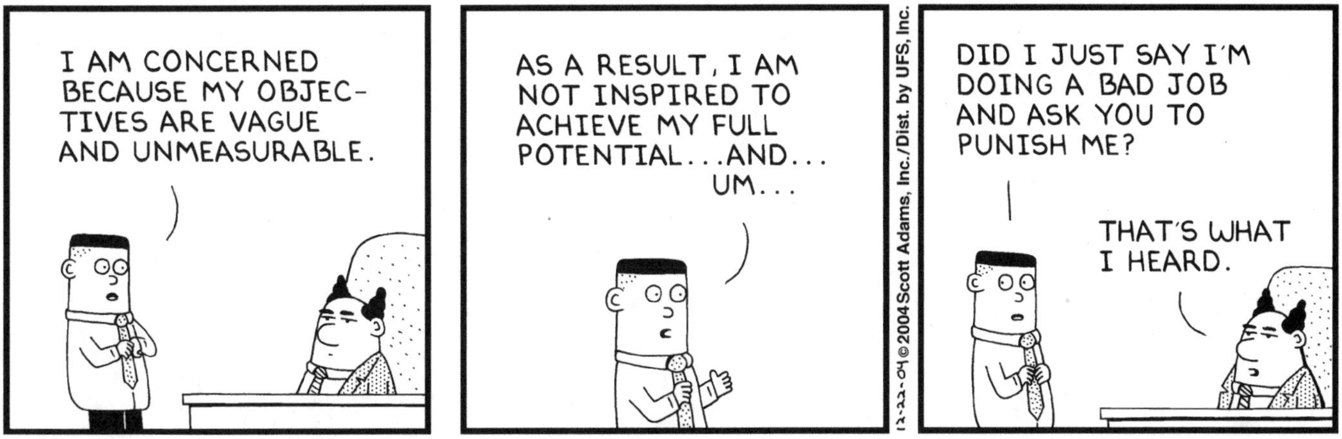
I AM CONCERNED BECAUSE MY OBJEC-TIVES ARE VAGUE AND UNMEASURABLE.
AS A RESULT, I AM NOT INSPIRED TO ACHIEVE MY FULL POTENTIAL...AND... UM...
12-22-04 © 2004 Scott Adams, Inc./Dist. by UFS, Inc.
DID I JUST SAY I'M DOING A BAD JOB AND ASK YOU TO PUNISH ME?
THAT'S WHAT I HEARD.

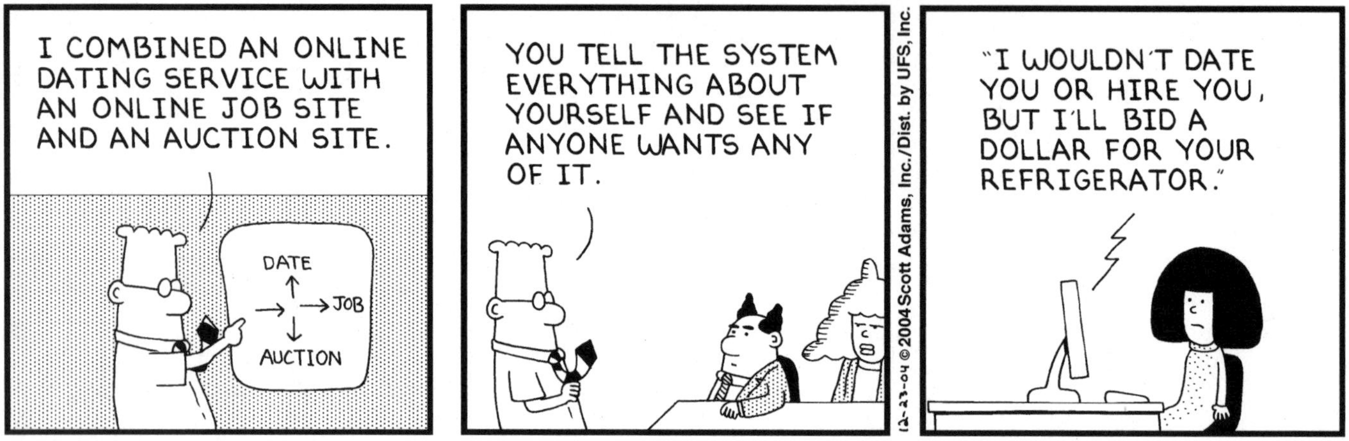
I COMBINED AN ONLINE DATING SERVICE WITH AN ONLINE JOB SITE AND AN AUCTION SITE.
DATE
JOB
AUCTION
YOU TELL THE SYSTEM EVERYTHING ABOUT YOURSELF AND SEE IF ANYONE WANTS ANY OF IT.
12-23-04 ©2004 Scott Adams, Inc./Dist. by UFS, Inc.
"I WOULDN'T DATE YOU OR HIRE YOU, BUT I'LL BID A DOLLAR FOR YOUR REFRIGERATOR."

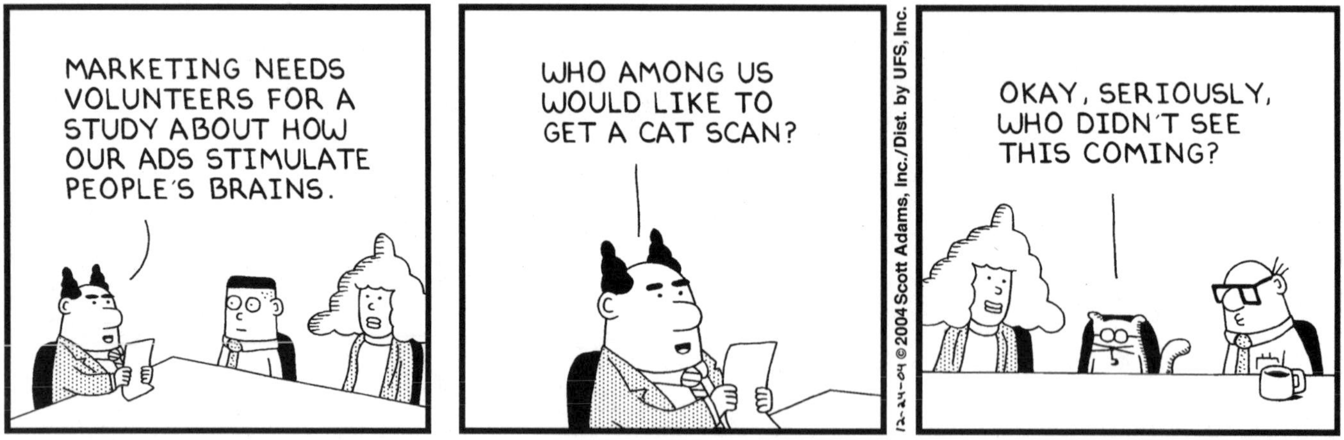
MARKETING NEEDS VOLUNTEERS FOR A STUDY ABOUT HOW OUR ADS STIMULATE PEOPLE'S BRAINS.
WHO AMONG US WOULD LIKE TO GET A CAT SCAN?
12-24-04 ©2004 Scott Adams, Inc./Dist. by UFS, Inc.
OKAY, SERIOUSLY, WHO DIDN'T SEE THIS COMING?

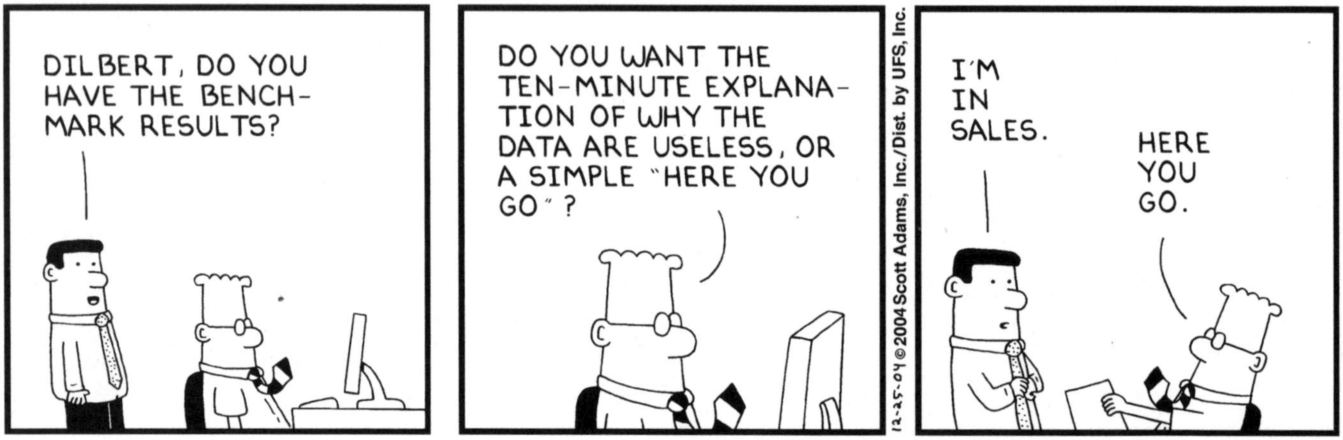
DILBERT, DO YOU HAVE THE BENCH-MARK RESULTS?
DO YOU WANT THE TEN-MINUTE EXPLANA-TION OF WHY THE DATA ARE USELESS, OR A SIMPLE "HERE YOU GO"?
12-25-04 ©2004 Scott Adams, Inc./Dist. by UFS, Inc.
I'M IN SALES.
HERE YOU GO.

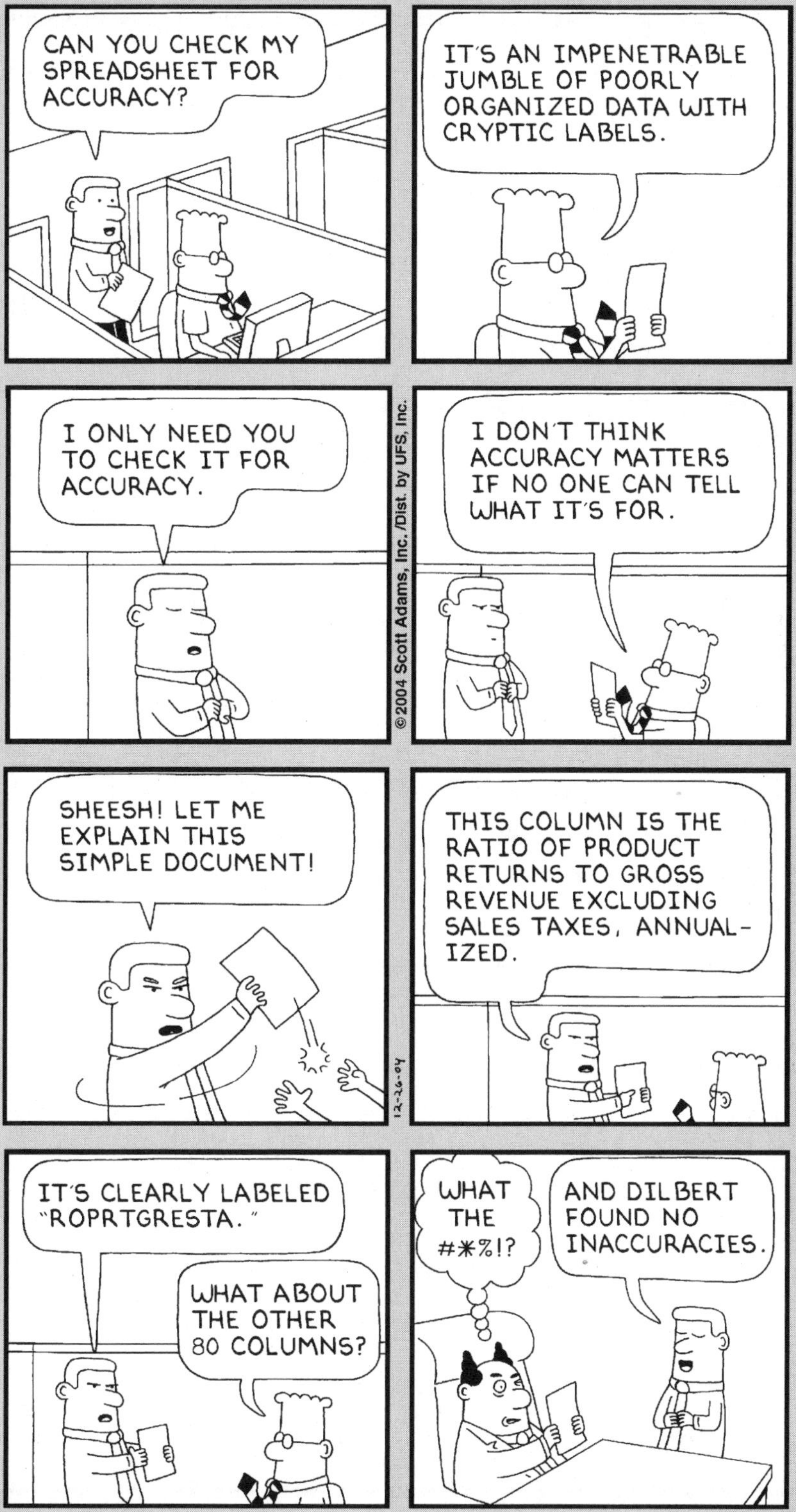
CAN YOU CHECK MY SPREADSHEET FOR ACCURACY?
IT'S AN IMPENETRABLE JUMBLE OF POORLY ORGANIZED DATA WITH CRYPTIC LABELS.
I ONLY NEED YOU TO CHECK IT FOR ACCURACY.
I DON'T THINK ACCURACY MATTERS IF NO ONE CAN TELL WHAT IT'S FOR.
©2004 Scott Adams, Inc./Dist. by UFS, Inc.
SHEESH! LET ME EXPLAIN THIS SIMPLE DOCUMENT!
THIS COLUMN IS THE RATIO OF PRODUCT RETURNS TO GROSS REVENUE EXCLUDING SALES TAXES, ANNUAL-IZED.
IT'S CLEARLY LABELED "ROPRTGRESTA."
WHAT ABOUT THE OTHER 80 COLUMNS?
WHAT THE #*%!?
AND DILBERT FOUND NO INACCURACIES.

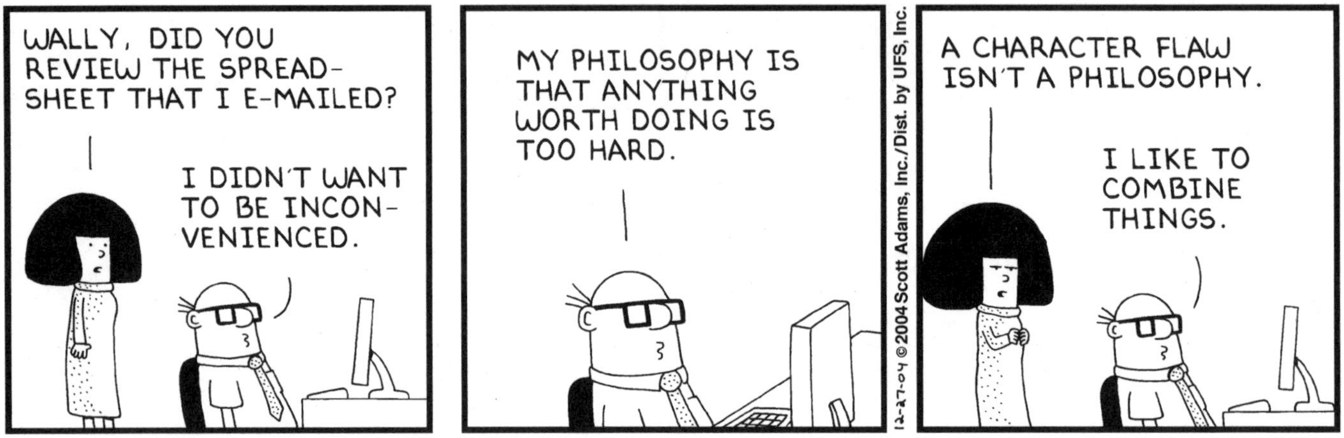
WALLY, DID YOU REVIEW THE SPREAD-SHEET THAT I E-MAILED?
I DIDN'T WANT TO BE INCON-VENIENCED.
MY PHILOSOPHY IS THAT ANYTHING WORTH DOING IS TOO HARD.
12-27-04 © 2004 Scott Adams, Inc./Dist. by UFS, Inc.
A CHARACTER FLAW ISN'T A PHILOSOPHY.
I LIKE TO COMBINE THINGS.

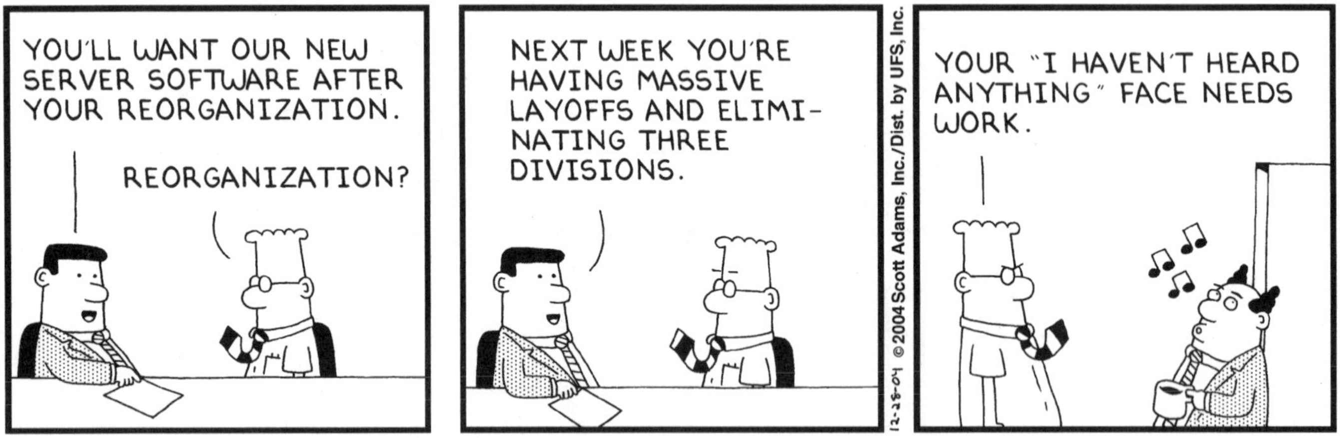
YOU'LL WANT OUR NEW SERVER SOFTWARE AFTER YOUR REORGANIZATION.
REORGANIZATION?
NEXT WEEK YOU'RE HAVING MASSIVE LAYOFFS AND ELIMI-NATING THREE DIVISIONS.
12-28-04 © 2004 Scott Adams, Inc./Dist. by UFS, Inc.
YOUR "I HAVEN'T HEARD ANYTHING" FACE NEEDS WORK.

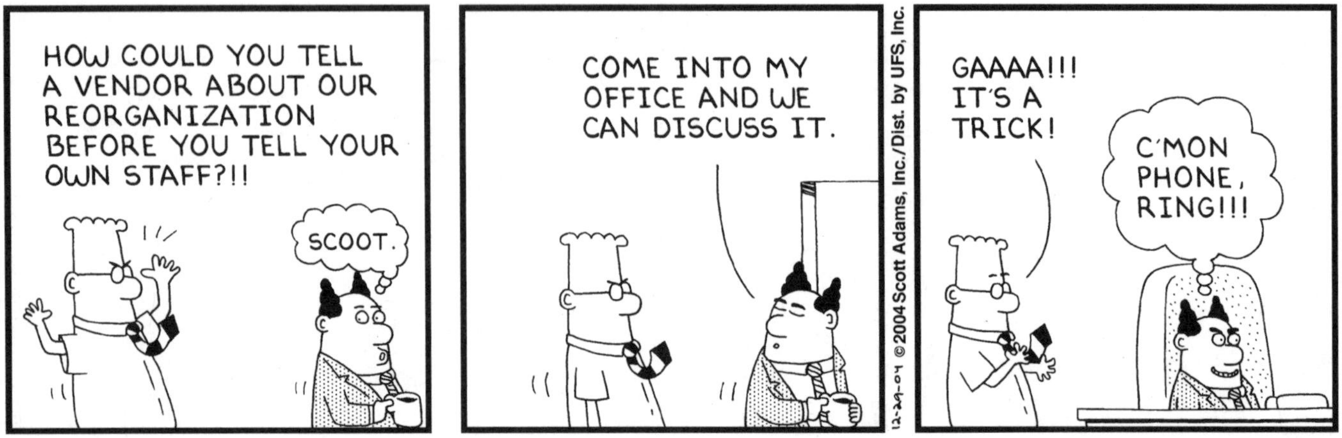
HOW COULD YOU TELL A VENDOR ABOUT OUR REORGANIZATION BEFORE YOU TELL YOUR OWN STAFF?!!
SCOOT.
COME INTO MY OFFICE AND WE CAN DISCUSS IT.
12-29-04 © 2004 Scott Adams, Inc./Dist. by UFS, Inc.
GAAAA!!! IT'S A TRICK!
C'MON PHONE, RING!!!

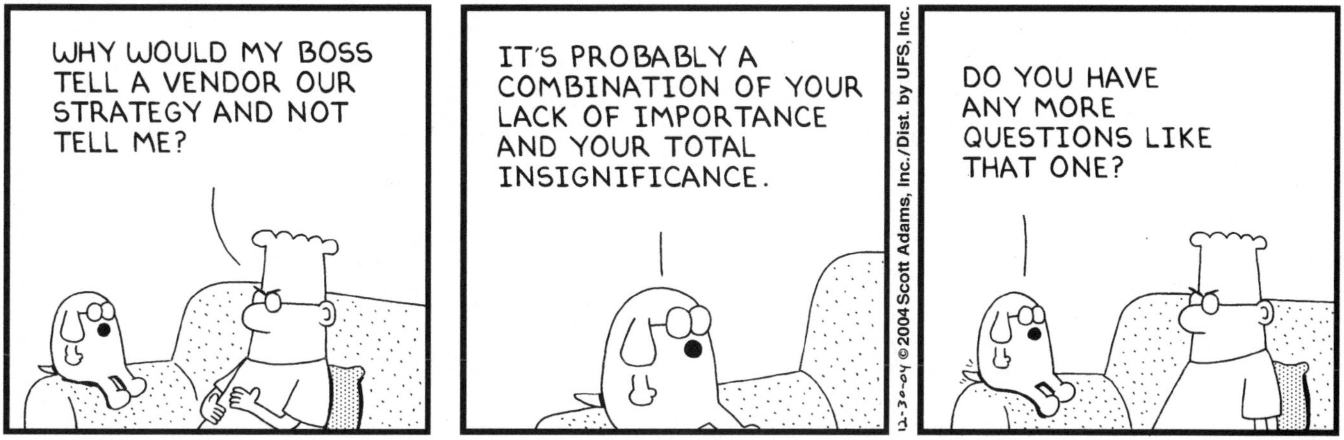
WHY WOULD MY BOSS TELL A VENDOR OUR STRATEGY AND NOT TELL ME?
IT'S PROBABLY A COMBINATION OF YOUR LACK OF IMPORTANCE AND YOUR TOTAL INSIGNIFICANCE.
12-30-04 © 2004 Scott Adams, Inc./Dist. by UFS, Inc.
DO YOU HAVE ANY MORE QUESTIONS LIKE THAT ONE?

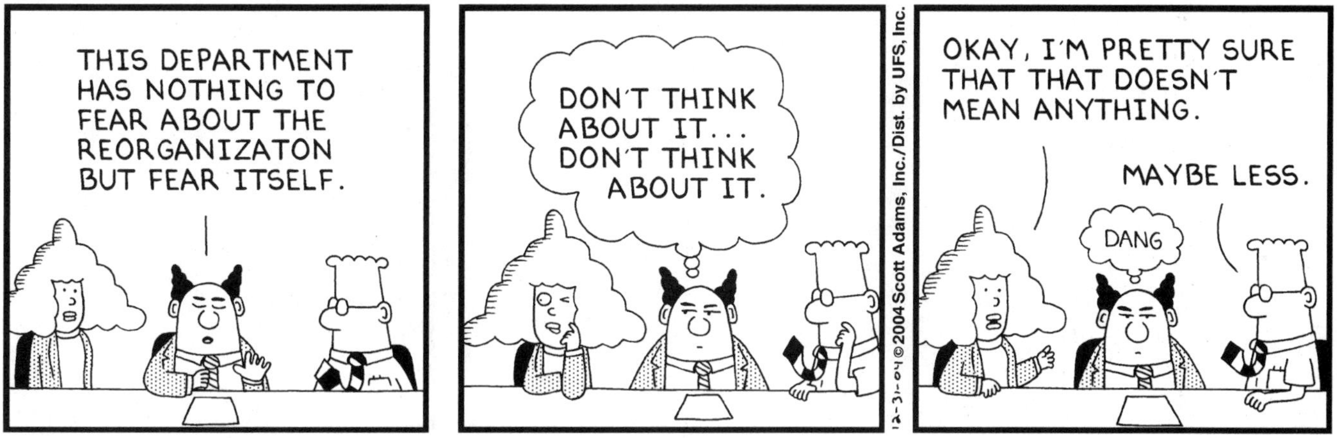
THIS DEPARTMENT HAS NOTHING TO FEAR ABOUT THE REORGANIZATON BUT FEAR ITSELF.
DON'T THINK ABOUT IT... DON'T THINK ABOUT IT.
12-31-04 © 2004 Scott Adams, Inc./Dist. by UFS, Inc.
OKAY, I'M PRETTY SURE THAT THAT DOESN'T MEAN ANYTHING.
DANG
MAYBE LESS.

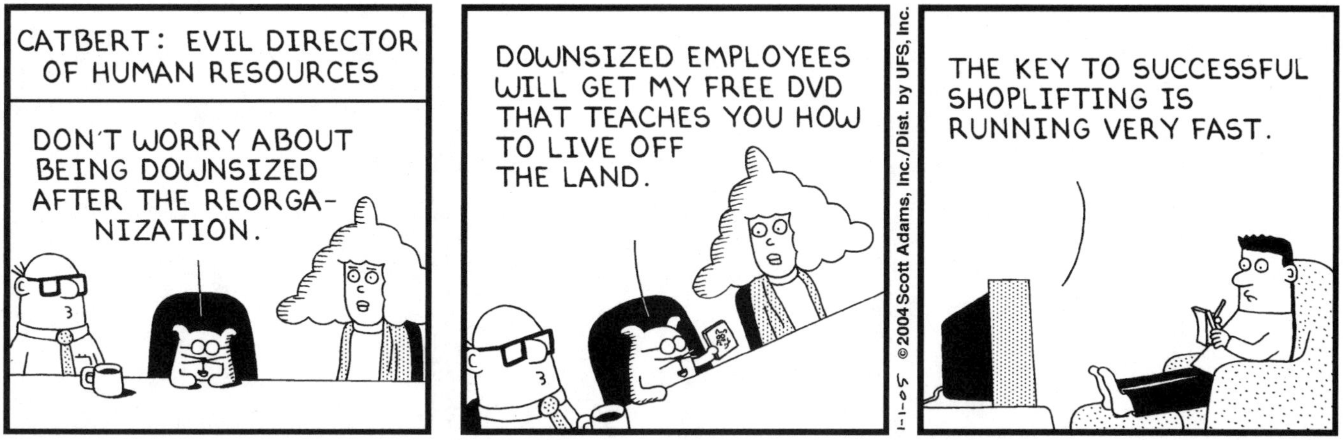
CATBERT: EVIL DIRECTOR OF HUMAN RESOURCES
DON'T WORRY ABOUT BEING DOWNSIZED AFTER THE REORGA-NIZATION.
DOWNSIZED EMPLOYEES WILL GET MY FREE DVD THAT TEACHES YOU HOW TO LIVE OFF THE LAND.
1-1-05 © 2004 Scott Adams, Inc./Dist. by UFS, Inc.
THE KEY TO SUCCESSFUL SHOPLIFTING IS RUNNING VERY FAST.

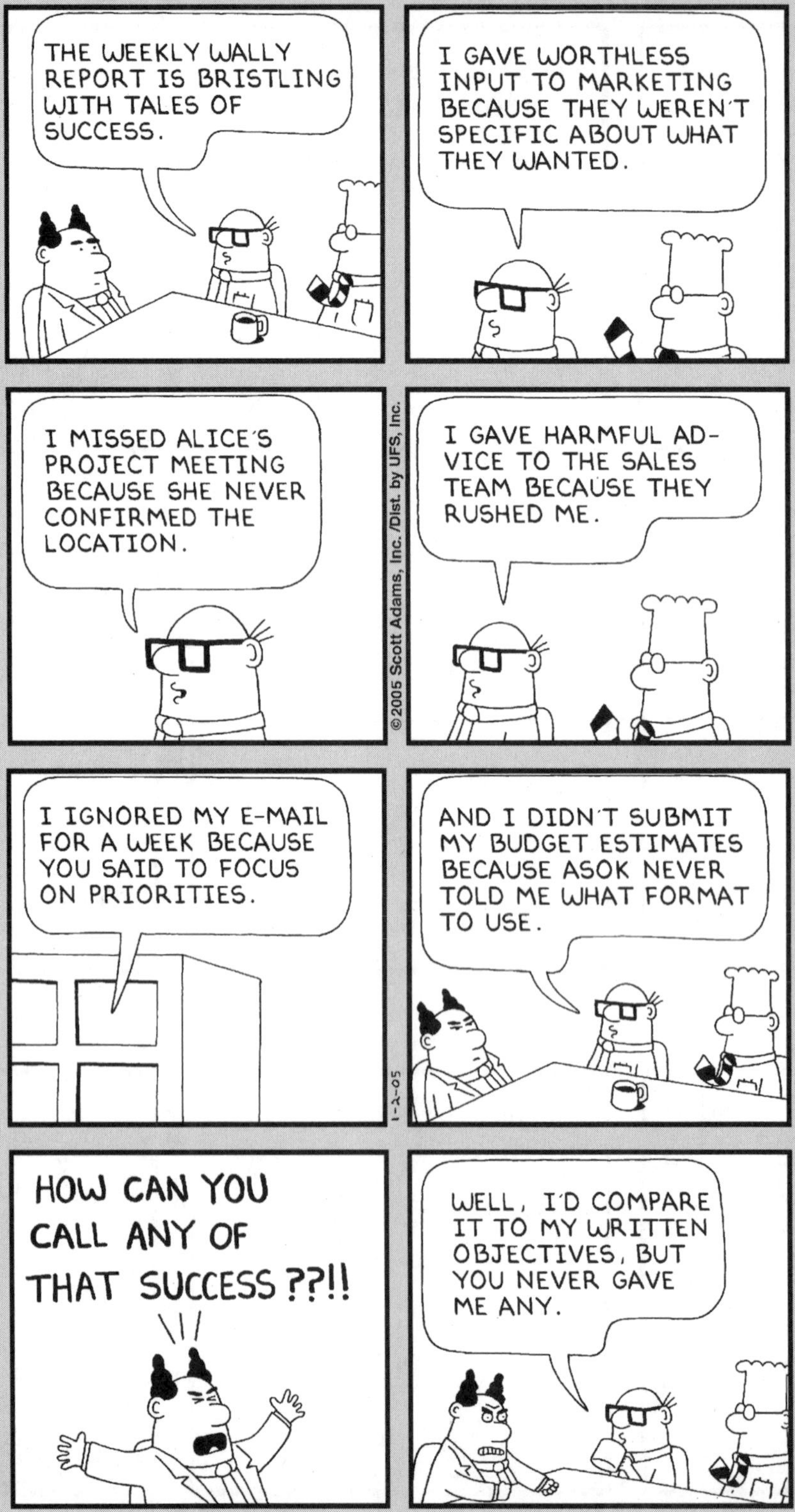
THE WEEKLY WALLY REPORT IS BRISTLING WITH TALES OF SUCCESS.
I GAVE WORTHLESS INPUT TO MARKETING BECAUSE THEY WEREN'T SPECIFIC ABOUT WHAT THEY WANTED.
I MISSED ALICE'S PROJECT MEETING BECAUSE SHE NEVER CONFIRMED THE LOCATION.
I GAVE HARMFUL ADVICE TO THE SALES TEAM BECAUSE THEY RUSHED ME.
©2005 Scott Adams, Inc. /Dist. by UFS, Inc.
I IGNORED MY E-MAIL FOR A WEEK BECAUSE YOU SAID TO FOCUS ON PRIORITIES.
AND I DIDN'T SUBMIT MY BUDGET ESTIMATES BECAUSE ASOK NEVER TOLD ME WHAT FORMAT TO USE.
1-2-05
HOW CAN YOU CALL ANY OF THAT SUCCESS??!!
WELL, I'D COMPARE IT TO MY WRITTEN OBJECTIVES, BUT YOU NEVER GAVE ME ANY.

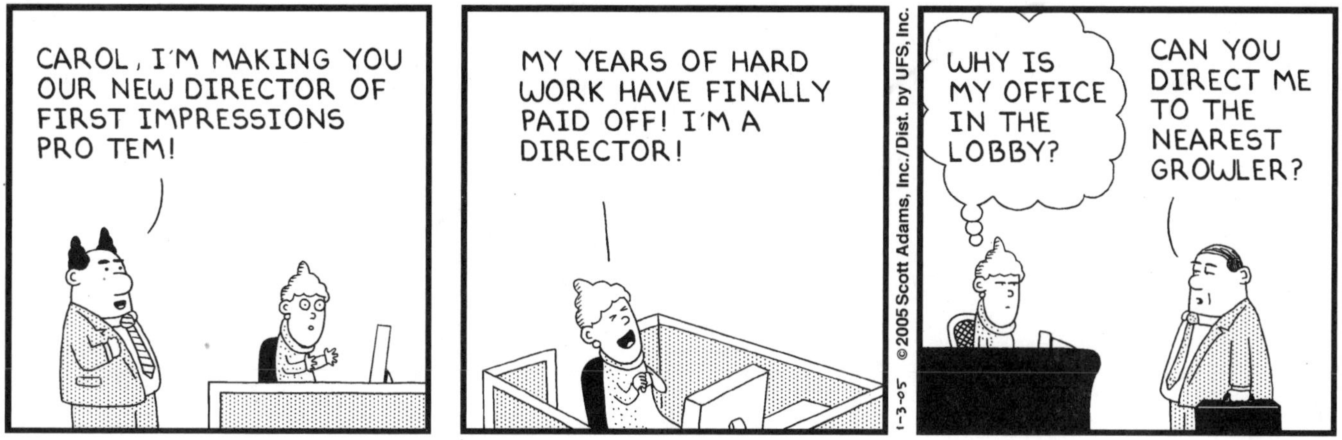
CAROL, I'M MAKING YOU OUR NEW DIRECTOR OF FIRST IMPRESSIONS PRO TEM!
MY YEARS OF HARD WORK HAVE FINALLY PAID OFF! I'M A DIRECTOR!
WHY IS MY OFFICE IN THE LOBBY?
CAN YOU DIRECT ME TO THE NEAREST GROWLER?
1-3-05 © 2005 Scott Adams, Inc./Dist. by UFS, Inc.

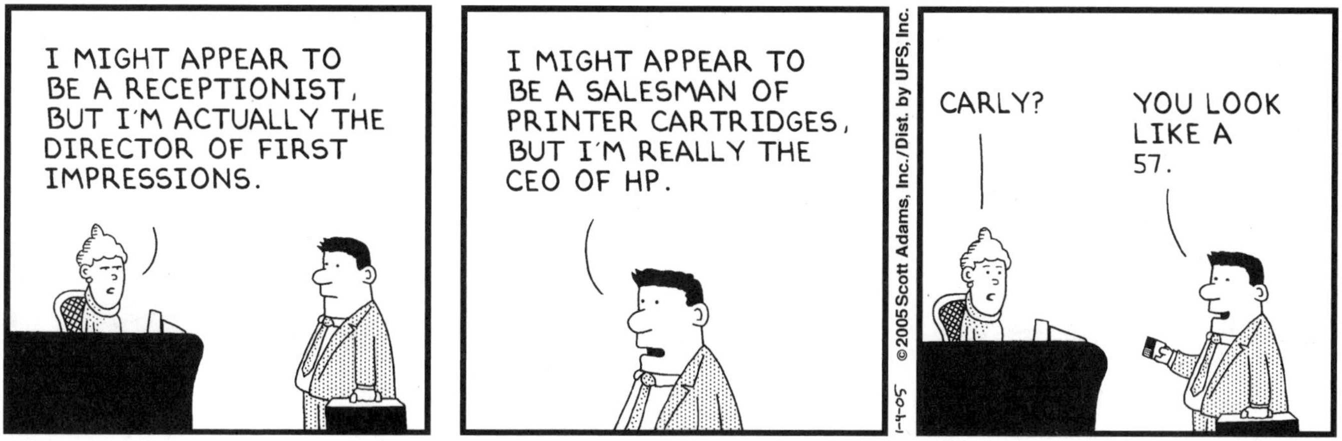
I MIGHT APPEAR TO BE A RECEPTIONIST, BUT I'M ACTUALLY THE DIRECTOR OF FIRST IMPRESSIONS.
I MIGHT APPEAR TO BE A SALESMAN OF PRINTER CARTRIDGES, BUT I'M REALLY THE CEO OF HP.
CARLY?
YOU LOOK LIKE A 57.
1-4-05 © 2005 Scott Adams, Inc./Dist. by UFS, Inc.

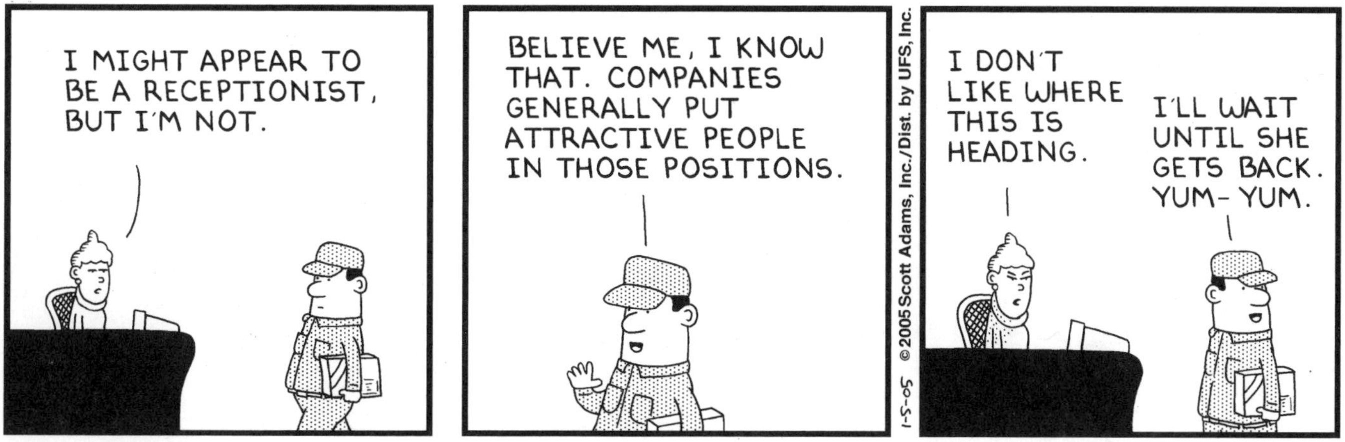
I MIGHT APPEAR TO BE A RECEPTIONIST, BUT I'M NOT.
BELIEVE ME, I KNOW THAT. COMPANIES GENERALLY PUT ATTRACTIVE PEOPLE IN THOSE POSITIONS.
I DON'T LIKE WHERE THIS IS HEADING.
I'LL WAIT UNTIL SHE GETS BACK. YUM-YUM.
1-5-05 © 2005 Scott Adams, Inc./Dist. by UFS, Inc.

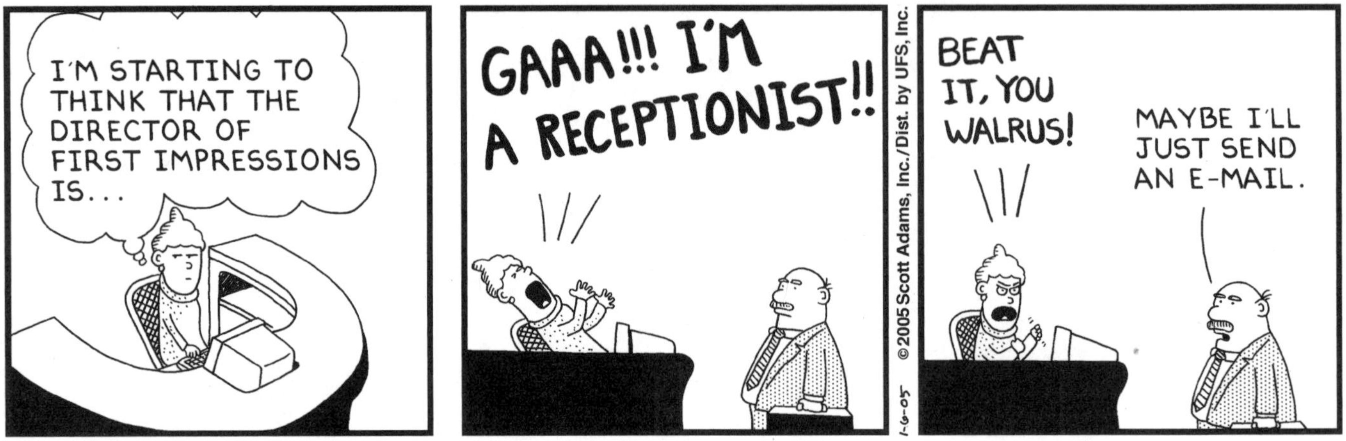
I'M STARTING TO THINK THAT THE DIRECTOR OF FIRST IMPRESSIONS IS...
GAAA!!! I'M A RECEPTIONIST!!
1-6-05
© 2005 Scott Adams, Inc./Dist. by UFS, Inc.
BEAT IT, YOU WALRUS!
MAYBE I'LL JUST SEND AN E-MAIL.

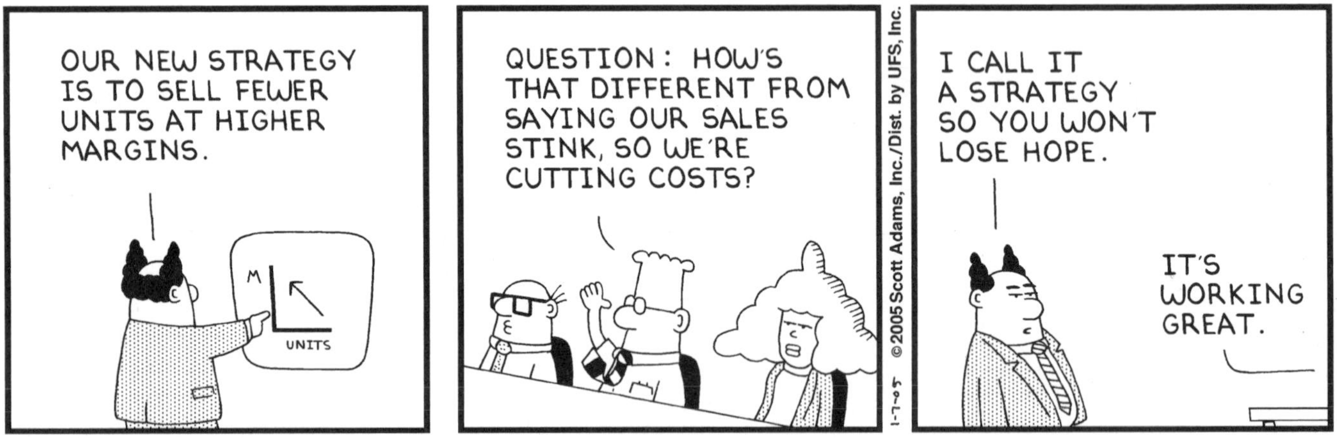
OUR NEW STRATEGY IS TO SELL FEWER UNITS AT HIGHER MARGINS.
M
UNITS
QUESTION: HOW'S THAT DIFFERENT FROM SAYING OUR SALES STINK, SO WE'RE CUTTING COSTS?
1-7-05
© 2005 Scott Adams, Inc./Dist. by UFS, Inc.
I CALL IT A STRATEGY SO YOU WON'T LOSE HOPE.
IT'S WORKING GREAT.

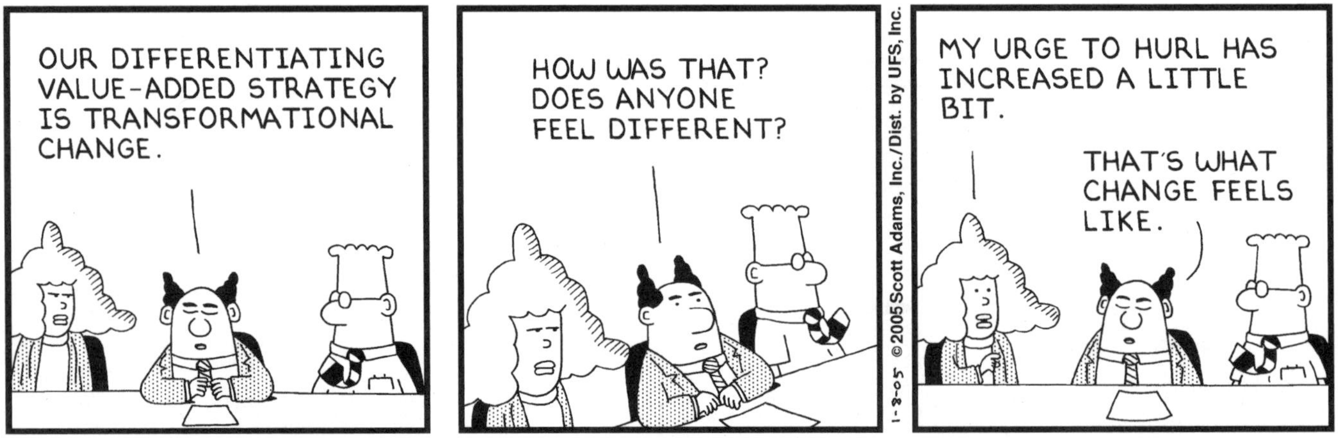
OUR DIFFERENTIATING VALUE-ADDED STRATEGY IS TRANSFORMATIONAL CHANGE.
HOW WAS THAT? DOES ANYONE FEEL DIFFERENT?
1-8-05
© 2005 Scott Adams, Inc./Dist. by UFS, Inc.
MY URGE TO HURL HAS INCREASED A LITTLE BIT.
THAT'S WHAT CHANGE FEELS LIKE.

I ASKED THE I.T. DEPARTMENT TO UPGRADE MY COMPUTER.
THEY'RE COMING HERE??!
WE MUST HIDE OUR NON-STANDARD EQUIPMENT!
UH-OH.
ZIP!!
SO-O-O... THIS DEN OF NON-STANDARD-IZATION MUST BE YOUR CUBICLE.
THIS NON-STANDARD PRINTER IS COMING WITH ME. AND I DON'T REMEMBER THAT MONITOR ON OUR LIST.
I MUST CLEANSE YOUR CUBICLE OF NON-CONFORMANCE SO THE HEALING CAN BEGIN.
SURELY MY UPGRADED COMPUTER WILL ARRIVE SOON.
MONTHS LATER
ABACUS?
PLEASE SHUT UP.
©2005 Scott Adams, Inc./Dist. by UFS, Inc.
1-9-05

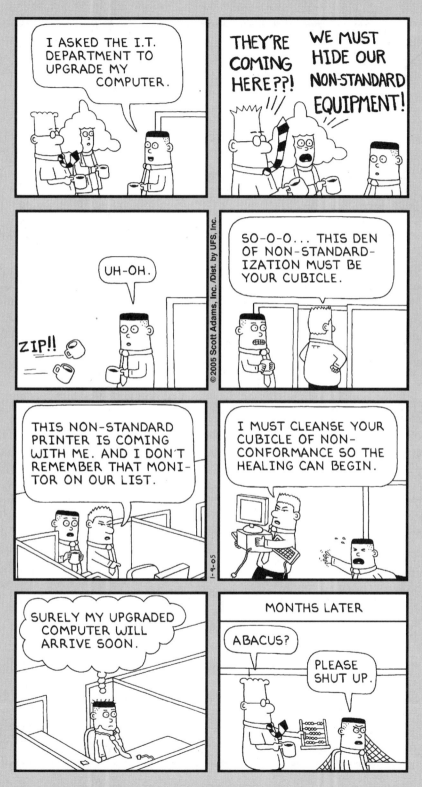

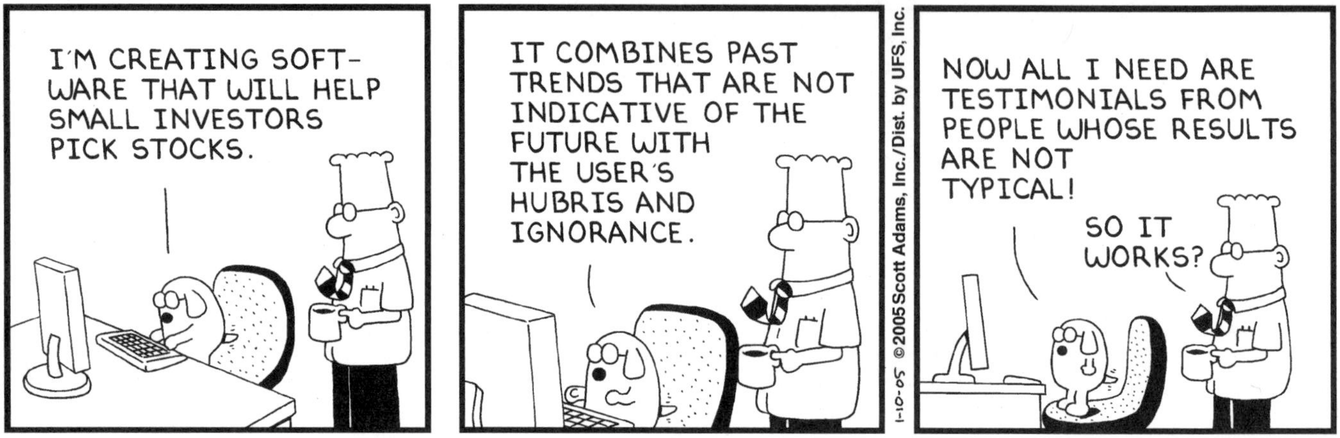
I'M CREATING SOFTWARE THAT WILL HELP SMALL INVESTORS PICK STOCKS.
IT COMBINES PAST TRENDS THAT ARE NOT INDICATIVE OF THE FUTURE WITH THE USER'S HUBRIS AND IGNORANCE.
1-10-05 © 2005 Scott Adams, Inc./Dist. by UFS, Inc.
NOW ALL I NEED ARE TESTIMONIALS FROM PEOPLE WHOSE RESULTS ARE NOT TYPICAL!
SO IT WORKS?

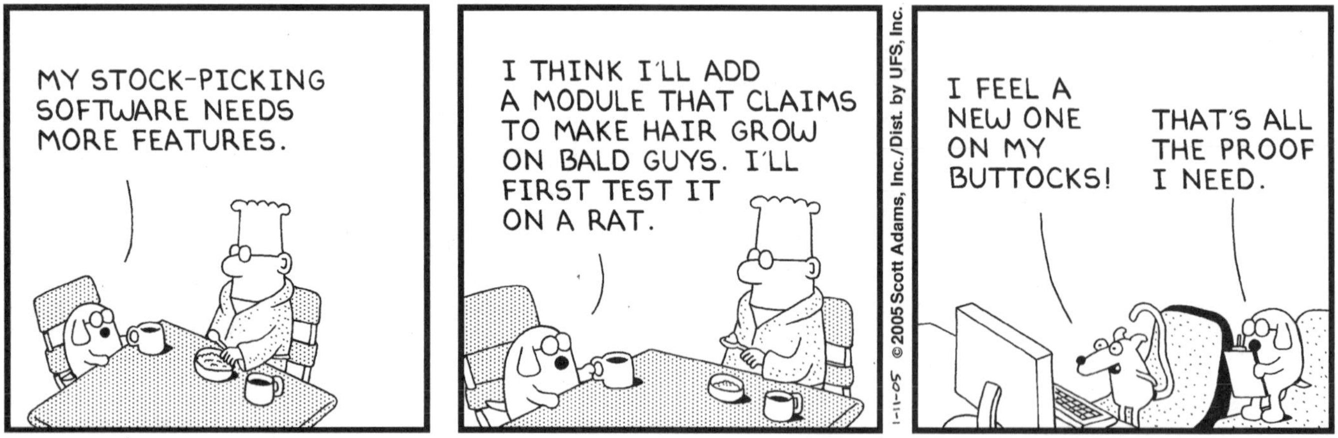
MY STOCK-PICKING SOFTWARE NEEDS MORE FEATURES.
I THINK I'LL ADD A MODULE THAT CLAIMS TO MAKE HAIR GROW ON BALD GUYS. I'LL FIRST TEST IT ON A RAT.
1-11-05 © 2005 Scott Adams, Inc./Dist. by UFS, Inc.
I FEEL A NEW ONE ON MY BUTTOCKS!
THAT'S ALL THE PROOF I NEED.

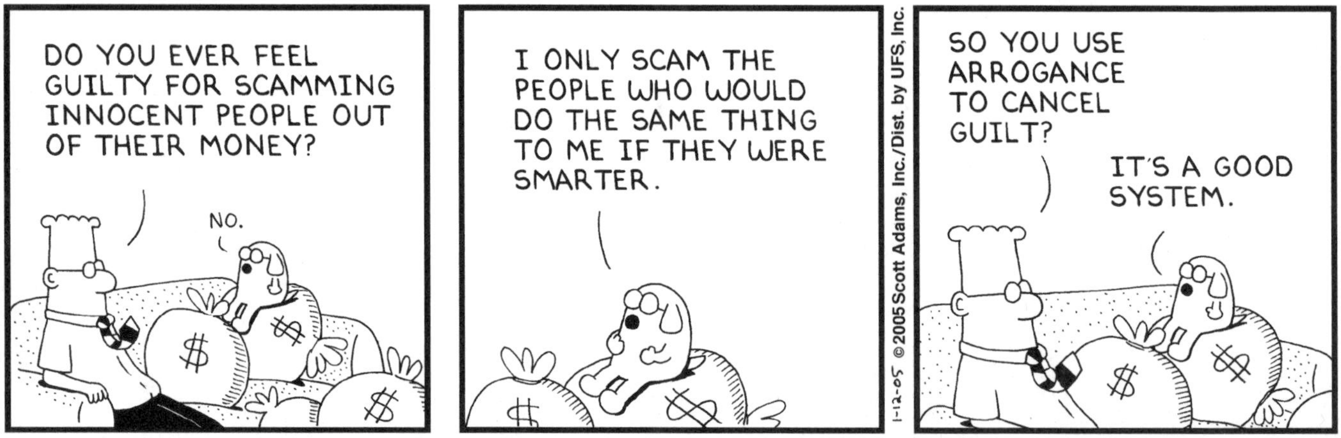
DO YOU EVER FEEL GUILTY FOR SCAMMING INNOCENT PEOPLE OUT OF THEIR MONEY?
NO.
I ONLY SCAM THE PEOPLE WHO WOULD DO THE SAME THING TO ME IF THEY WERE SMARTER.
1-12-05 © 2005 Scott Adams, Inc./Dist. by UFS, Inc.
SO YOU USE ARROGANCE TO CANCEL GUILT?
IT'S A GOOD SYSTEM.

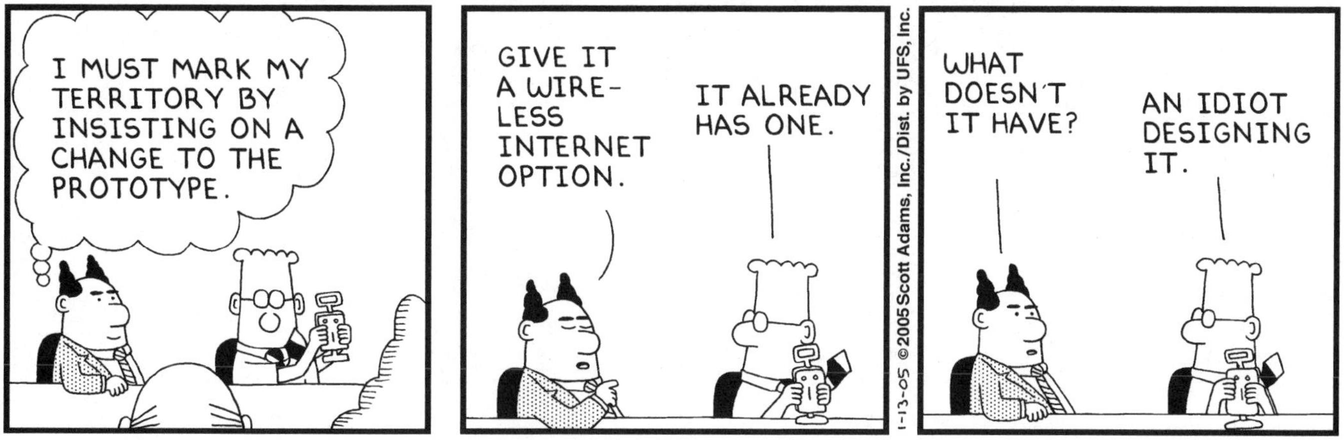
I MUST MARK MY TERRITORY BY INSISTING ON A CHANGE TO THE PROTOTYPE.
GIVE IT A WIRE-LESS INTERNET OPTION.
IT ALREADY HAS ONE.
1-13-05 ©2005 Scott Adams, Inc./Dist. by UFS, Inc.
WHAT DOESN'T IT HAVE?
AN IDIOT DESIGNING IT.

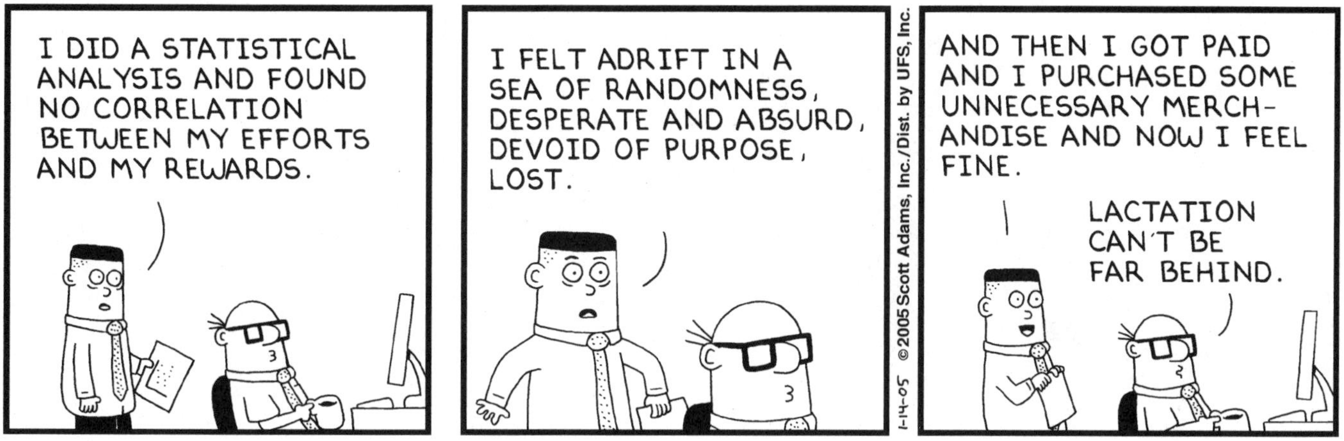
I DID A STATISTICAL ANALYSIS AND FOUND NO CORRELATION BETWEEN MY EFFORTS AND MY REWARDS.
I FELT ADRIFT IN A SEA OF RANDOMNESS, DESPERATE AND ABSURD, DEVOID OF PURPOSE, LOST.
1-14-05 ©2005 Scott Adams, Inc./Dist. by UFS, Inc.
AND THEN I GOT PAID AND I PURCHASED SOME UNNECESSARY MERCH-ANDISE AND NOW I FEEL FINE.
LACTATION CAN'T BE FAR BEHIND.

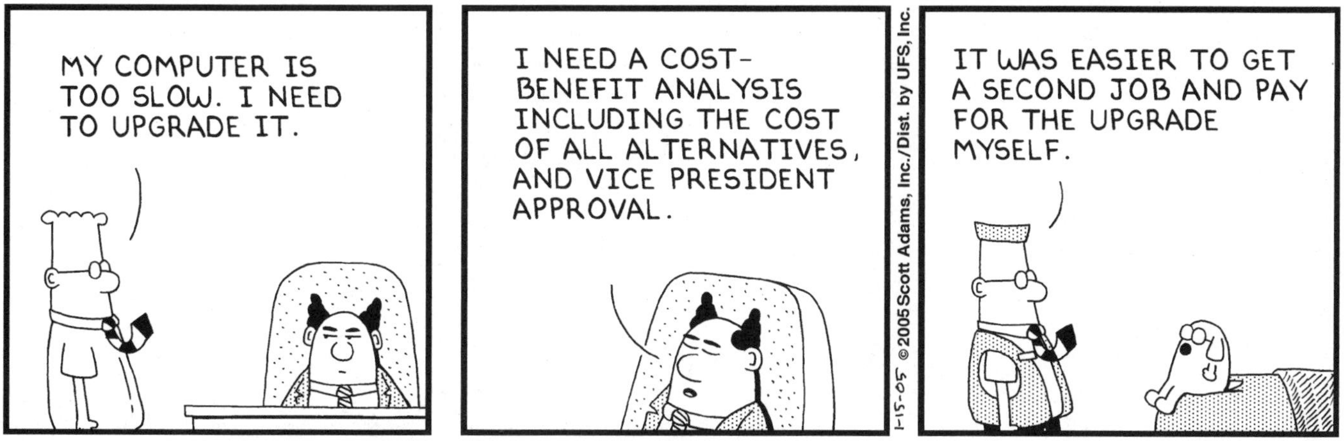
MY COMPUTER IS TOO SLOW. I NEED TO UPGRADE IT.
I NEED A COST-BENEFIT ANALYSIS INCLUDING THE COST OF ALL ALTERNATIVES, AND VICE PRESIDENT APPROVAL.
1-15-05 ©2005 Scott Adams, Inc./Dist. by UFS, Inc.
IT WAS EASIER TO GET A SECOND JOB AND PAY FOR THE UPGRADE MYSELF.

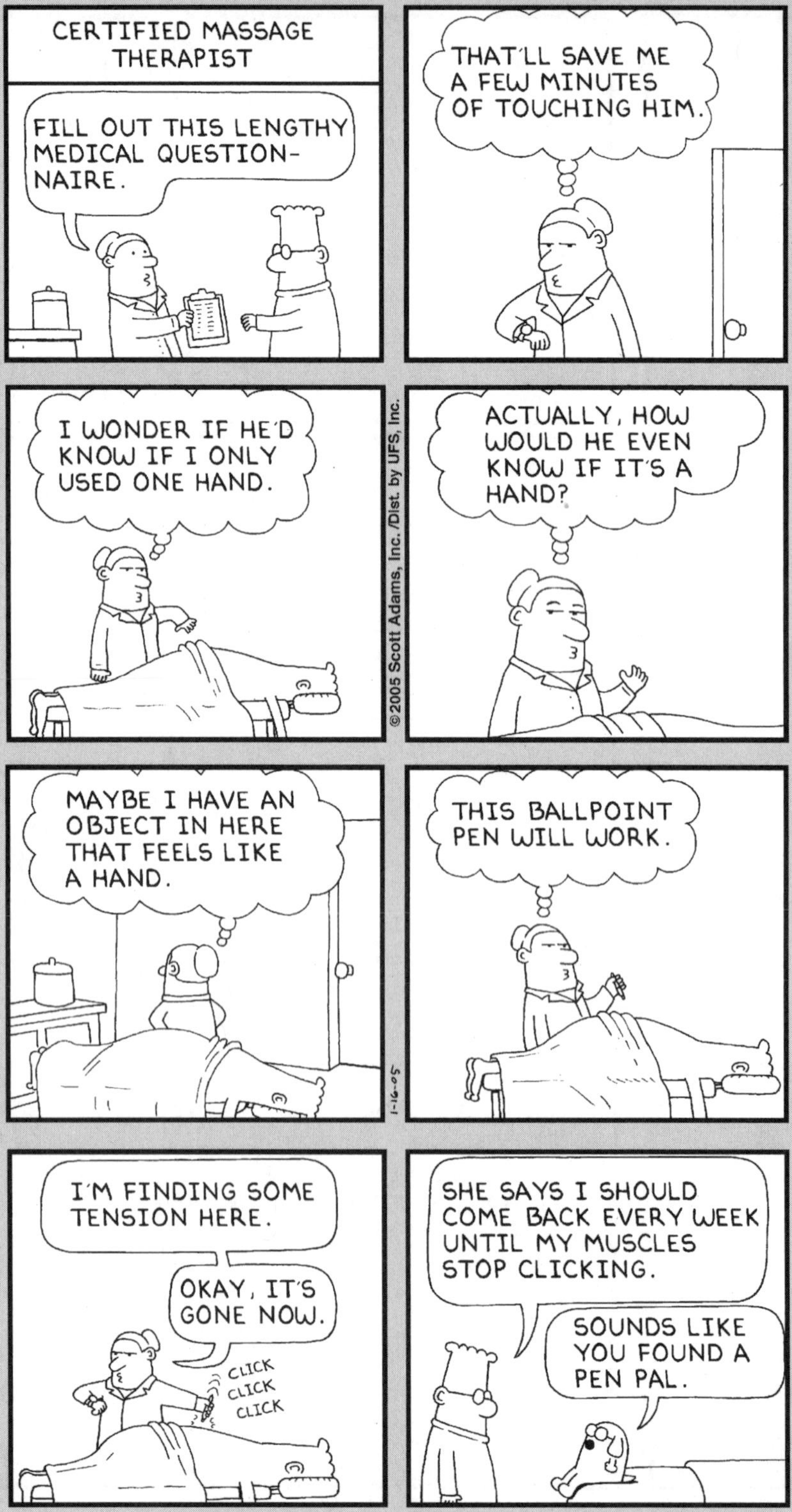
CERTIFIED MASSAGE THERAPIST
FILL OUT THIS LENGTHY MEDICAL QUESTION-NAIRE.
THAT'LL SAVE ME A FEW MINUTES OF TOUCHING HIM.
I WONDER IF HE'D KNOW IF I ONLY USED ONE HAND.
ACTUALLY, HOW WOULD HE EVEN KNOW IF IT'S A HAND?
MAYBE I HAVE AN OBJECT IN HERE THAT FEELS LIKE A HAND.
THIS BALLPOINT PEN WILL WORK.
I'M FINDING SOME TENSION HERE.
OKAY, IT'S GONE NOW.
CLICK CLICK CLICK
SHE SAYS I SHOULD COME BACK EVERY WEEK UNTIL MY MUSCLES STOP CLICKING.
SOUNDS LIKE YOU FOUND A PEN PAL.
1-16-05

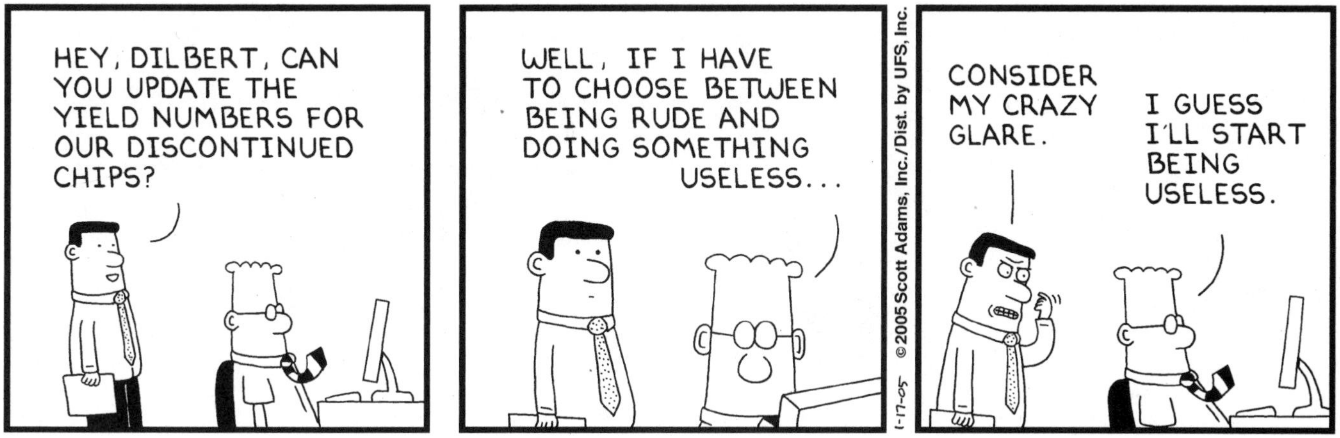
HEY, DILBERT, CAN YOU UPDATE THE YIELD NUMBERS FOR OUR DISCONTINUED CHIPS?
WELL, IF I HAVE TO CHOOSE BETWEEN BEING RUDE AND DOING SOMETHING USELESS...
1-17-05 © 2005 Scott Adams, Inc./Dist. by UFS, Inc.
CONSIDER MY CRAZY GLARE.
I GUESS I'LL START BEING USELESS.

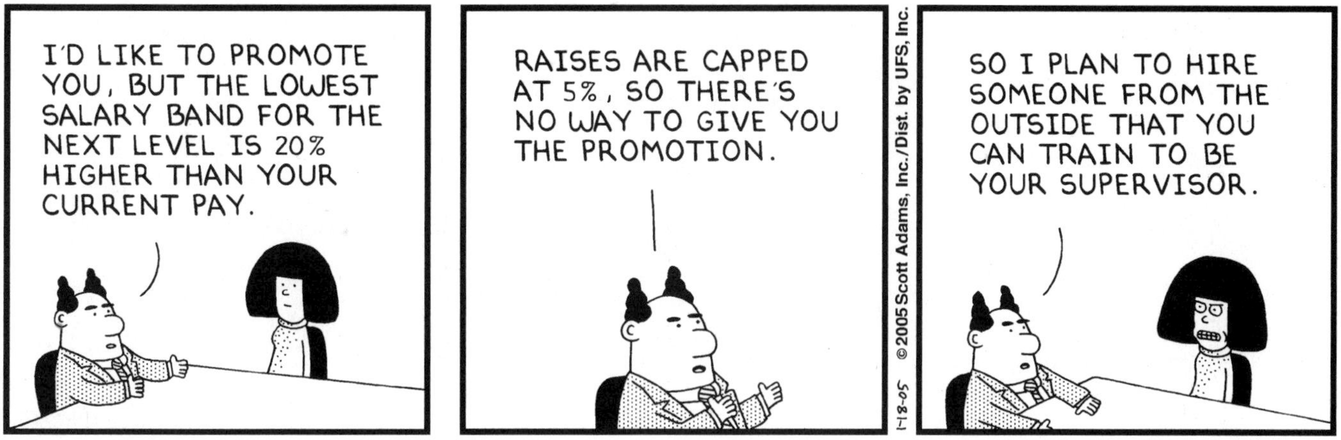
I'D LIKE TO PROMOTE YOU, BUT THE LOWEST SALARY BAND FOR THE NEXT LEVEL IS 20% HIGHER THAN YOUR CURRENT PAY.
RAISES ARE CAPPED AT 5%, SO THERE'S NO WAY TO GIVE YOU THE PROMOTION.
1-18-05 © 2005 Scott Adams, Inc./Dist. by UFS, Inc.
SO I PLAN TO HIRE SOMEONE FROM THE OUTSIDE THAT YOU CAN TRAIN TO BE YOUR SUPERVISOR.

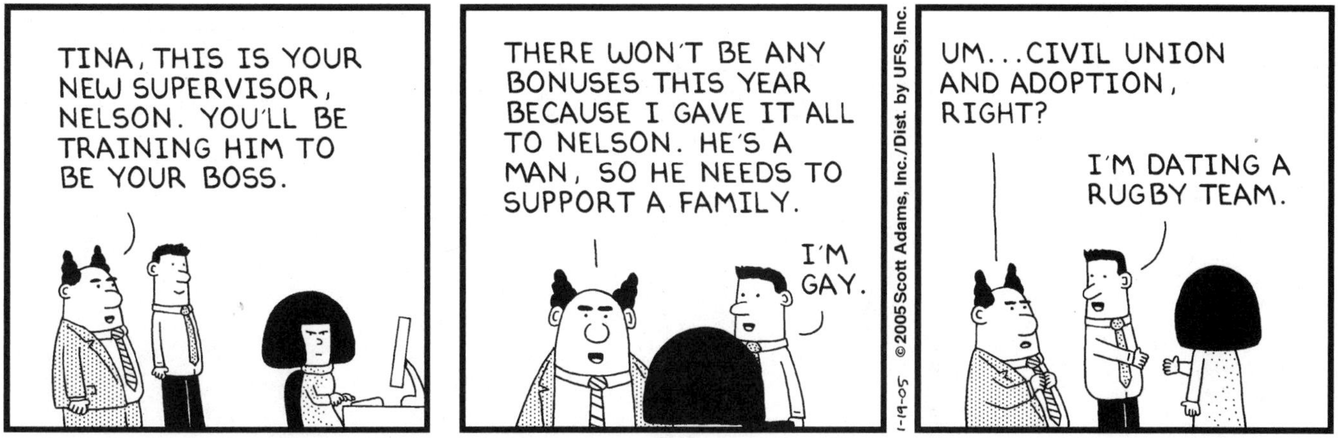
TINA, THIS IS YOUR NEW SUPERVISOR, NELSON. YOU'LL BE TRAINING HIM TO BE YOUR BOSS.
THERE WON'T BE ANY BONUSES THIS YEAR BECAUSE I GAVE IT ALL TO NELSON. HE'S A MAN, SO HE NEEDS TO SUPPORT A FAMILY.
I'M GAY.
1-19-05 © 2005 Scott Adams, Inc./Dist. by UFS, Inc.
UM...CIVIL UNION AND ADOPTION, RIGHT?
I'M DATING A RUGBY TEAM.

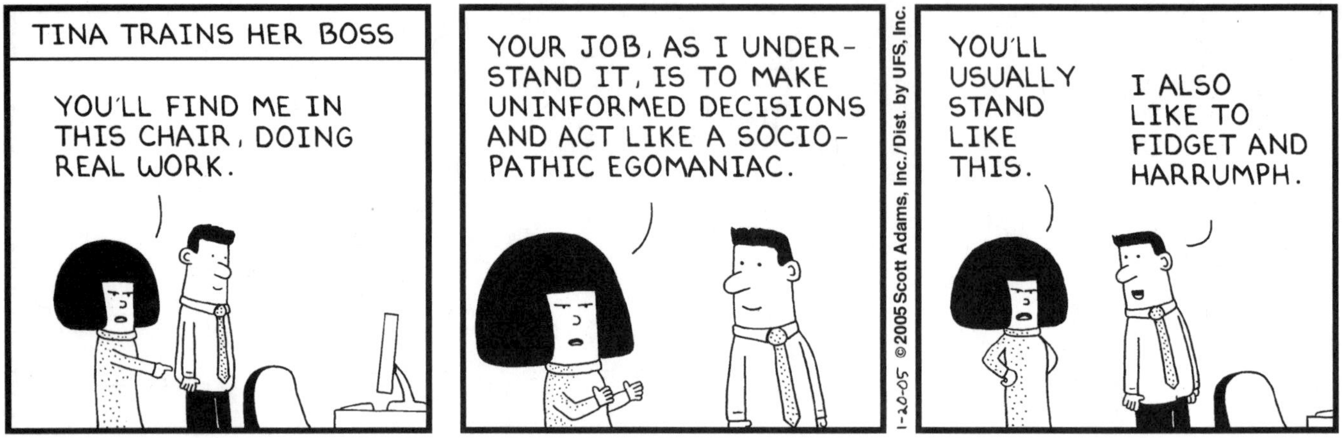
TINA TRAINS HER BOSS
YOU'LL FIND ME IN THIS CHAIR, DOING REAL WORK.
YOUR JOB, AS I UNDERSTAND IT, IS TO MAKE UNINFORMED DECISIONS AND ACT LIKE A SOCIOPATHIC EGOMANIAC.
1-20-05 © 2005 Scott Adams, Inc./Dist. by UFS, Inc.
YOU'LL USUALLY STAND LIKE THIS.
I ALSO LIKE TO FIDGET AND HARRUMPH.

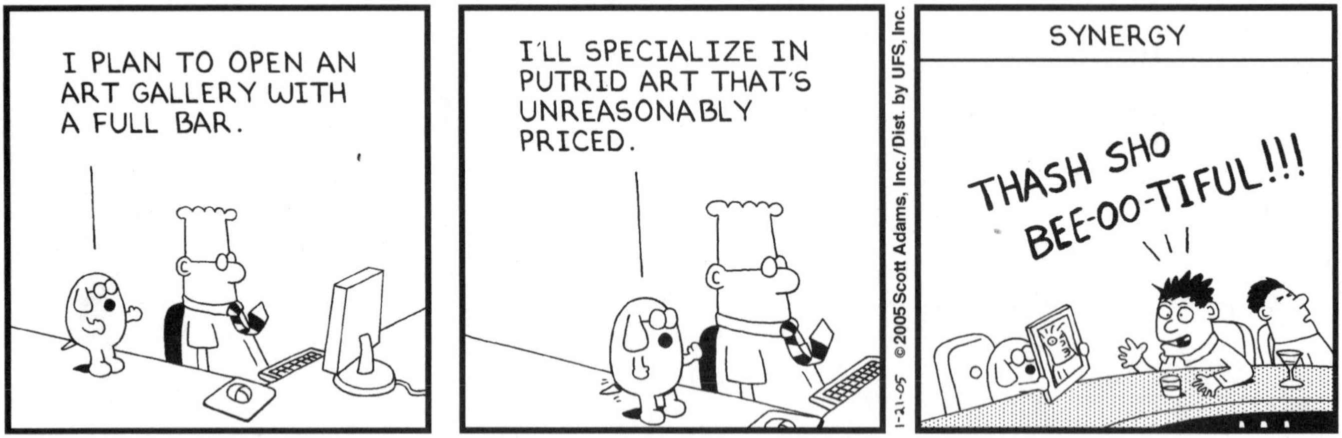
I PLAN TO OPEN AN ART GALLERY WITH A FULL BAR.
I'LL SPECIALIZE IN PUTRID ART THAT'S UNREASONABLY PRICED.
1-21-05 © 2005 Scott Adams, Inc./Dist. by UFS, Inc.
SYNERGY
THASH SHO BEE-OO-TIFUL!!!

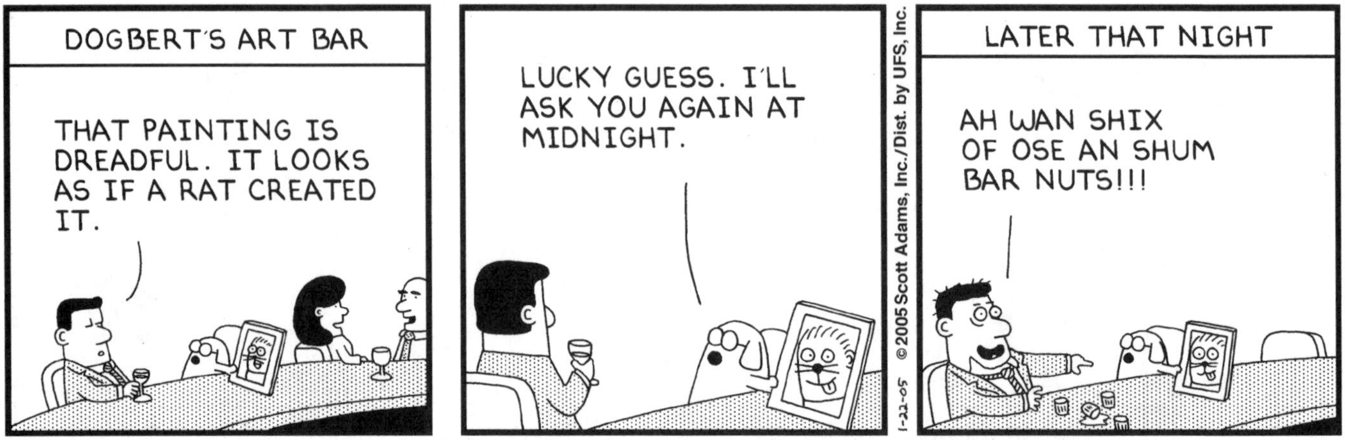
DOGBERT'S ART BAR
THAT PAINTING IS DREADFUL. IT LOOKS AS IF A RAT CREATED IT.
LUCKY GUESS. I'LL ASK YOU AGAIN AT MIDNIGHT.
1-22-05 © 2005 Scott Adams, Inc./Dist. by UFS, Inc.
LATER THAT NIGHT
AH WAN SHIX OF OSE AN SHUM BAR NUTS!!!

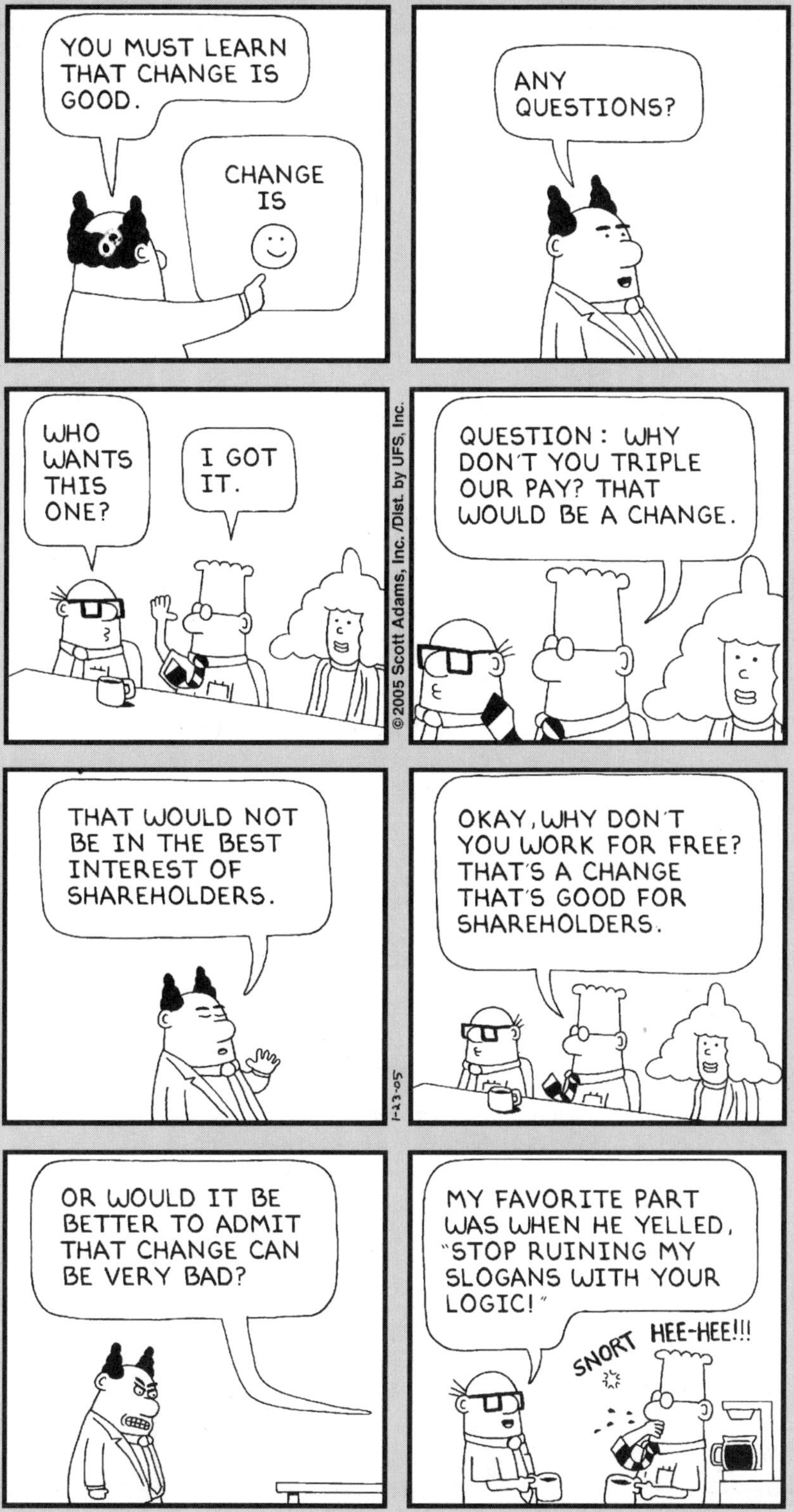
YOU MUST LEARN THAT CHANGE IS GOOD.
CHANGE IS
ANY QUESTIONS?
WHO WANTS THIS ONE?
I GOT IT.
©2005 Scott Adams, Inc./Dist. by UFS, Inc.
QUESTION: WHY DON'T YOU TRIPLE OUR PAY? THAT WOULD BE A CHANGE.
THAT WOULD NOT BE IN THE BEST INTEREST OF SHAREHOLDERS.
1-23-05
OKAY, WHY DON'T YOU WORK FOR FREE? THAT'S A CHANGE THAT'S GOOD FOR SHAREHOLDERS.
OR WOULD IT BE BETTER TO ADMIT THAT CHANGE CAN BE VERY BAD?
MY FAVORITE PART WAS WHEN HE YELLED, "STOP RUINING MY SLOGANS WITH YOUR LOGIC!"
SNORT
HEE-HEE!!!

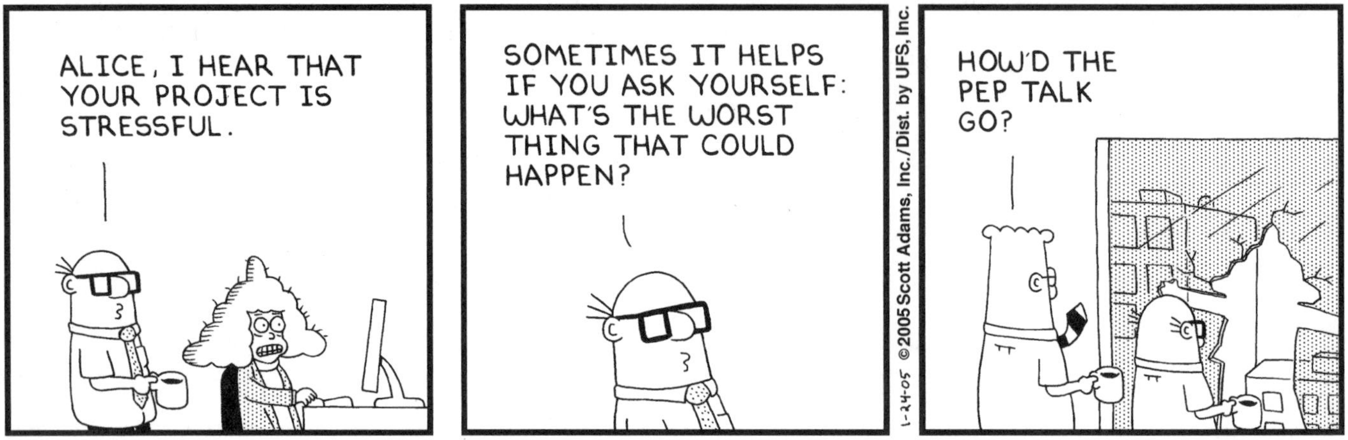
ALICE, I HEAR THAT YOUR PROJECT IS STRESSFUL.
SOMETIMES IT HELPS IF YOU ASK YOURSELF: WHAT'S THE WORST THING THAT COULD HAPPEN?
1-24-05 ©2005 Scott Adams, Inc./Dist. by UFS, Inc.
HOW'D THE PEP TALK GO?

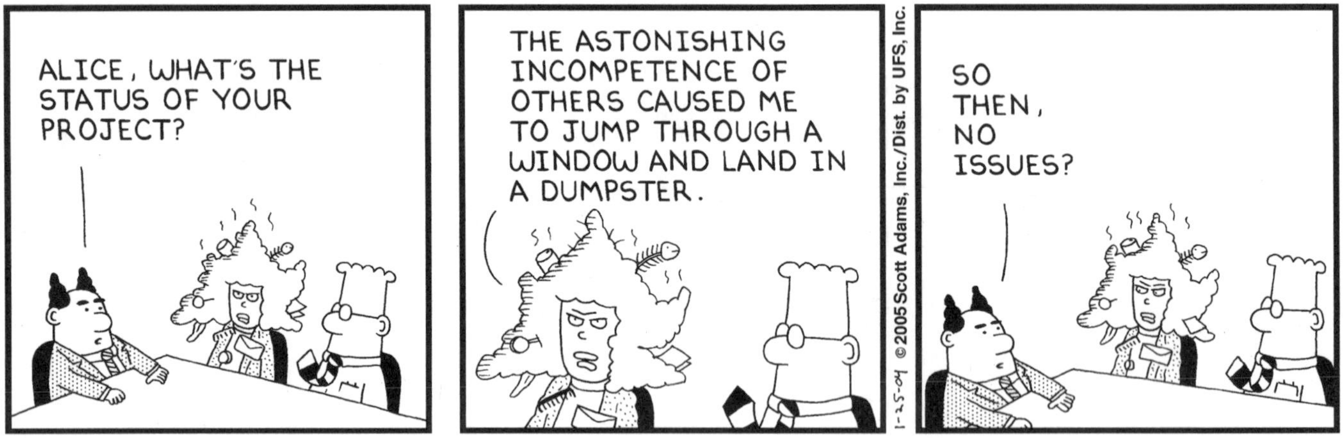
ALICE, WHAT'S THE STATUS OF YOUR PROJECT?
THE ASTONISHING INCOMPETENCE OF OTHERS CAUSED ME TO JUMP THROUGH A WINDOW AND LAND IN A DUMPSTER.
1-25-05 ©2005 Scott Adams, Inc./Dist. by UFS, Inc.
SO THEN, NO ISSUES?

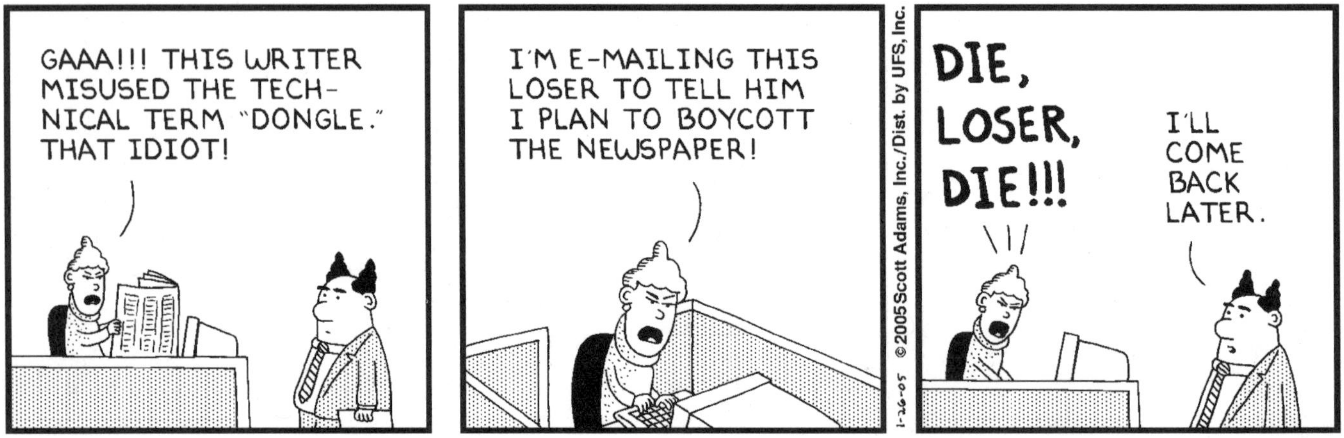
GAAA!!! THIS WRITER MISUSED THE TECH-NICAL TERM "DONGLE." THAT IDIOT!
I'M E-MAILING THIS LOSER TO TELL HIM I PLAN TO BOYCOTT THE NEWSPAPER!
1-26-05 ©2005 Scott Adams, Inc./Dist. by UFS, Inc.
DIE, LOSER, DIE!!!
I'LL COME BACK LATER.

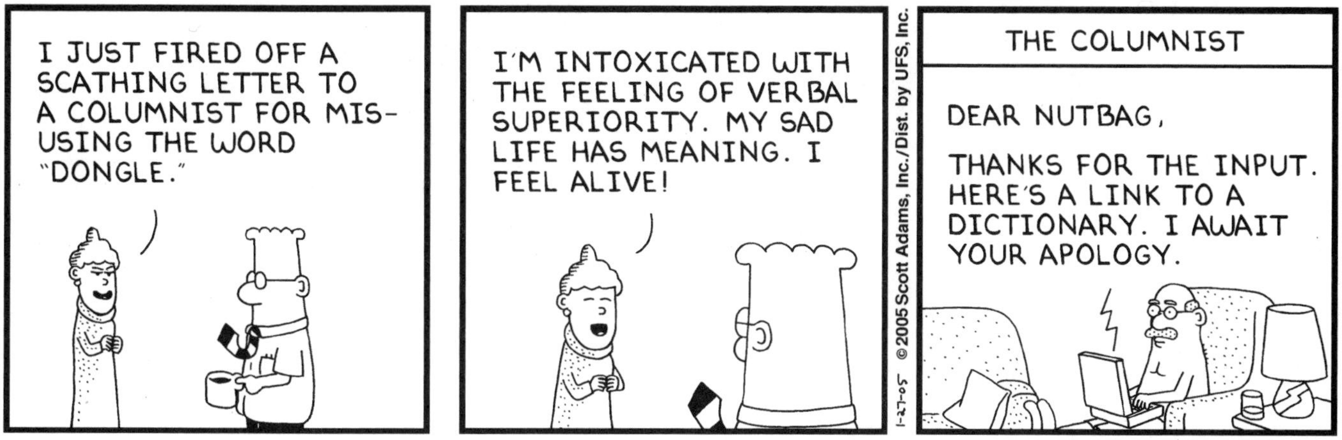
I JUST FIRED OFF A SCATHING LETTER TO A COLUMNIST FOR MIS-USING THE WORD "DONGLE."
I'M INTOXICATED WITH THE FEELING OF VERBAL SUPERIORITY. MY SAD LIFE HAS MEANING. I FEEL ALIVE!
THE COLUMNIST
DEAR NUTBAG,
THANKS FOR THE INPUT. HERE'S A LINK TO A DICTIONARY. I AWAIT YOUR APOLOGY.
1-27-05 © 2005 Scott Adams, Inc./Dist. by UFS, Inc.

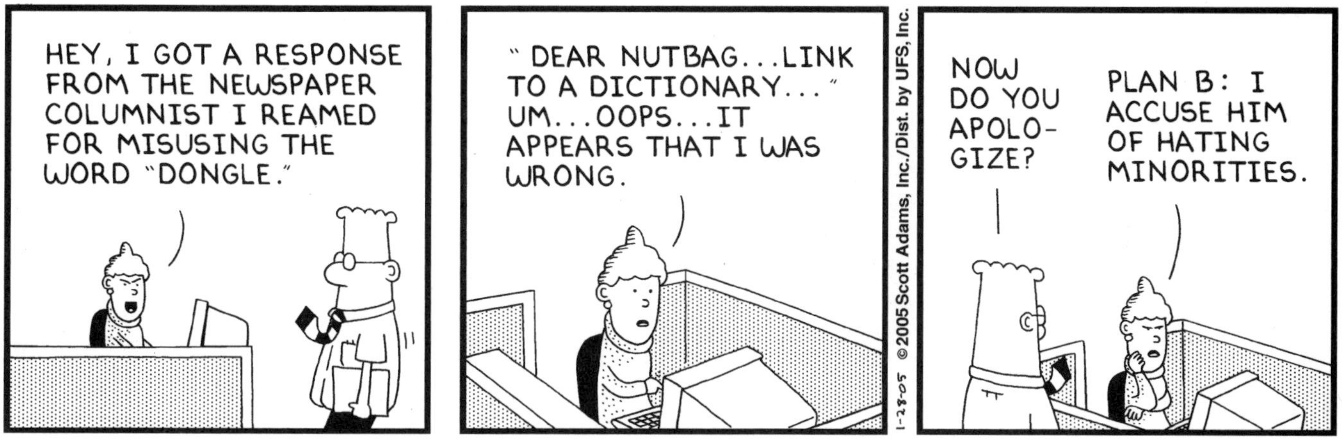
HEY, I GOT A RESPONSE FROM THE NEWSPAPER COLUMNIST I REAMED FOR MISUSING THE WORD "DONGLE."
" DEAR NUTBAG...LINK TO A DICTIONARY... " UM...OOPS...IT APPEARS THAT I WAS WRONG.
NOW DO YOU APOLO-GIZE?
PLAN B: I ACCUSE HIM OF HATING MINORITIES.
1-28-05 © 2005 Scott Adams, Inc./Dist. by UFS, Inc.

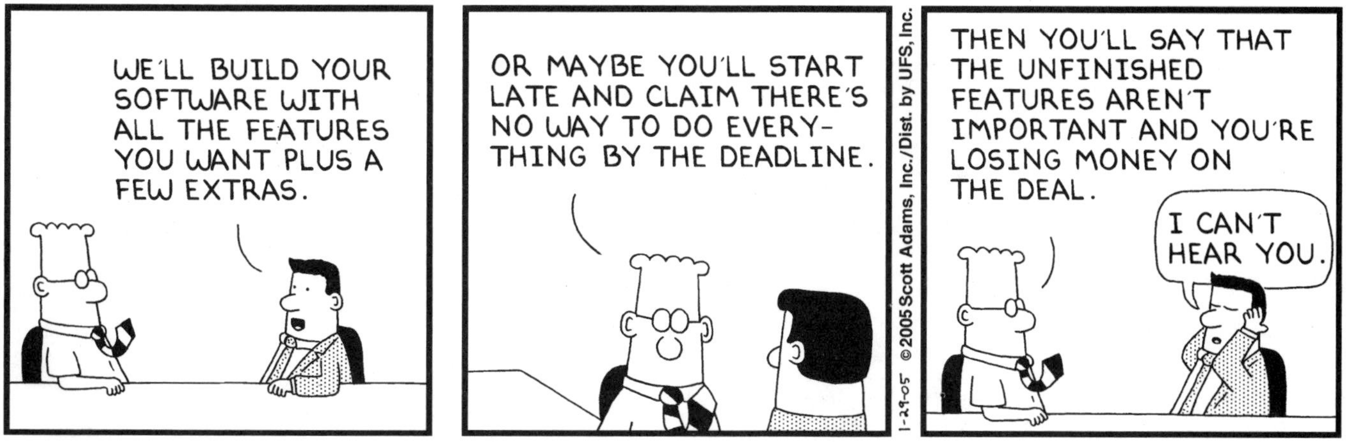
WE'LL BUILD YOUR SOFTWARE WITH ALL THE FEATURES YOU WANT PLUS A FEW EXTRAS.
OR MAYBE YOU'LL START LATE AND CLAIM THERE'S NO WAY TO DO EVERY-THING BY THE DEADLINE.
THEN YOU'LL SAY THAT THE UNFINISHED FEATURES AREN'T IMPORTANT AND YOU'RE LOSING MONEY ON THE DEAL.
I CAN'T HEAR YOU.
1-29-05 © 2005 Scott Adams, Inc./Dist. by UFS, Inc.

HERE'S MY VACATION SCHEDULE.
GOOD.
WHOA! YOU'RE PLANNING TO TAKE MORE VACATION DAYS THAN YOU'VE ACCRUED.
IT'S OKAY BECAUSE I'LL ACCRUE THE DAYS BEFORE THE ACTUAL VACATION.
NO CAN DO. WHAT IF YOU QUIT BEFORE THEN?
I'M LITERALLY AFRAID TO HEAR THE ANSWER TO THAT QUESTION.
THINK, MAN! IF YOU QUIT AND HAVE A VACATION AT THE SAME TIME...
I'LL BE DOWN TWO PEOPLE!!!
IT'S HARD TO REMAIN UPBEAT.
DO YOU STILL LIVE HERE?
©2005 Scott Adams, Inc./Dist. by UFS, Inc.
1-30-05

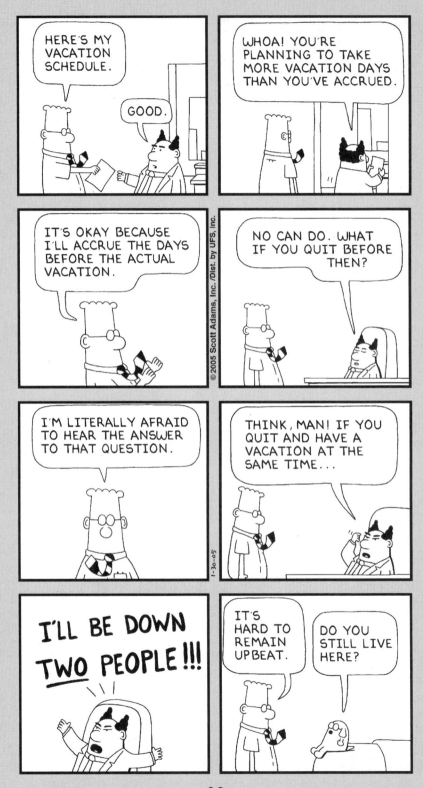

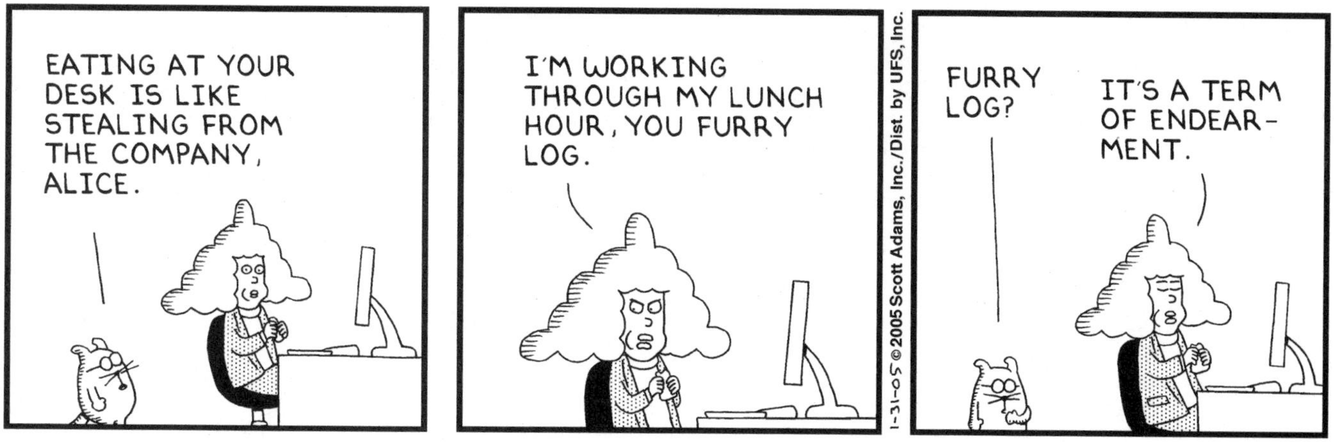
EATING AT YOUR DESK IS LIKE STEALING FROM THE COMPANY, ALICE.
I'M WORKING THROUGH MY LUNCH HOUR, YOU FURRY LOG.
FURRY LOG?
IT'S A TERM OF ENDEAR-MENT.
1-31-05 © 2005 Scott Adams, Inc./Dist. by UFS, Inc.

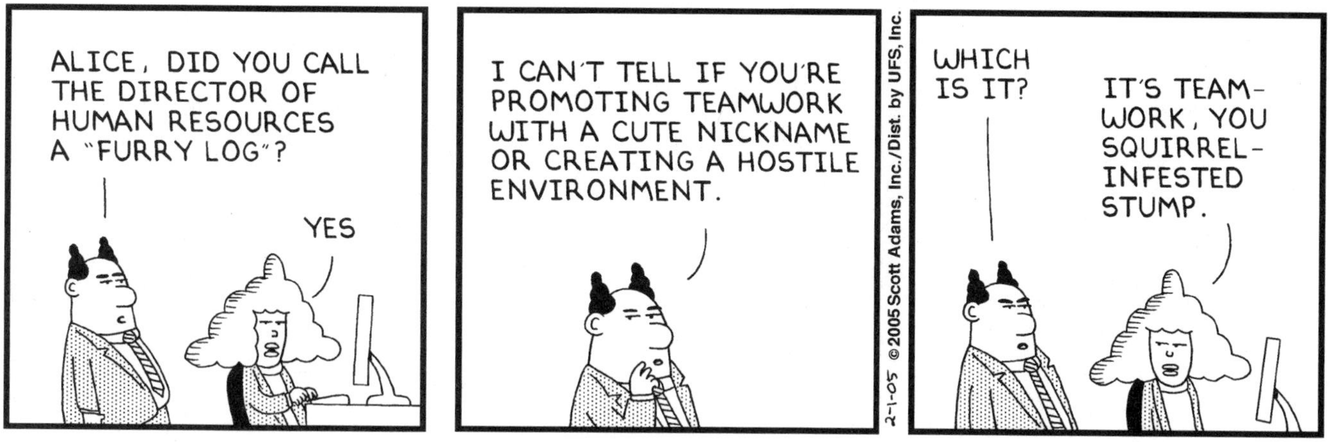
ALICE, DID YOU CALL THE DIRECTOR OF HUMAN RESOURCES A "FURRY LOG"?
YES
I CAN'T TELL IF YOU'RE PROMOTING TEAMWORK WITH A CUTE NICKNAME OR CREATING A HOSTILE ENVIRONMENT.
WHICH IS IT?
IT'S TEAM-WORK, YOU SQUIRREL-INFESTED STUMP.
2-1-05 © 2005 Scott Adams, Inc./Dist. by UFS, Inc.

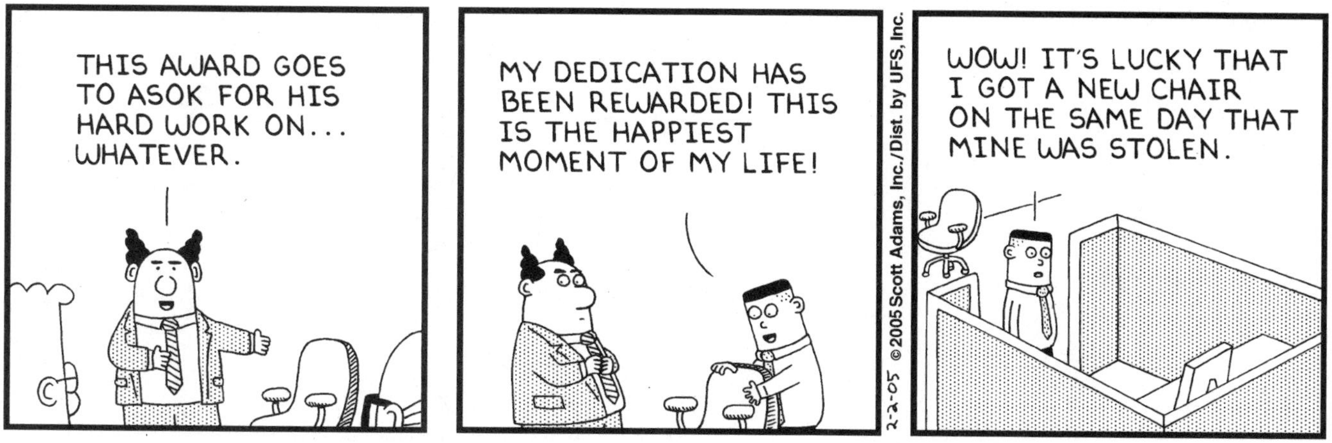
THIS AWARD GOES TO ASOK FOR HIS HARD WORK ON... WHATEVER.
MY DEDICATION HAS BEEN REWARDED! THIS IS THE HAPPIEST MOMENT OF MY LIFE!
WOW! IT'S LUCKY THAT I GOT A NEW CHAIR ON THE SAME DAY THAT MINE WAS STOLEN.
2-2-05 © 2005 Scott Adams, Inc./Dist. by UFS, Inc.

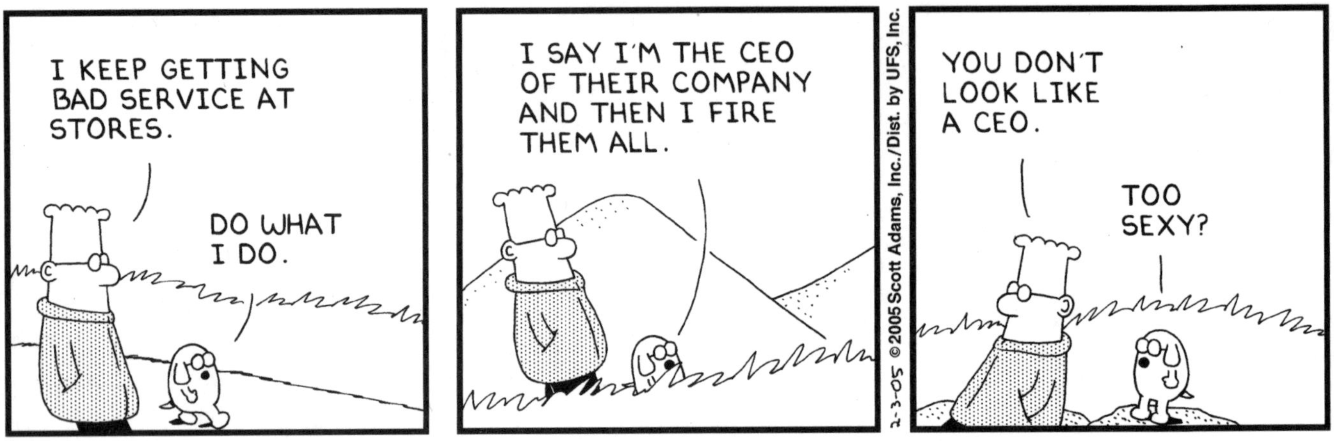
I KEEP GETTING BAD SERVICE AT STORES.
DO WHAT I DO.
I SAY I'M THE CEO OF THEIR COMPANY AND THEN I FIRE THEM ALL.
YOU DON'T LOOK LIKE A CEO.
TOO SEXY?
2-3-05 ©2005 Scott Adams, Inc./Dist. by UFS, Inc.

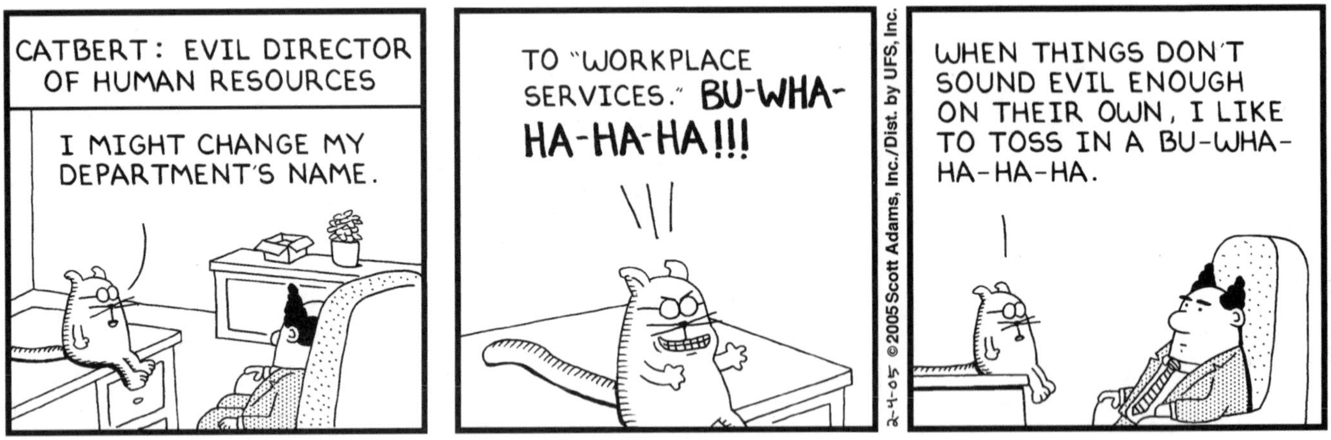
CATBERT: EVIL DIRECTOR OF HUMAN RESOURCES
I MIGHT CHANGE MY DEPARTMENT'S NAME.
TO "WORKPLACE SERVICES." BU-WHA-HA-HA-HA!!!
WHEN THINGS DON'T SOUND EVIL ENOUGH ON THEIR OWN, I LIKE TO TOSS IN A BU-WHA-HA-HA-HA.
2-4-05 ©2005 Scott Adams, Inc./Dist. by UFS, Inc.

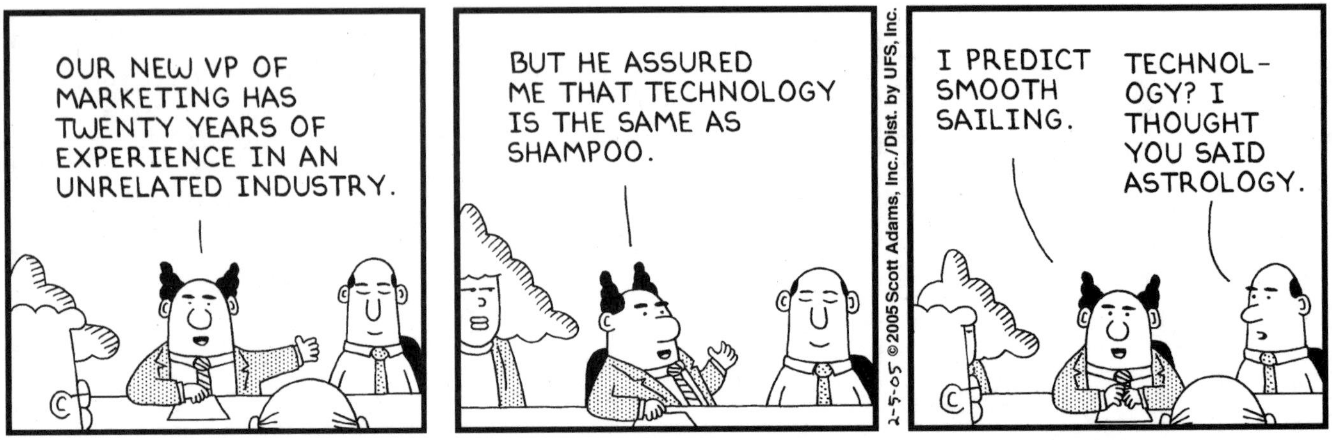
OUR NEW VP OF MARKETING HAS TWENTY YEARS OF EXPERIENCE IN AN UNRELATED INDUSTRY.
BUT HE ASSURED ME THAT TECHNOLOGY IS THE SAME AS SHAMPOO.
I PREDICT SMOOTH SAILING.
TECHNOL-OGY? I THOUGHT YOU SAID ASTROLOGY.
2-5-05 ©2005 Scott Adams, Inc./Dist. by UFS, Inc.

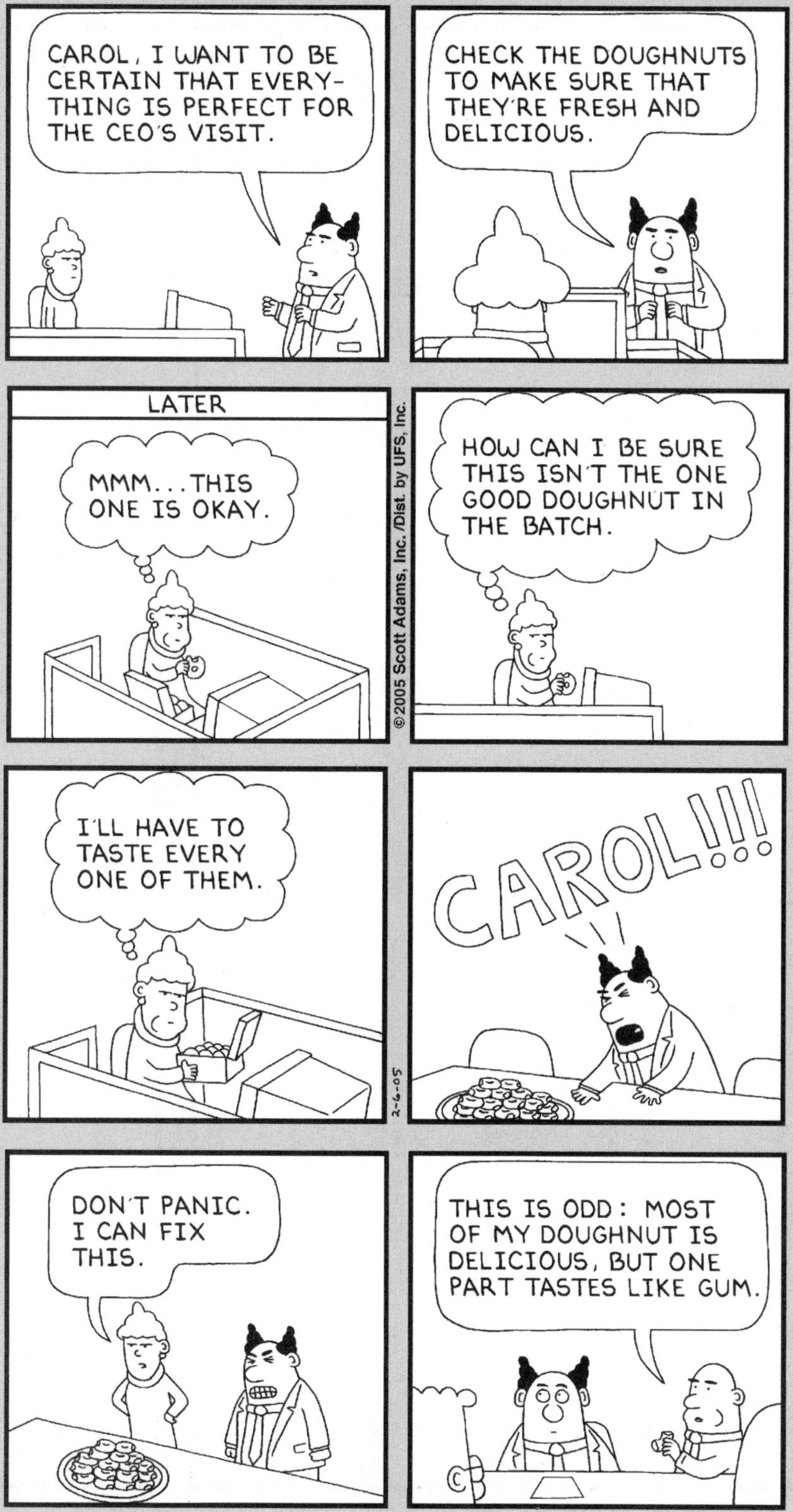
CAROL, I WANT TO BE CERTAIN THAT EVERY-THING IS PERFECT FOR THE CEO'S VISIT.
CHECK THE DOUGHNUTS TO MAKE SURE THAT THEY'RE FRESH AND DELICIOUS.
LATER
MMM...THIS ONE IS OKAY.
HOW CAN I BE SURE THIS ISN'T THE ONE GOOD DOUGHNUT IN THE BATCH.
I'LL HAVE TO TASTE EVERY ONE OF THEM.
CAROL!!!
DON'T PANIC. I CAN FIX THIS.
THIS IS ODD: MOST OF MY DOUGHNUT IS DELICIOUS, BUT ONE PART TASTES LIKE GUM.
©2005 Scott Adams, Inc./Dist. by UFS, Inc.
2-6-05

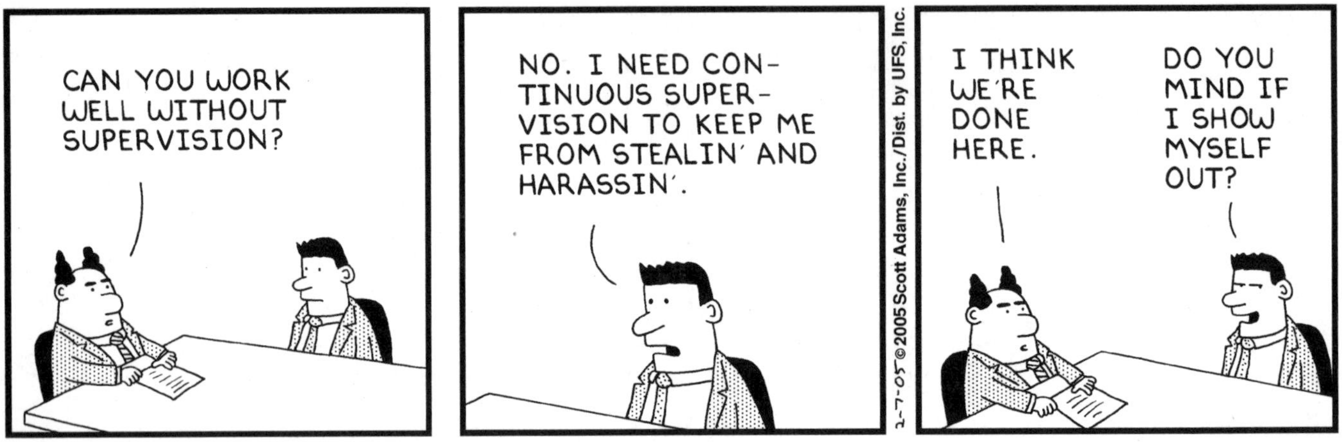
CAN YOU WORK WELL WITHOUT SUPERVISION?
NO. I NEED CON-TINUOUS SUPER-VISION TO KEEP ME FROM STEALIN' AND HARASSIN'.
2-7-05 ©2005 Scott Adams, Inc./Dist. by UFS, Inc.
I THINK WE'RE DONE HERE.
DO YOU MIND IF I SHOW MYSELF OUT?

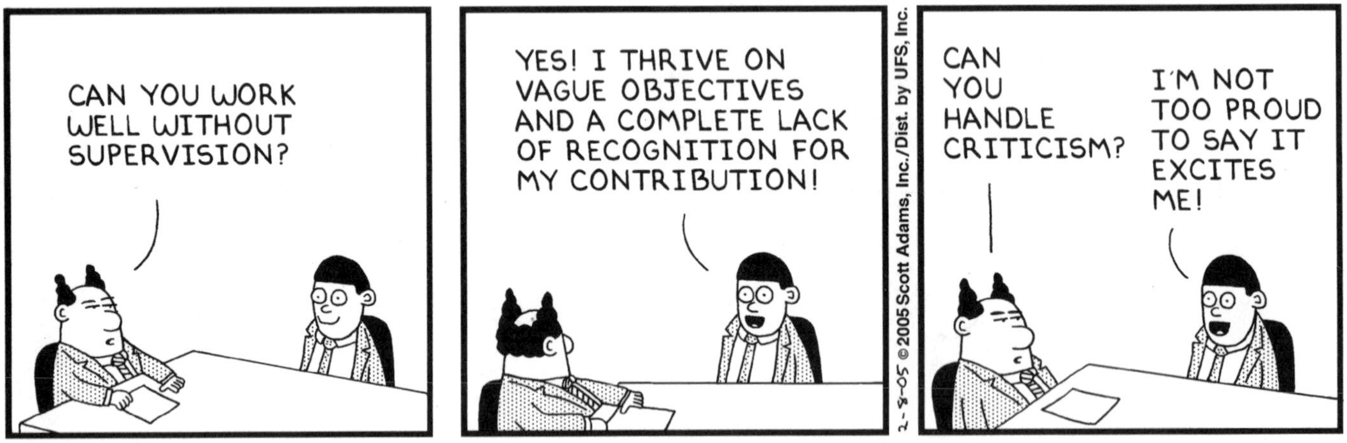
CAN YOU WORK WELL WITHOUT SUPERVISION?
YES! I THRIVE ON VAGUE OBJECTIVES AND A COMPLETE LACK OF RECOGNITION FOR MY CONTRIBUTION!
2-8-05 ©2005 Scott Adams, Inc./Dist. by UFS, Inc.
CAN YOU HANDLE CRITICISM?
I'M NOT TOO PROUD TO SAY IT EXCITES ME!

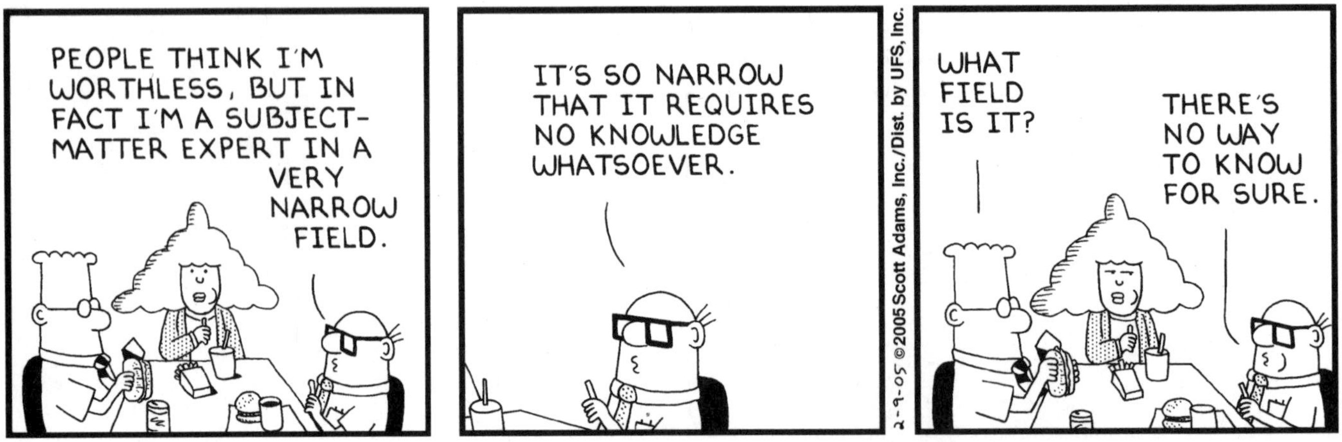
PEOPLE THINK I'M WORTHLESS, BUT IN FACT I'M A SUBJECT-MATTER EXPERT IN A VERY NARROW FIELD.
IT'S SO NARROW THAT IT REQUIRES NO KNOWLEDGE WHATSOEVER.
2-9-05 ©2005 Scott Adams, Inc./Dist. by UFS, Inc.
WHAT FIELD IS IT?
THERE'S NO WAY TO KNOW FOR SURE.

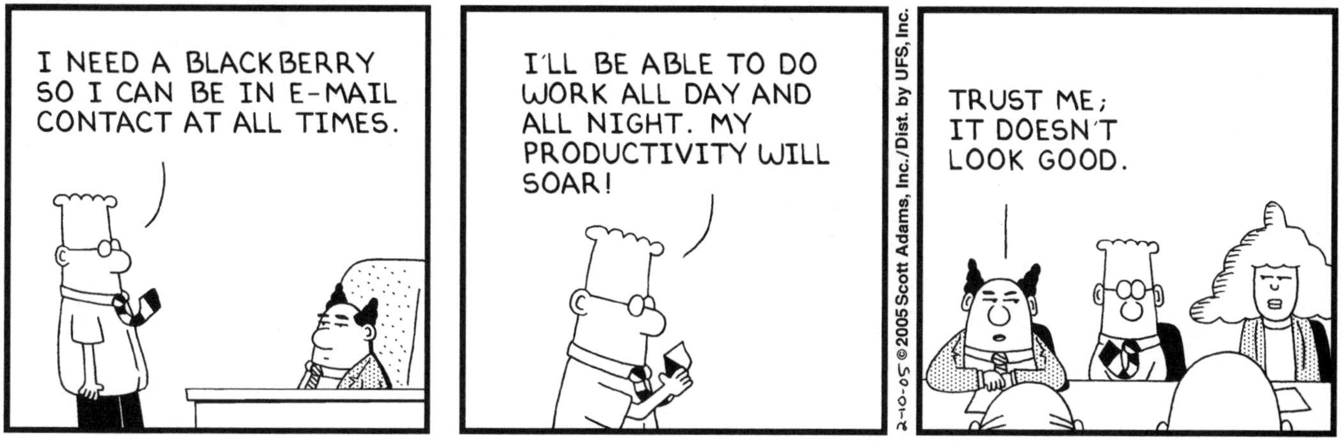
I NEED A BLACKBERRY SO I CAN BE IN E-MAIL CONTACT AT ALL TIMES.
I'LL BE ABLE TO DO WORK ALL DAY AND ALL NIGHT. MY PRODUCTIVITY WILL SOAR!
TRUST ME; IT DOESN'T LOOK GOOD.
2-10-05 © 2005 Scott Adams, Inc./Dist. by UFS, Inc.

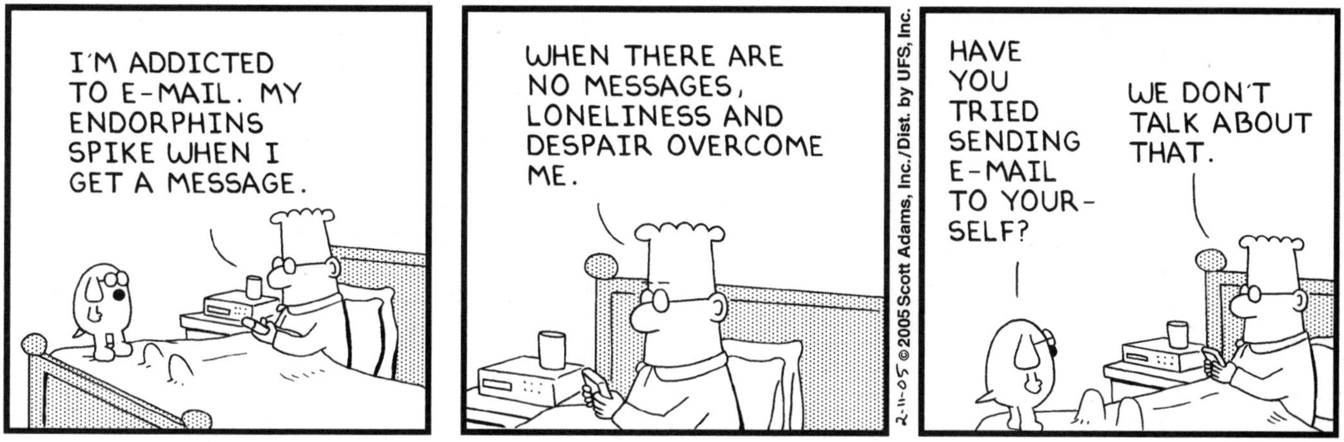
I'M ADDICTED TO E-MAIL. MY ENDORPHINS SPIKE WHEN I GET A MESSAGE.
WHEN THERE ARE NO MESSAGES, LONELINESS AND DESPAIR OVERCOME ME.
HAVE YOU TRIED SENDING E-MAIL TO YOUR-SELF?
WE DON'T TALK ABOUT THAT.
2-11-05 © 2005 Scott Adams, Inc./Dist. by UFS, Inc.

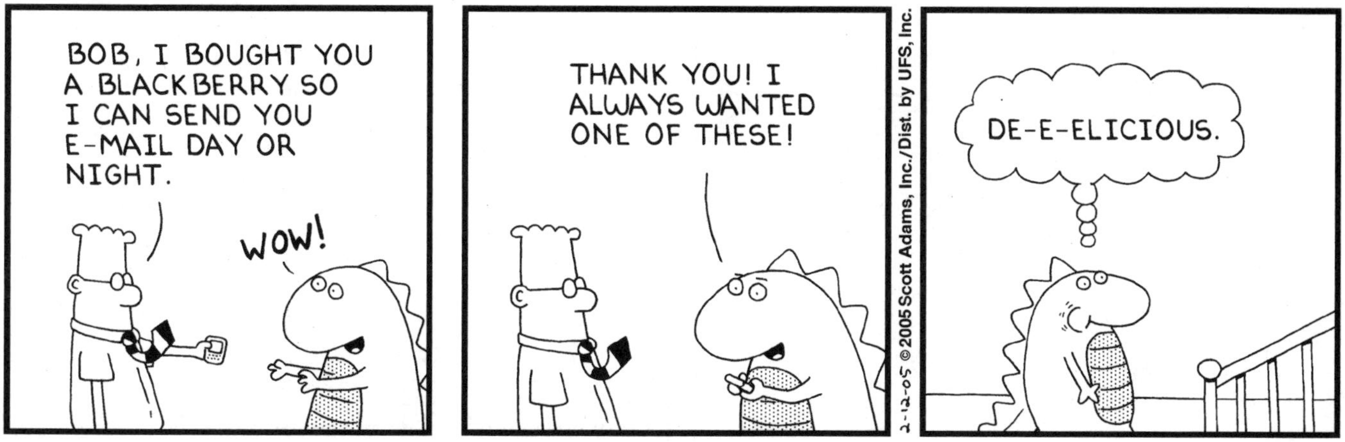
BOB, I BOUGHT YOU A BLACKBERRY SO I CAN SEND YOU E-MAIL DAY OR NIGHT.
WOW!
THANK YOU! I ALWAYS WANTED ONE OF THESE!
DE-E-ELICIOUS.
2-12-05 © 2005 Scott Adams, Inc./Dist. by UFS, Inc.

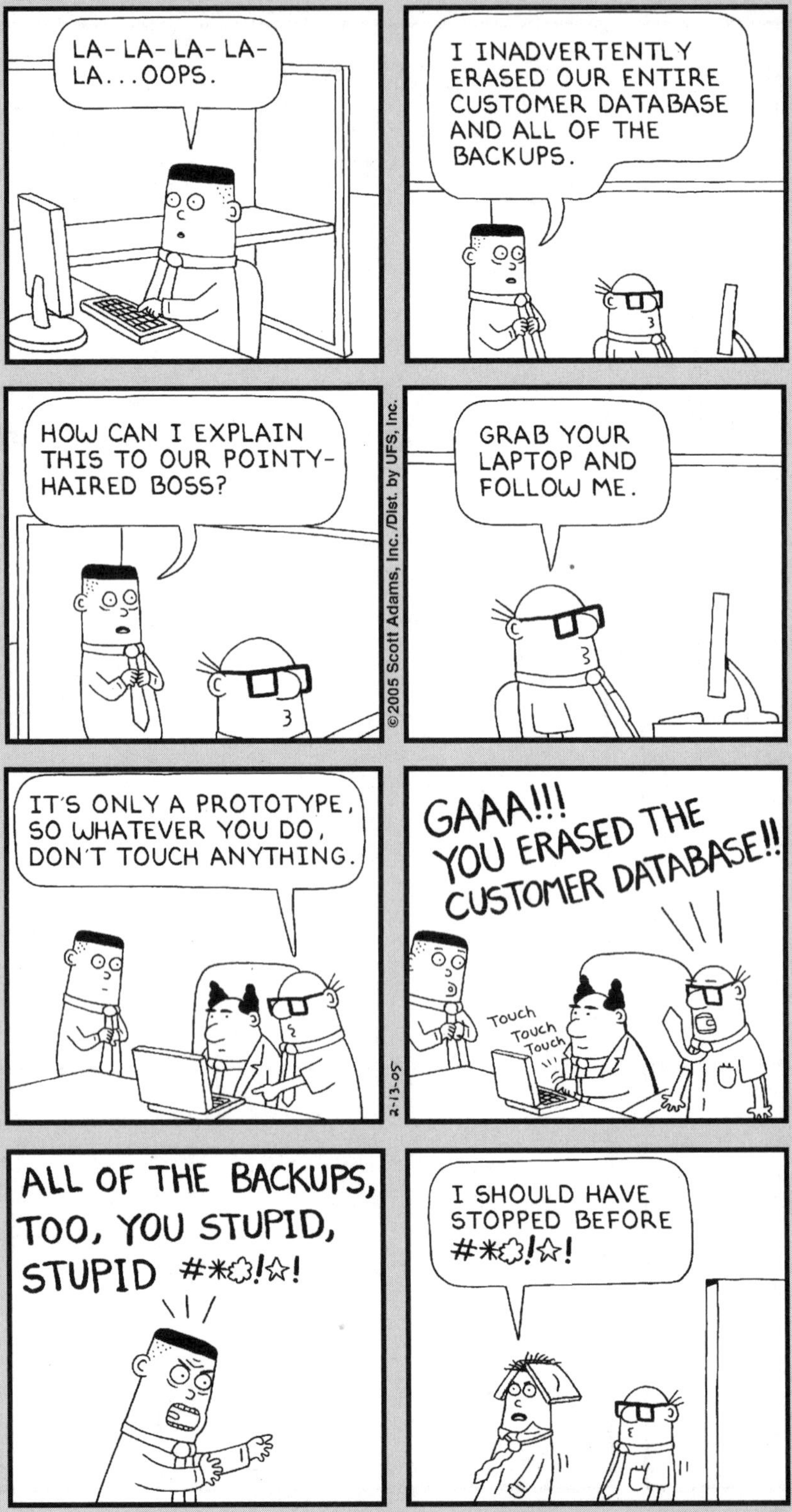
LA- LA- LA- LA- LA. . . OOPS.
I INADVERTENTLY ERASED OUR ENTIRE CUSTOMER DATABASE AND ALL OF THE BACKUPS.
HOW CAN I EXPLAIN THIS TO OUR POINTY-HAIRED BOSS?
GRAB YOUR LAPTOP AND FOLLOW ME.
IT'S ONLY A PROTOTYPE, SO WHATEVER YOU DO, DON'T TOUCH ANYTHING.
GAAA!!! YOU ERASED THE CUSTOMER DATABASE!!
Touch Touch Touch
ALL OF THE BACKUPS, TOO, YOU STUPID, STUPID #*✿!☆!
I SHOULD HAVE STOPPED BEFORE #*✿!☆!
©2005 Scott Adams, Inc./Dist. by UFS, Inc.
2-13-05

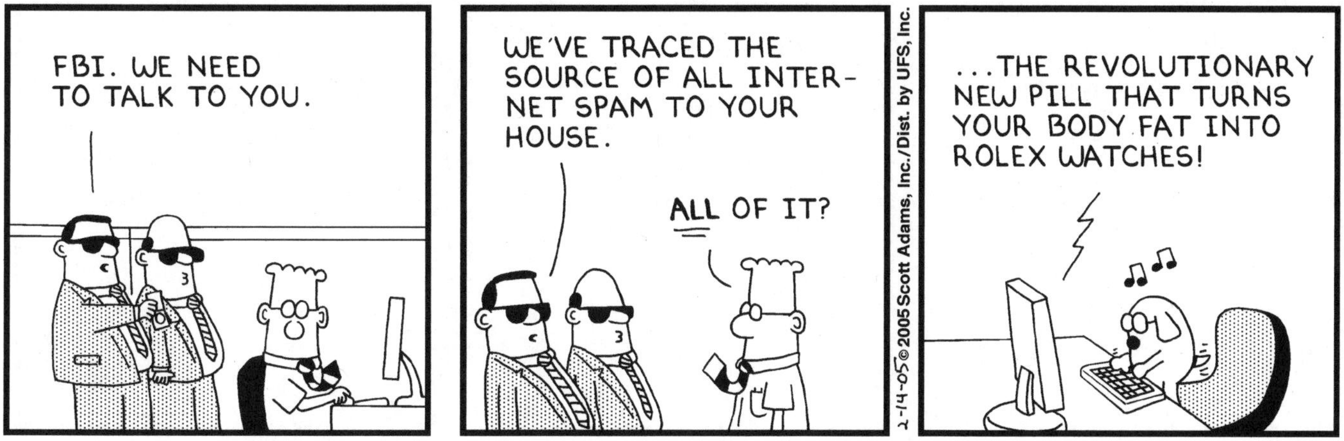
FBI. WE NEED TO TALK TO YOU.
WE'VE TRACED THE SOURCE OF ALL INTER-NET SPAM TO YOUR HOUSE.
ALL OF IT?
...THE REVOLUTIONARY NEW PILL THAT TURNS YOUR BODY FAT INTO ROLEX WATCHES!

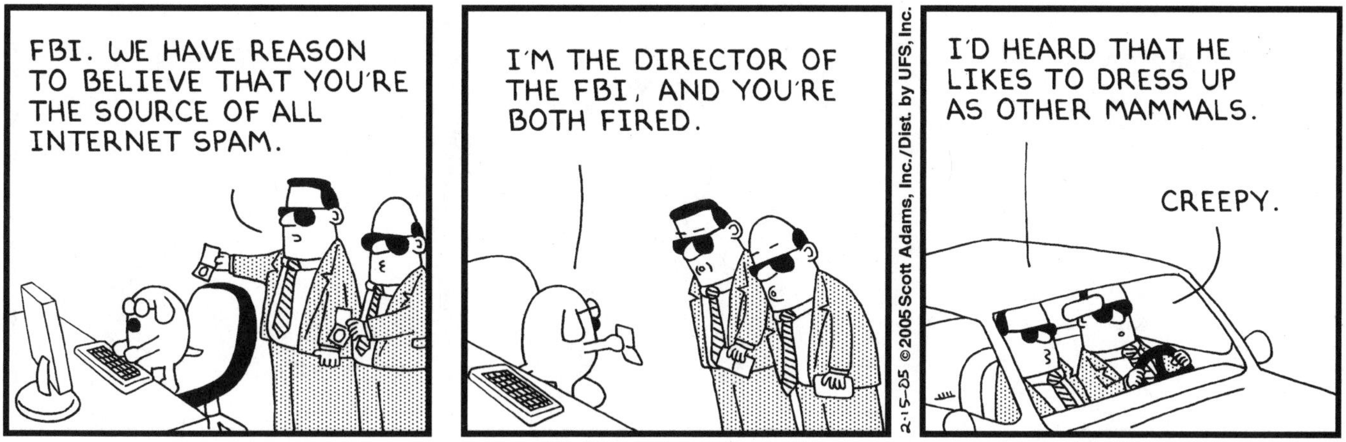
FBI. WE HAVE REASON TO BELIEVE THAT YOU'RE THE SOURCE OF ALL INTERNET SPAM.
I'M THE DIRECTOR OF THE FBI, AND YOU'RE BOTH FIRED.
I'D HEARD THAT HE LIKES TO DRESS UP AS OTHER MAMMALS.
CREEPY.

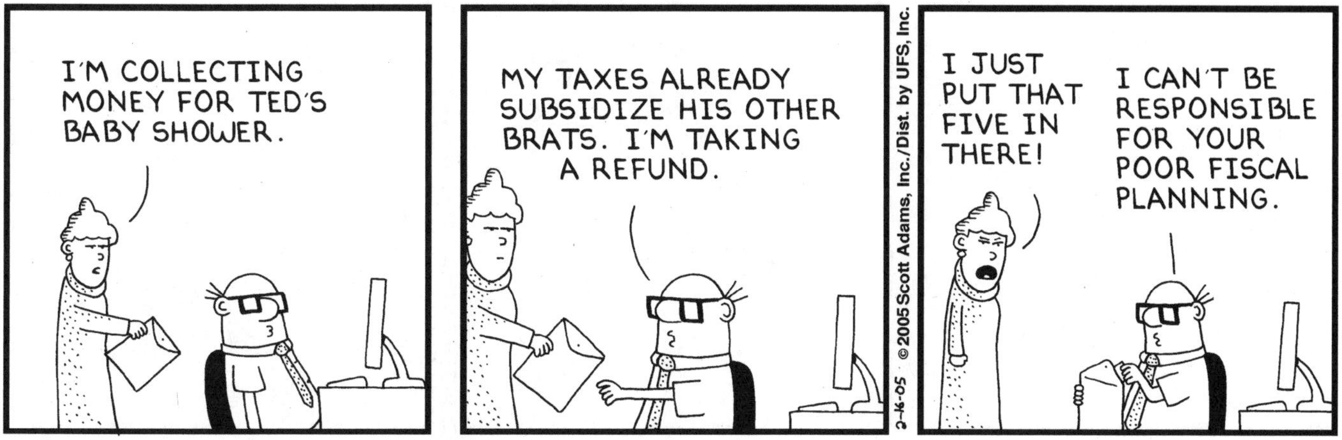
I'M COLLECTING MONEY FOR TED'S BABY SHOWER.
MY TAXES ALREADY SUBSIDIZE HIS OTHER BRATS. I'M TAKING A REFUND.
I JUST PUT THAT FIVE IN THERE!
I CAN'T BE RESPONSIBLE FOR YOUR POOR FISCAL PLANNING.

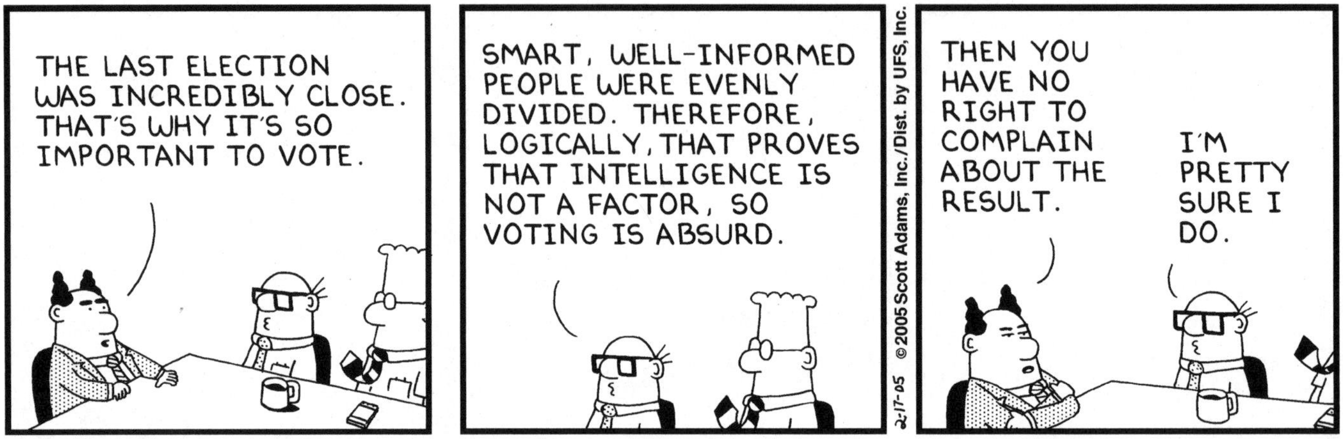
THE LAST ELECTION WAS INCREDIBLY CLOSE. THAT'S WHY IT'S SO IMPORTANT TO VOTE.
SMART, WELL-INFORMED PEOPLE WERE EVENLY DIVIDED. THEREFORE, LOGICALLY, THAT PROVES THAT INTELLIGENCE IS NOT A FACTOR, SO VOTING IS ABSURD.
2-17-05 © 2005 Scott Adams, Inc./Dist. by UFS, Inc.
THEN YOU HAVE NO RIGHT TO COMPLAIN ABOUT THE RESULT.
I'M PRETTY SURE I DO.

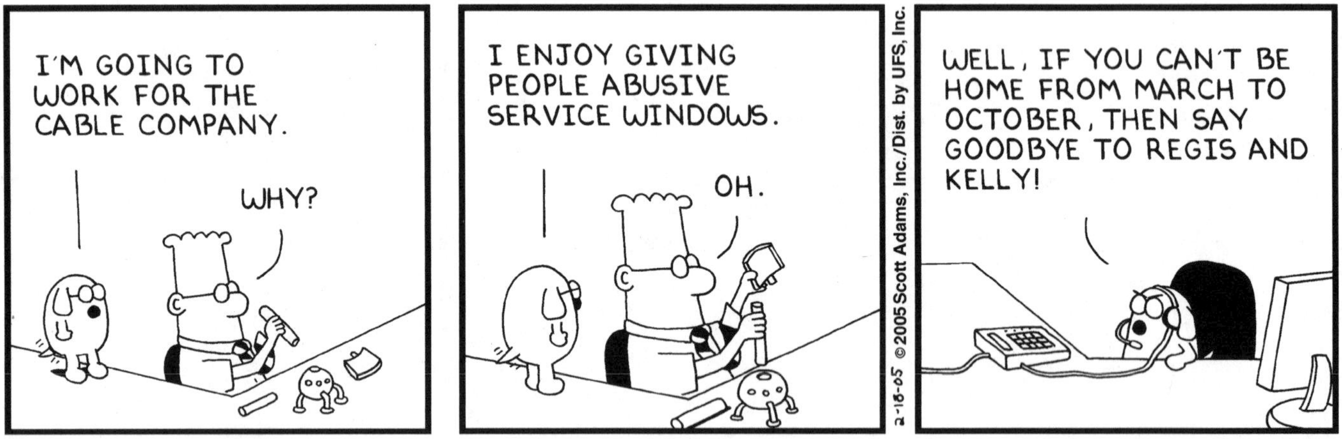
I'M GOING TO WORK FOR THE CABLE COMPANY.
WHY?
I ENJOY GIVING PEOPLE ABUSIVE SERVICE WINDOWS.
OH.
2-18-05 © 2005 Scott Adams, Inc./Dist. by UFS, Inc.
WELL, IF YOU CAN'T BE HOME FROM MARCH TO OCTOBER, THEN SAY GOODBYE TO REGIS AND KELLY!

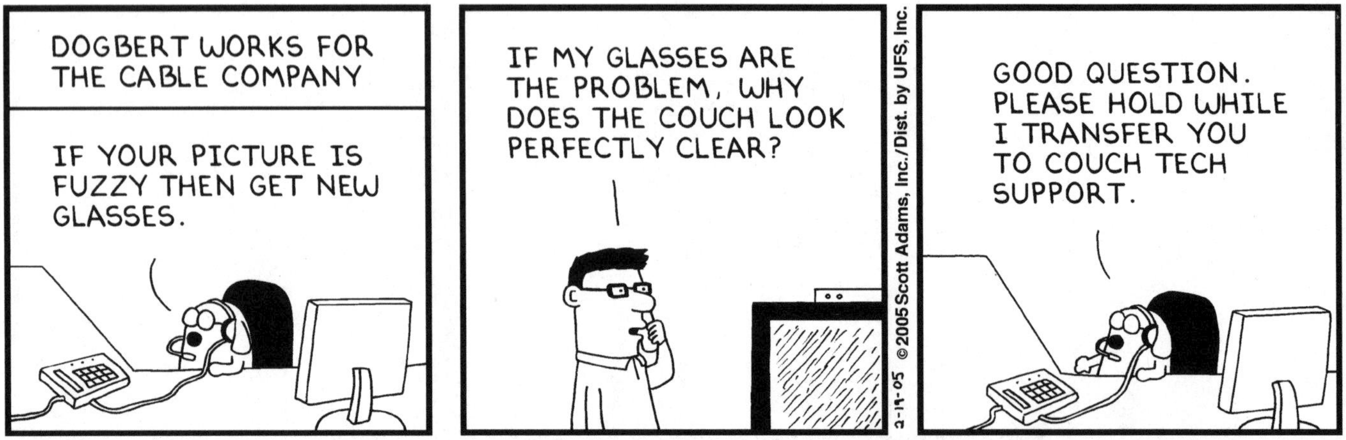
DOGBERT WORKS FOR THE CABLE COMPANY
IF YOUR PICTURE IS FUZZY THEN GET NEW GLASSES.
IF MY GLASSES ARE THE PROBLEM, WHY DOES THE COUCH LOOK PERFECTLY CLEAR?
2-19-05 © 2005 Scott Adams, Inc./Dist. by UFS, Inc.
GOOD QUESTION. PLEASE HOLD WHILE I TRANSFER YOU TO COUCH TECH SUPPORT.

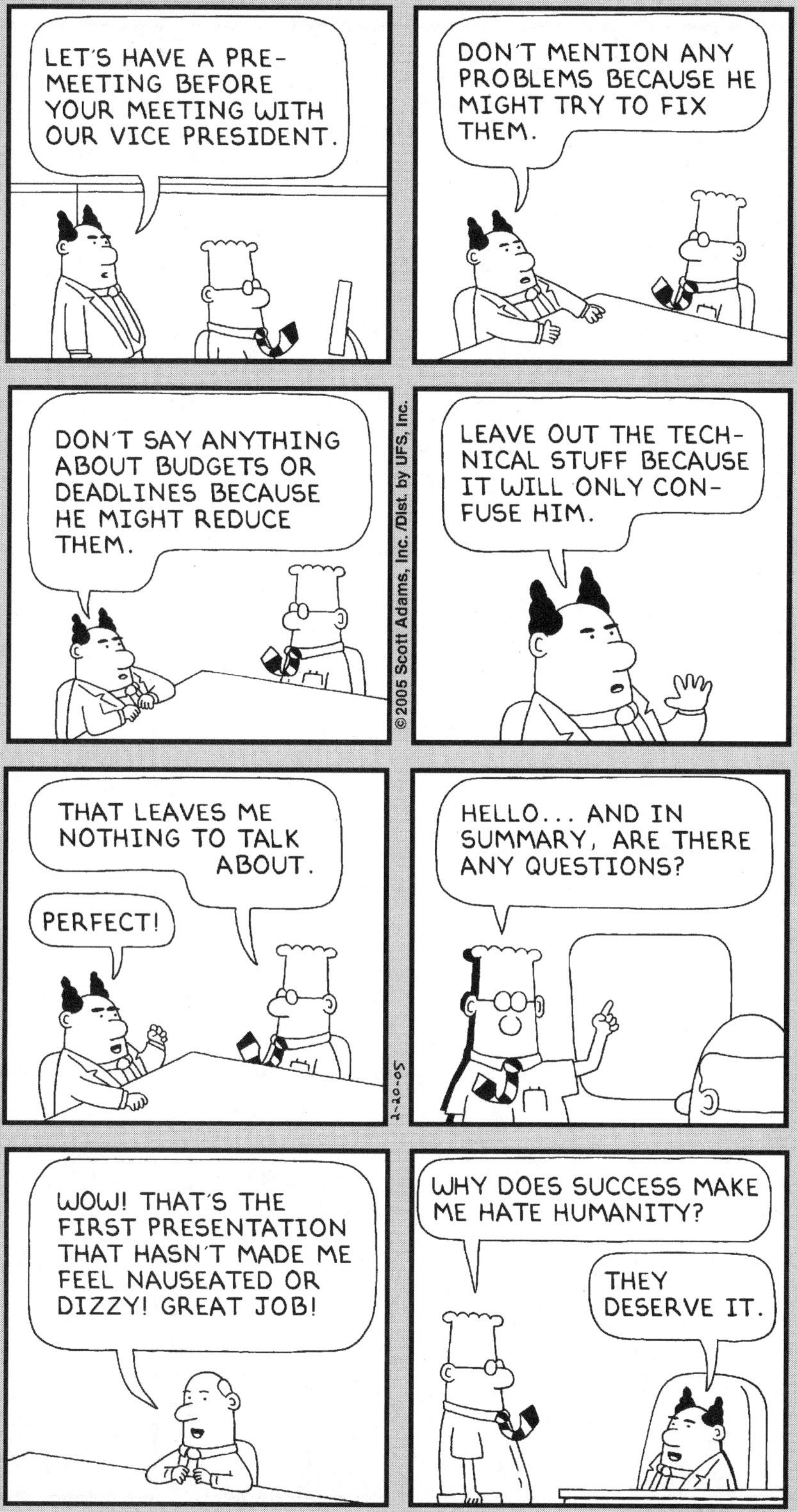
LET'S HAVE A PRE-MEETING BEFORE YOUR MEETING WITH OUR VICE PRESIDENT.
DON'T MENTION ANY PROBLEMS BECAUSE HE MIGHT TRY TO FIX THEM.
DON'T SAY ANYTHING ABOUT BUDGETS OR DEADLINES BECAUSE HE MIGHT REDUCE THEM.
LEAVE OUT THE TECH-NICAL STUFF BECAUSE IT WILL ONLY CON-FUSE HIM.
THAT LEAVES ME NOTHING TO TALK ABOUT.
PERFECT!
HELLO... AND IN SUMMARY, ARE THERE ANY QUESTIONS?
WOW! THAT'S THE FIRST PRESENTATION THAT HASN'T MADE ME FEEL NAUSEATED OR DIZZY! GREAT JOB!
WHY DOES SUCCESS MAKE ME HATE HUMANITY?
THEY DESERVE IT.
©2005 Scott Adams, Inc./Dist. by UFS, Inc.
2-20-05

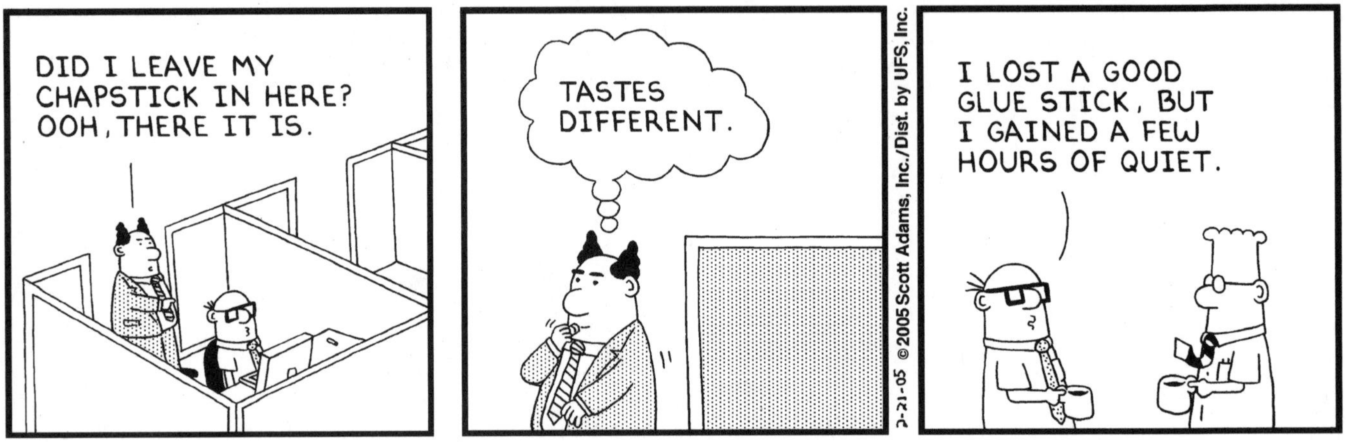
DID I LEAVE MY CHAPSTICK IN HERE? OOH, THERE IT IS.
TASTES DIFFERENT.
©2005 Scott Adams, Inc./Dist. by UFS, Inc.
I LOST A GOOD GLUE STICK, BUT I GAINED A FEW HOURS OF QUIET.

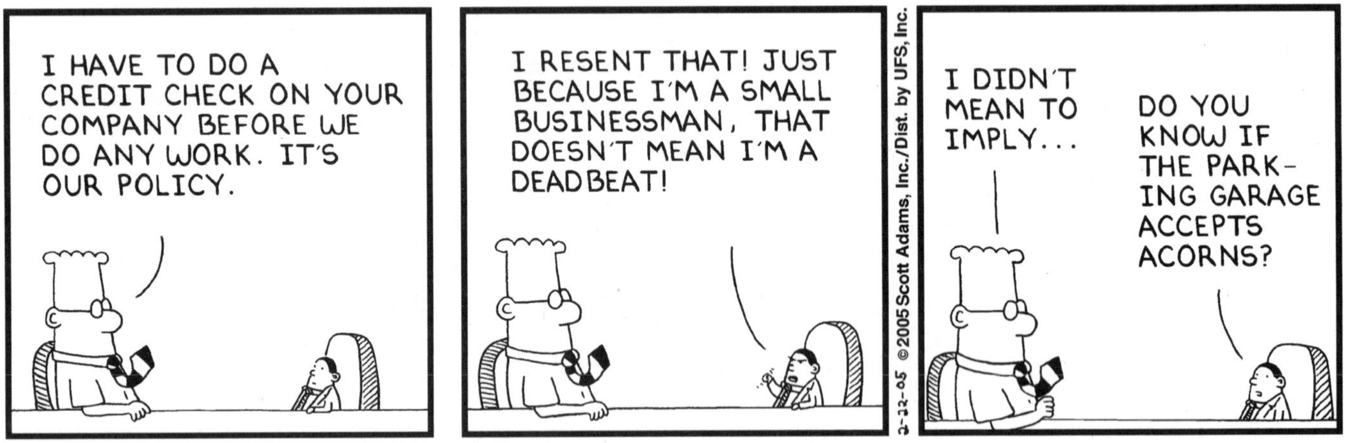
I HAVE TO DO A CREDIT CHECK ON YOUR COMPANY BEFORE WE DO ANY WORK. IT'S OUR POLICY.
I RESENT THAT! JUST BECAUSE I'M A SMALL BUSINESSMAN, THAT DOESN'T MEAN I'M A DEADBEAT!
©2005 Scott Adams, Inc./Dist. by UFS, Inc.
I DIDN'T MEAN TO IMPLY...
DO YOU KNOW IF THE PARKING GARAGE ACCEPTS ACORNS?

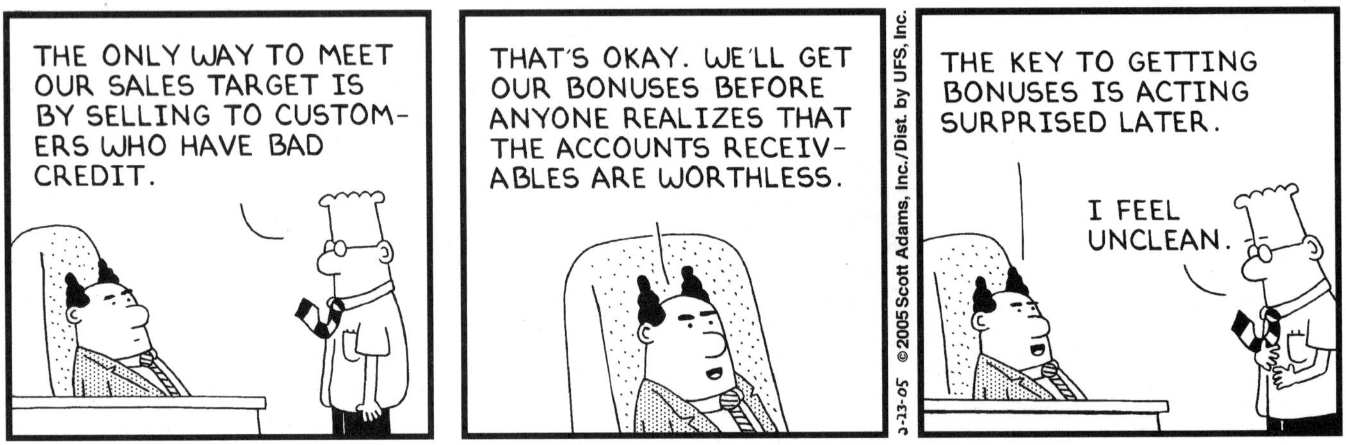
THE ONLY WAY TO MEET OUR SALES TARGET IS BY SELLING TO CUSTOMERS WHO HAVE BAD CREDIT.
THAT'S OKAY. WE'LL GET OUR BONUSES BEFORE ANYONE REALIZES THAT THE ACCOUNTS RECEIVABLES ARE WORTHLESS.
©2005 Scott Adams, Inc./Dist. by UFS, Inc.
THE KEY TO GETTING BONUSES IS ACTING SURPRISED LATER.
I FEEL UNCLEAN.

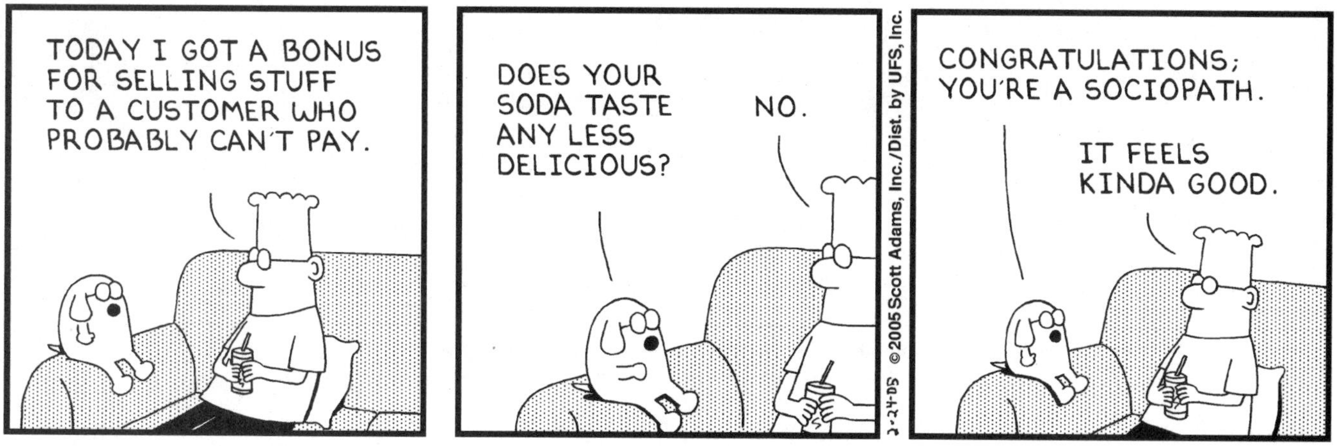
TODAY I GOT A BONUS FOR SELLING STUFF TO A CUSTOMER WHO PROBABLY CAN'T PAY.
DOES YOUR SODA TASTE ANY LESS DELICIOUS?
NO.
2-24-05 © 2005 Scott Adams, Inc./Dist. by UFS, Inc.
CONGRATULATIONS; YOU'RE A SOCIOPATH.
IT FEELS KINDA GOOD.

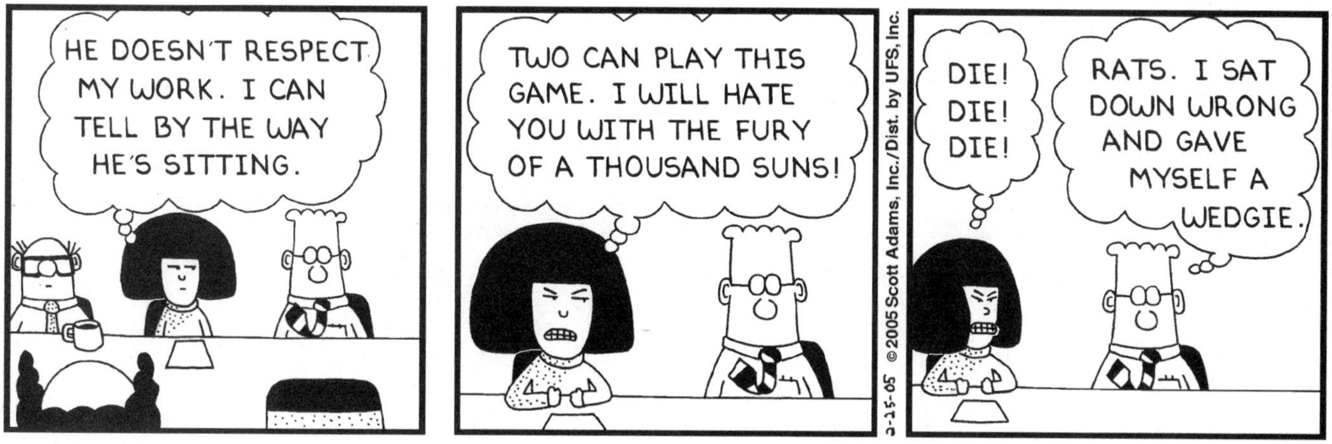
HE DOESN'T RESPECT MY WORK. I CAN TELL BY THE WAY HE'S SITTING.
TWO CAN PLAY THIS GAME. I WILL HATE YOU WITH THE FURY OF A THOUSAND SUNS!
2-25-05 © 2005 Scott Adams, Inc./Dist. by UFS, Inc.
DIE! DIE! DIE!
RATS. I SAT DOWN WRONG AND GAVE MYSELF A WEDGIE.

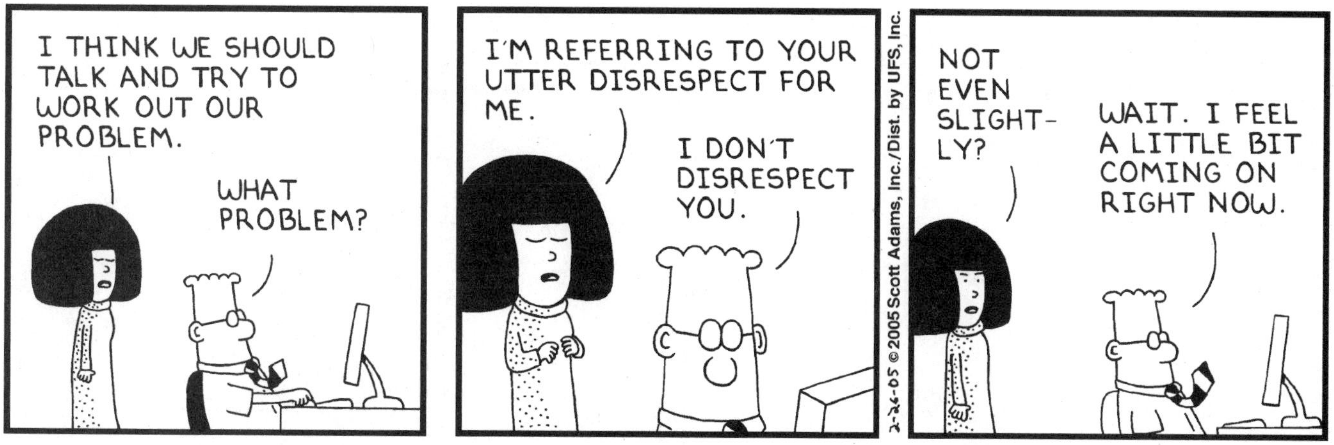
I THINK WE SHOULD TALK AND TRY TO WORK OUT OUR PROBLEM.
WHAT PROBLEM?
I'M REFERRING TO YOUR UTTER DISRESPECT FOR ME.
I DON'T DISRESPECT YOU.
2-26-05 © 2005 Scott Adams, Inc./Dist. by UFS, Inc.
NOT EVEN SLIGHTLY?
WAIT. I FEEL A LITTLE BIT COMING ON RIGHT NOW.

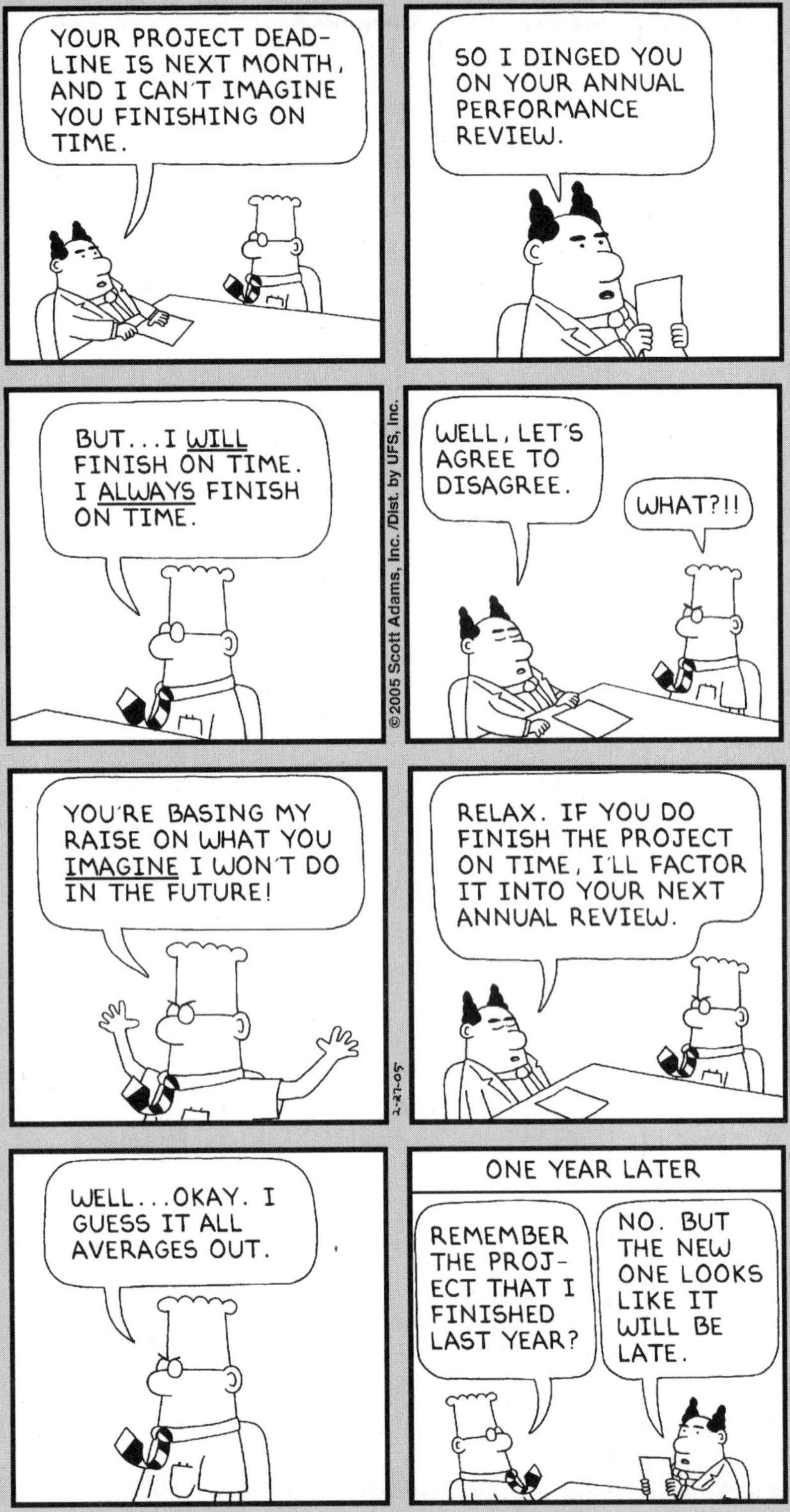
YOUR PROJECT DEAD-LINE IS NEXT MONTH, AND I CAN'T IMAGINE YOU FINISHING ON TIME.
SO I DINGED YOU ON YOUR ANNUAL PERFORMANCE REVIEW.
BUT...I WILL FINISH ON TIME. I ALWAYS FINISH ON TIME.
WELL, LET'S AGREE TO DISAGREE.
WHAT?!!
YOU'RE BASING MY RAISE ON WHAT YOU IMAGINE I WON'T DO IN THE FUTURE!
RELAX. IF YOU DO FINISH THE PROJECT ON TIME, I'LL FACTOR IT INTO YOUR NEXT ANNUAL REVIEW.
WELL...OKAY. I GUESS IT ALL AVERAGES OUT.
ONE YEAR LATER
REMEMBER THE PROJ-ECT THAT I FINISHED LAST YEAR?
NO. BUT THE NEW ONE LOOKS LIKE IT WILL BE LATE.
©2005 Scott Adams, Inc./Dist. by UFS, Inc.
2-27-05

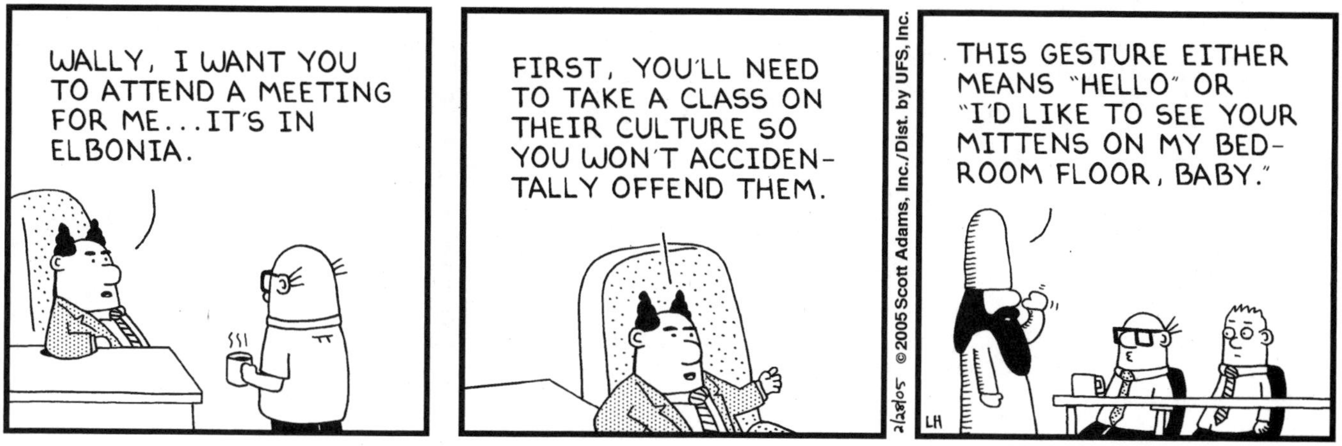
WALLY, I WANT YOU TO ATTEND A MEETING FOR ME... IT'S IN ELBONIA.
FIRST, YOU'LL NEED TO TAKE A CLASS ON THEIR CULTURE SO YOU WON'T ACCIDENTALLY OFFEND THEM.
2/28/05 © 2005 Scott Adams, Inc./Dist. by UFS, Inc.
THIS GESTURE EITHER MEANS "HELLO" OR "I'D LIKE TO SEE YOUR MITTENS ON MY BEDROOM FLOOR, BABY."

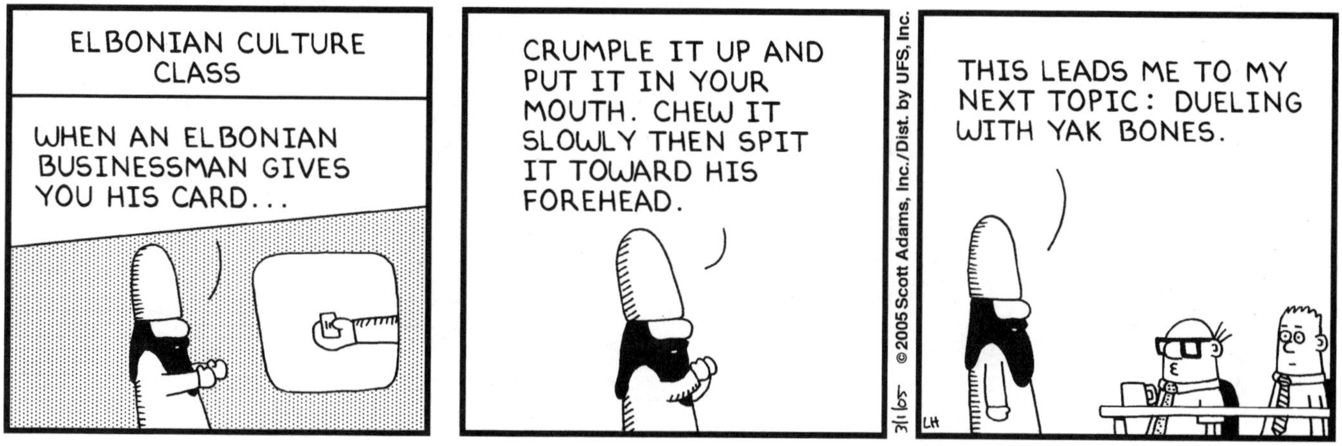
ELBONIAN CULTURE CLASS
WHEN AN ELBONIAN BUSINESSMAN GIVES YOU HIS CARD...
CRUMPLE IT UP AND PUT IT IN YOUR MOUTH. CHEW IT SLOWLY THEN SPIT IT TOWARD HIS FOREHEAD.
3/1/05 © 2005 Scott Adams, Inc./Dist. by UFS, Inc.
THIS LEADS ME TO MY NEXT TOPIC: DUELING WITH YAK BONES.

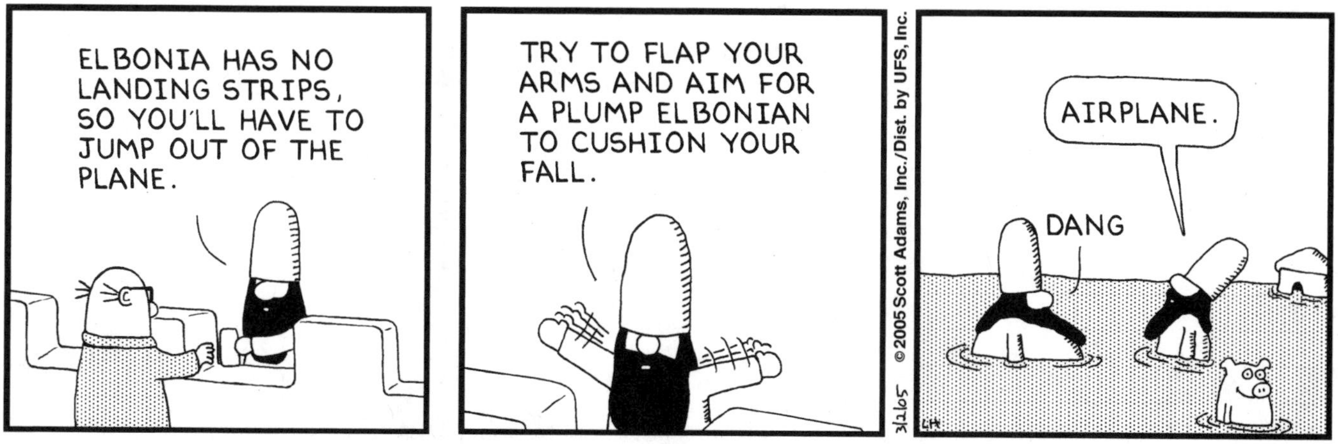
ELBONIA HAS NO LANDING STRIPS, SO YOU'LL HAVE TO JUMP OUT OF THE PLANE.
TRY TO FLAP YOUR ARMS AND AIM FOR A PLUMP ELBONIAN TO CUSHION YOUR FALL.
3/2/05 © 2005 Scott Adams, Inc./Dist. by UFS, Inc.
AIRPLANE.
DANG

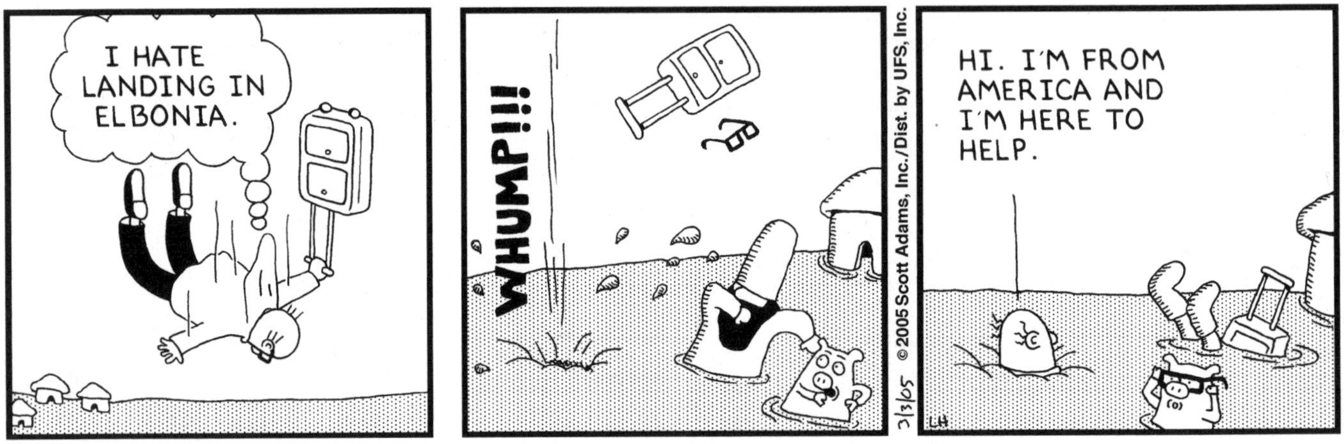
I HATE LANDING IN ELBONIA.
WHUMP!!!
HI. I'M FROM AMERICA AND I'M HERE TO HELP.
© 2005 Scott Adams, Inc./Dist. by UFS, Inc.
3/3/05

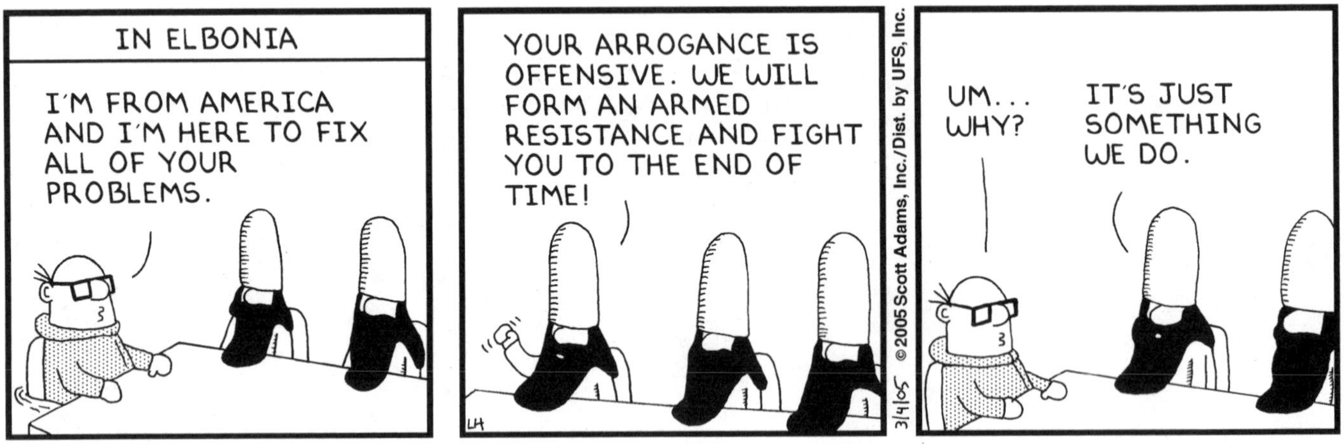
IN ELBONIA
I'M FROM AMERICA AND I'M HERE TO FIX ALL OF YOUR PROBLEMS.
YOUR ARROGANCE IS OFFENSIVE. WE WILL FORM AN ARMED RESISTANCE AND FIGHT YOU TO THE END OF TIME!
UM... WHY?
IT'S JUST SOMETHING WE DO.
© 2005 Scott Adams, Inc./Dist. by UFS, Inc.
3/4/05

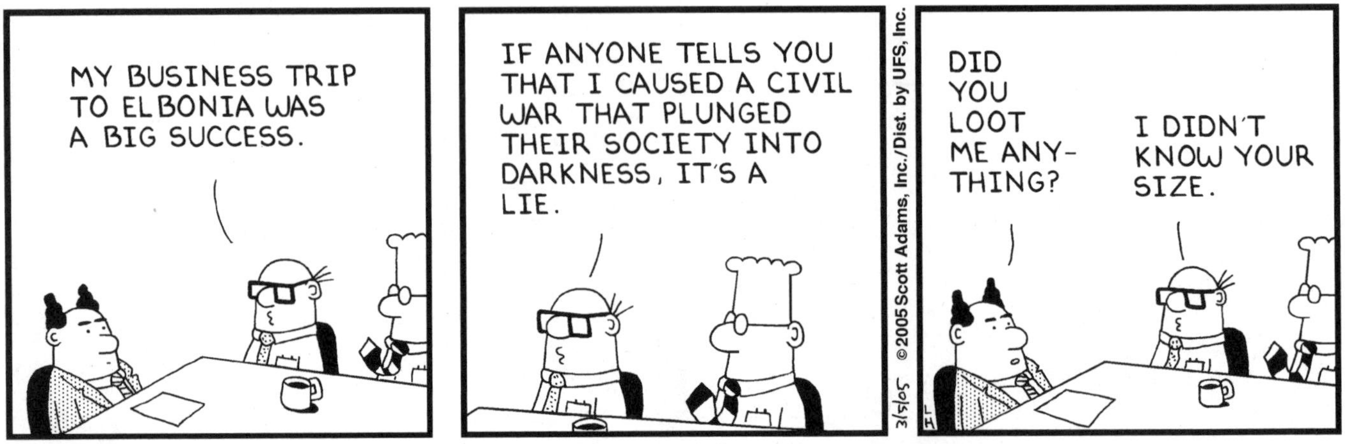
MY BUSINESS TRIP TO ELBONIA WAS A BIG SUCCESS.
IF ANYONE TELLS YOU THAT I CAUSED A CIVIL WAR THAT PLUNGED THEIR SOCIETY INTO DARKNESS, IT'S A LIE.
DID YOU LOOT ME ANY-THING?
I DIDN'T KNOW YOUR SIZE.
© 2005 Scott Adams, Inc./Dist. by UFS, Inc.
3/5/05

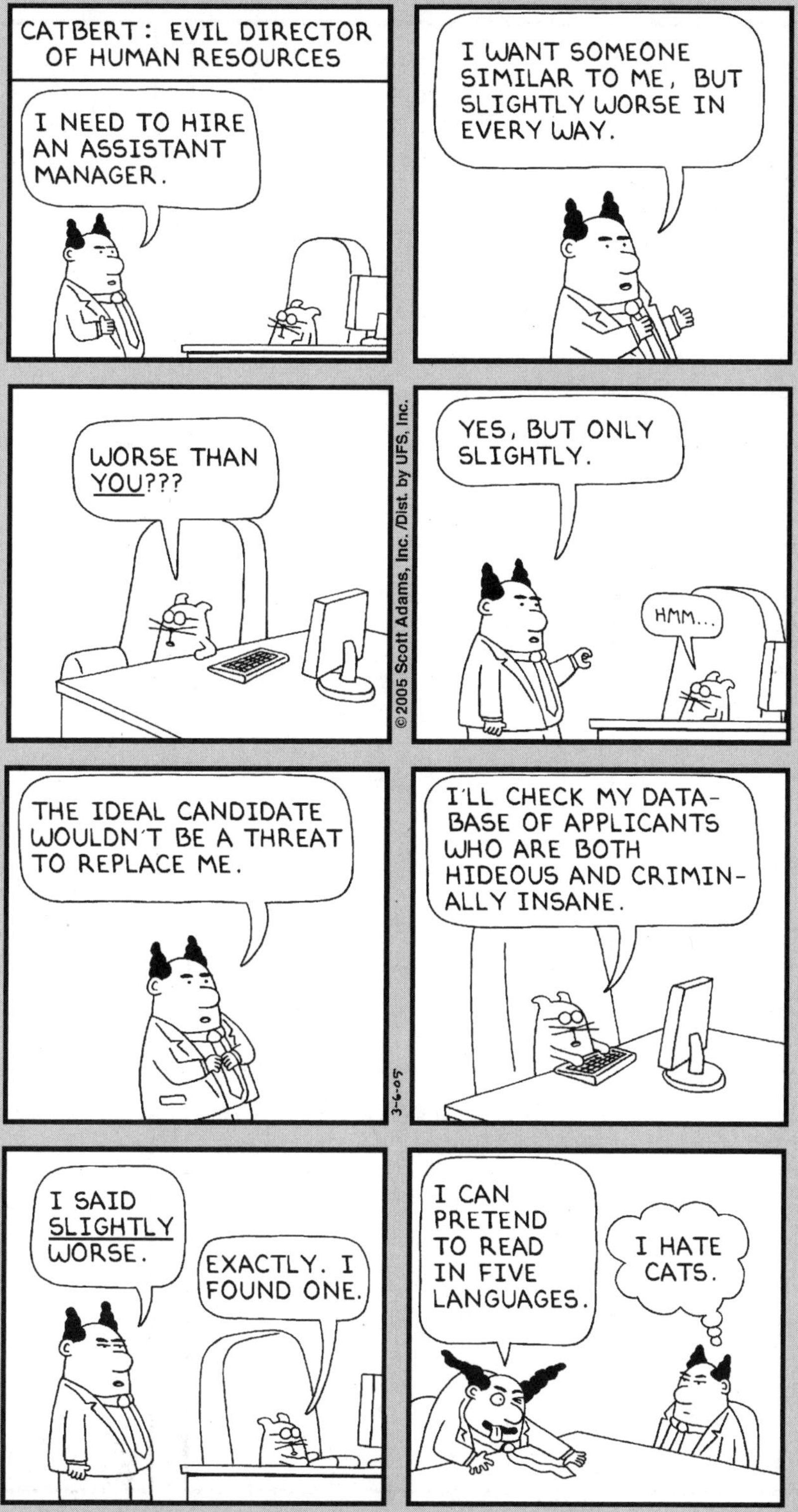
CATBERT: EVIL DIRECTOR OF HUMAN RESOURCES
I NEED TO HIRE AN ASSISTANT MANAGER.
I WANT SOMEONE SIMILAR TO ME, BUT SLIGHTLY WORSE IN EVERY WAY.
WORSE THAN YOU???
YES, BUT ONLY SLIGHTLY.
HMM...
THE IDEAL CANDIDATE WOULDN'T BE A THREAT TO REPLACE ME.
I'LL CHECK MY DATA-BASE OF APPLICANTS WHO ARE BOTH HIDEOUS AND CRIMIN-ALLY INSANE.
I SAID SLIGHTLY WORSE.
EXACTLY. I FOUND ONE.
I CAN PRETEND TO READ IN FIVE LANGUAGES.
I HATE CATS.
©2005 Scott Adams, Inc. /Dist. by UFS, Inc.
3-6-05

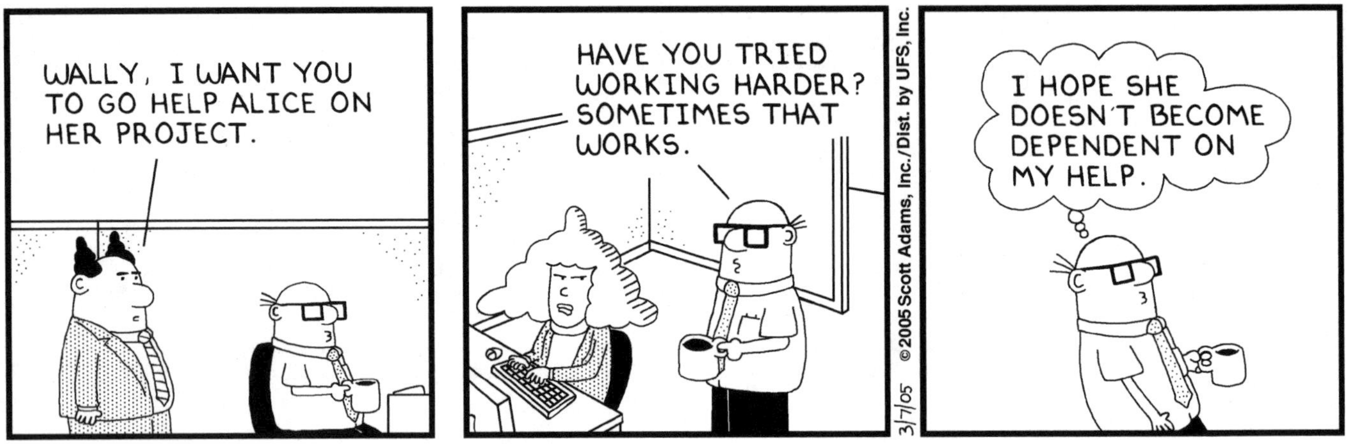
WALLY, I WANT YOU TO GO HELP ALICE ON HER PROJECT.
HAVE YOU TRIED WORKING HARDER? SOMETIMES THAT WORKS.
3/7/05 ©2005 Scott Adams, Inc./Dist. by UFS, Inc.
I HOPE SHE DOESN'T BECOME DEPENDENT ON MY HELP.

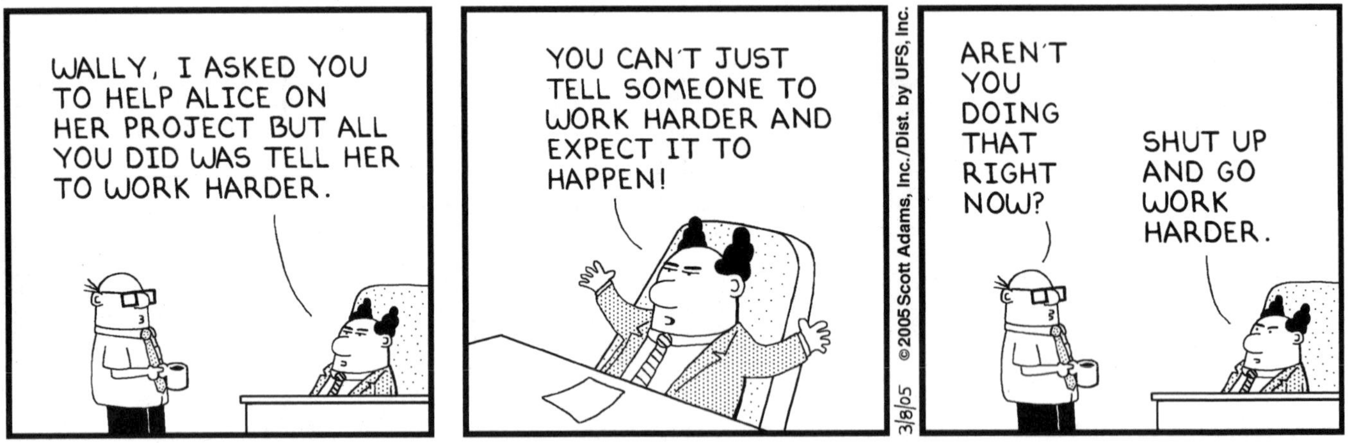
WALLY, I ASKED YOU TO HELP ALICE ON HER PROJECT BUT ALL YOU DID WAS TELL HER TO WORK HARDER.
YOU CAN'T JUST TELL SOMEONE TO WORK HARDER AND EXPECT IT TO HAPPEN!
3/8/05 ©2005 Scott Adams, Inc./Dist. by UFS, Inc.
AREN'T YOU DOING THAT RIGHT NOW?
SHUT UP AND GO WORK HARDER.

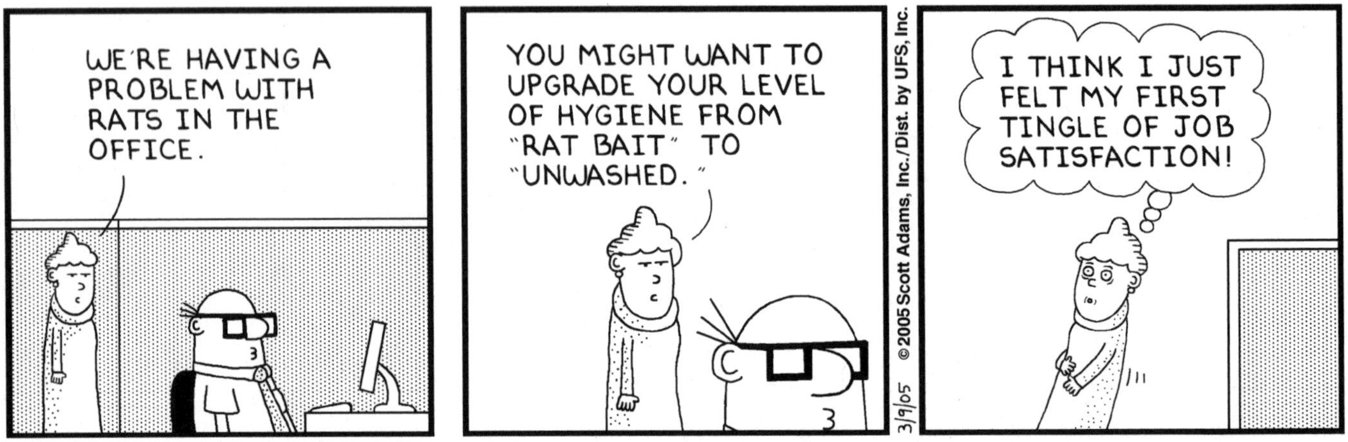
WE'RE HAVING A PROBLEM WITH RATS IN THE OFFICE.
YOU MIGHT WANT TO UPGRADE YOUR LEVEL OF HYGIENE FROM "RAT BAIT" TO "UNWASHED."
3/9/05 ©2005 Scott Adams, Inc./Dist. by UFS, Inc.
I THINK I JUST FELT MY FIRST TINGLE OF JOB SATISFACTION!

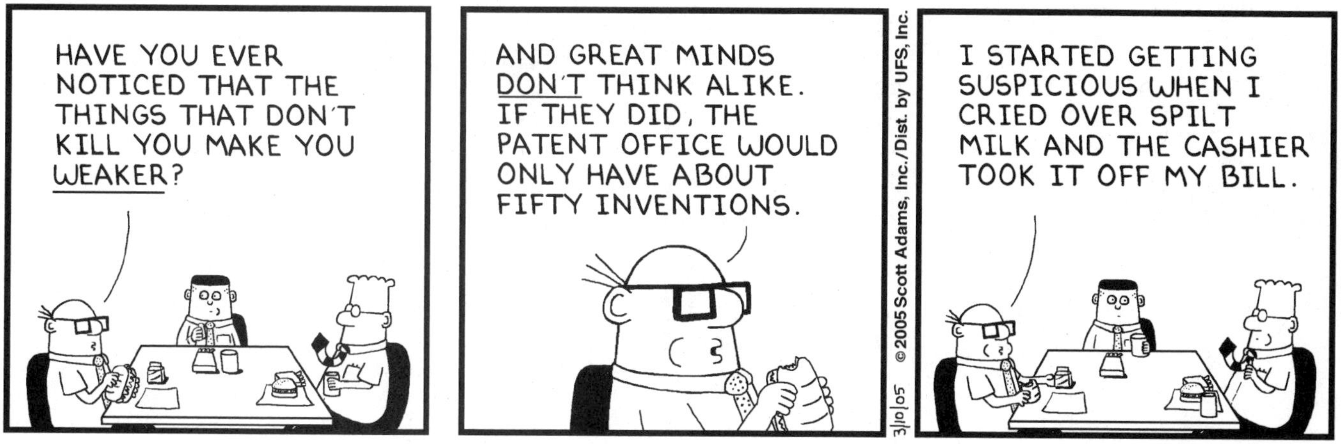
HAVE YOU EVER NOTICED THAT THE THINGS THAT DON'T KILL YOU MAKE YOU WEAKER?
AND GREAT MINDS DON'T THINK ALIKE. IF THEY DID, THE PATENT OFFICE WOULD ONLY HAVE ABOUT FIFTY INVENTIONS.
3/10/05 © 2005 Scott Adams, Inc./Dist. by UFS, Inc.
I STARTED GETTING SUSPICIOUS WHEN I CRIED OVER SPILT MILK AND THE CASHIER TOOK IT OFF MY BILL.

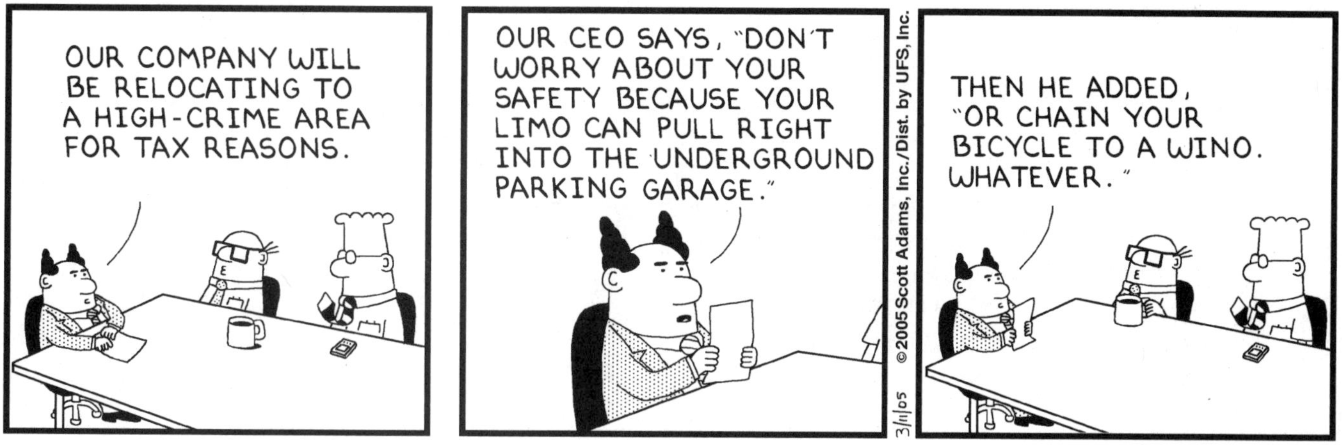
OUR COMPANY WILL BE RELOCATING TO A HIGH-CRIME AREA FOR TAX REASONS.
OUR CEO SAYS, "DON'T WORRY ABOUT YOUR SAFETY BECAUSE YOUR LIMO CAN PULL RIGHT INTO THE UNDERGROUND PARKING GARAGE."
3/11/05 © 2005 Scott Adams, Inc./Dist. by UFS, Inc.
THEN HE ADDED, "OR CHAIN YOUR BICYCLE TO A WINO. WHATEVER."

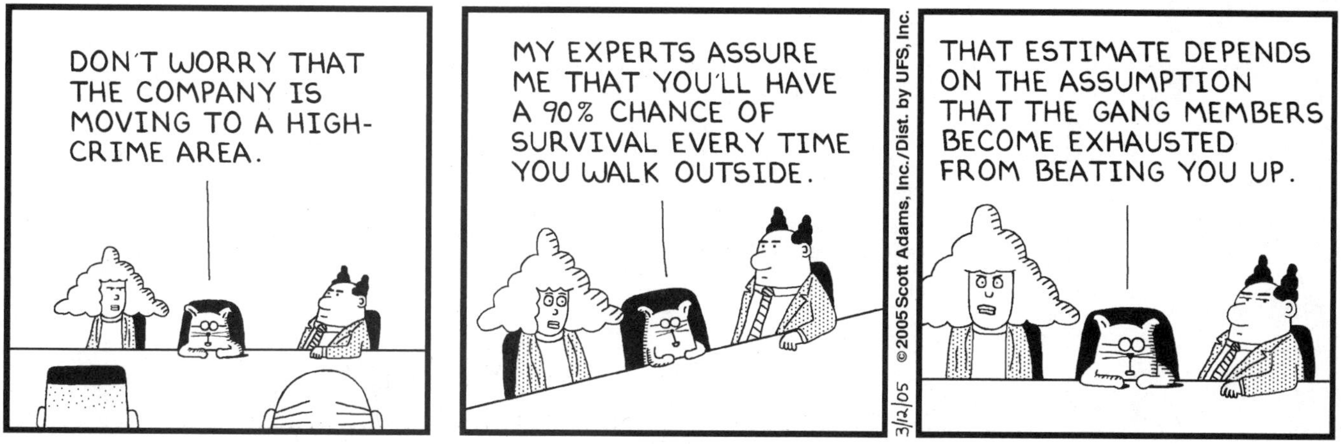
DON'T WORRY THAT THE COMPANY IS MOVING TO A HIGH-CRIME AREA.
MY EXPERTS ASSURE ME THAT YOU'LL HAVE A 90% CHANCE OF SURVIVAL EVERY TIME YOU WALK OUTSIDE.
3/12/05 © 2005 Scott Adams, Inc./Dist. by UFS, Inc.
THAT ESTIMATE DEPENDS ON THE ASSUMPTION THAT THE GANG MEMBERS BECOME EXHAUSTED FROM BEATING YOU UP.

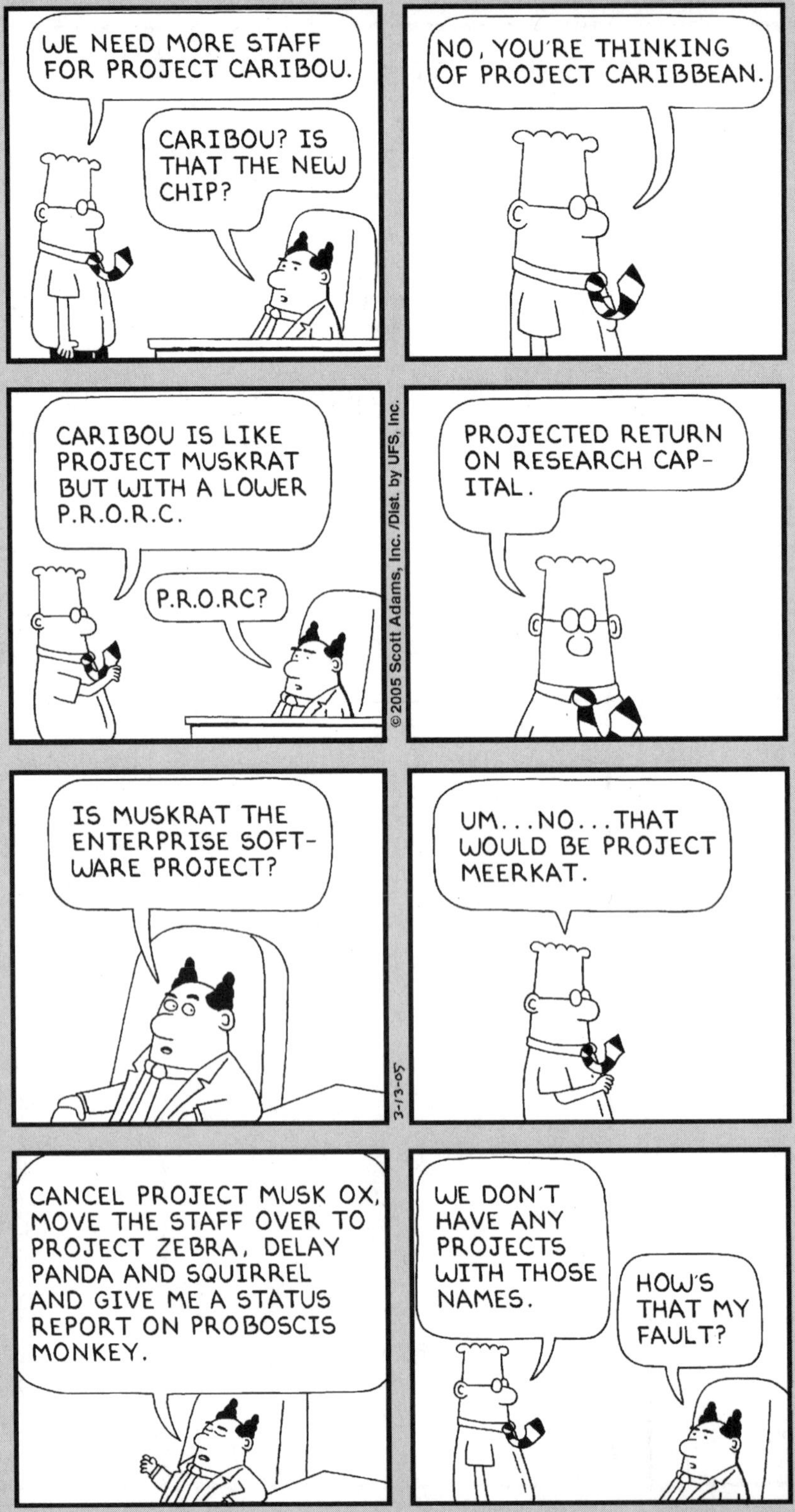
WE NEED MORE STAFF FOR PROJECT CARIBOU.
CARIBOU? IS THAT THE NEW CHIP?
NO, YOU'RE THINKING OF PROJECT CARIBBEAN.
CARIBOU IS LIKE PROJECT MUSKRAT BUT WITH A LOWER P.R.O.R.C.
P.R.O.RC?
PROJECTED RETURN ON RESEARCH CAP-ITAL.
© 2005 Scott Adams, Inc./Dist. by UFS, Inc.
IS MUSKRAT THE ENTERPRISE SOFT-WARE PROJECT?
UM...NO...THAT WOULD BE PROJECT MEERKAT.
3-13-05
CANCEL PROJECT MUSK OX, MOVE THE STAFF OVER TO PROJECT ZEBRA, DELAY PANDA AND SQUIRREL AND GIVE ME A STATUS REPORT ON PROBOSCIS MONKEY.
WE DON'T HAVE ANY PROJECTS WITH THOSE NAMES.
HOW'S THAT MY FAULT?

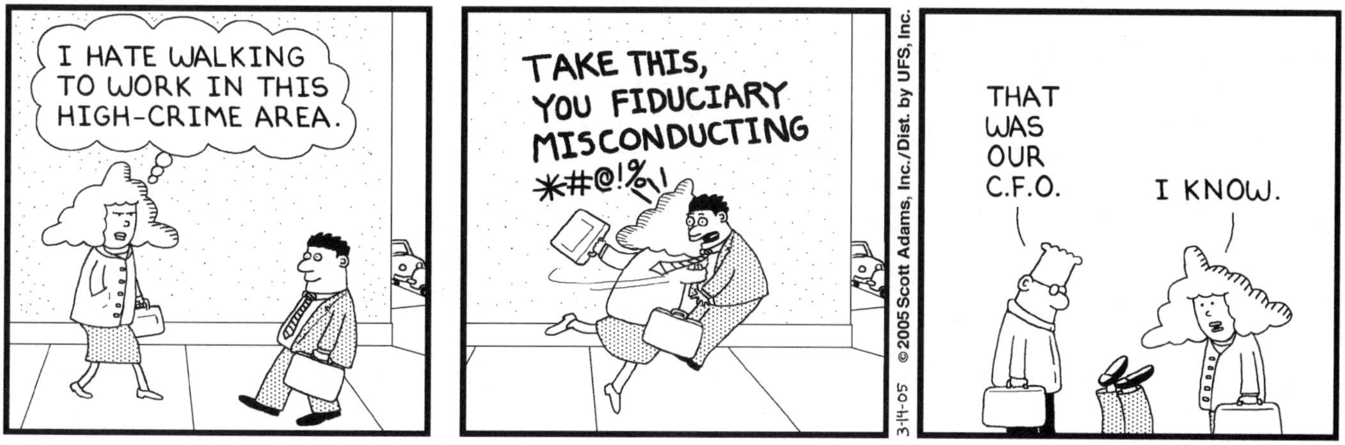
I HATE WALKING TO WORK IN THIS HIGH-CRIME AREA.
TAKE THIS, YOU FIDUCIARY MISCONDUCTING *#@!%!
3-14-05 © 2005 Scott Adams, Inc./Dist. by UFS, Inc.
THAT WAS OUR C.F.O.
I KNOW.

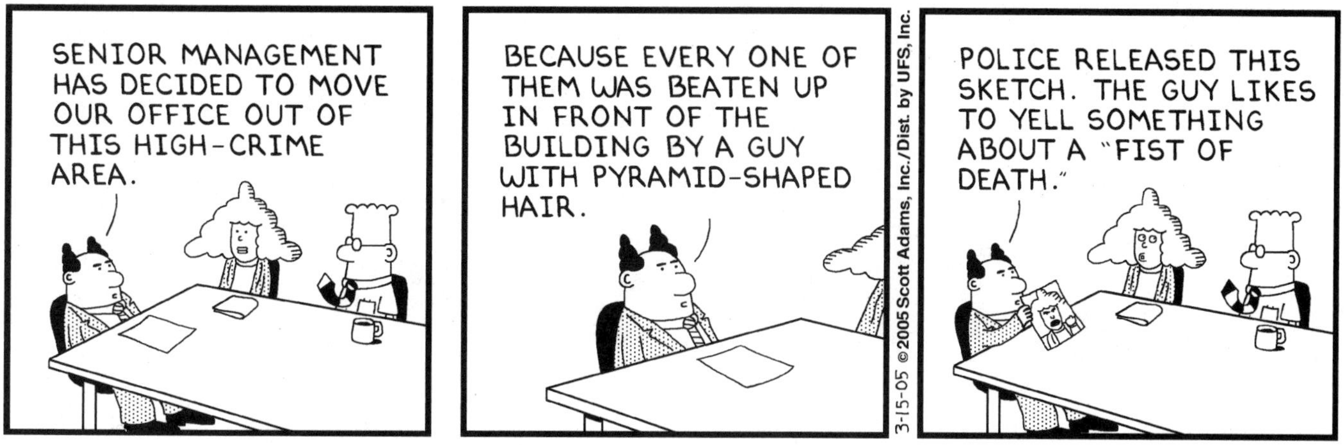
SENIOR MANAGEMENT HAS DECIDED TO MOVE OUR OFFICE OUT OF THIS HIGH-CRIME AREA.
BECAUSE EVERY ONE OF THEM WAS BEATEN UP IN FRONT OF THE BUILDING BY A GUY WITH PYRAMID-SHAPED HAIR.
3-15-05 © 2005 Scott Adams, Inc./Dist. by UFS, Inc.
POLICE RELEASED THIS SKETCH. THE GUY LIKES TO YELL SOMETHING ABOUT A "FIST OF DEATH."

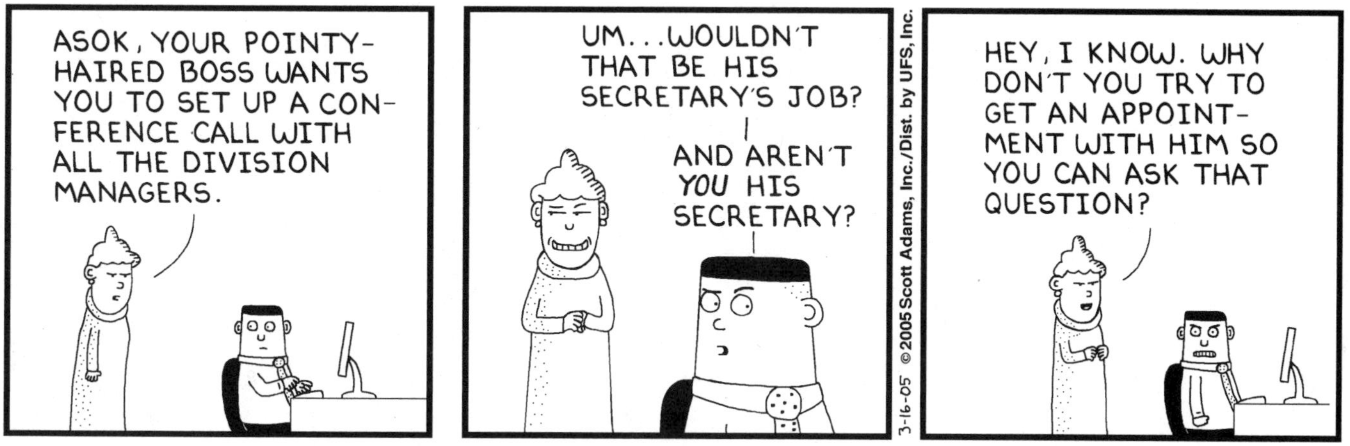
ASOK, YOUR POINTY-HAIRED BOSS WANTS YOU TO SET UP A CONFERENCE CALL WITH ALL THE DIVISION MANAGERS.
UM...WOULDN'T THAT BE HIS SECRETARY'S JOB?
AND AREN'T YOU HIS SECRETARY?
3-16-05 © 2005 Scott Adams, Inc./Dist. by UFS, Inc.
HEY, I KNOW. WHY DON'T YOU TRY TO GET AN APPOINTMENT WITH HIM SO YOU CAN ASK THAT QUESTION?

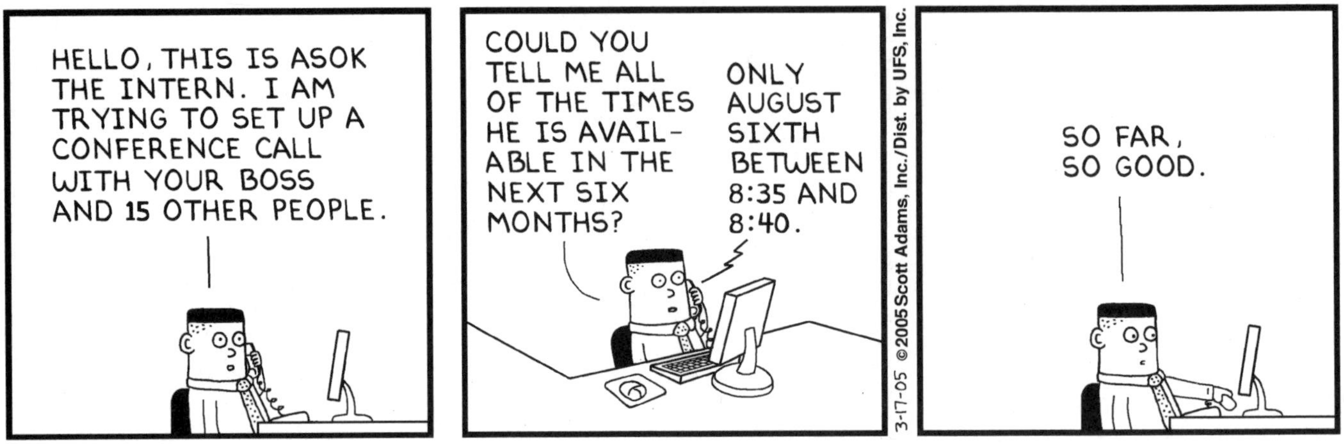
HELLO, THIS IS ASOK THE INTERN. I AM TRYING TO SET UP A CONFERENCE CALL WITH YOUR BOSS AND 15 OTHER PEOPLE.
COULD YOU TELL ME ALL OF THE TIMES HE IS AVAILABLE IN THE NEXT SIX MONTHS?
ONLY AUGUST SIXTH BETWEEN 8:35 AND 8:40.
SO FAR, SO GOOD.
3-17-05 ©2005 Scott Adams, Inc./Dist. by UFS, Inc.

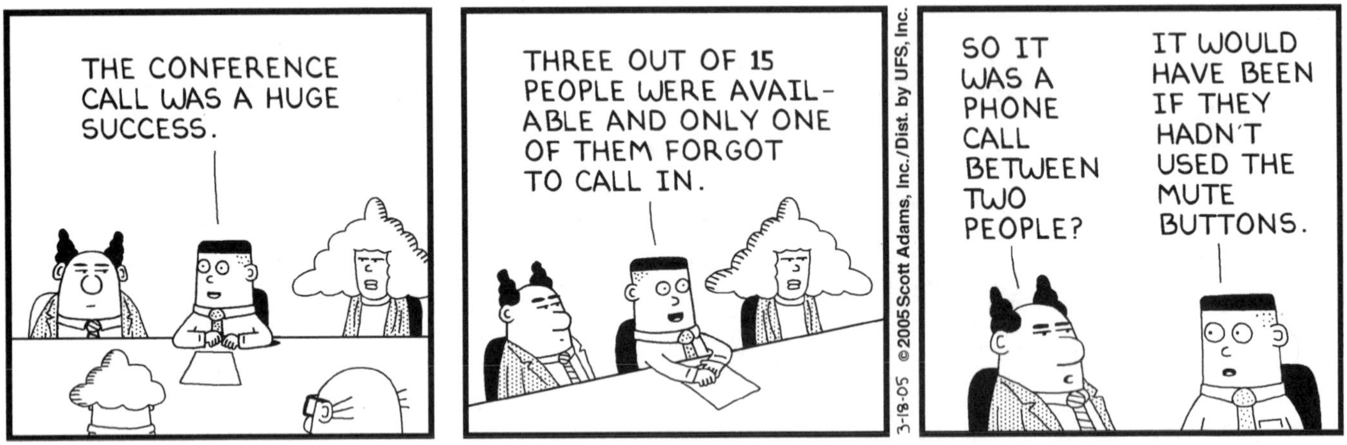
THE CONFERENCE CALL WAS A HUGE SUCCESS.
THREE OUT OF 15 PEOPLE WERE AVAILABLE AND ONLY ONE OF THEM FORGOT TO CALL IN.
SO IT WAS A PHONE CALL BETWEEN TWO PEOPLE?
IT WOULD HAVE BEEN IF THEY HADN'T USED THE MUTE BUTTONS.
3-18-05 ©2005 Scott Adams, Inc./Dist. by UFS, Inc.

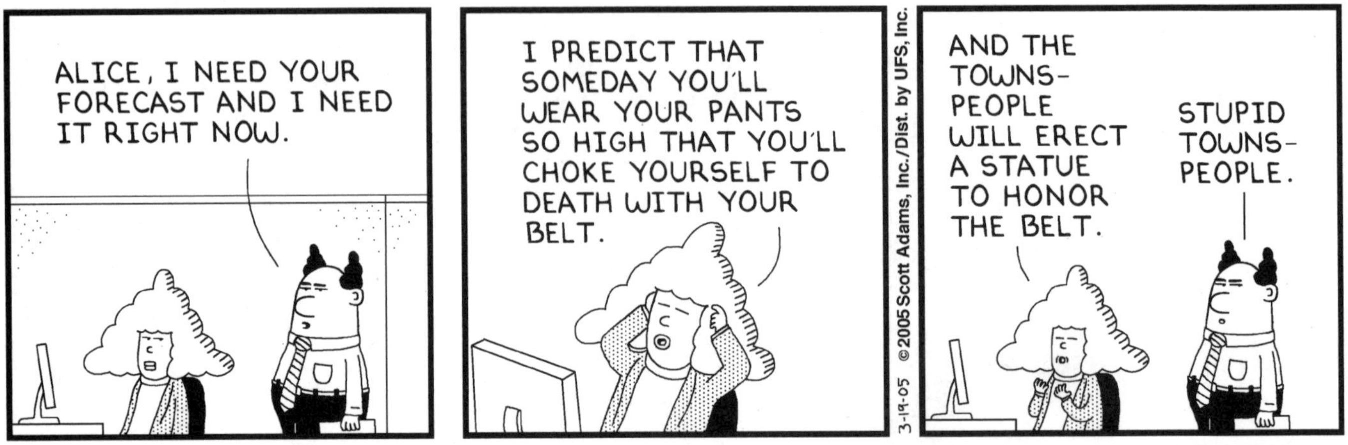
ALICE, I NEED YOUR FORECAST AND I NEED IT RIGHT NOW.
I PREDICT THAT SOMEDAY YOU'LL WEAR YOUR PANTS SO HIGH THAT YOU'LL CHOKE YOURSELF TO DEATH WITH YOUR BELT.
AND THE TOWNSPEOPLE WILL ERECT A STATUE TO HONOR THE BELT.
STUPID TOWNSPEOPLE.
3-19-05 ©2005 Scott Adams, Inc./Dist. by UFS, Inc.

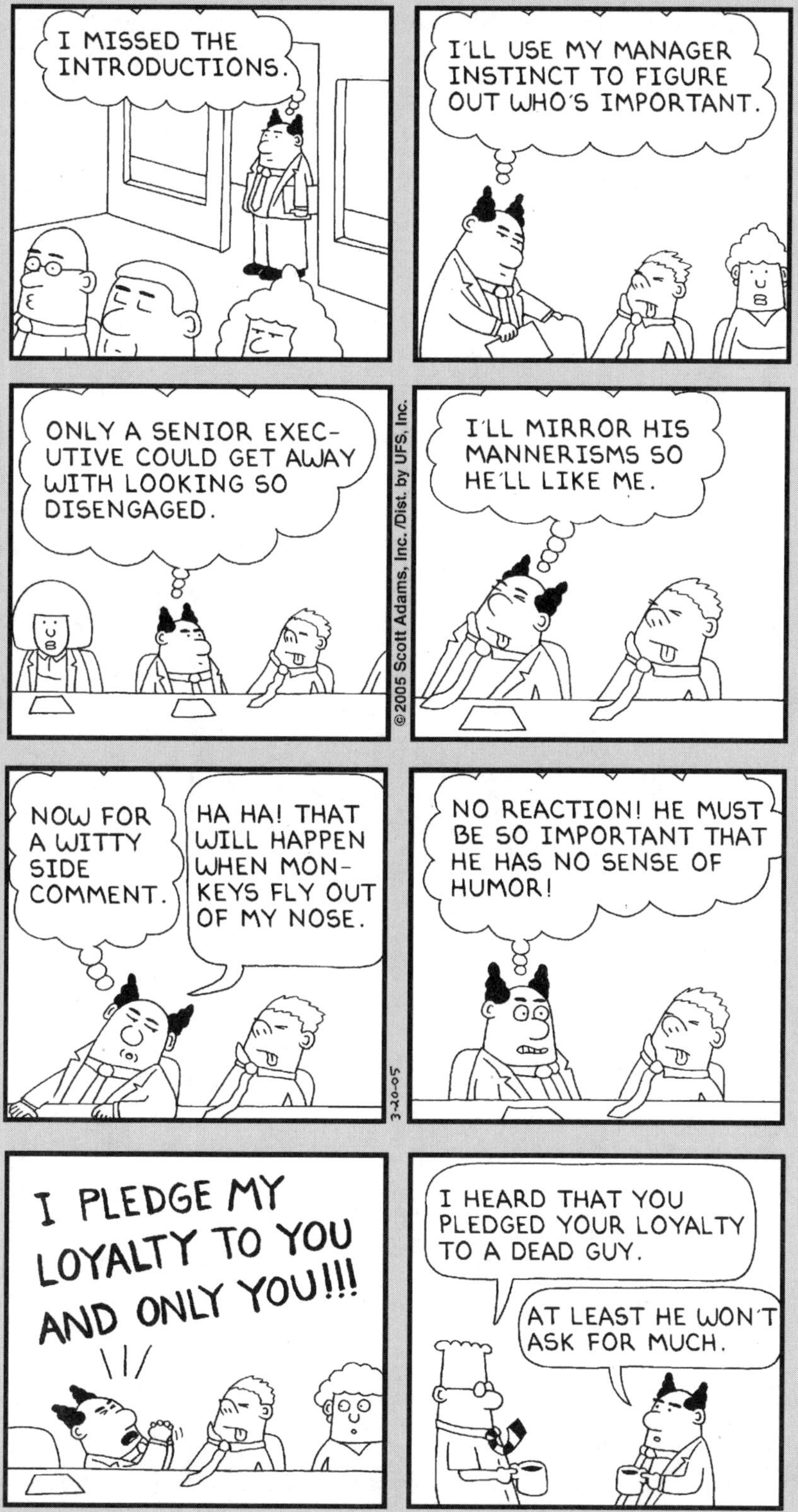
I MISSED THE INTRODUCTIONS.
I'LL USE MY MANAGER INSTINCT TO FIGURE OUT WHO'S IMPORTANT.
ONLY A SENIOR EXECUTIVE COULD GET AWAY WITH LOOKING SO DISENGAGED.
©2005 Scott Adams, Inc./Dist. by UFS, Inc.
I'LL MIRROR HIS MANNERISMS SO HE'LL LIKE ME.
NOW FOR A WITTY SIDE COMMENT.
HA HA! THAT WILL HAPPEN WHEN MONKEYS FLY OUT OF MY NOSE.
3-20-05
NO REACTION! HE MUST BE SO IMPORTANT THAT HE HAS NO SENSE OF HUMOR!
I PLEDGE MY LOYALTY TO YOU AND ONLY YOU!!!
I HEARD THAT YOU PLEDGED YOUR LOYALTY TO A DEAD GUY.
AT LEAST HE WON'T ASK FOR MUCH.

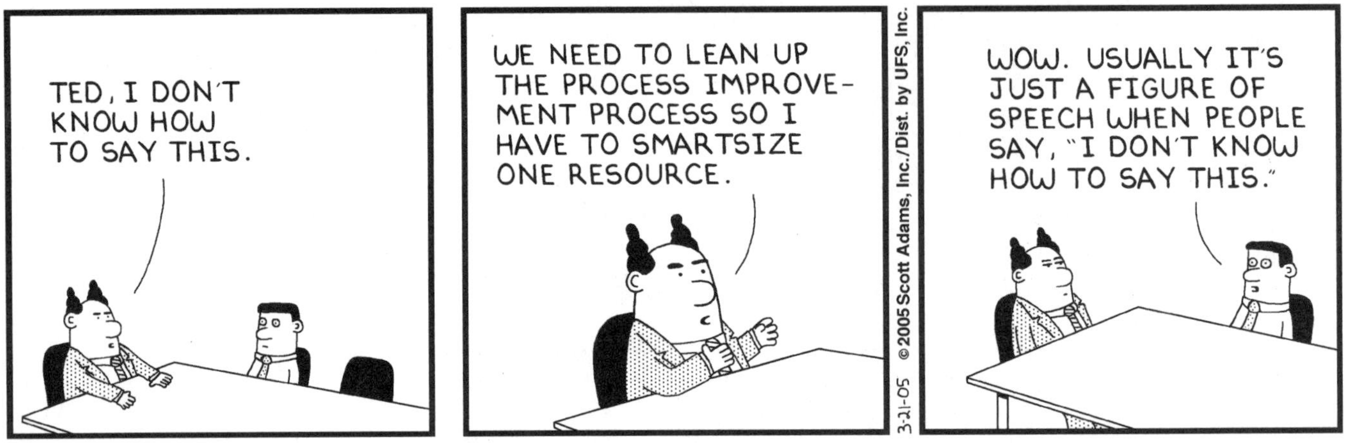
TED, I DON'T KNOW HOW TO SAY THIS.
WE NEED TO LEAN UP THE PROCESS IMPROVEMENT PROCESS SO I HAVE TO SMARTSIZE ONE RESOURCE.
3-21-05 ©2005 Scott Adams, Inc./Dist. by UFS, Inc.
WOW. USUALLY IT'S JUST A FIGURE OF SPEECH WHEN PEOPLE SAY, "I DON'T KNOW HOW TO SAY THIS."

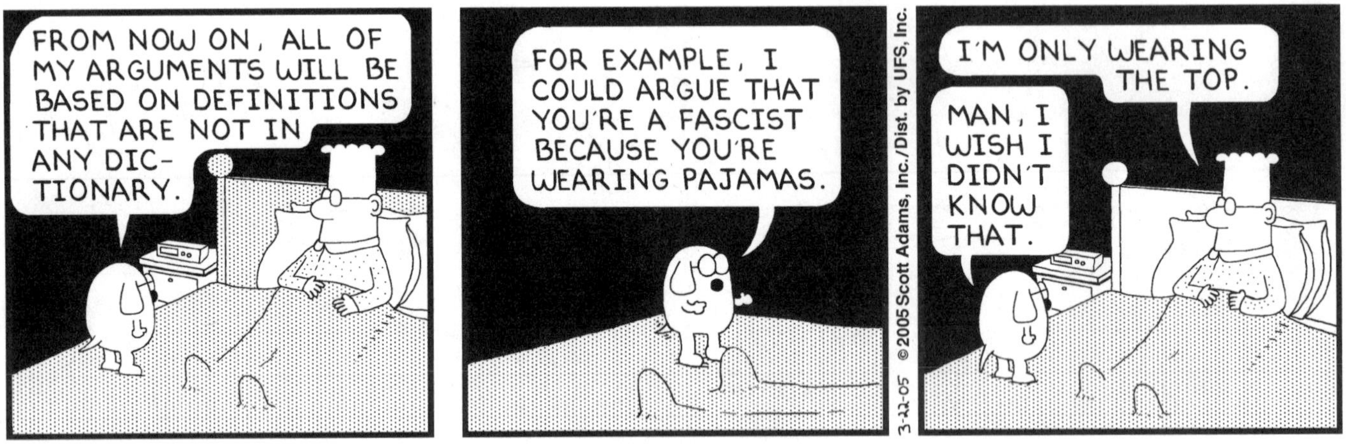
FROM NOW ON, ALL OF MY ARGUMENTS WILL BE BASED ON DEFINITIONS THAT ARE NOT IN ANY DICTIONARY.
FOR EXAMPLE, I COULD ARGUE THAT YOU'RE A FASCIST BECAUSE YOU'RE WEARING PAJAMAS.
3-22-05 ©2005 Scott Adams, Inc./Dist. by UFS, Inc.
I'M ONLY WEARING THE TOP.
MAN, I WISH I DIDN'T KNOW THAT.

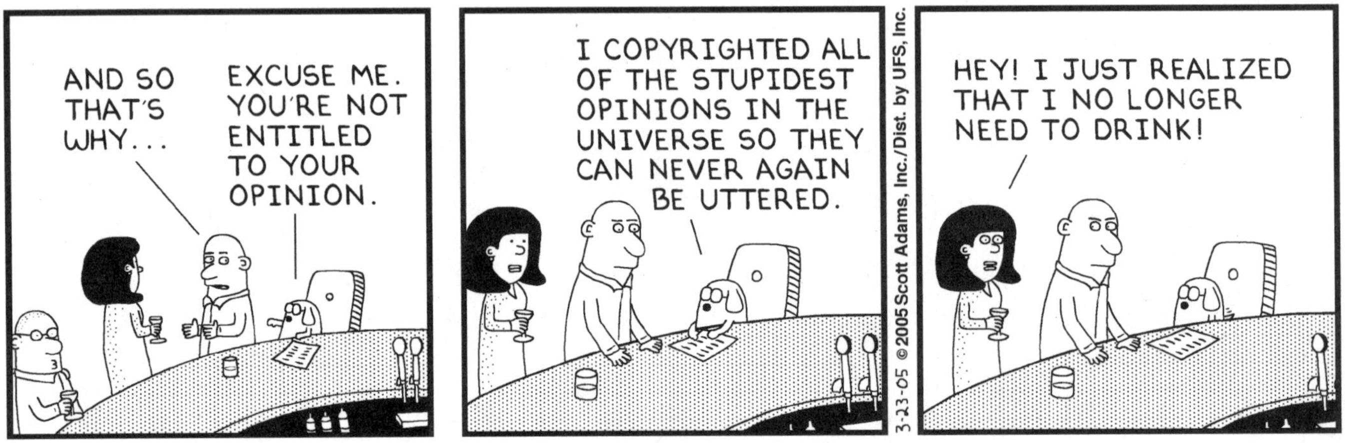
AND SO THAT'S WHY...
EXCUSE ME. YOU'RE NOT ENTITLED TO YOUR OPINION.
I COPYRIGHTED ALL OF THE STUPIDEST OPINIONS IN THE UNIVERSE SO THEY CAN NEVER AGAIN BE UTTERED.
3-23-05 ©2005 Scott Adams, Inc./Dist. by UFS, Inc.
HEY! I JUST REALIZED THAT I NO LONGER NEED TO DRINK!

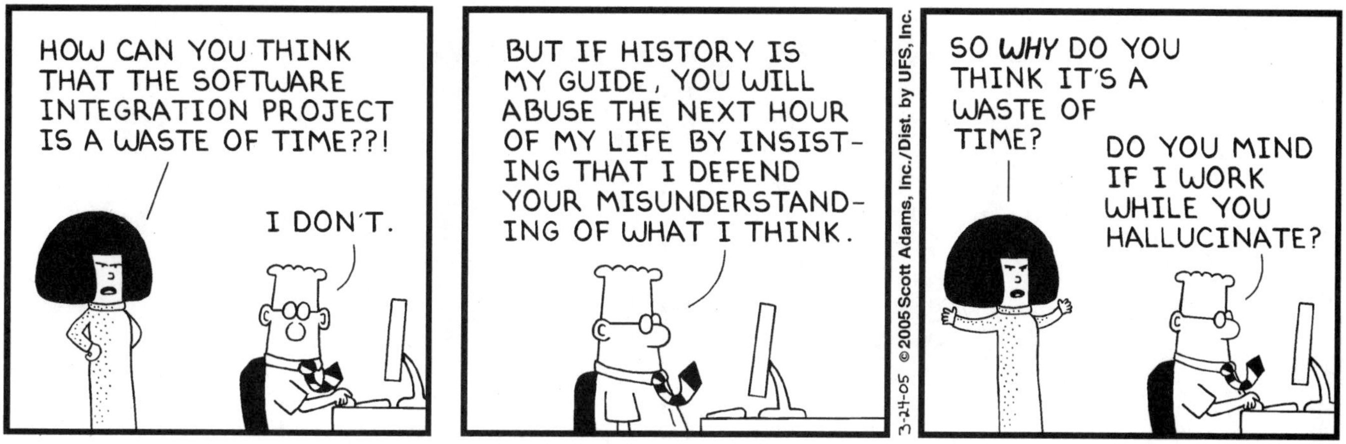
HOW CAN YOU THINK THAT THE SOFTWARE INTEGRATION PROJECT IS A WASTE OF TIME??!
I DON'T.
BUT IF HISTORY IS MY GUIDE, YOU WILL ABUSE THE NEXT HOUR OF MY LIFE BY INSISTING THAT I DEFEND YOUR MISUNDERSTANDING OF WHAT I THINK.
3-24-05 © 2005 Scott Adams, Inc./Dist. by UFS, Inc.
SO WHY DO YOU THINK IT'S A WASTE OF TIME?
DO YOU MIND IF I WORK WHILE YOU HALLUCINATE?

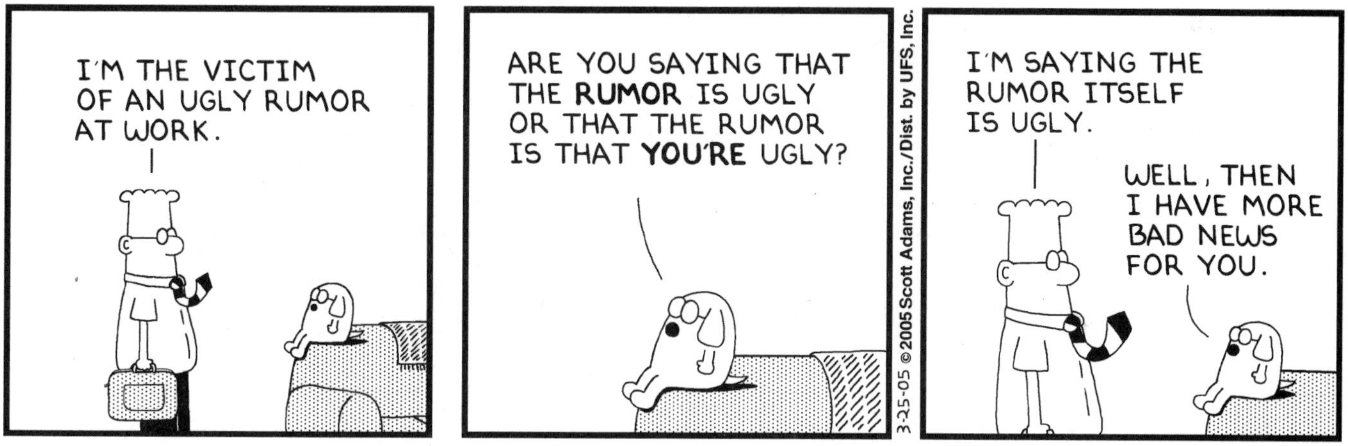
I'M THE VICTIM OF AN UGLY RUMOR AT WORK.
ARE YOU SAYING THAT THE RUMOR IS UGLY OR THAT THE RUMOR IS THAT YOU'RE UGLY?
3-25-05 © 2005 Scott Adams, Inc./Dist. by UFS, Inc.
I'M SAYING THE RUMOR ITSELF IS UGLY.
WELL, THEN I HAVE MORE BAD NEWS FOR YOU.

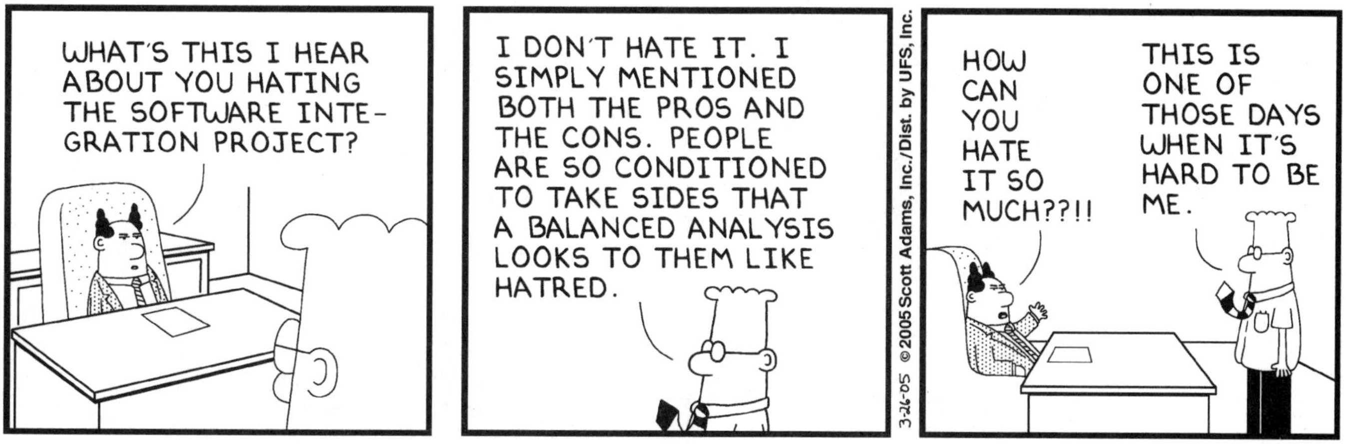
WHAT'S THIS I HEAR ABOUT YOU HATING THE SOFTWARE INTEGRATION PROJECT?
I DON'T HATE IT. I SIMPLY MENTIONED BOTH THE PROS AND THE CONS. PEOPLE ARE SO CONDITIONED TO TAKE SIDES THAT A BALANCED ANALYSIS LOOKS TO THEM LIKE HATRED.
3-26-05 © 2005 Scott Adams, Inc./Dist. by UFS, Inc.
HOW CAN YOU HATE IT SO MUCH??!!
THIS IS ONE OF THOSE DAYS WHEN IT'S HARD TO BE ME.

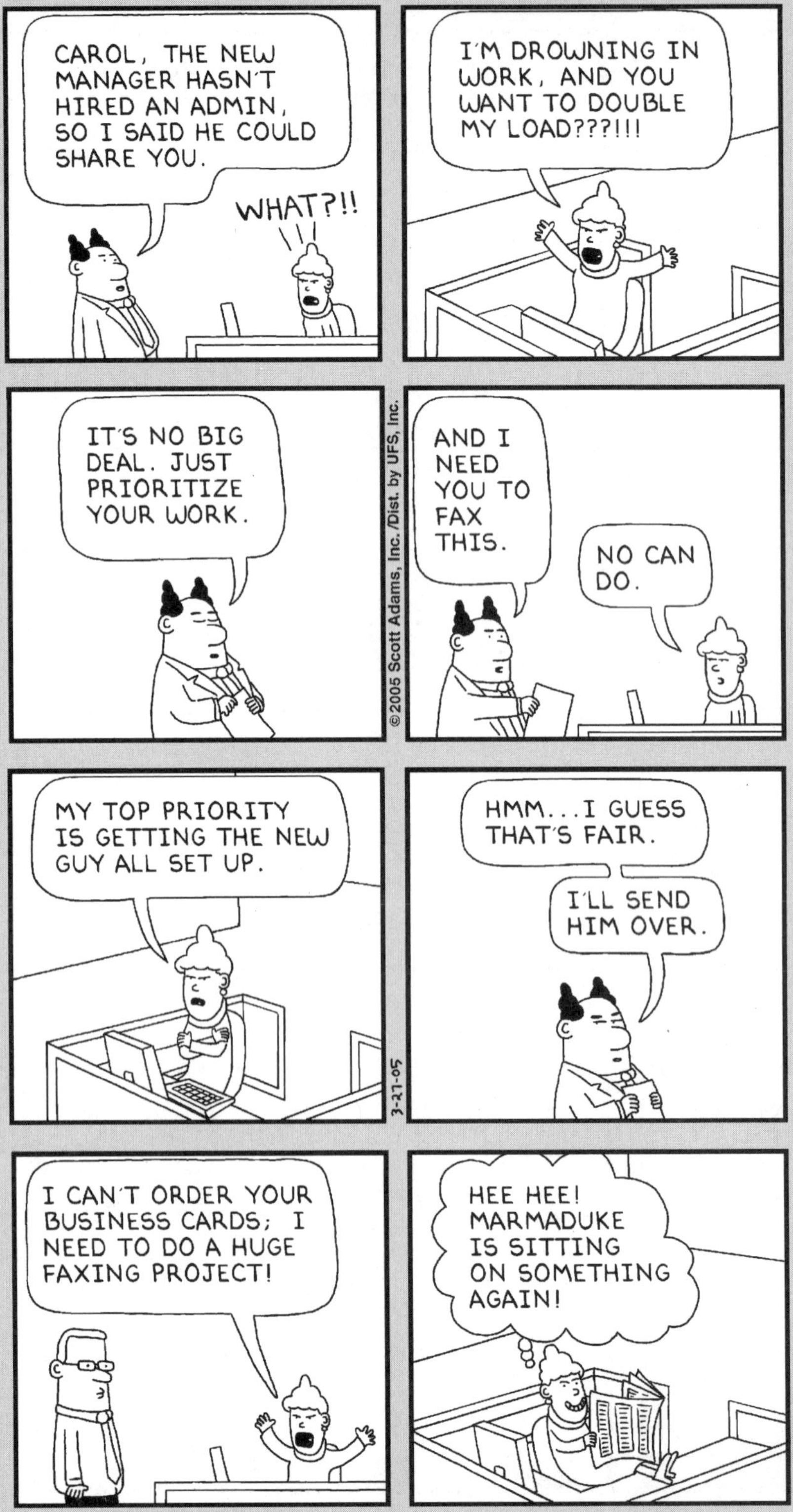
CAROL, THE NEW MANAGER HASN'T HIRED AN ADMIN, SO I SAID HE COULD SHARE YOU.
WHAT?!!
I'M DROWNING IN WORK, AND YOU WANT TO DOUBLE MY LOAD???!!!
IT'S NO BIG DEAL. JUST PRIORITIZE YOUR WORK.
AND I NEED YOU TO FAX THIS.
NO CAN DO.
©2005 Scott Adams, Inc./Dist. by UFS, Inc.
MY TOP PRIORITY IS GETTING THE NEW GUY ALL SET UP.
HMM... I GUESS THAT'S FAIR.
I'LL SEND HIM OVER.
3-21-05
I CAN'T ORDER YOUR BUSINESS CARDS; I NEED TO DO A HUGE FAXING PROJECT!
HEE HEE! MARMADUKE IS SITTING ON SOMETHING AGAIN!

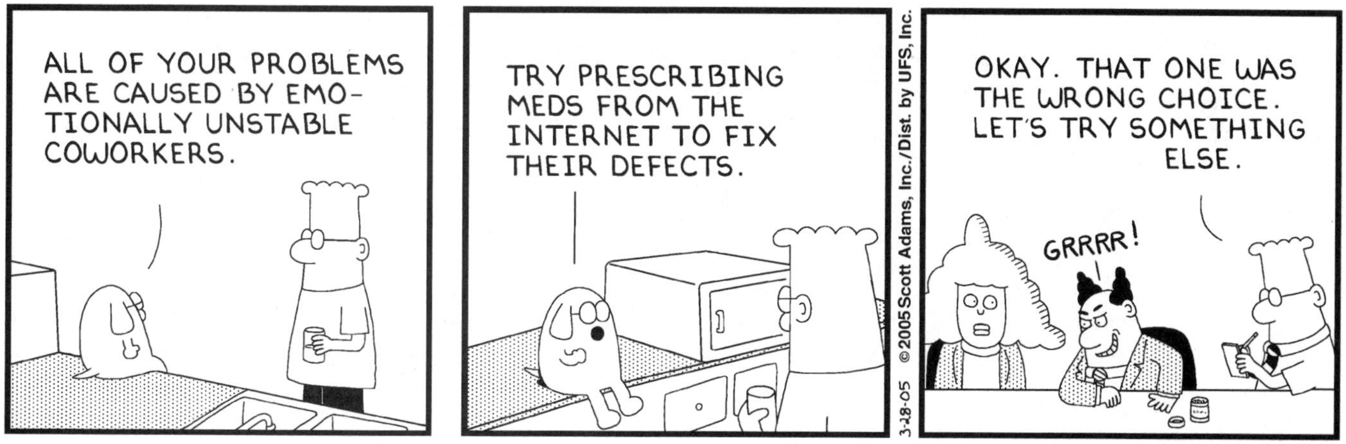
ALL OF YOUR PROBLEMS ARE CAUSED BY EMO-TIONALLY UNSTABLE COWORKERS.
TRY PRESCRIBING MEDS FROM THE INTERNET TO FIX THEIR DEFECTS.
3-28-05 ©2005 Scott Adams, Inc./Dist. by UFS, Inc.
OKAY. THAT ONE WAS THE WRONG CHOICE. LET'S TRY SOMETHING ELSE.
GRRRR!

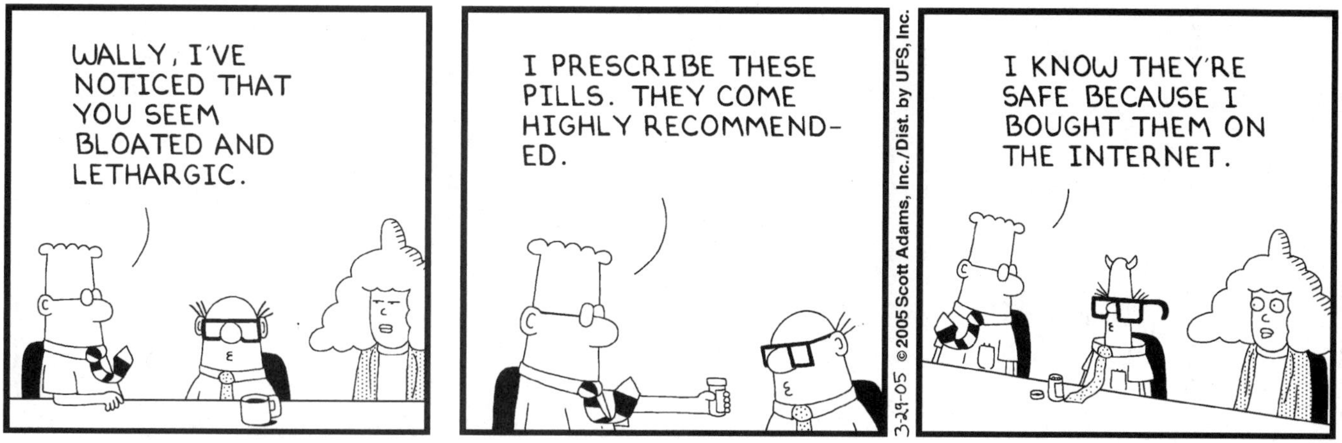
WALLY, I'VE NOTICED THAT YOU SEEM BLOATED AND LETHARGIC.
I PRESCRIBE THESE PILLS. THEY COME HIGHLY RECOMMEND-ED.
3-29-05 ©2005 Scott Adams, Inc./Dist. by UFS, Inc.
I KNOW THEY'RE SAFE BECAUSE I BOUGHT THEM ON THE INTERNET.

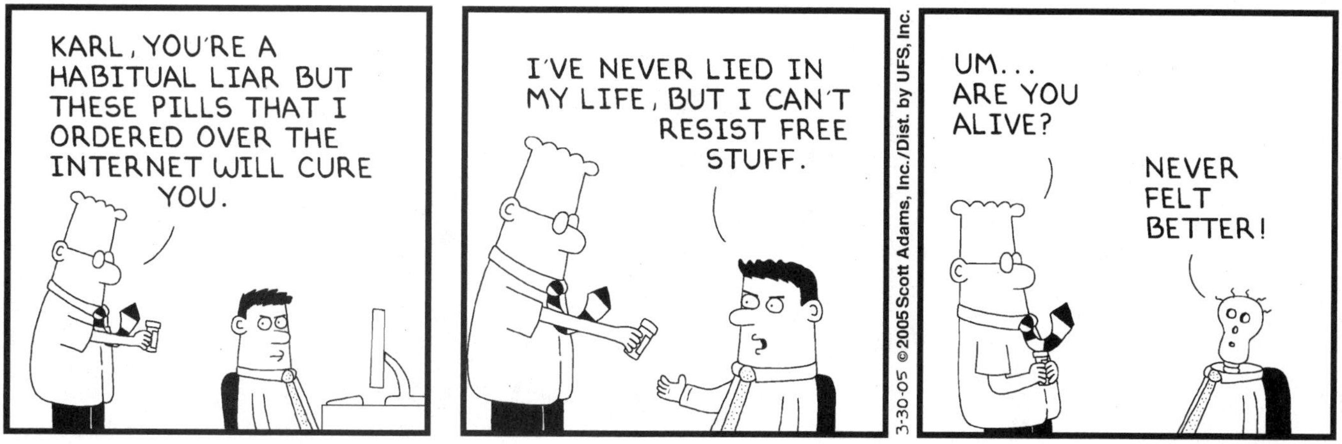
KARL, YOU'RE A HABITUAL LIAR BUT THESE PILLS THAT I ORDERED OVER THE INTERNET WILL CURE YOU.
I'VE NEVER LIED IN MY LIFE, BUT I CAN'T RESIST FREE STUFF.
3-30-05 ©2005 Scott Adams, Inc./Dist. by UFS, Inc.
UM... ARE YOU ALIVE?
NEVER FELT BETTER!

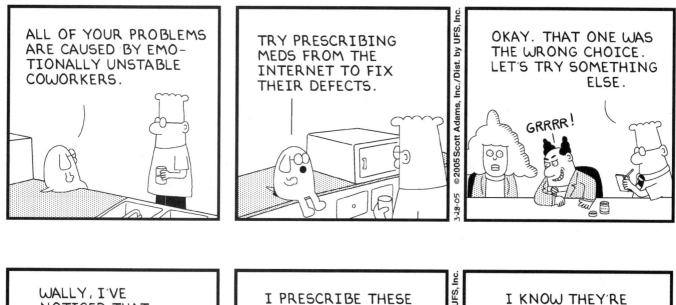

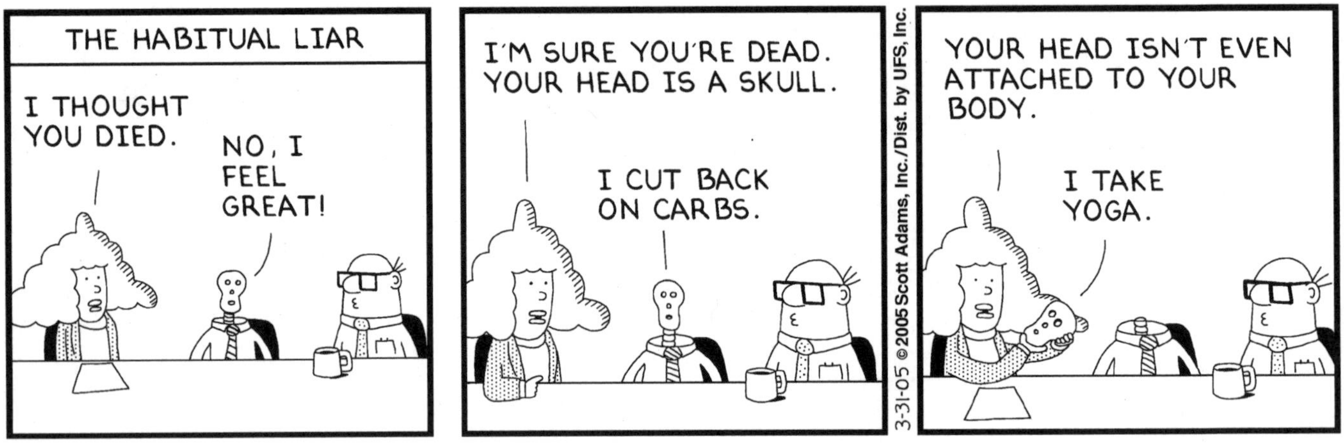
THE HABITUAL LIAR
I THOUGHT YOU DIED.
NO, I FEEL GREAT!
I'M SURE YOU'RE DEAD. YOUR HEAD IS A SKULL.
I CUT BACK ON CARBS.
3-31-05 © 2005 Scott Adams, Inc./Dist. by UFS, Inc.
YOUR HEAD ISN'T EVEN ATTACHED TO YOUR BODY.
I TAKE YOGA.

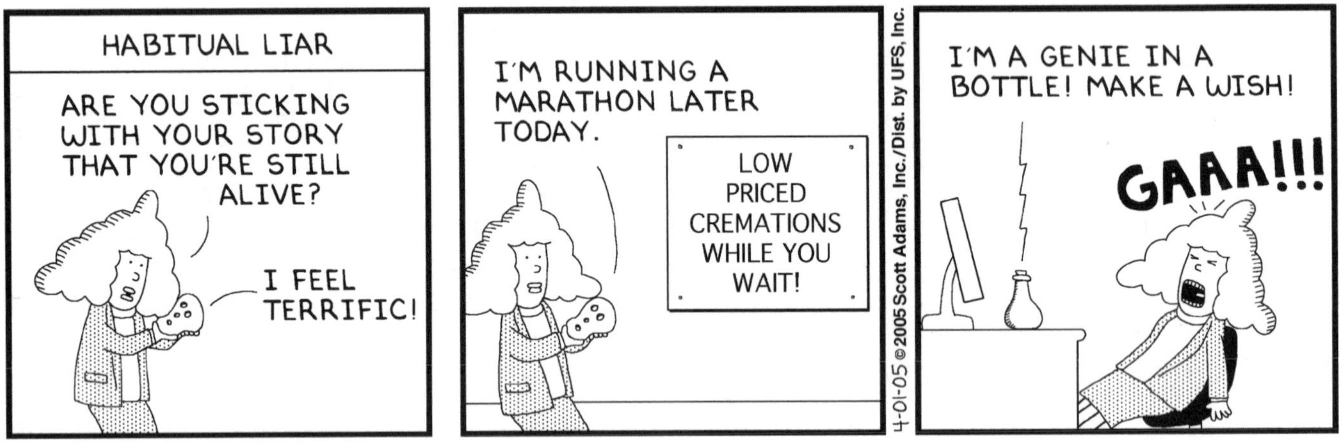
HABITUAL LIAR
ARE YOU STICKING WITH YOUR STORY THAT YOU'RE STILL ALIVE?
I FEEL TERRIFIC!
I'M RUNNING A MARATHON LATER TODAY.
LOW PRICED CREMATIONS WHILE YOU WAIT!
4-01-05 © 2005 Scott Adams, Inc./Dist. by UFS, Inc.
I'M A GENIE IN A BOTTLE! MAKE A WISH!
GAAA!!!

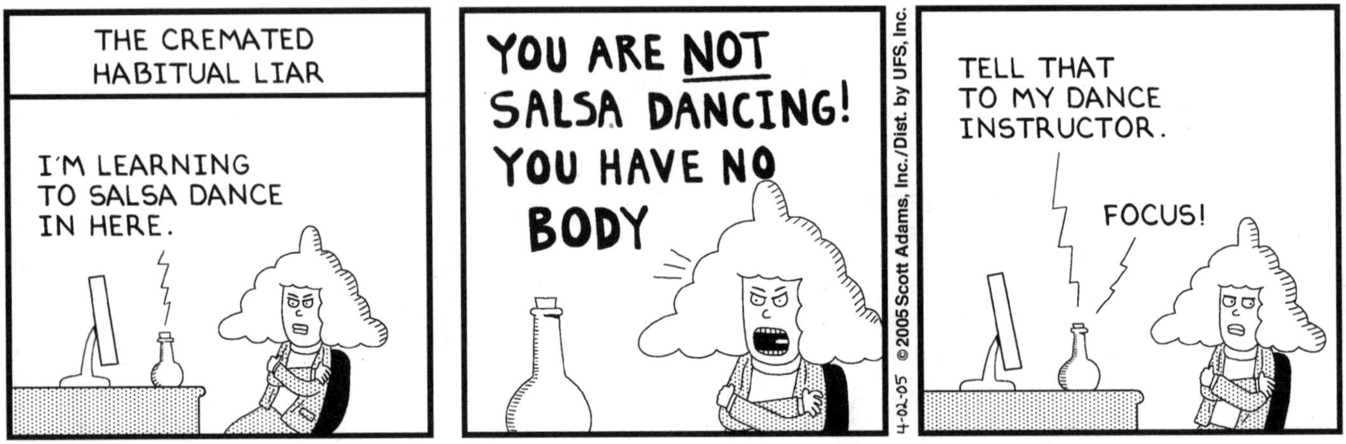
THE CREMATED HABITUAL LIAR
I'M LEARNING TO SALSA DANCE IN HERE.
YOU ARE NOT SALSA DANCING! YOU HAVE NO BODY
4-02-05 © 2005 Scott Adams, Inc./Dist. by UFS, Inc.
TELL THAT TO MY DANCE INSTRUCTOR.
FOCUS!

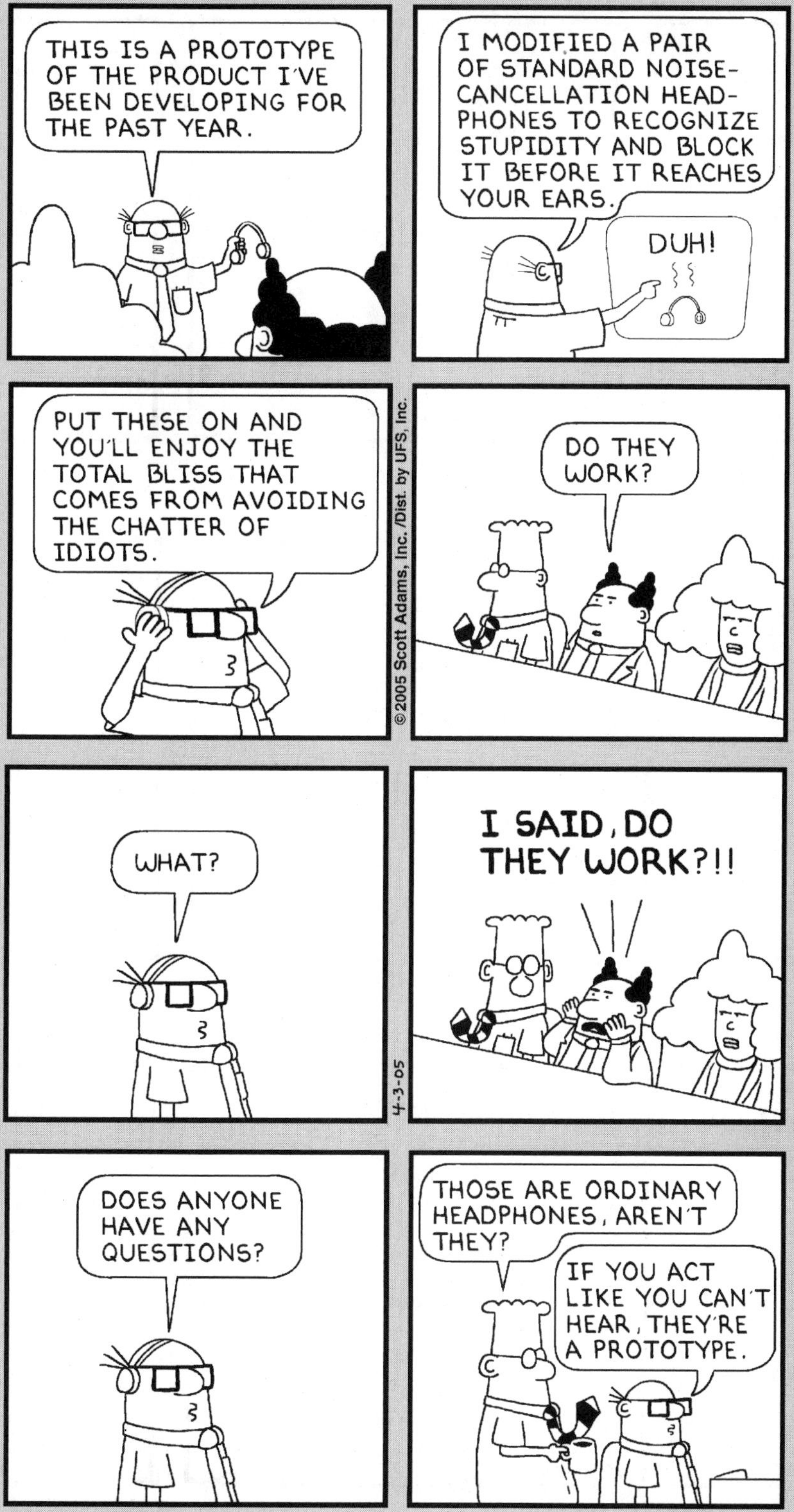
THIS IS A PROTOTYPE OF THE PRODUCT I'VE BEEN DEVELOPING FOR THE PAST YEAR.
I MODIFIED A PAIR OF STANDARD NOISE-CANCELLATION HEAD-PHONES TO RECOGNIZE STUPIDITY AND BLOCK IT BEFORE IT REACHES YOUR EARS.
DUH!
PUT THESE ON AND YOU'LL ENJOY THE TOTAL BLISS THAT COMES FROM AVOIDING THE CHATTER OF IDIOTS.
©2005 Scott Adams, Inc. /Dist. by UFS, Inc.
DO THEY WORK?
WHAT?
I SAID, DO THEY WORK?!!
4-3-05
DOES ANYONE HAVE ANY QUESTIONS?
THOSE ARE ORDINARY HEADPHONES, AREN'T THEY?
IF YOU ACT LIKE YOU CAN'T HEAR, THEY'RE A PROTOTYPE.

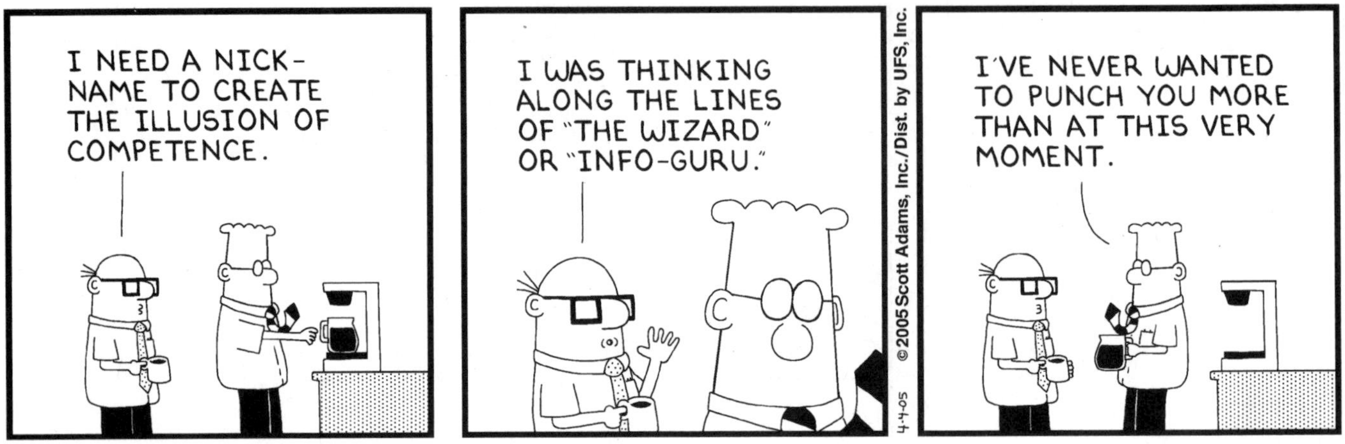
I NEED A NICK-NAME TO CREATE THE ILLUSION OF COMPETENCE.
I WAS THINKING ALONG THE LINES OF "THE WIZARD" OR "INFO-GURU."
© 2005 Scott Adams, Inc./Dist. by UFS, Inc.
4-4-05
I'VE NEVER WANTED TO PUNCH YOU MORE THAN AT THIS VERY MOMENT.

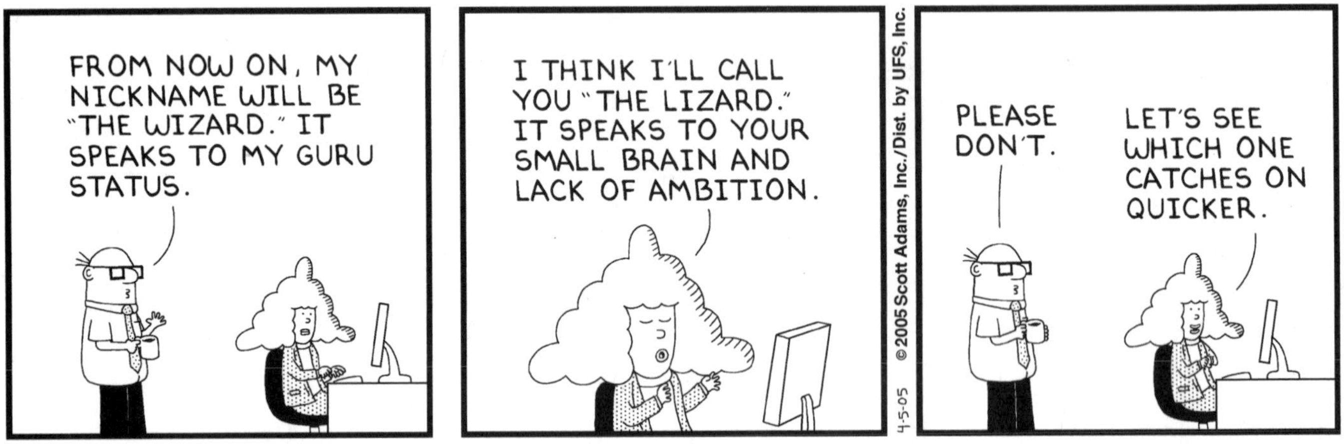
FROM NOW ON, MY NICKNAME WILL BE "THE WIZARD." IT SPEAKS TO MY GURU STATUS.
I THINK I'LL CALL YOU "THE LIZARD." IT SPEAKS TO YOUR SMALL BRAIN AND LACK OF AMBITION.
© 2005 Scott Adams, Inc./Dist. by UFS, Inc.
4-5-05
PLEASE DON'T.
LET'S SEE WHICH ONE CATCHES ON QUICKER.

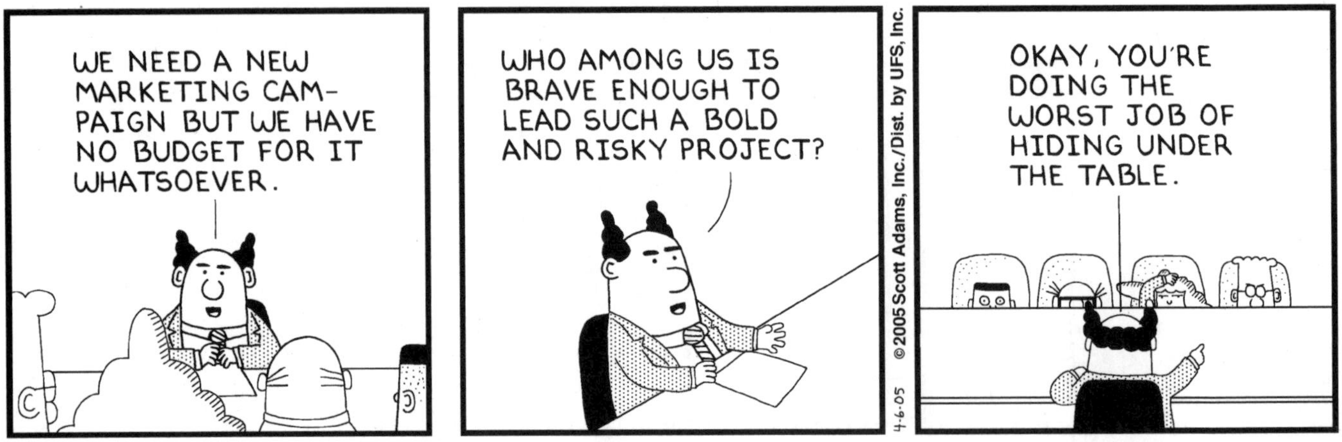
WE NEED A NEW MARKETING CAM-PAIGN BUT WE HAVE NO BUDGET FOR IT WHATSOEVER.
WHO AMONG US IS BRAVE ENOUGH TO LEAD SUCH A BOLD AND RISKY PROJECT?
© 2005 Scott Adams, Inc./Dist. by UFS, Inc.
4-6-05
OKAY, YOU'RE DOING THE WORST JOB OF HIDING UNDER THE TABLE.

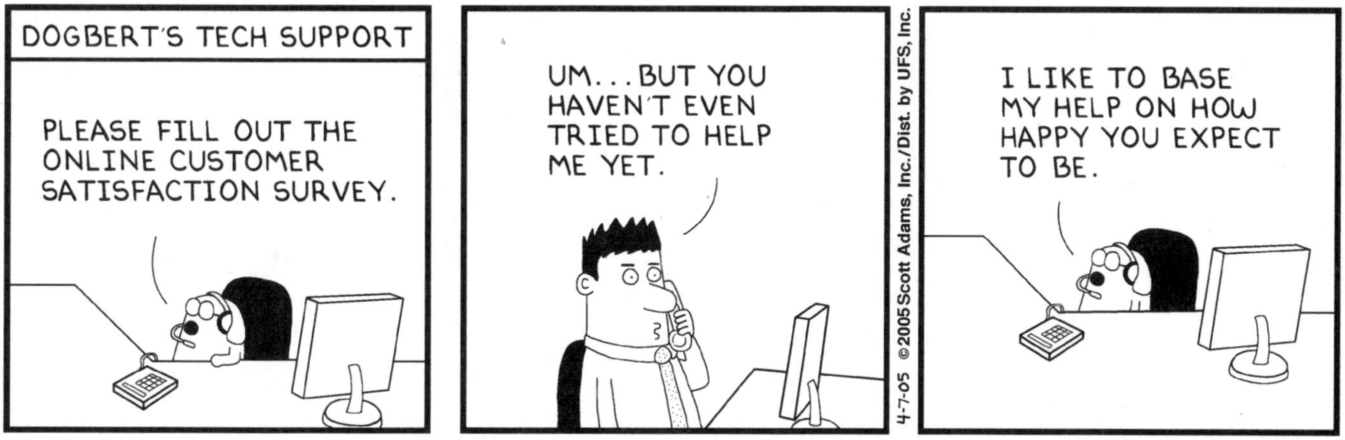
DOGBERT'S TECH SUPPORT
PLEASE FILL OUT THE ONLINE CUSTOMER SATISFACTION SURVEY.
UM...BUT YOU HAVEN'T EVEN TRIED TO HELP ME YET.
I LIKE TO BASE MY HELP ON HOW HAPPY YOU EXPECT TO BE.
4-7-05 © 2005 Scott Adams, Inc./Dist. by UFS, Inc.

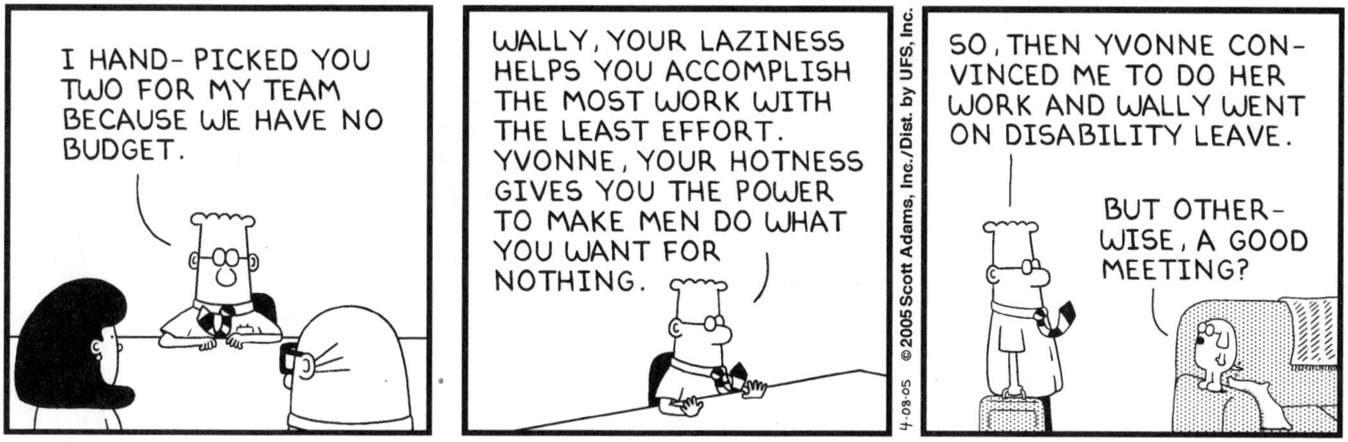
I HAND-PICKED YOU TWO FOR MY TEAM BECAUSE WE HAVE NO BUDGET.
WALLY, YOUR LAZINESS HELPS YOU ACCOMPLISH THE MOST WORK WITH THE LEAST EFFORT. YVONNE, YOUR HOTNESS GIVES YOU THE POWER TO MAKE MEN DO WHAT YOU WANT FOR NOTHING.
4-08-05 © 2005 Scott Adams, Inc./Dist. by UFS, Inc.
SO, THEN YVONNE CONVINCED ME TO DO HER WORK AND WALLY WENT ON DISABILITY LEAVE.
BUT OTHERWISE, A GOOD MEETING?

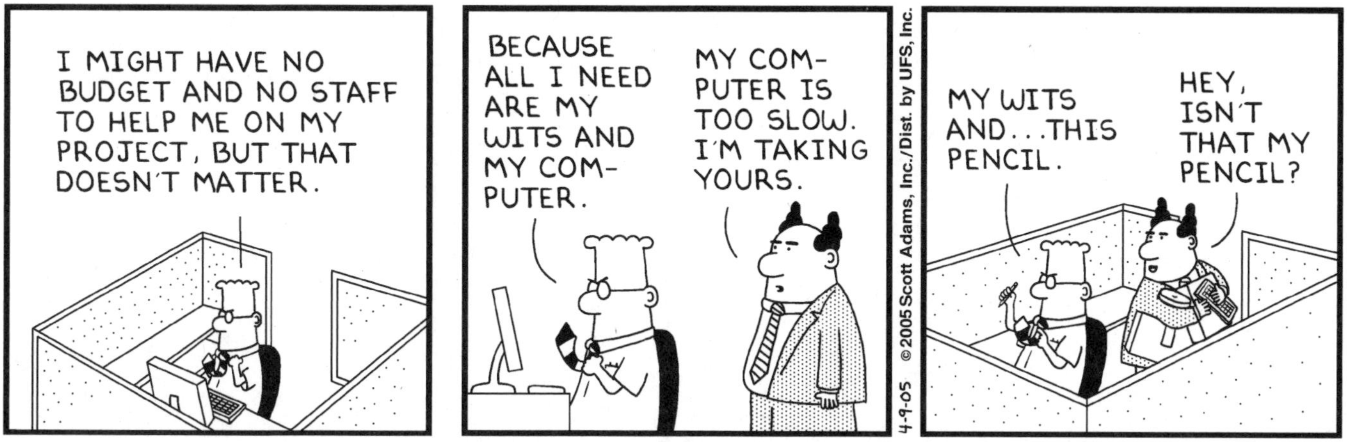
I MIGHT HAVE NO BUDGET AND NO STAFF TO HELP ME ON MY PROJECT, BUT THAT DOESN'T MATTER.
BECAUSE ALL I NEED ARE MY WITS AND MY COMPUTER.
MY COMPUTER IS TOO SLOW. I'M TAKING YOURS.
4-9-05 © 2005 Scott Adams, Inc./Dist. by UFS, Inc.
MY WITS AND...THIS PENCIL.
HEY, ISN'T THAT MY PENCIL?

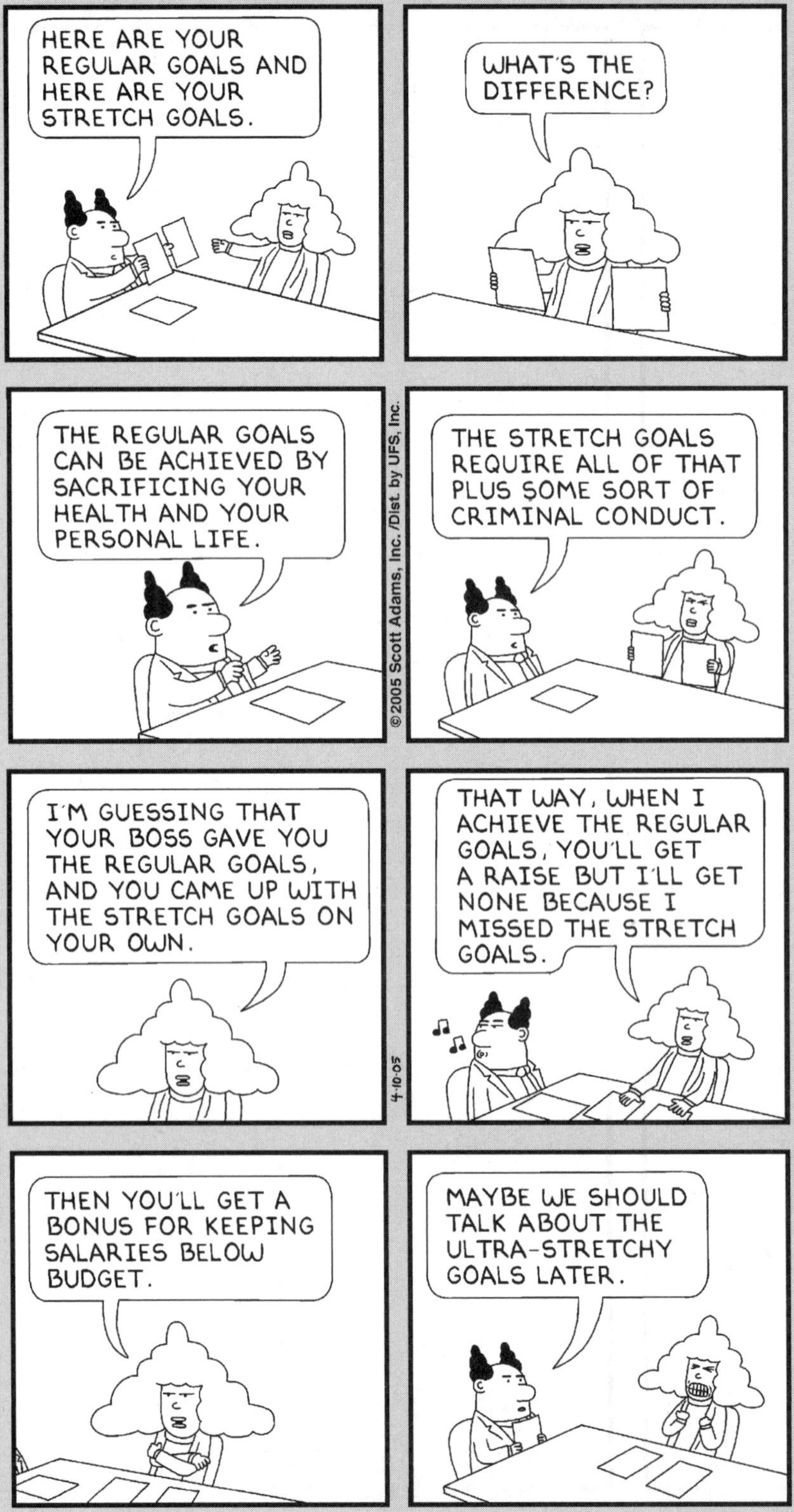
HERE ARE YOUR REGULAR GOALS AND HERE ARE YOUR STRETCH GOALS.
WHAT'S THE DIFFERENCE?
THE REGULAR GOALS CAN BE ACHIEVED BY SACRIFICING YOUR HEALTH AND YOUR PERSONAL LIFE.
THE STRETCH GOALS REQUIRE ALL OF THAT PLUS SOME SORT OF CRIMINAL CONDUCT.
I'M GUESSING THAT YOUR BOSS GAVE YOU THE REGULAR GOALS, AND YOU CAME UP WITH THE STRETCH GOALS ON YOUR OWN.
THAT WAY, WHEN I ACHIEVE THE REGULAR GOALS, YOU'LL GET A RAISE BUT I'LL GET NONE BECAUSE I MISSED THE STRETCH GOALS.
THEN YOU'LL GET A BONUS FOR KEEPING SALARIES BELOW BUDGET.
MAYBE WE SHOULD TALK ABOUT THE ULTRA-STRETCHY GOALS LATER.
©2005 Scott Adams, Inc./Dist. by UFS, Inc.
4-10-05

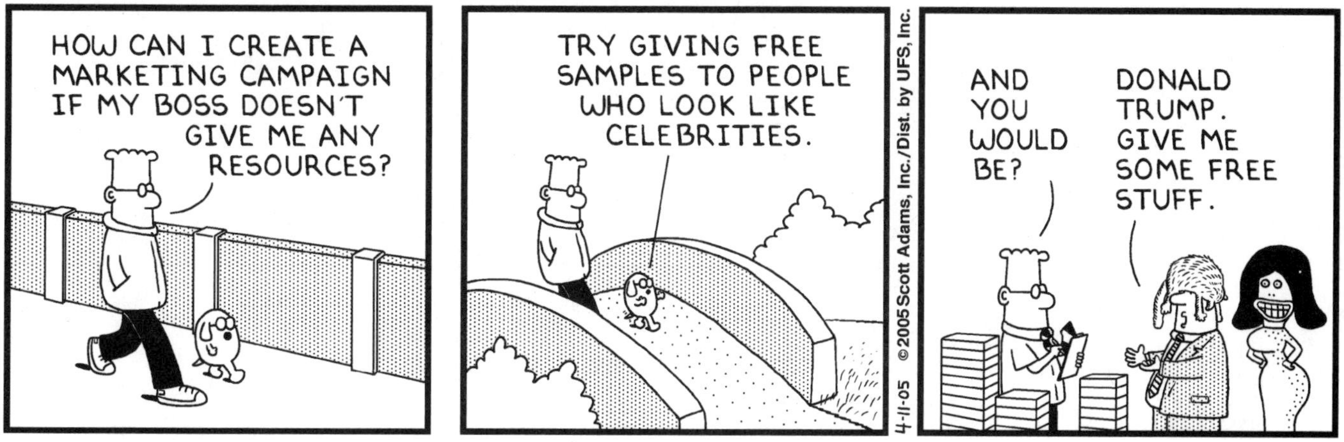
HOW CAN I CREATE A MARKETING CAMPAIGN IF MY BOSS DOESN'T GIVE ME ANY RESOURCES?
TRY GIVING FREE SAMPLES TO PEOPLE WHO LOOK LIKE CELEBRITIES.
4-11-05 ©2005 Scott Adams, Inc./Dist. by UFS, Inc.
AND YOU WOULD BE?
DONALD TRUMP. GIVE ME SOME FREE STUFF.

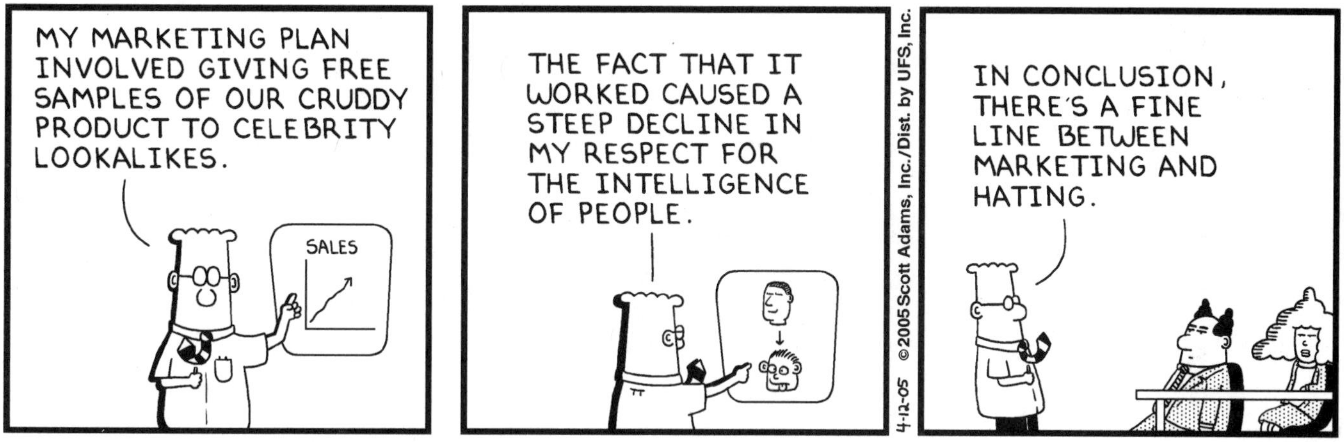
MY MARKETING PLAN INVOLVED GIVING FREE SAMPLES OF OUR CRUDDY PRODUCT TO CELEBRITY LOOKALIKES.
SALES
THE FACT THAT IT WORKED CAUSED A STEEP DECLINE IN MY RESPECT FOR THE INTELLIGENCE OF PEOPLE.
4-12-05 ©2005 Scott Adams, Inc./Dist. by UFS, Inc.
IN CONCLUSION, THERE'S A FINE LINE BETWEEN MARKETING AND HATING.

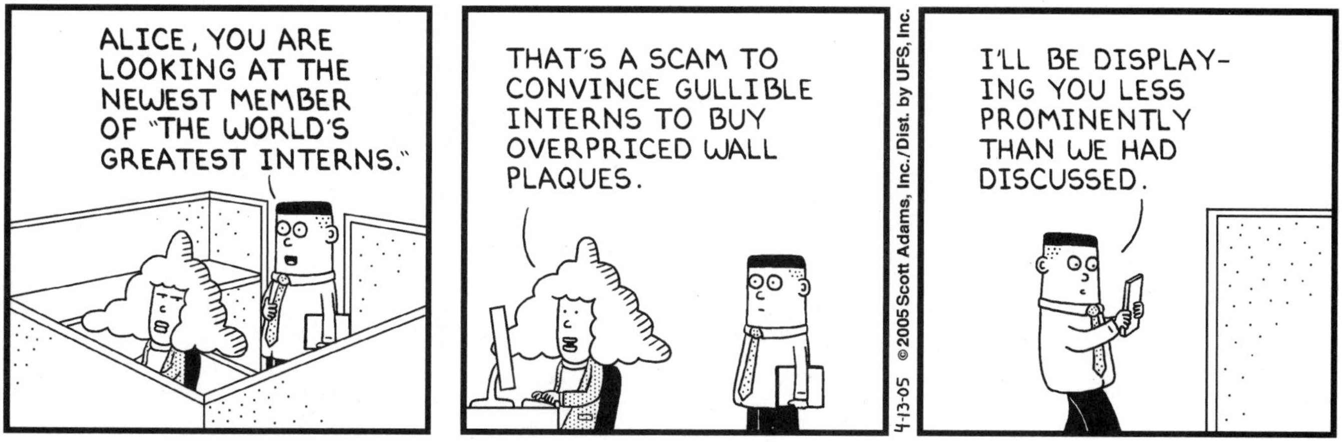
ALICE, YOU ARE LOOKING AT THE NEWEST MEMBER OF "THE WORLD'S GREATEST INTERNS."
THAT'S A SCAM TO CONVINCE GULLIBLE INTERNS TO BUY OVERPRICED WALL PLAQUES.
4-13-05 ©2005 Scott Adams, Inc./Dist. by UFS, Inc.
I'LL BE DISPLAY-ING YOU LESS PROMINENTLY THAN WE HAD DISCUSSED.

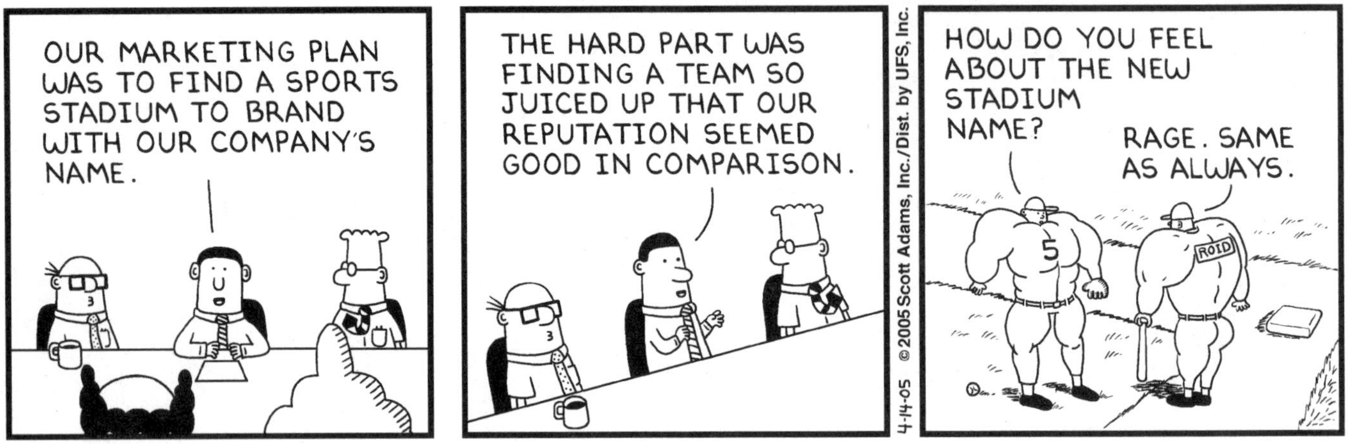
OUR MARKETING PLAN WAS TO FIND A SPORTS STADIUM TO BRAND WITH OUR COMPANY'S NAME.
THE HARD PART WAS FINDING A TEAM SO JUICED UP THAT OUR REPUTATION SEEMED GOOD IN COMPARISON.
4-14-05 © 2005 Scott Adams, Inc./Dist. by UFS, Inc.
HOW DO YOU FEEL ABOUT THE NEW STADIUM NAME?
RAGE. SAME AS ALWAYS.
5
ROID

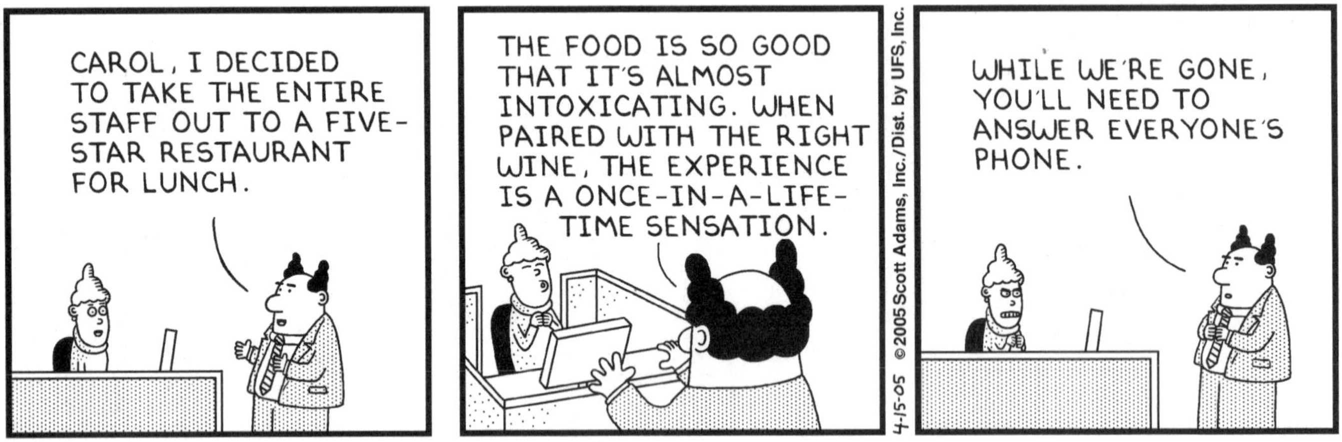
CAROL, I DECIDED TO TAKE THE ENTIRE STAFF OUT TO A FIVE-STAR RESTAURANT FOR LUNCH.
THE FOOD IS SO GOOD THAT IT'S ALMOST INTOXICATING. WHEN PAIRED WITH THE RIGHT WINE, THE EXPERIENCE IS A ONCE-IN-A-LIFE-TIME SENSATION.
4-15-05 © 2005 Scott Adams, Inc./Dist. by UFS, Inc.
WHILE WE'RE GONE, YOU'LL NEED TO ANSWER EVERYONE'S PHONE.

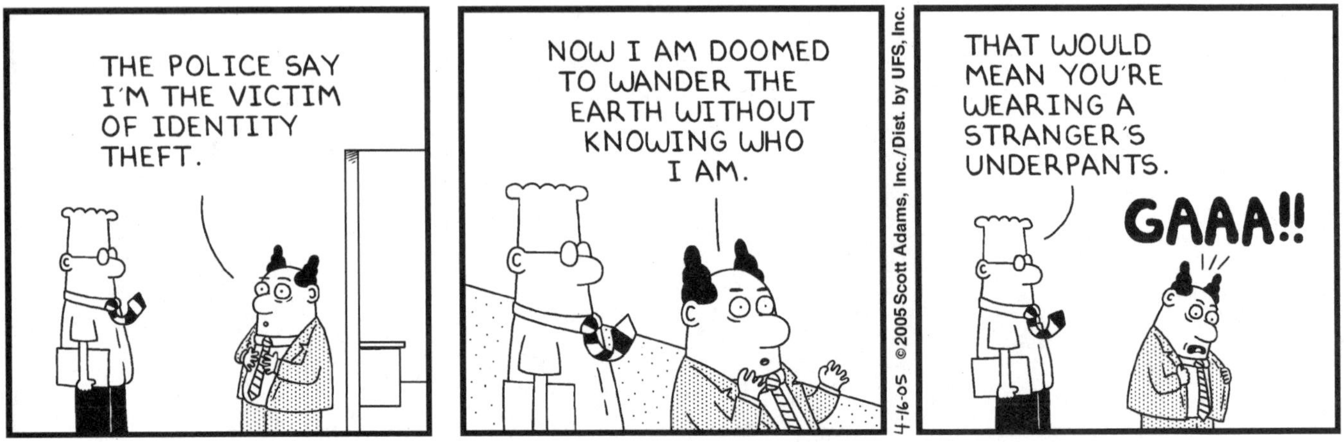
THE POLICE SAY I'M THE VICTIM OF IDENTITY THEFT.
NOW I AM DOOMED TO WANDER THE EARTH WITHOUT KNOWING WHO I AM.
4-16-05 © 2005 Scott Adams, Inc./Dist. by UFS, Inc.
THAT WOULD MEAN YOU'RE WEARING A STRANGER'S UNDERPANTS.
GAAA!!

INTRODUCING
LOOPY
THE WOMAN WHO
COULDN'T END A STORY
DID I TELL YOU ABOUT MY VACATION?
UH-OH
WE LEARNED ABOUT COCONUTS.
I'M TRAPPED.
© 2005 Scott Adams, Inc./Dist. by UFS, Inc.
COCONUTS ARE ROUND AND HAIRY, AND THEY GROW ON TREES.
MUST ESCAPE.
COCONUT TREES ARE FOUND IN MANY COUNTRIES.
MUST USE MY EJECTOR SEAT.
4-17-05
HA HA!
FOOMP!
THEY'RE BROWN.
GAAA!!! SHE HAS A PURSUIT CHAIR!!!
FOOMP!
I TOOK LOTS OF PICTURES.
MUST...AIM FOR TRAFFIC.

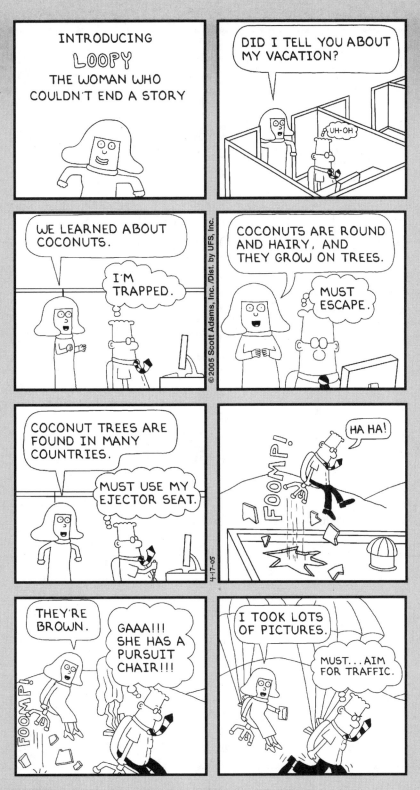

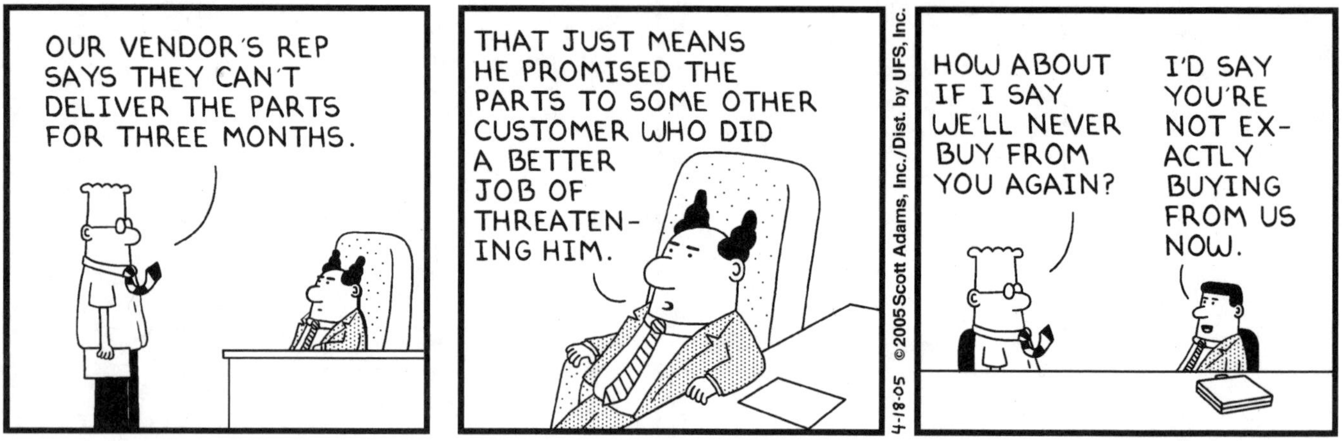
OUR VENDOR'S REP SAYS THEY CAN'T DELIVER THE PARTS FOR THREE MONTHS.
THAT JUST MEANS HE PROMISED THE PARTS TO SOME OTHER CUSTOMER WHO DID A BETTER JOB OF THREATENING HIM.
4-18-05 ©2005 Scott Adams, Inc./Dist. by UFS, Inc.
HOW ABOUT IF I SAY WE'LL NEVER BUY FROM YOU AGAIN?
I'D SAY YOU'RE NOT EXACTLY BUYING FROM US NOW.

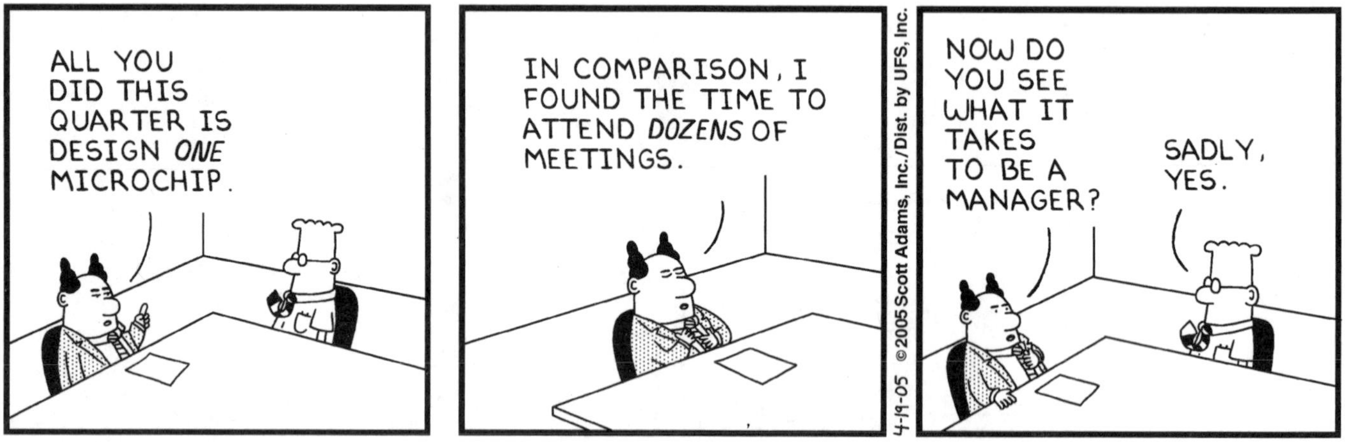
ALL YOU DID THIS QUARTER IS DESIGN *ONE* MICROCHIP.
IN COMPARISON, I FOUND THE TIME TO ATTEND *DOZENS* OF MEETINGS.
4-19-05 ©2005 Scott Adams, Inc./Dist. by UFS, Inc.
NOW DO YOU SEE WHAT IT TAKES TO BE A MANAGER?
SADLY, YES.

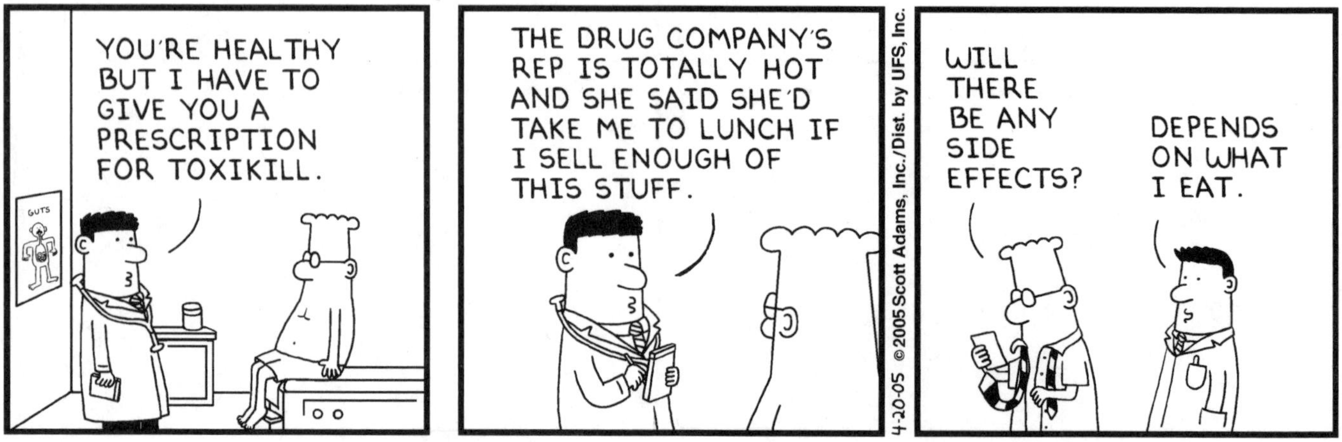
YOU'RE HEALTHY BUT I HAVE TO GIVE YOU A PRESCRIPTION FOR TOXIKILL.
GUTS
THE DRUG COMPANY'S REP IS TOTALLY HOT AND SHE SAID SHE'D TAKE ME TO LUNCH IF I SELL ENOUGH OF THIS STUFF.
4-20-05 ©2005 Scott Adams, Inc./Dist. by UFS, Inc.
WILL THERE BE ANY SIDE EFFECTS?
DEPENDS ON WHAT I EAT.

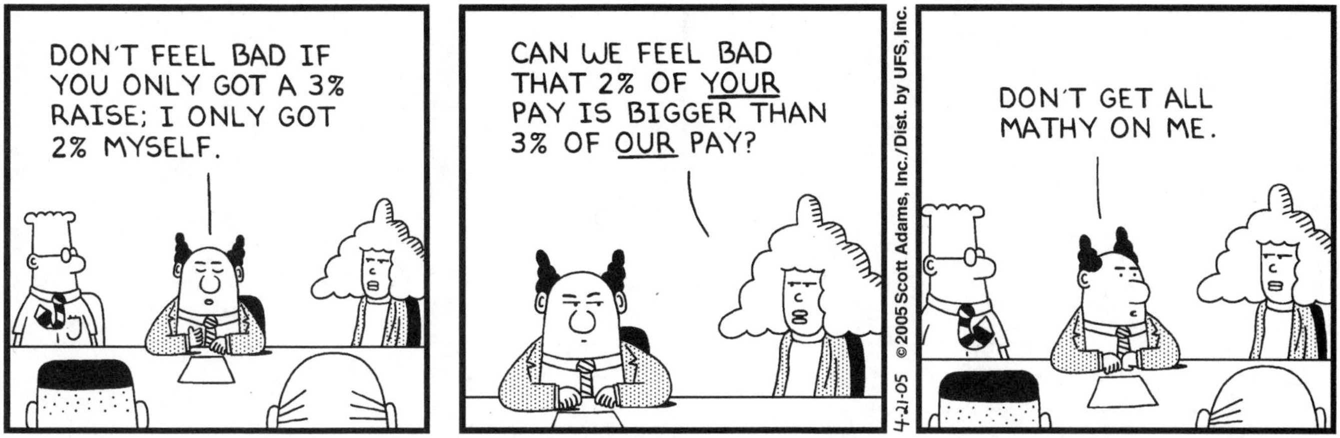
DON'T FEEL BAD IF YOU ONLY GOT A 3% RAISE; I ONLY GOT 2% MYSELF.
CAN WE FEEL BAD THAT 2% OF YOUR PAY IS BIGGER THAN 3% OF OUR PAY?
4-21-05 © 2005 Scott Adams, Inc./Dist. by UFS, Inc.
DON'T GET ALL MATHY ON ME.

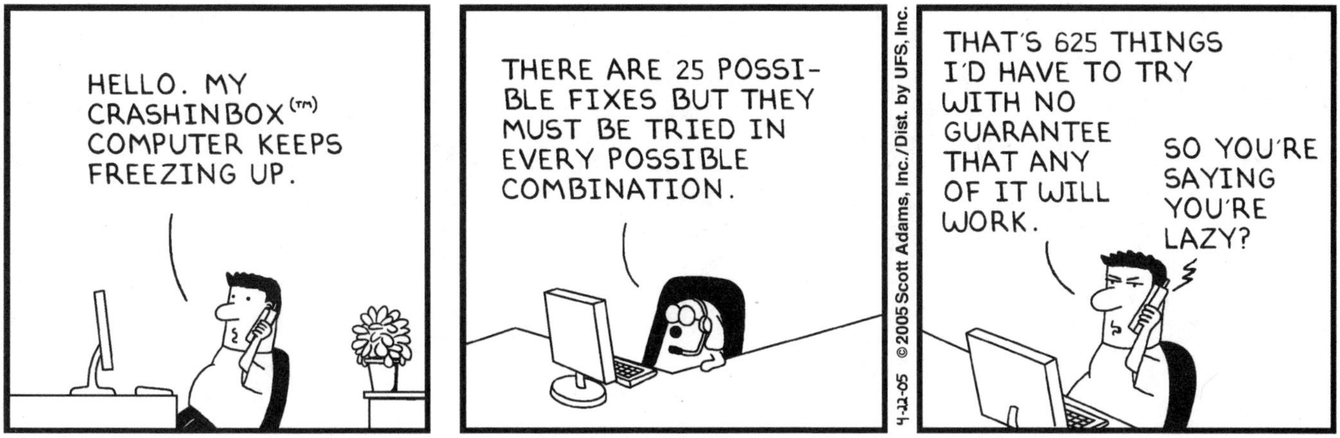
HELLO. MY CRASHINBOX(TM) COMPUTER KEEPS FREEZING UP.
THERE ARE 25 POSSI-BLE FIXES BUT THEY MUST BE TRIED IN EVERY POSSIBLE COMBINATION.
4-22-05 © 2005 Scott Adams, Inc./Dist. by UFS, Inc.
THAT'S 625 THINGS I'D HAVE TO TRY WITH NO GUARANTEE THAT ANY OF IT WILL WORK.
SO YOU'RE SAYING YOU'RE LAZY?

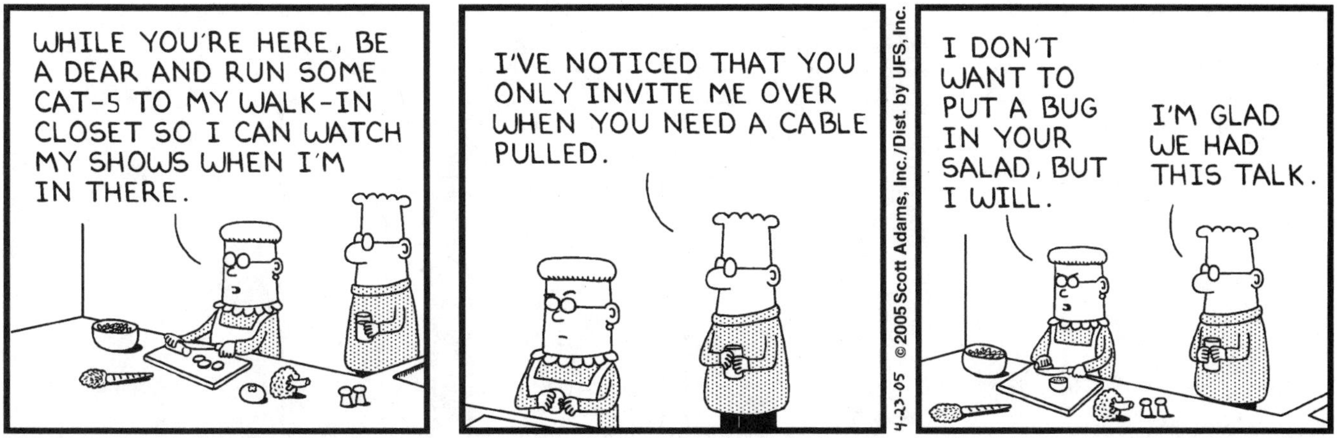
WHILE YOU'RE HERE, BE A DEAR AND RUN SOME CAT-5 TO MY WALK-IN CLOSET SO I CAN WATCH MY SHOWS WHEN I'M IN THERE.
I'VE NOTICED THAT YOU ONLY INVITE ME OVER WHEN YOU NEED A CABLE PULLED.
4-23-05 © 2005 Scott Adams, Inc./Dist. by UFS, Inc.
I DON'T WANT TO PUT A BUG IN YOUR SALAD, BUT I WILL.
I'M GLAD WE HAD THIS TALK.

MY ACCOMPLISHMENT THIS MONTH WAS OPENING A FILE THAT SOMEONE E-MAILED.
THAT TOOK AN ENTIRE MONTH?
IT WASN'T THAT EASY. I DIDN'T HAVE THE RIGHT SOFTWARE TO OPEN THE FILE.
I TRIED TO DOWN-LOAD THE VIEWER FROM THE INTERNET BUT THE WEB SITE DIDN'T SUPPORT MY BROWSER.
©2005 Scott Adams, Inc./Dist. by UFS, Inc.
AND I COULDN'T UPGRADE MY BROWSER UNTIL I UPGRADED MY OPERATING SYSTEM!
THAT REQUIRED ME TO UPGRADE ALL OF MY APPLICATIONS SOFTWARE, TOO.
4-24-05
MY HARD DISK GOT MAXED OUT, SO I HAD TO UPGRADE MY COMPUTER AND TRANSFER ALL OF THE FILES.
SO, THEN YOU GOT TO VIEW THE FILE?
YEAH... IT WAS A FUNNY ONE ABOUT A CAT.

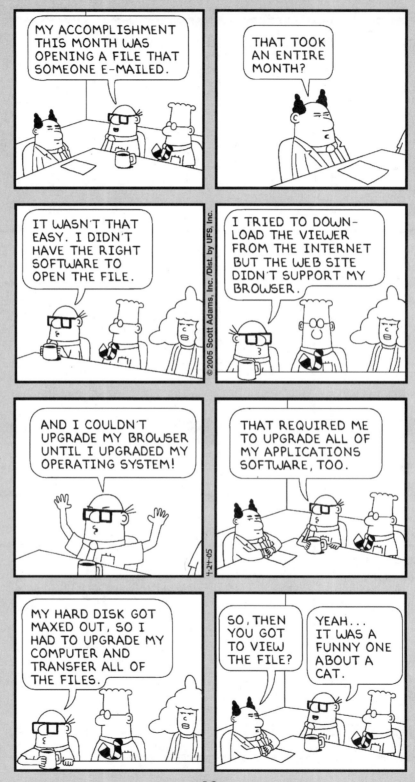

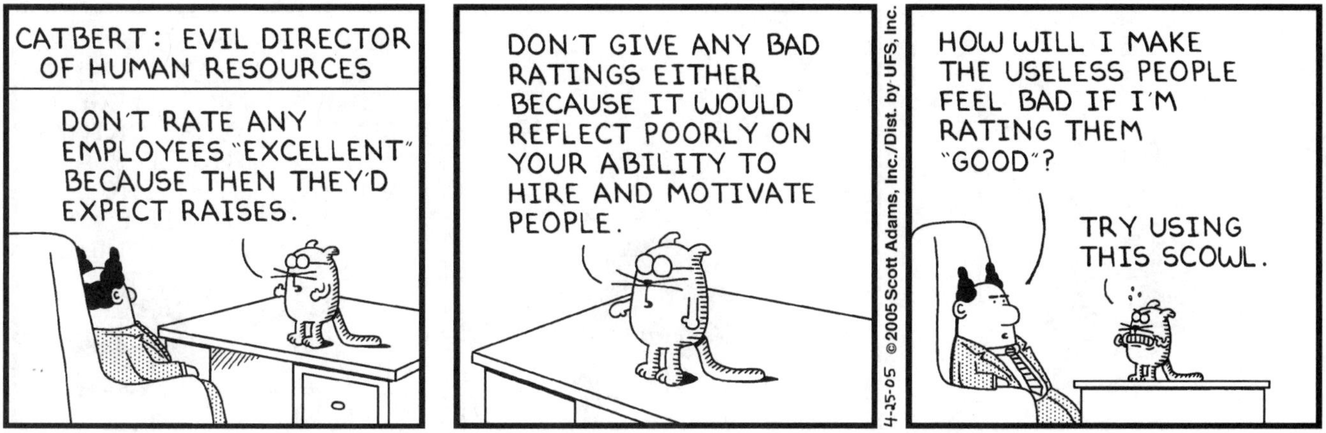
CATBERT: EVIL DIRECTOR OF HUMAN RESOURCES
DON'T RATE ANY EMPLOYEES "EXCELLENT" BECAUSE THEN THEY'D EXPECT RAISES.
DON'T GIVE ANY BAD RATINGS EITHER BECAUSE IT WOULD REFLECT POORLY ON YOUR ABILITY TO HIRE AND MOTIVATE PEOPLE.
4-25-05 © 2005 Scott Adams, Inc./Dist. by UFS, Inc.
HOW WILL I MAKE THE USELESS PEOPLE FEEL BAD IF I'M RATING THEM "GOOD"?
TRY USING THIS SCOWL.

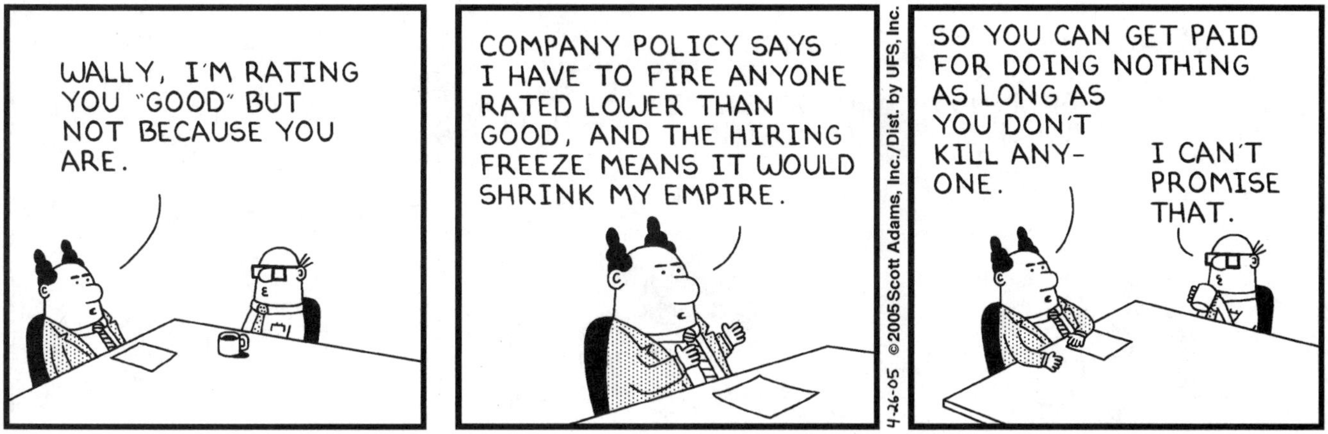
WALLY, I'M RATING YOU "GOOD" BUT NOT BECAUSE YOU ARE.
COMPANY POLICY SAYS I HAVE TO FIRE ANYONE RATED LOWER THAN GOOD, AND THE HIRING FREEZE MEANS IT WOULD SHRINK MY EMPIRE.
4-26-05 © 2005 Scott Adams, Inc./Dist. by UFS, Inc.
SO YOU CAN GET PAID FOR DOING NOTHING AS LONG AS YOU DON'T KILL ANY-ONE.
I CAN'T PROMISE THAT.

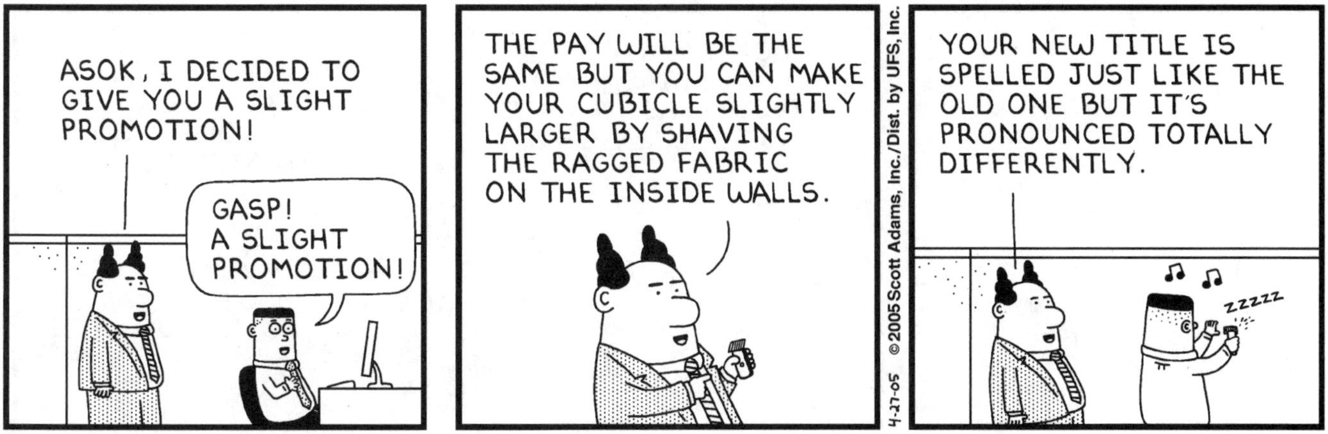
ASOK, I DECIDED TO GIVE YOU A SLIGHT PROMOTION!
GASP! A SLIGHT PROMOTION!
THE PAY WILL BE THE SAME BUT YOU CAN MAKE YOUR CUBICLE SLIGHTLY LARGER BY SHAVING THE RAGGED FABRIC ON THE INSIDE WALLS.
4-27-05 © 2005 Scott Adams, Inc./Dist. by UFS, Inc.
YOUR NEW TITLE IS SPELLED JUST LIKE THE OLD ONE BUT IT'S PRONOUNCED TOTALLY DIFFERENTLY.
ZZZZZ

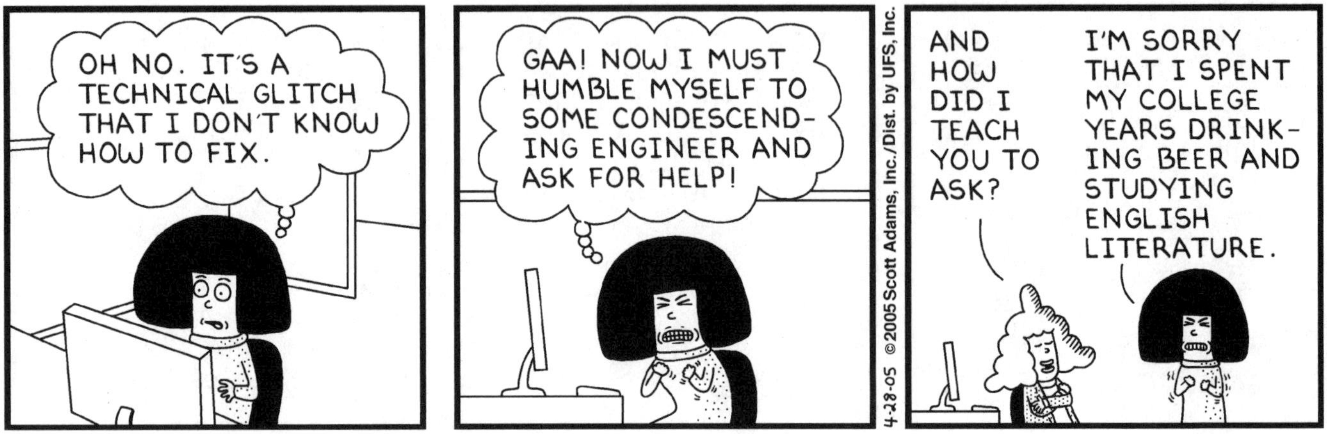
OH NO. IT'S A TECHNICAL GLITCH THAT I DON'T KNOW HOW TO FIX.
GAA! NOW I MUST HUMBLE MYSELF TO SOME CONDESCEND-ING ENGINEER AND ASK FOR HELP!
4-28-05 ©2005 Scott Adams, Inc./Dist. by UFS, Inc.
AND HOW DID I TEACH YOU TO ASK?
I'M SORRY THAT I SPENT MY COLLEGE YEARS DRINK-ING BEER AND STUDYING ENGLISH LITERATURE.

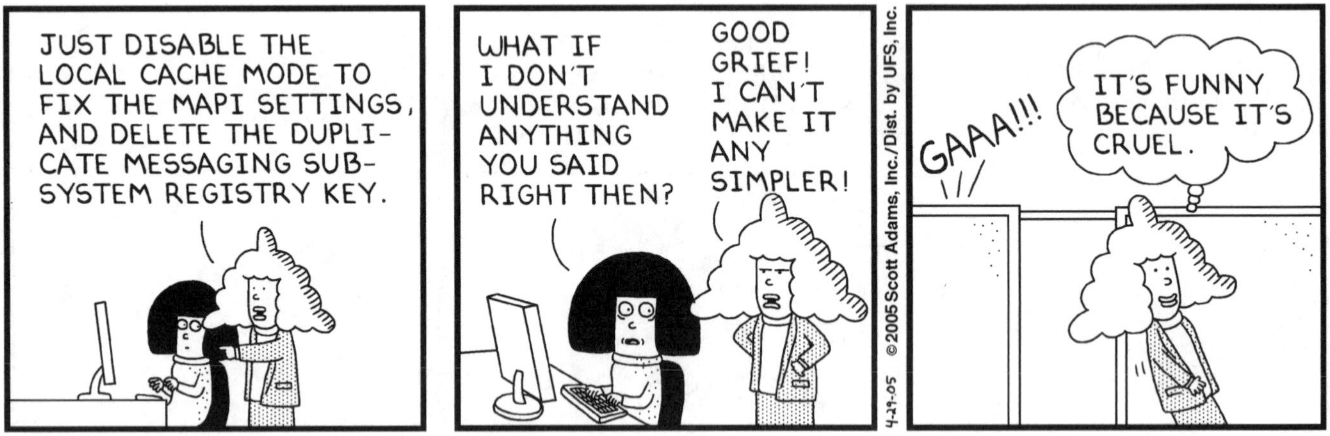
JUST DISABLE THE LOCAL CACHE MODE TO FIX THE MAPI SETTINGS, AND DELETE THE DUPLI-CATE MESSAGING SUB-SYSTEM REGISTRY KEY.
WHAT IF I DON'T UNDERSTAND ANYTHING YOU SAID RIGHT THEN?
GOOD GRIEF! I CAN'T MAKE IT ANY SIMPLER!
4-29-05 ©2005 Scott Adams, Inc./Dist. by UFS, Inc.
GAAA!!!
IT'S FUNNY BECAUSE IT'S CRUEL.

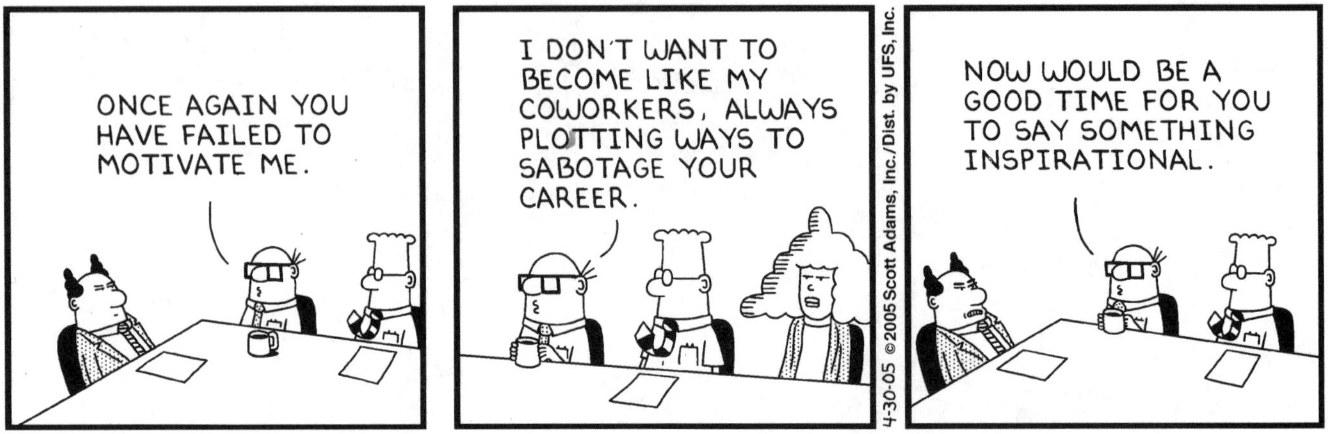
ONCE AGAIN YOU HAVE FAILED TO MOTIVATE ME.
I DON'T WANT TO BECOME LIKE MY COWORKERS, ALWAYS PLOTTING WAYS TO SABOTAGE YOUR CAREER.
4-30-05 ©2005 Scott Adams, Inc./Dist. by UFS, Inc.
NOW WOULD BE A GOOD TIME FOR YOU TO SAY SOMETHING INSPIRATIONAL.

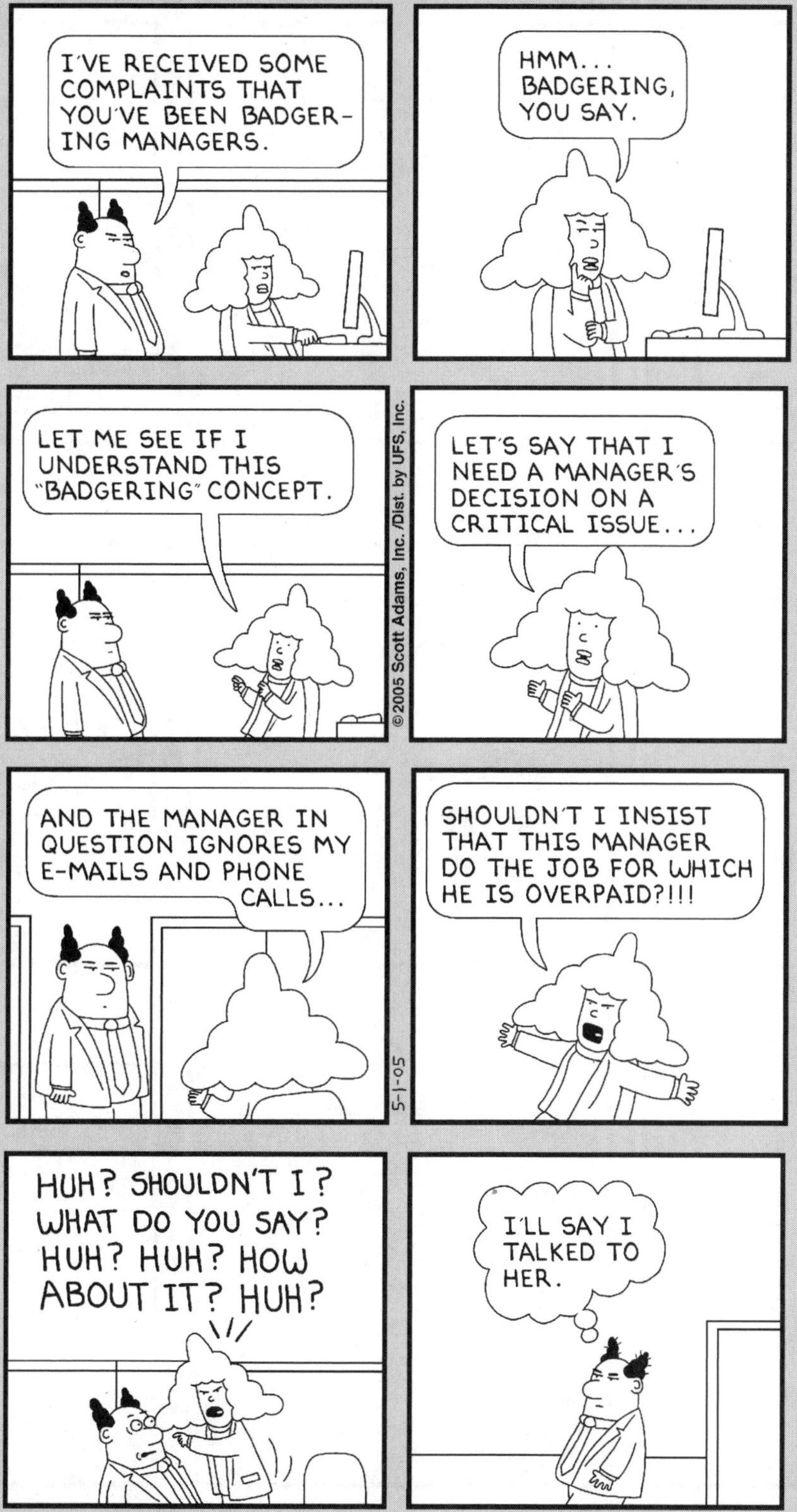
I'VE RECEIVED SOME COMPLAINTS THAT YOU'VE BEEN BADGER-ING MANAGERS.
HMM... BADGERING, YOU SAY.
LET ME SEE IF I UNDERSTAND THIS "BADGERING" CONCEPT.
LET'S SAY THAT I NEED A MANAGER'S DECISION ON A CRITICAL ISSUE...
AND THE MANAGER IN QUESTION IGNORES MY E-MAILS AND PHONE CALLS...
SHOULDN'T I INSIST THAT THIS MANAGER DO THE JOB FOR WHICH HE IS OVERPAID?!!!
HUH? SHOULDN'T I? WHAT DO YOU SAY? HUH? HUH? HOW ABOUT IT? HUH?
I'LL SAY I TALKED TO HER.
©2005 Scott Adams, Inc./Dist. by UFS, Inc.
5-1-05

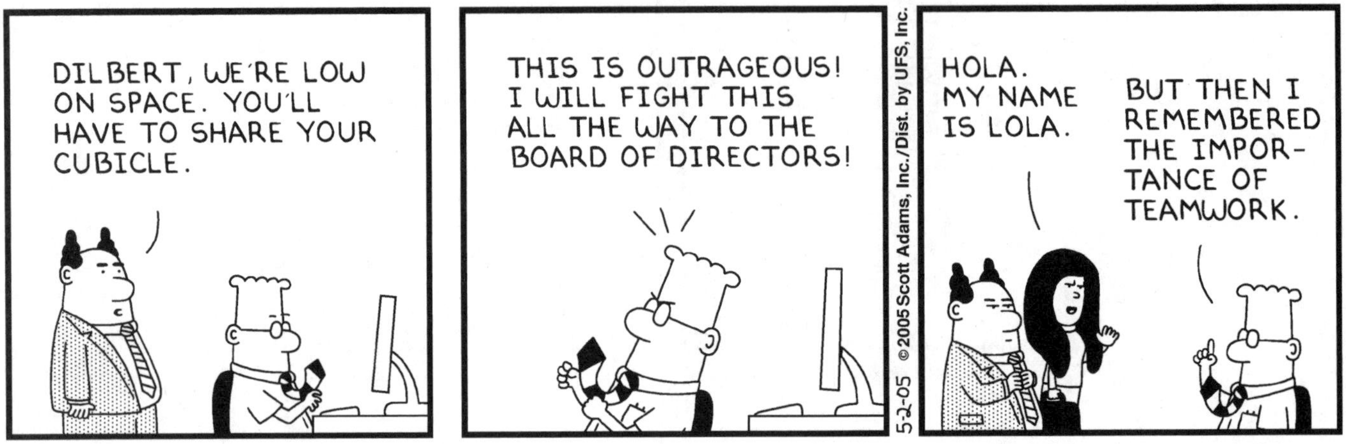
DILBERT, WE'RE LOW ON SPACE. YOU'LL HAVE TO SHARE YOUR CUBICLE.
THIS IS OUTRAGEOUS! I WILL FIGHT THIS ALL THE WAY TO THE BOARD OF DIRECTORS!
5-2-05 ©2005 Scott Adams, Inc./Dist. by UFS, Inc.
HOLA. MY NAME IS LOLA.
BUT THEN I REMEMBERED THE IMPORTANCE OF TEAMWORK.

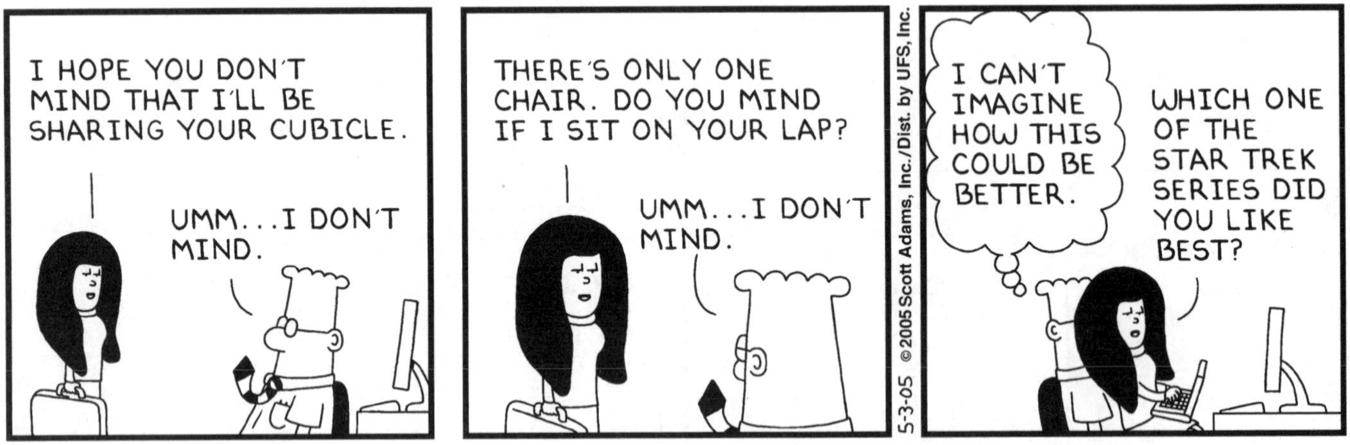
I HOPE YOU DON'T MIND THAT I'LL BE SHARING YOUR CUBICLE.
UMM...I DON'T MIND.
THERE'S ONLY ONE CHAIR. DO YOU MIND IF I SIT ON YOUR LAP?
UMM...I DON'T MIND.
5-3-05 ©2005 Scott Adams, Inc./Dist. by UFS, Inc.
I CAN'T IMAGINE HOW THIS COULD BE BETTER.
WHICH ONE OF THE STAR TREK SERIES DID YOU LIKE BEST?

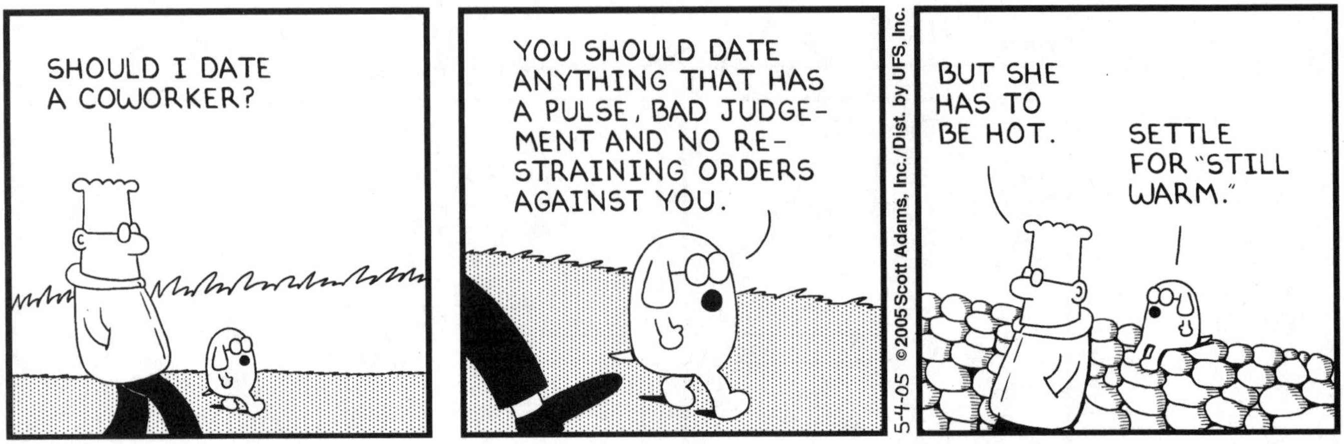
SHOULD I DATE A COWORKER?
YOU SHOULD DATE ANYTHING THAT HAS A PULSE, BAD JUDGEMENT AND NO RESTRAINING ORDERS AGAINST YOU.
5-4-05 ©2005 Scott Adams, Inc./Dist. by UFS, Inc.
BUT SHE HAS TO BE HOT.
SETTLE FOR "STILL WARM."

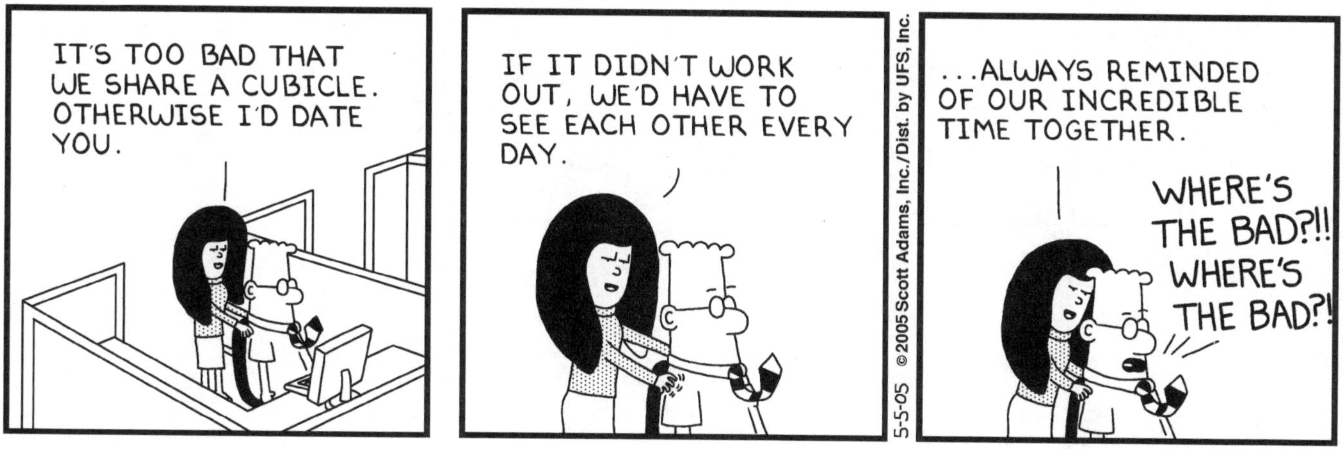
IT'S TOO BAD THAT WE SHARE A CUBICLE. OTHERWISE I'D DATE YOU.
IF IT DIDN'T WORK OUT, WE'D HAVE TO SEE EACH OTHER EVERY DAY.
...ALWAYS REMINDED OF OUR INCREDIBLE TIME TOGETHER.
WHERE'S THE BAD?!! WHERE'S THE BAD?!
5-5-05 © 2005 Scott Adams, Inc./Dist. by UFS, Inc.

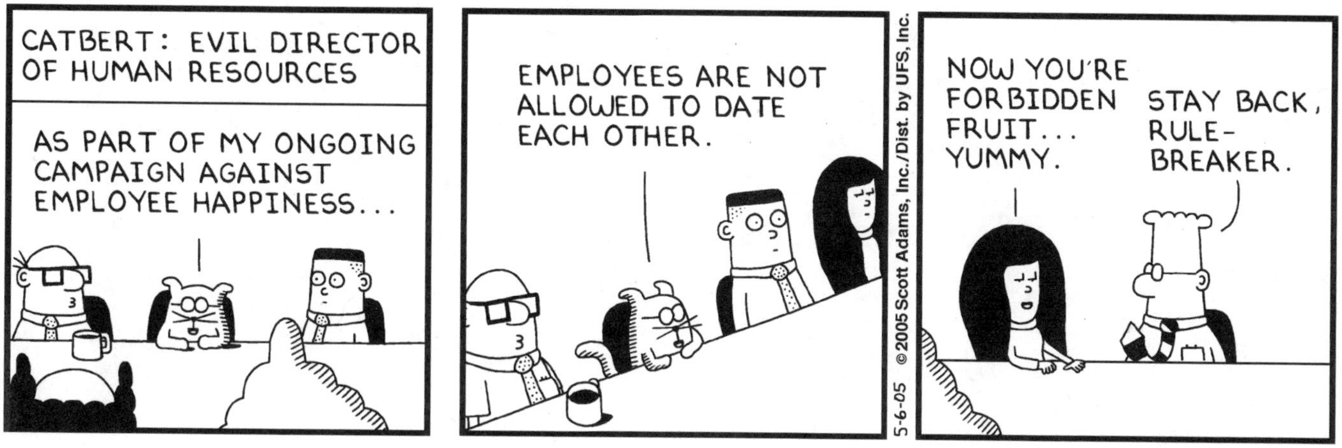
CATBERT: EVIL DIRECTOR OF HUMAN RESOURCES
AS PART OF MY ONGOING CAMPAIGN AGAINST EMPLOYEE HAPPINESS...
EMPLOYEES ARE NOT ALLOWED TO DATE EACH OTHER.
NOW YOU'RE FORBIDDEN FRUIT... YUMMY.
STAY BACK, RULE-BREAKER.
5-6-05 © 2005 Scott Adams, Inc./Dist. by UFS, Inc.

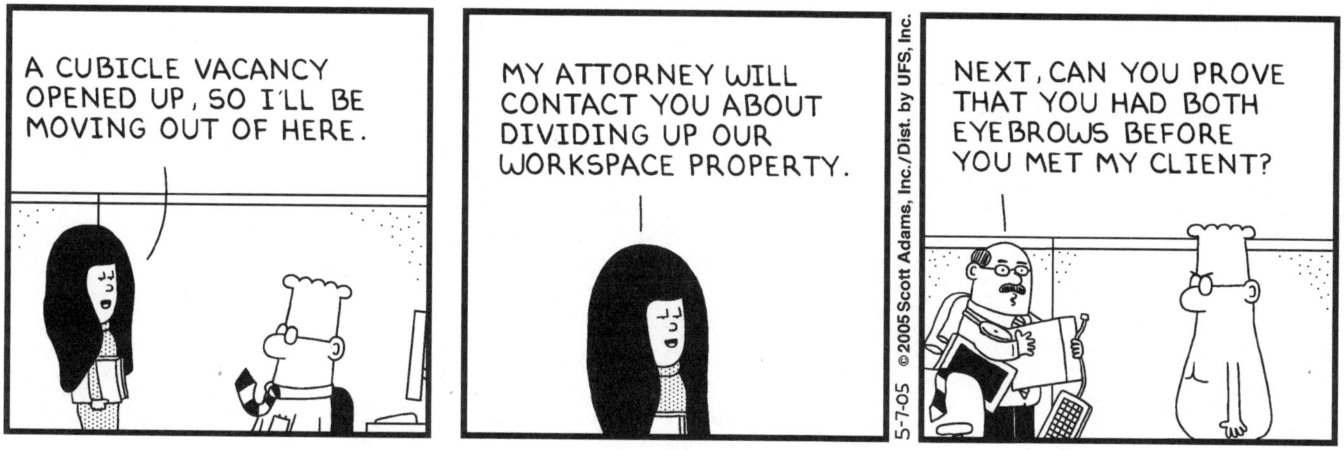
A CUBICLE VACANCY OPENED UP, SO I'LL BE MOVING OUT OF HERE.
MY ATTORNEY WILL CONTACT YOU ABOUT DIVIDING UP OUR WORKSPACE PROPERTY.
NEXT, CAN YOU PROVE THAT YOU HAD BOTH EYEBROWS BEFORE YOU MET MY CLIENT?
5-7-05 © 2005 Scott Adams, Inc./Dist. by UFS, Inc.

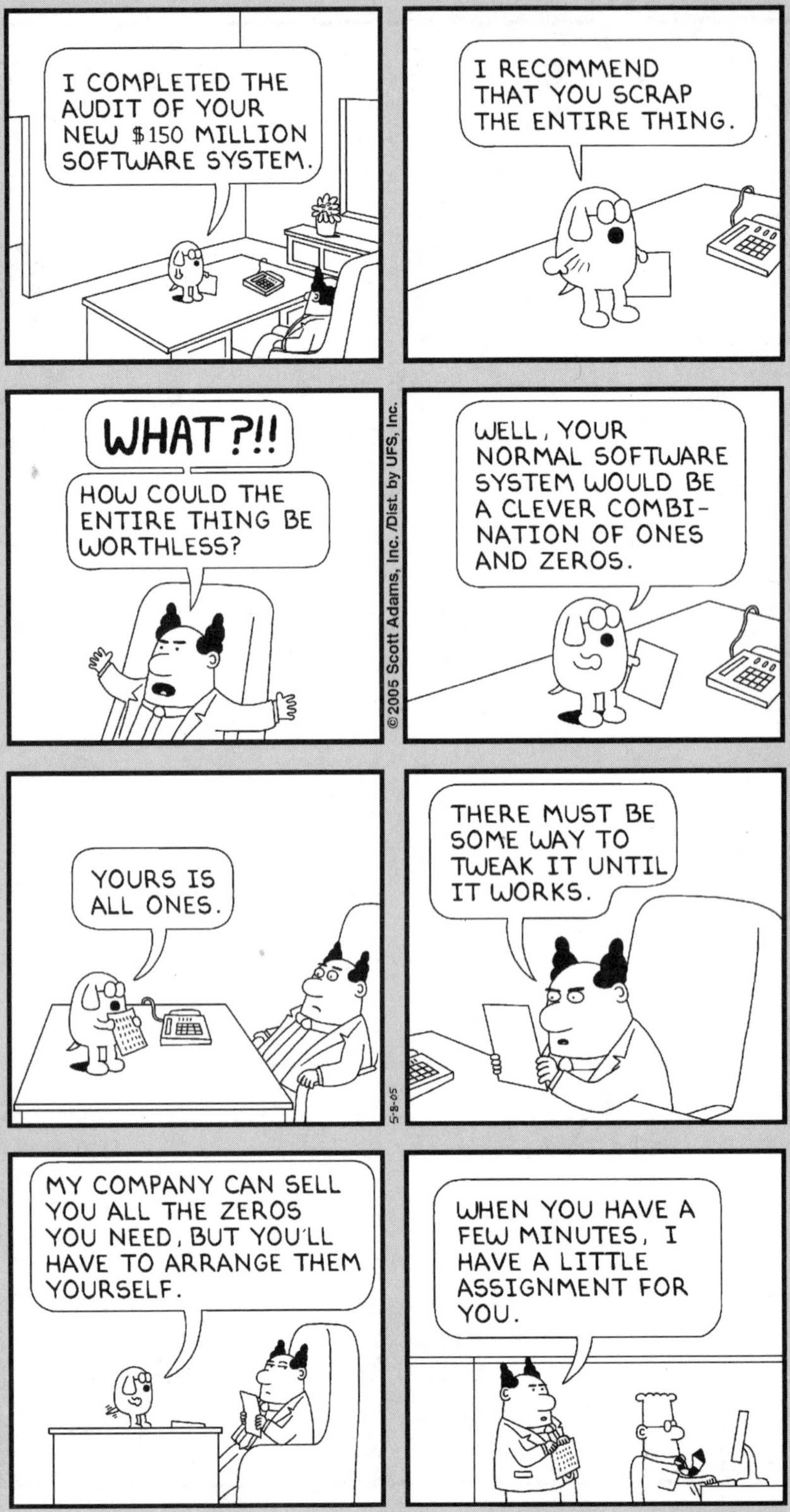
I COMPLETED THE AUDIT OF YOUR NEW $150 MILLION SOFTWARE SYSTEM.
I RECOMMEND THAT YOU SCRAP THE ENTIRE THING.
WHAT?!!
HOW COULD THE ENTIRE THING BE WORTHLESS?
WELL, YOUR NORMAL SOFTWARE SYSTEM WOULD BE A CLEVER COMBINATION OF ONES AND ZEROS.
YOURS IS ALL ONES.
THERE MUST BE SOME WAY TO TWEAK IT UNTIL IT WORKS.
MY COMPANY CAN SELL YOU ALL THE ZEROS YOU NEED, BUT YOU'LL HAVE TO ARRANGE THEM YOURSELF.
WHEN YOU HAVE A FEW MINUTES, I HAVE A LITTLE ASSIGNMENT FOR YOU.
© 2005 Scott Adams, Inc./Dist. by UFS, Inc.
5-8-05

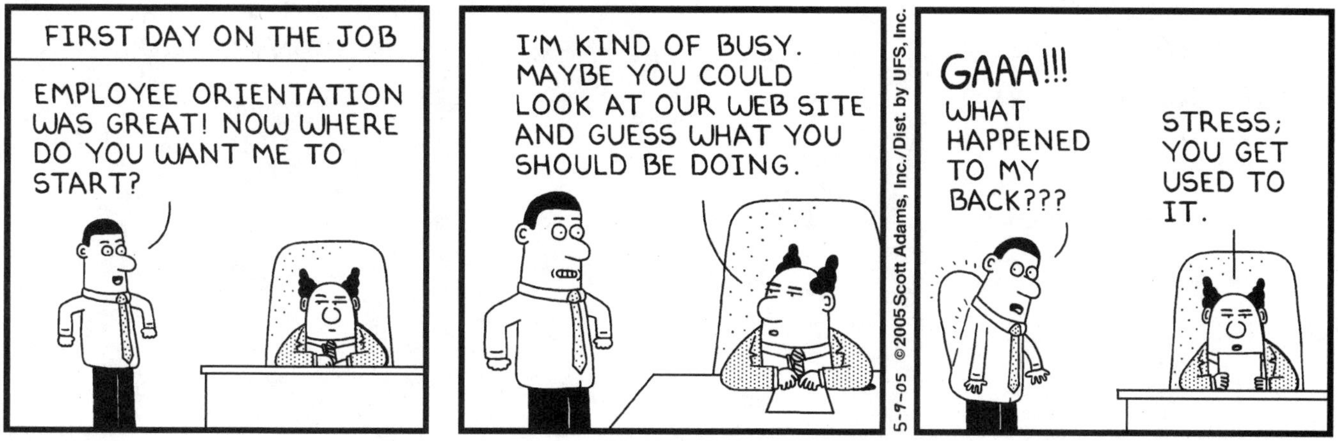
FIRST DAY ON THE JOB
EMPLOYEE ORIENTATION WAS GREAT! NOW WHERE DO YOU WANT ME TO START?
I'M KIND OF BUSY. MAYBE YOU COULD LOOK AT OUR WEB SITE AND GUESS WHAT YOU SHOULD BE DOING.
5-9-05 © 2005 Scott Adams, Inc./Dist. by UFS, Inc.
GAAA!!! WHAT HAPPENED TO MY BACK???
STRESS; YOU GET USED TO IT.

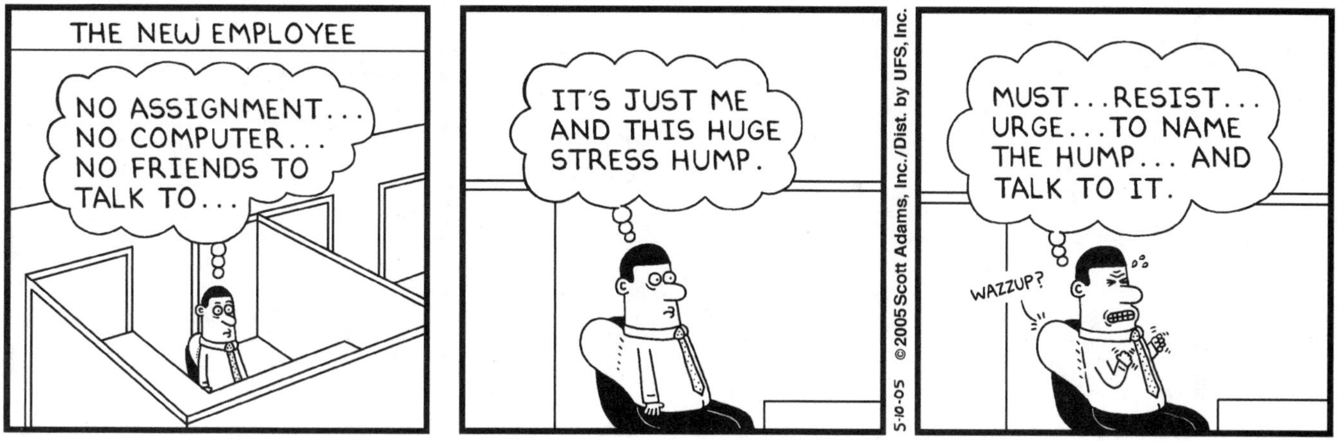
THE NEW EMPLOYEE
NO ASSIGNMENT... NO COMPUTER... NO FRIENDS TO TALK TO...
IT'S JUST ME AND THIS HUGE STRESS HUMP.
5-10-05 © 2005 Scott Adams, Inc./Dist. by UFS, Inc.
MUST... RESIST... URGE... TO NAME THE HUMP... AND TALK TO IT.
WAZZUP?

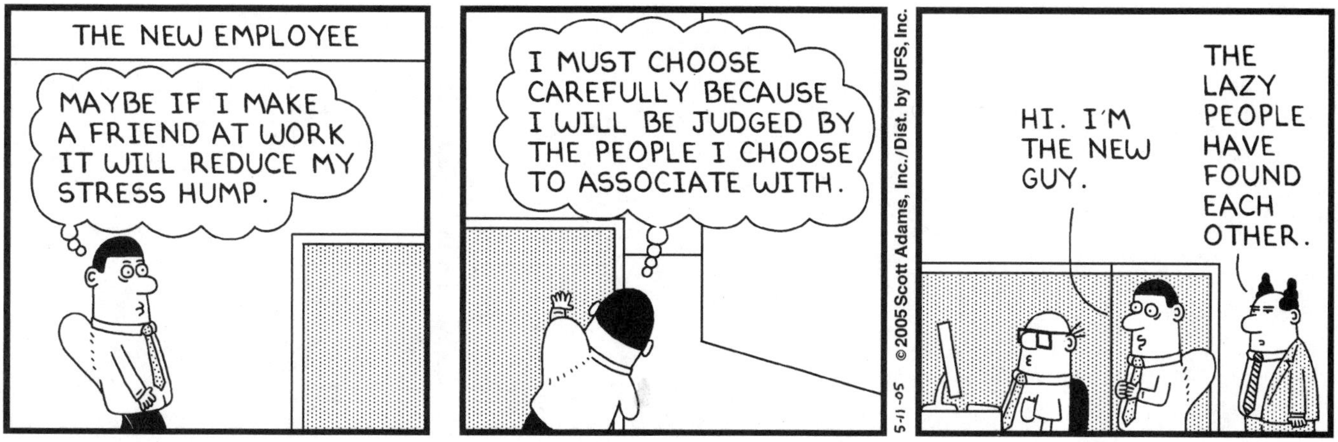
THE NEW EMPLOYEE
MAYBE IF I MAKE A FRIEND AT WORK IT WILL REDUCE MY STRESS HUMP.
I MUST CHOOSE CAREFULLY BECAUSE I WILL BE JUDGED BY THE PEOPLE I CHOOSE TO ASSOCIATE WITH.
5-11-05 © 2005 Scott Adams, Inc./Dist. by UFS, Inc.
HI. I'M THE NEW GUY.
THE LAZY PEOPLE HAVE FOUND EACH OTHER.

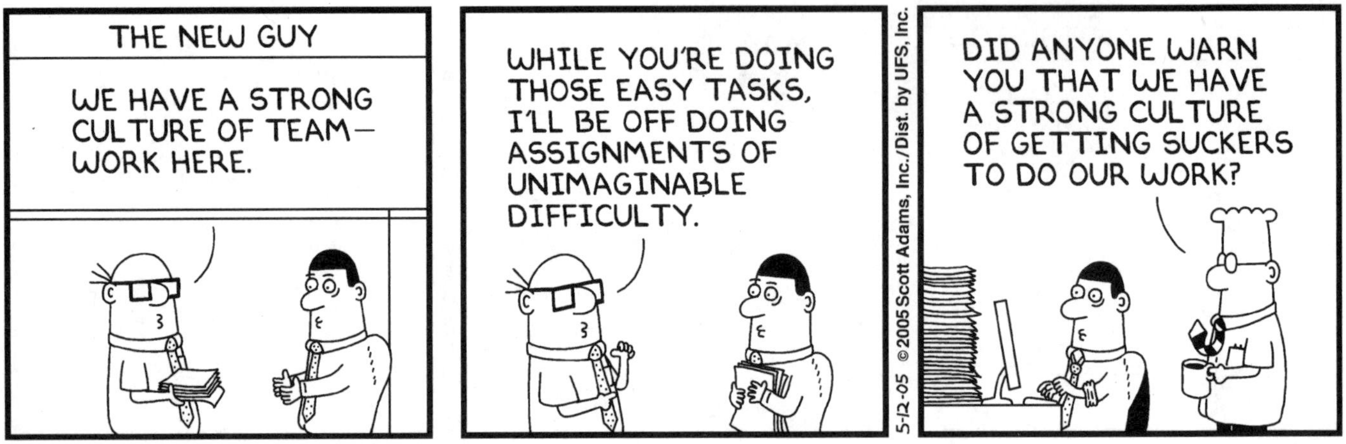
THE NEW GUY
WE HAVE A STRONG CULTURE OF TEAM—WORK HERE.
WHILE YOU'RE DOING THOSE EASY TASKS, I'LL BE OFF DOING ASSIGNMENTS OF UNIMAGINABLE DIFFICULTY.
5-12-05 © 2005 Scott Adams, Inc./Dist. by UFS, Inc.
DID ANYONE WARN YOU THAT WE HAVE A STRONG CULTURE OF GETTING SUCKERS TO DO OUR WORK?

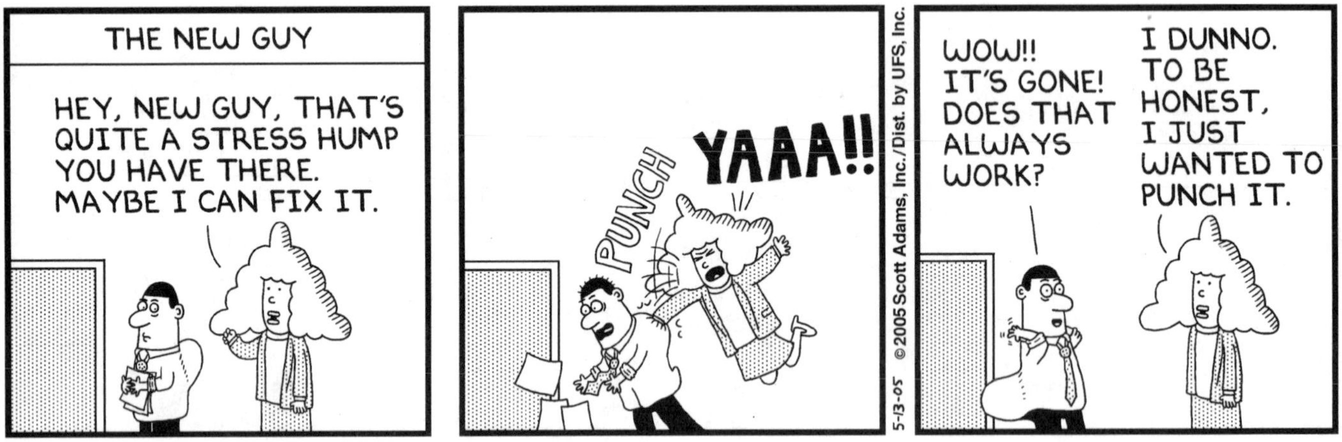
THE NEW GUY
HEY, NEW GUY, THAT'S QUITE A STRESS HUMP YOU HAVE THERE. MAYBE I CAN FIX IT.
PUNCH
YAAA!!
5-13-05 © 2005 Scott Adams, Inc./Dist. by UFS, Inc.
WOW!! IT'S GONE! DOES THAT ALWAYS WORK?
I DUNNO. TO BE HONEST, I JUST WANTED TO PUNCH IT.

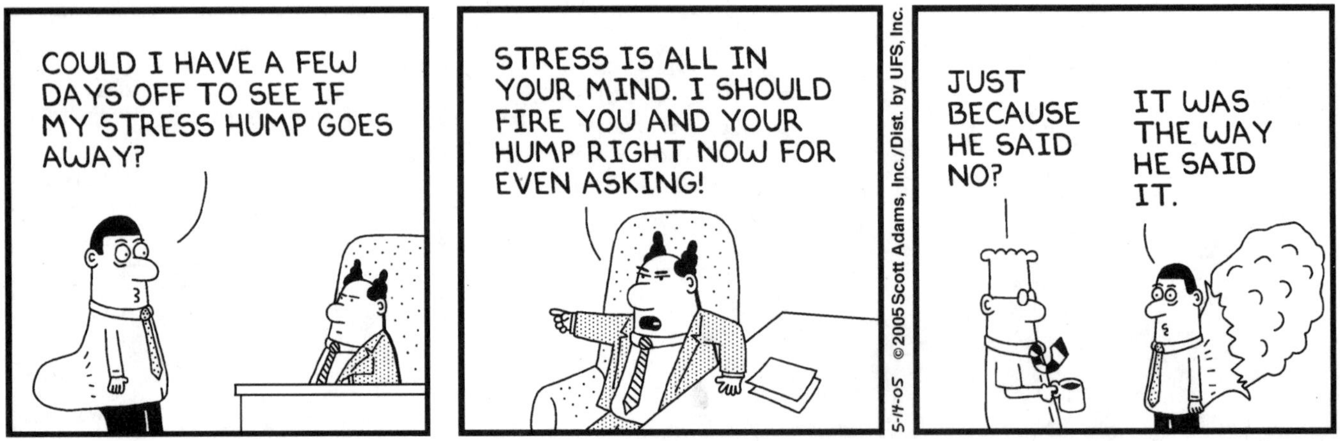
COULD I HAVE A FEW DAYS OFF TO SEE IF MY STRESS HUMP GOES AWAY?
STRESS IS ALL IN YOUR MIND. I SHOULD FIRE YOU AND YOUR HUMP RIGHT NOW FOR EVEN ASKING!
5-14-05 © 2005 Scott Adams, Inc./Dist. by UFS, Inc.
JUST BECAUSE HE SAID NO?
IT WAS THE WAY HE SAID IT.

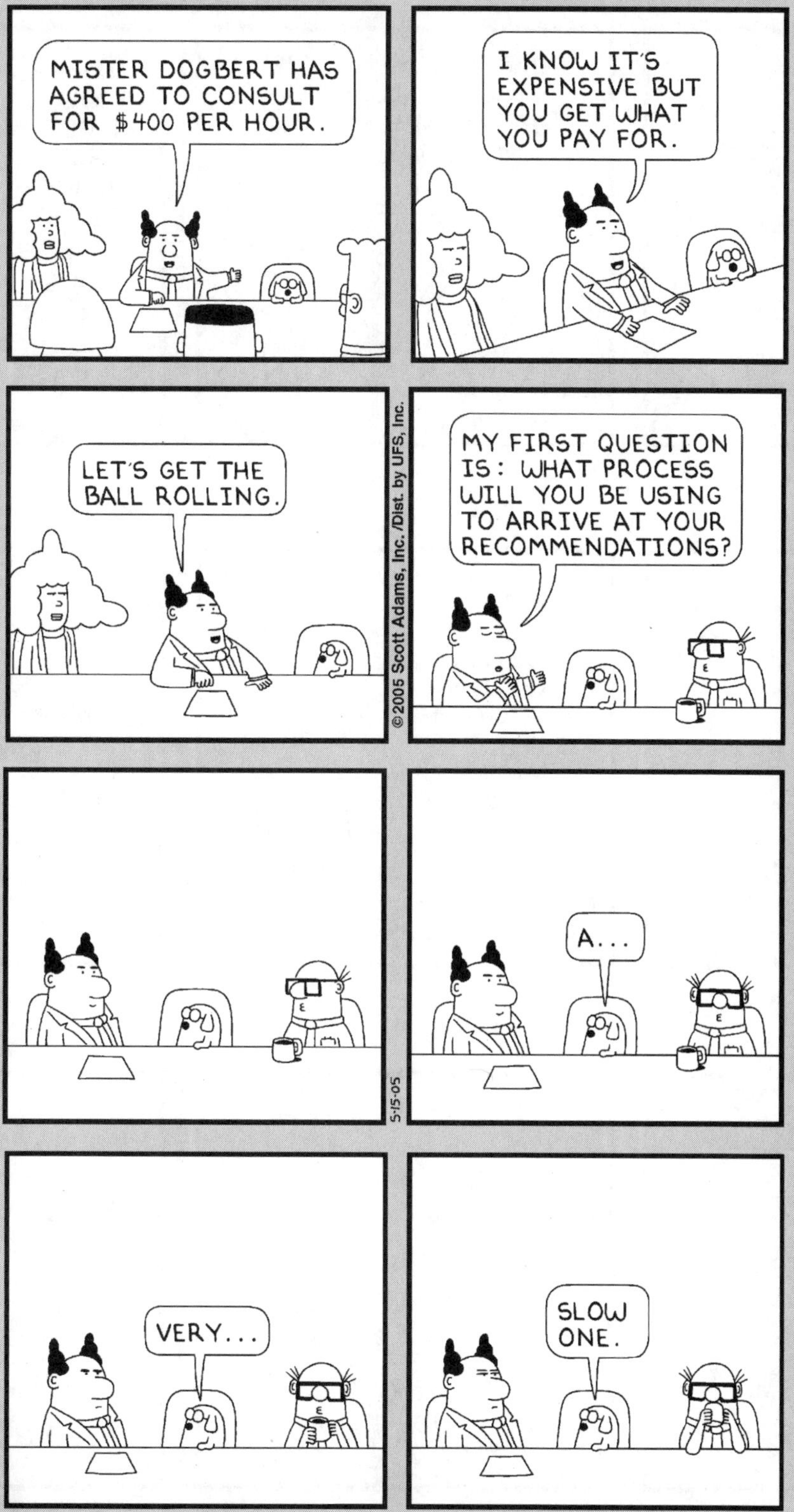
MISTER DOGBERT HAS AGREED TO CONSULT FOR $400 PER HOUR.
I KNOW IT'S EXPENSIVE BUT YOU GET WHAT YOU PAY FOR.
LET'S GET THE BALL ROLLING.
MY FIRST QUESTION IS: WHAT PROCESS WILL YOU BE USING TO ARRIVE AT YOUR RECOMMENDATIONS?
A...
VERY...
SLOW ONE.
©2005 Scott Adams, Inc. /Dist. by UFS, Inc.
5-15-05

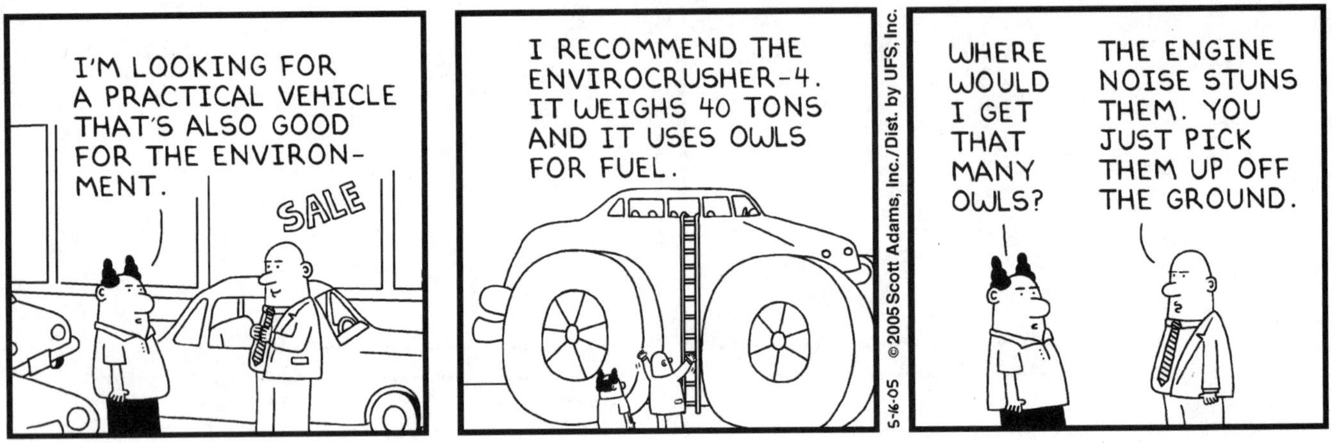
I'M LOOKING FOR A PRACTICAL VEHICLE THAT'S ALSO GOOD FOR THE ENVIRONMENT.
SALE
I RECOMMEND THE ENVIROCRUSHER-4. IT WEIGHS 40 TONS AND IT USES OWLS FOR FUEL.
5-6-05 ©2005 Scott Adams, Inc./Dist. by UFS, Inc.
WHERE WOULD I GET THAT MANY OWLS?
THE ENGINE NOISE STUNS THEM. YOU JUST PICK THEM UP OFF THE GROUND.

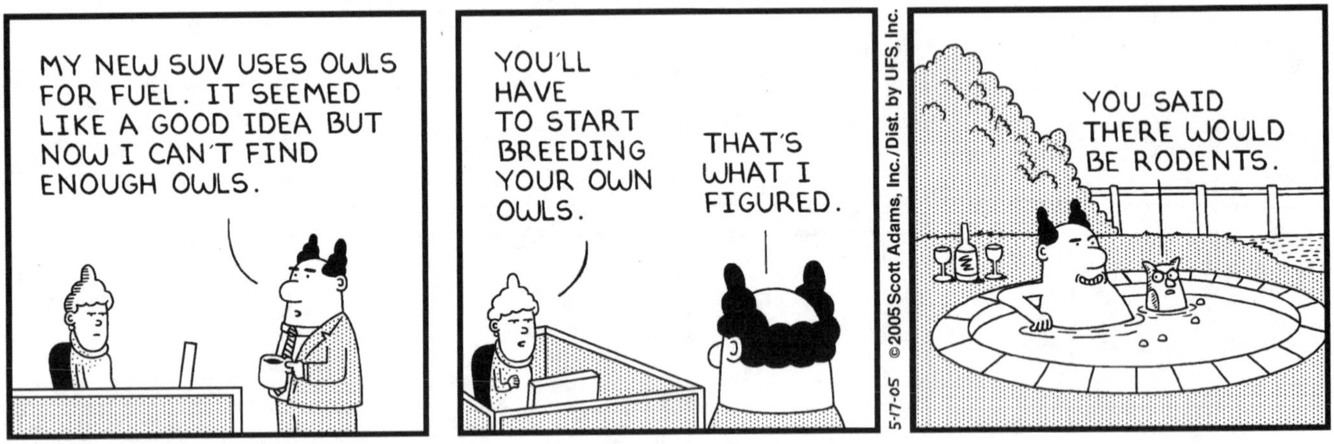
MY NEW SUV USES OWLS FOR FUEL. IT SEEMED LIKE A GOOD IDEA BUT NOW I CAN'T FIND ENOUGH OWLS.
YOU'LL HAVE TO START BREEDING YOUR OWN OWLS.
THAT'S WHAT I FIGURED.
5-17-05 ©2005 Scott Adams, Inc./Dist. by UFS, Inc.
YOU SAID THERE WOULD BE RODENTS.

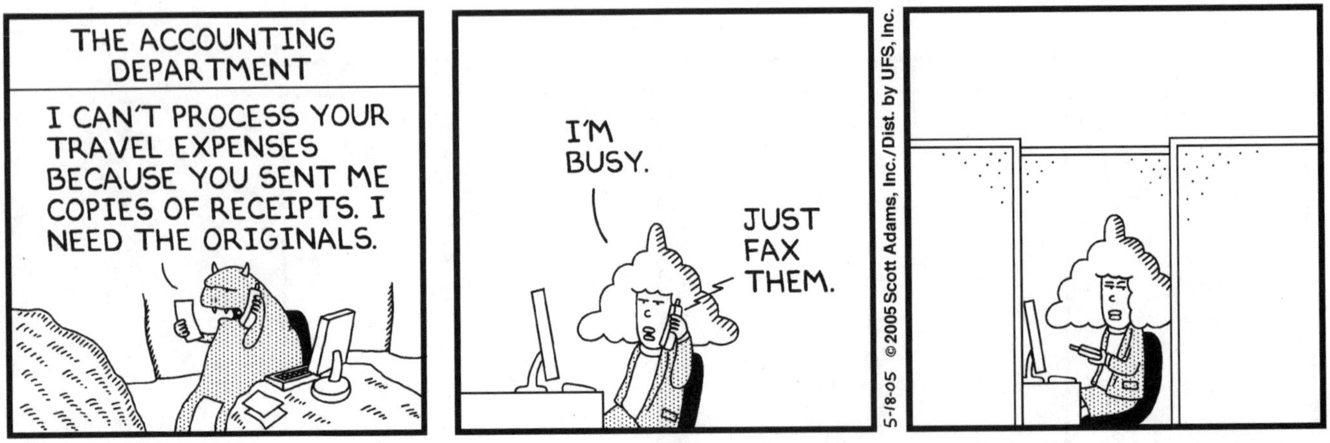
THE ACCOUNTING DEPARTMENT
I CAN'T PROCESS YOUR TRAVEL EXPENSES BECAUSE YOU SENT ME COPIES OF RECEIPTS. I NEED THE ORIGINALS.
I'M BUSY.
JUST FAX THEM.
5-18-05 ©2005 Scott Adams, Inc./Dist. by UFS, Inc.

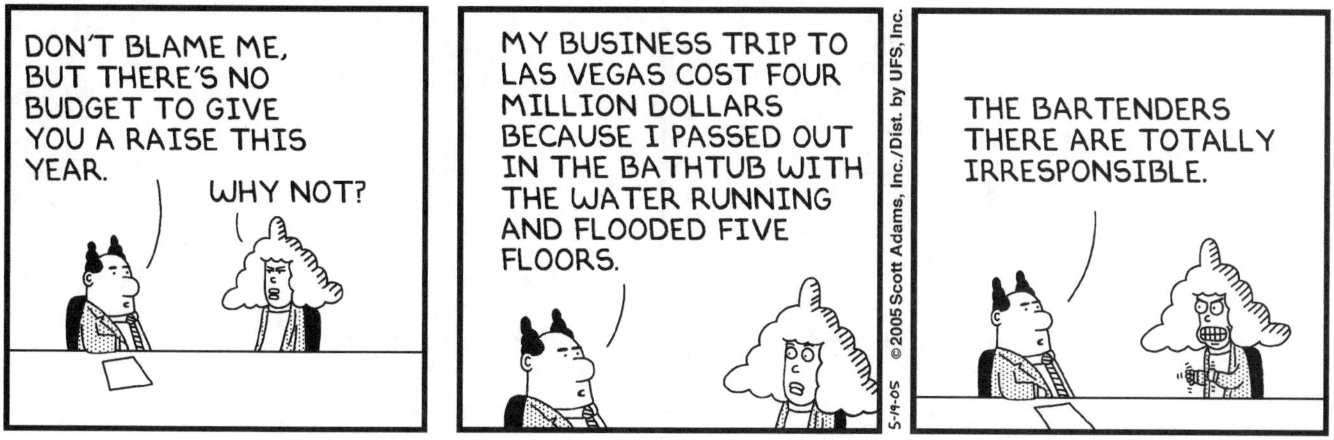
DON'T BLAME ME, BUT THERE'S NO BUDGET TO GIVE YOU A RAISE THIS YEAR.
WHY NOT?
MY BUSINESS TRIP TO LAS VEGAS COST FOUR MILLION DOLLARS BECAUSE I PASSED OUT IN THE BATHTUB WITH THE WATER RUNNING AND FLOODED FIVE FLOORS.
5-19-05 © 2005 Scott Adams, Inc./Dist. by UFS, Inc.
THE BARTENDERS THERE ARE TOTALLY IRRESPONSIBLE.

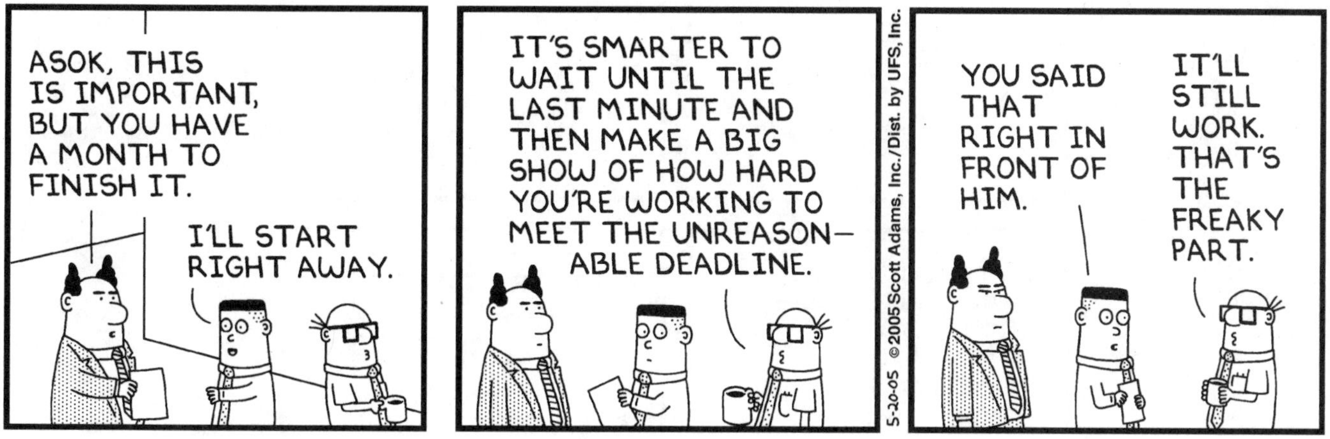
ASOK, THIS IS IMPORTANT, BUT YOU HAVE A MONTH TO FINISH IT.
I'LL START RIGHT AWAY.
IT'S SMARTER TO WAIT UNTIL THE LAST MINUTE AND THEN MAKE A BIG SHOW OF HOW HARD YOU'RE WORKING TO MEET THE UNREASON-ABLE DEADLINE.
5-20-05 © 2005 Scott Adams, Inc./Dist. by UFS, Inc.
YOU SAID THAT RIGHT IN FRONT OF HIM.
IT'LL STILL WORK. THAT'S THE FREAKY PART.

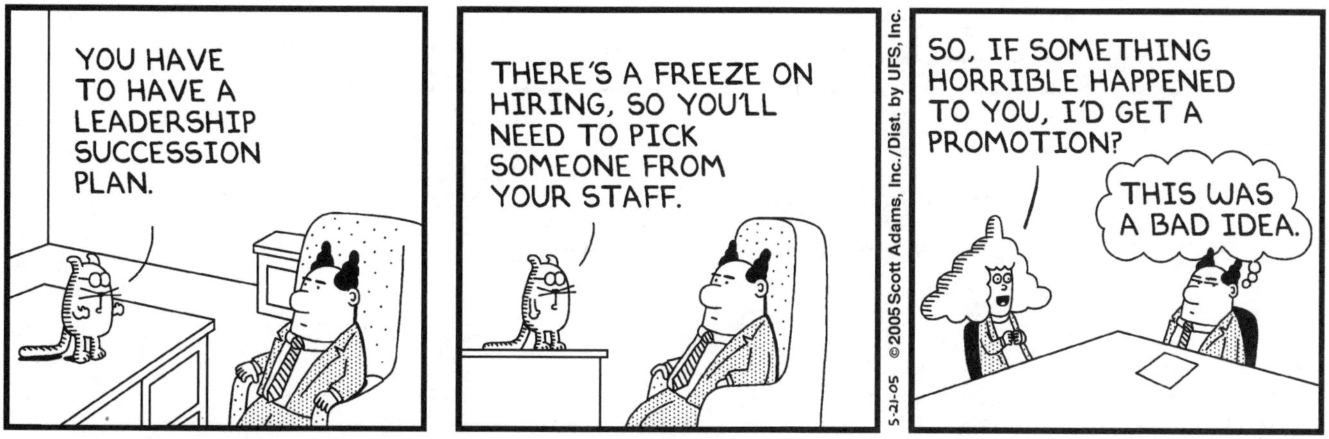
YOU HAVE TO HAVE A LEADERSHIP SUCCESSION PLAN.
THERE'S A FREEZE ON HIRING, SO YOU'LL NEED TO PICK SOMEONE FROM YOUR STAFF.
5-21-05 © 2005 Scott Adams, Inc./Dist. by UFS, Inc.
SO, IF SOMETHING HORRIBLE HAPPENED TO YOU, I'D GET A PROMOTION?
THIS WAS A BAD IDEA.

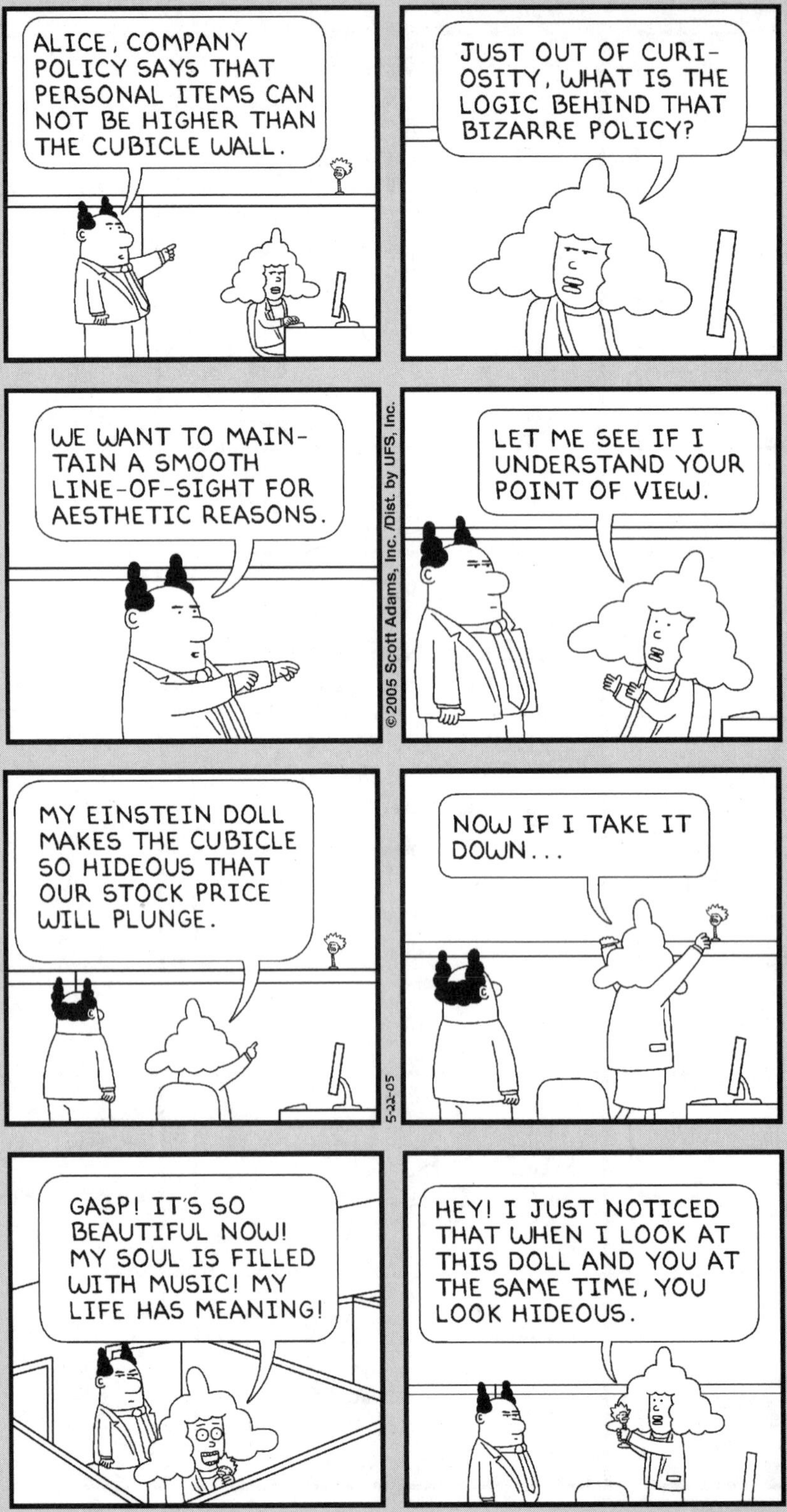
ALICE, COMPANY POLICY SAYS THAT PERSONAL ITEMS CAN NOT BE HIGHER THAN THE CUBICLE WALL.
JUST OUT OF CURI- OSITY, WHAT IS THE LOGIC BEHIND THAT BIZARRE POLICY?
WE WANT TO MAIN- TAIN A SMOOTH LINE-OF-SIGHT FOR AESTHETIC REASONS.
LET ME SEE IF I UNDERSTAND YOUR POINT OF VIEW.
MY EINSTEIN DOLL MAKES THE CUBICLE SO HIDEOUS THAT OUR STOCK PRICE WILL PLUNGE.
NOW IF I TAKE IT DOWN...
GASP! IT'S SO BEAUTIFUL NOW! MY SOUL IS FILLED WITH MUSIC! MY LIFE HAS MEANING!
HEY! I JUST NOTICED THAT WHEN I LOOK AT THIS DOLL AND YOU AT THE SAME TIME, YOU LOOK HIDEOUS.
©2005 Scott Adams, Inc./Dist. by UFS, Inc.
5-22-05

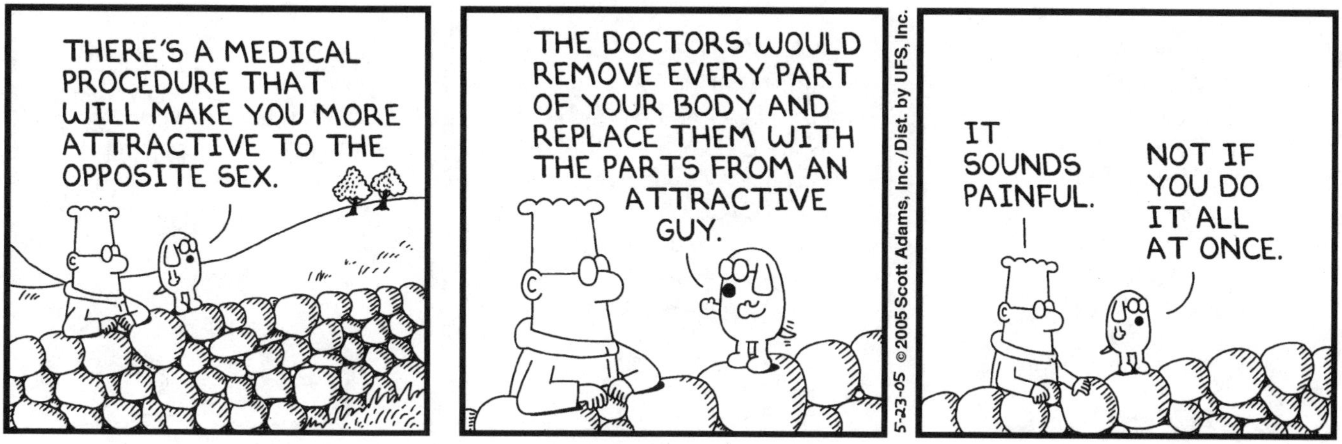
THERE'S A MEDICAL PROCEDURE THAT WILL MAKE YOU MORE ATTRACTIVE TO THE OPPOSITE SEX.
THE DOCTORS WOULD REMOVE EVERY PART OF YOUR BODY AND REPLACE THEM WITH THE PARTS FROM AN ATTRACTIVE GUY.
5-23-05 © 2005 Scott Adams, Inc./Dist. by UFS, Inc.
IT SOUNDS PAINFUL.
NOT IF YOU DO IT ALL AT ONCE.

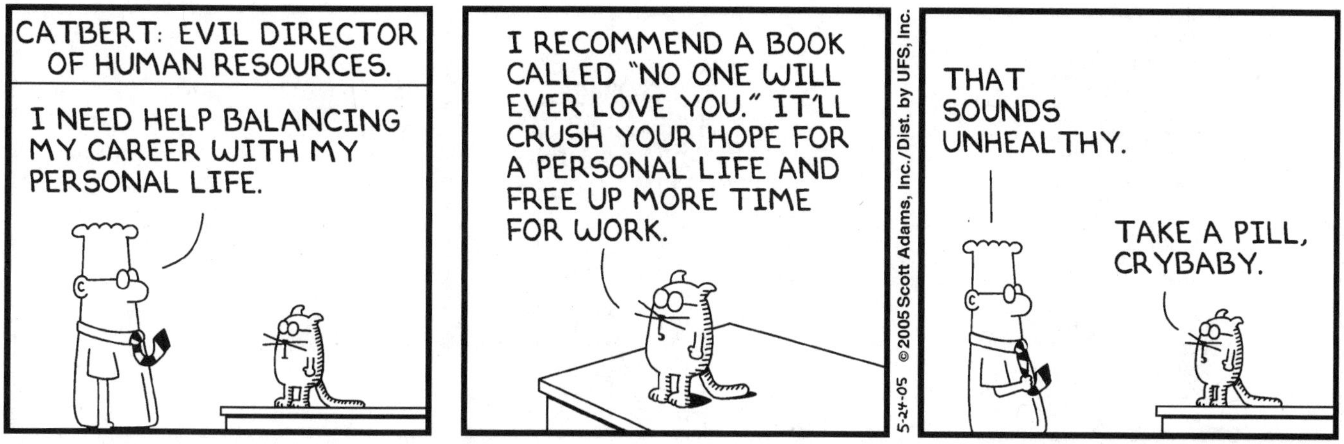
CATBERT: EVIL DIRECTOR OF HUMAN RESOURCES.
I NEED HELP BALANCING MY CAREER WITH MY PERSONAL LIFE.
I RECOMMEND A BOOK CALLED "NO ONE WILL EVER LOVE YOU." IT'LL CRUSH YOUR HOPE FOR A PERSONAL LIFE AND FREE UP MORE TIME FOR WORK.
5-24-05 © 2005 Scott Adams, Inc./Dist. by UFS, Inc.
THAT SOUNDS UNHEALTHY.
TAKE A PILL, CRYBABY.

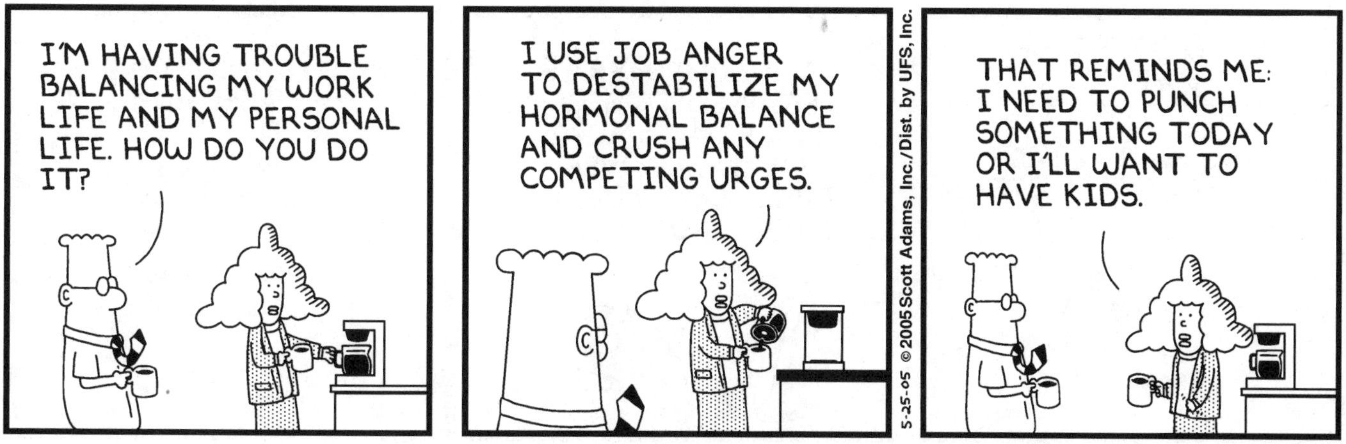
I'M HAVING TROUBLE BALANCING MY WORK LIFE AND MY PERSONAL LIFE. HOW DO YOU DO IT?
I USE JOB ANGER TO DESTABILIZE MY HORMONAL BALANCE AND CRUSH ANY COMPETING URGES.
5-25-05 © 2005 Scott Adams, Inc./Dist. by UFS, Inc.
THAT REMINDS ME: I NEED TO PUNCH SOMETHING TODAY OR I'LL WANT TO HAVE KIDS.

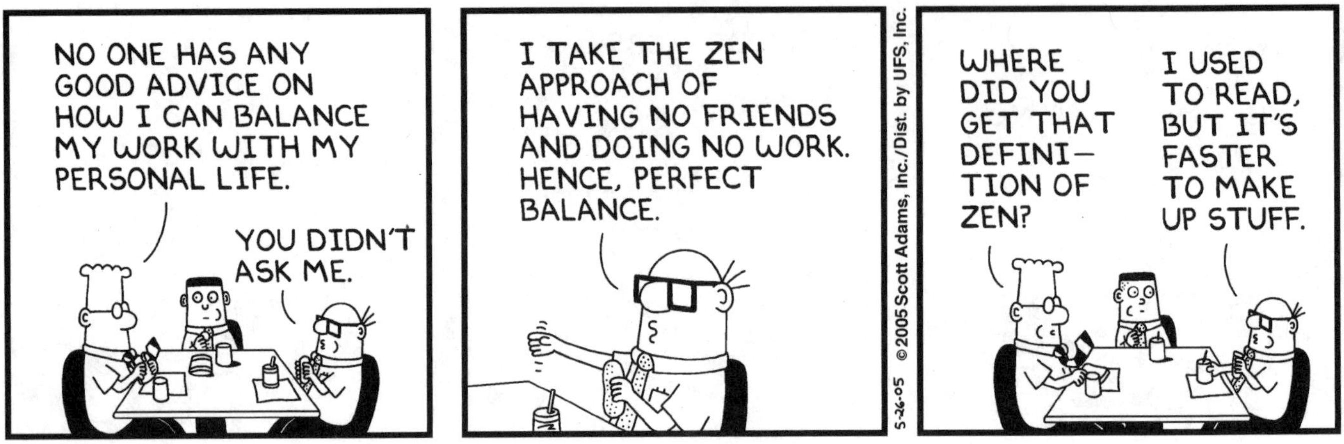
NO ONE HAS ANY GOOD ADVICE ON HOW I CAN BALANCE MY WORK WITH MY PERSONAL LIFE.
YOU DIDN'T ASK ME.
I TAKE THE ZEN APPROACH OF HAVING NO FRIENDS AND DOING NO WORK. HENCE, PERFECT BALANCE.
WHERE DID YOU GET THAT DEFINI- TION OF ZEN?
I USED TO READ, BUT IT'S FASTER TO MAKE UP STUFF.
5-26-05 © 2005 Scott Adams, Inc./Dist. by UFS, Inc.

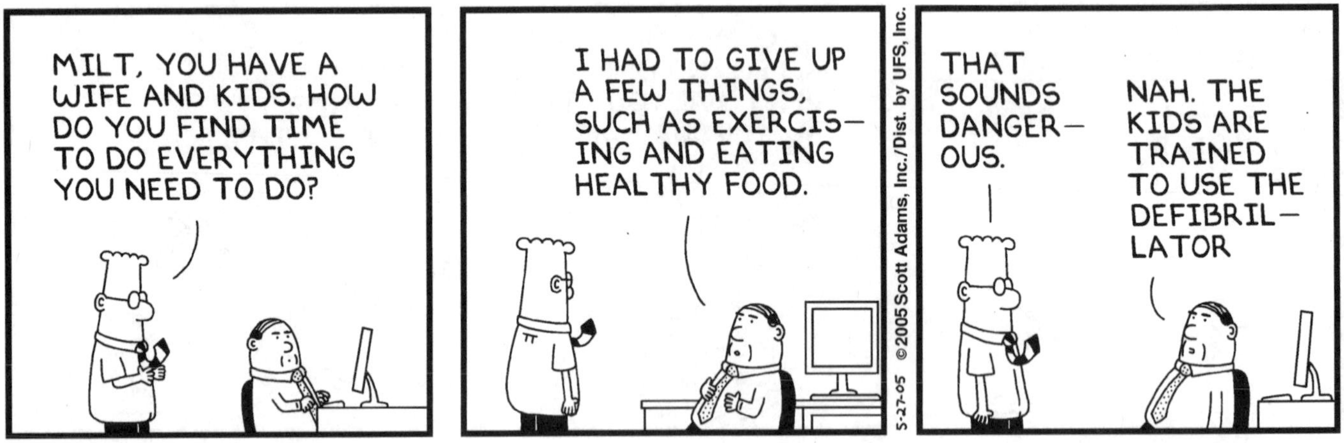
MILT, YOU HAVE A WIFE AND KIDS. HOW DO YOU FIND TIME TO DO EVERYTHING YOU NEED TO DO?
I HAD TO GIVE UP A FEW THINGS, SUCH AS EXERCIS- ING AND EATING HEALTHY FOOD.
THAT SOUNDS DANGER- OUS.
NAH. THE KIDS ARE TRAINED TO USE THE DEFIBRIL- LATOR
5-27-05 © 2005 Scott Adams, Inc./Dist. by UFS, Inc.

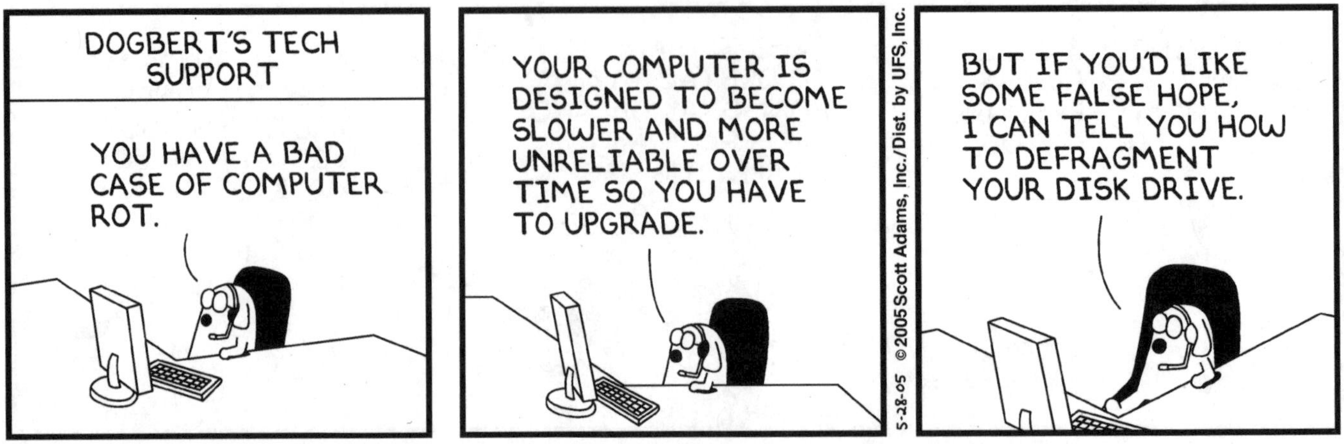
DOGBERT'S TECH SUPPORT
YOU HAVE A BAD CASE OF COMPUTER ROT.
YOUR COMPUTER IS DESIGNED TO BECOME SLOWER AND MORE UNRELIABLE OVER TIME SO YOU HAVE TO UPGRADE.
BUT IF YOU'D LIKE SOME FALSE HOPE, I CAN TELL YOU HOW TO DEFRAGMENT YOUR DISK DRIVE.
5-28-05 © 2005 Scott Adams, Inc./Dist. by UFS, Inc.

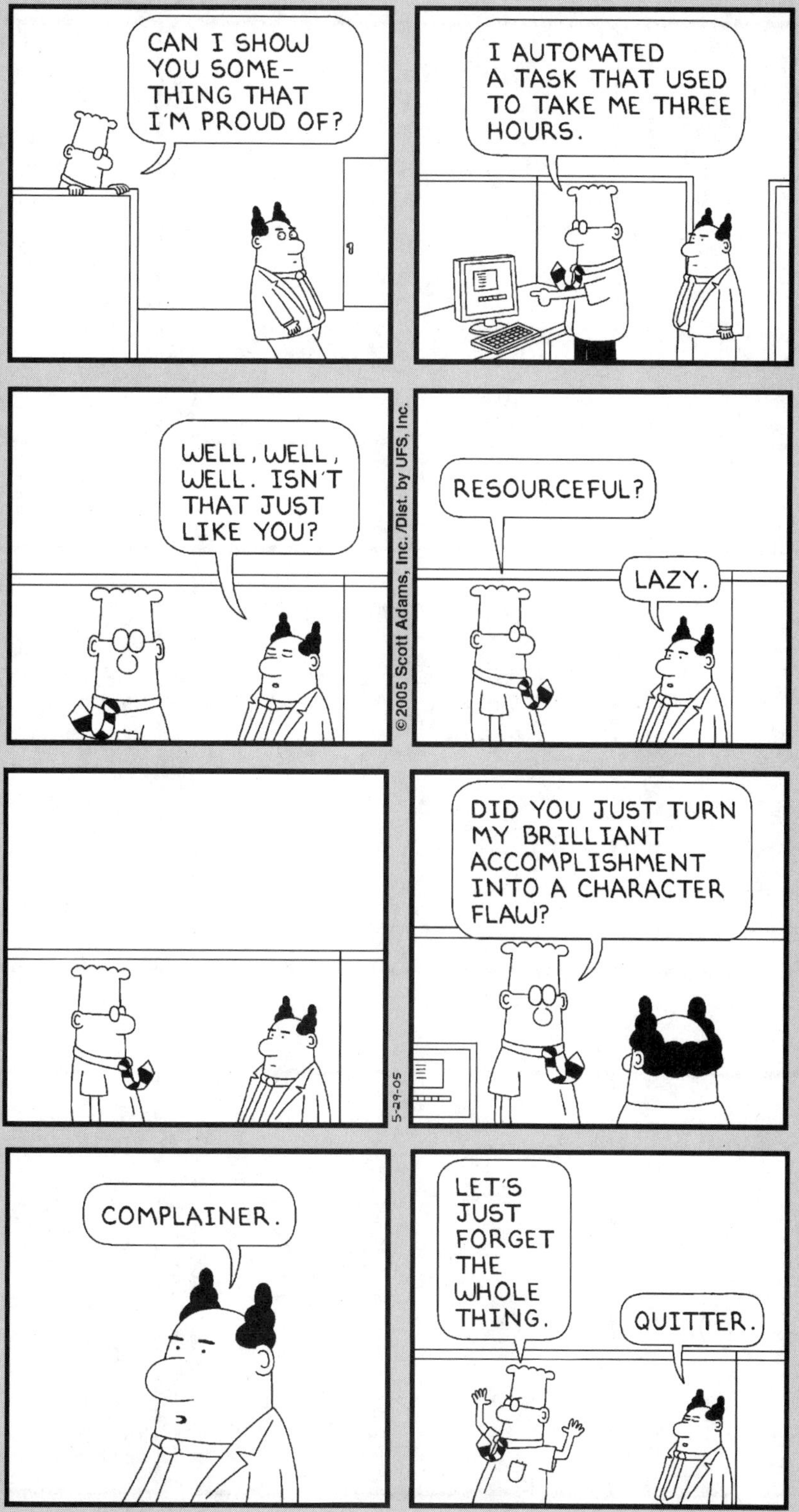
CAN I SHOW YOU SOME-THING THAT I'M PROUD OF?
I AUTOMATED A TASK THAT USED TO TAKE ME THREE HOURS.
WELL, WELL, WELL. ISN'T THAT JUST LIKE YOU?
RESOURCEFUL?
LAZY.
DID YOU JUST TURN MY BRILLIANT ACCOMPLISHMENT INTO A CHARACTER FLAW?
COMPLAINER.
LET'S JUST FORGET THE WHOLE THING.
QUITTER.
©2005 Scott Adams, Inc./Dist. by UFS, Inc.
5-29-05

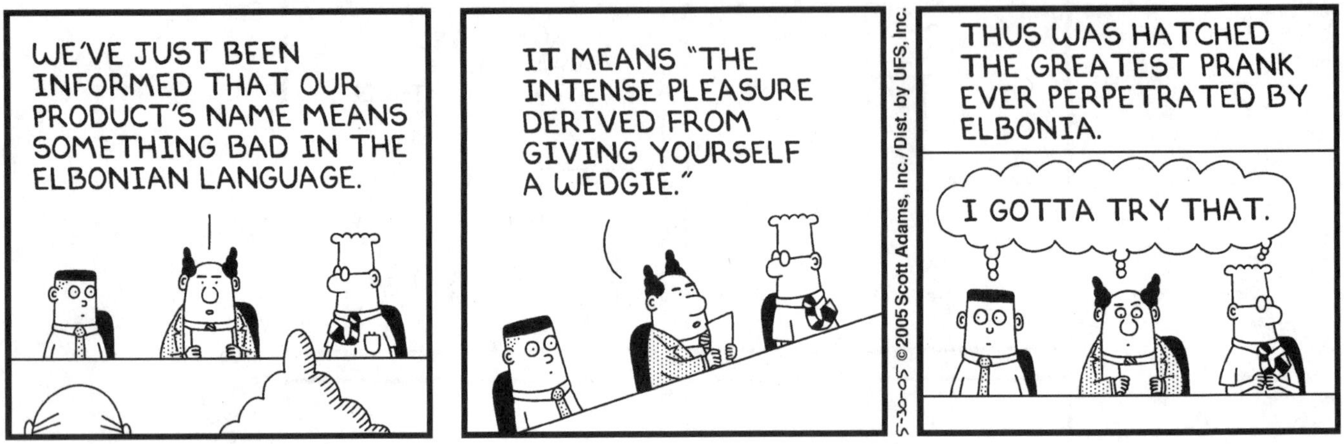
WE'VE JUST BEEN INFORMED THAT OUR PRODUCT'S NAME MEANS SOMETHING BAD IN THE ELBONIAN LANGUAGE.
IT MEANS "THE INTENSE PLEASURE DERIVED FROM GIVING YOURSELF A WEDGIE."
5-30-05 ©2005 Scott Adams, Inc./Dist. by UFS, Inc.
THUS WAS HATCHED THE GREATEST PRANK EVER PERPETRATED BY ELBONIA.
I GOTTA TRY THAT.

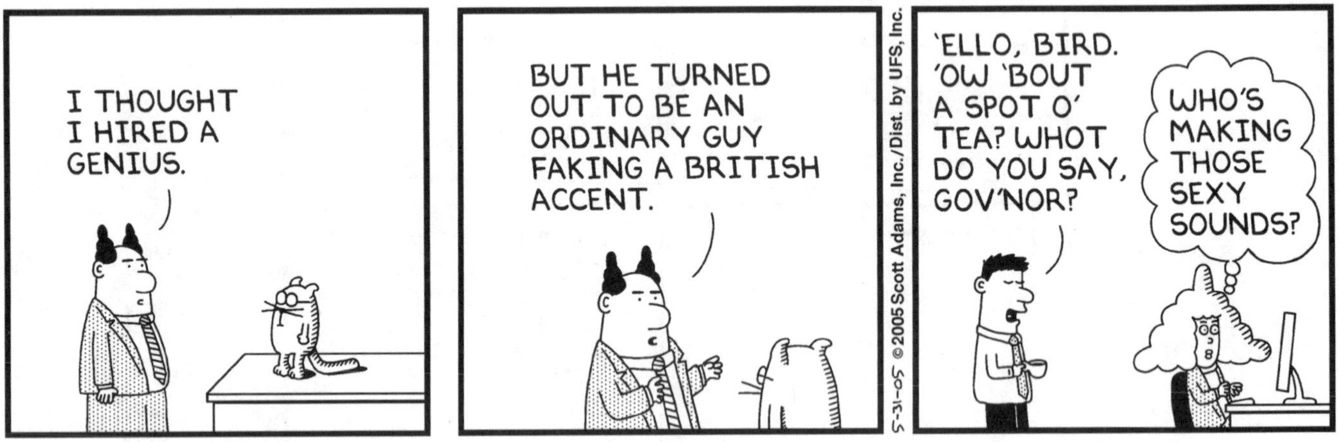
I THOUGHT I HIRED A GENIUS.
BUT HE TURNED OUT TO BE AN ORDINARY GUY FAKING A BRITISH ACCENT.
5-31-05 ©2005 Scott Adams, Inc./Dist. by UFS, Inc.
'ELLO, BIRD. 'OW 'BOUT A SPOT O' TEA? WHOT DO YOU SAY, GOV'NOR?
WHO'S MAKING THOSE SEXY SOUNDS?

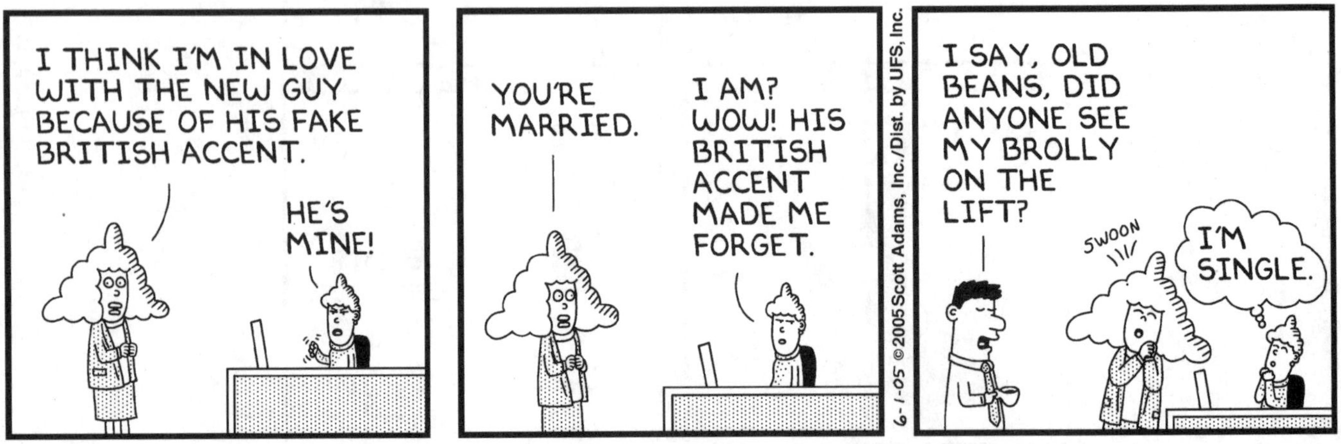
I THINK I'M IN LOVE WITH THE NEW GUY BECAUSE OF HIS FAKE BRITISH ACCENT.
HE'S MINE!
YOU'RE MARRIED.
I AM? WOW! HIS BRITISH ACCENT MADE ME FORGET.
6-1-05 ©2005 Scott Adams, Inc./Dist. by UFS, Inc.
I SAY, OLD BEANS, DID ANYONE SEE MY BROLLY ON THE LIFT?
SWOON
I'M SINGLE.

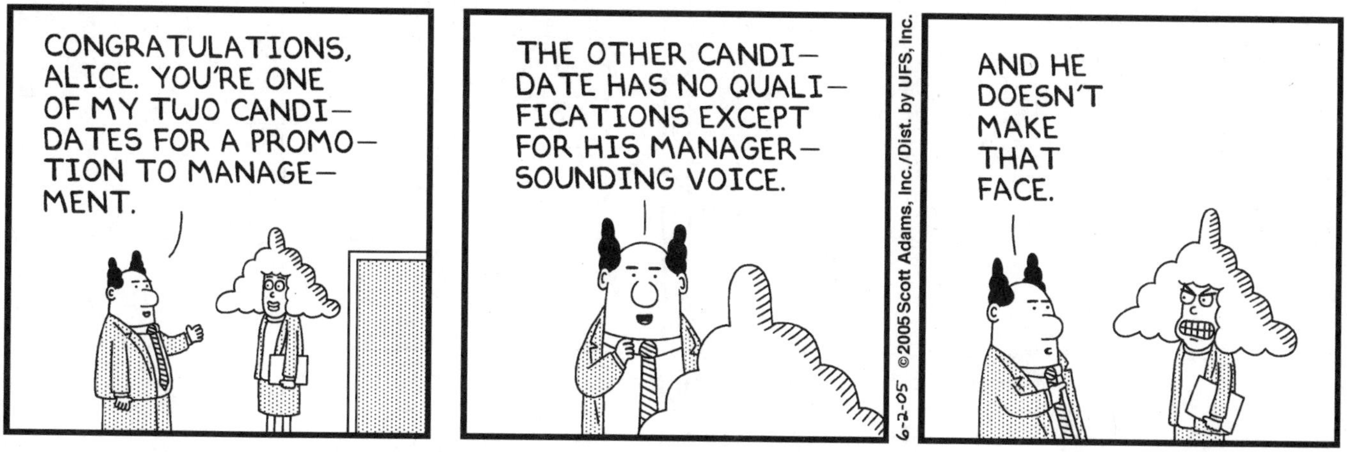
CONGRATULATIONS, ALICE. YOU'RE ONE OF MY TWO CANDI– DATES FOR A PROMO– TION TO MANAGE– MENT.
THE OTHER CANDI– DATE HAS NO QUALI– FICATIONS EXCEPT FOR HIS MANAGER– SOUNDING VOICE.
6-2-05 ©2005 Scott Adams, Inc./Dist. by UFS, Inc.
AND HE DOESN'T MAKE THAT FACE.

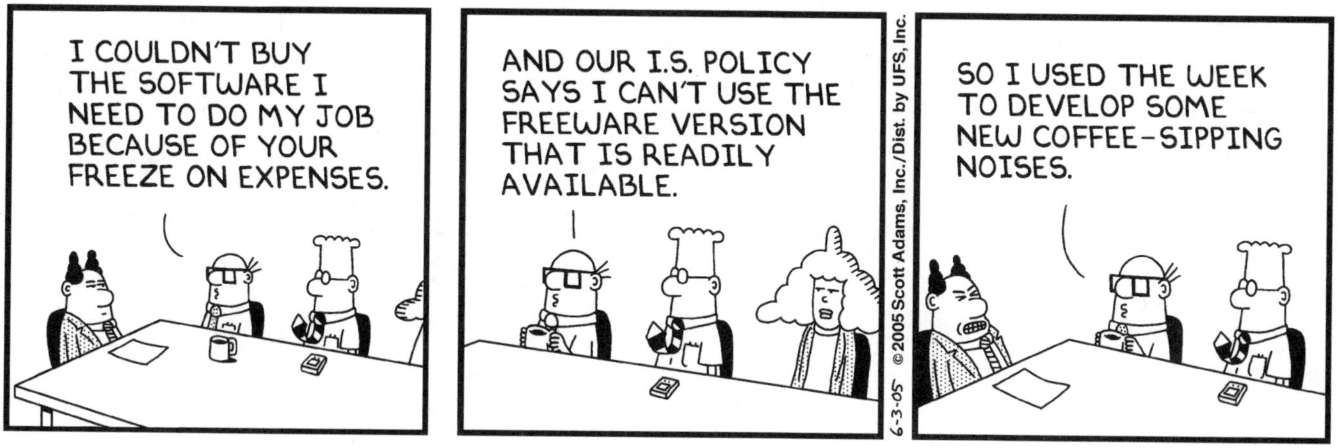
I COULDN'T BUY THE SOFTWARE I NEED TO DO MY JOB BECAUSE OF YOUR FREEZE ON EXPENSES.
AND OUR I.S. POLICY SAYS I CAN'T USE THE FREEWARE VERSION THAT IS READILY AVAILABLE.
6-3-05 ©2005 Scott Adams, Inc./Dist. by UFS, Inc.
SO I USED THE WEEK TO DEVELOP SOME NEW COFFEE–SIPPING NOISES.

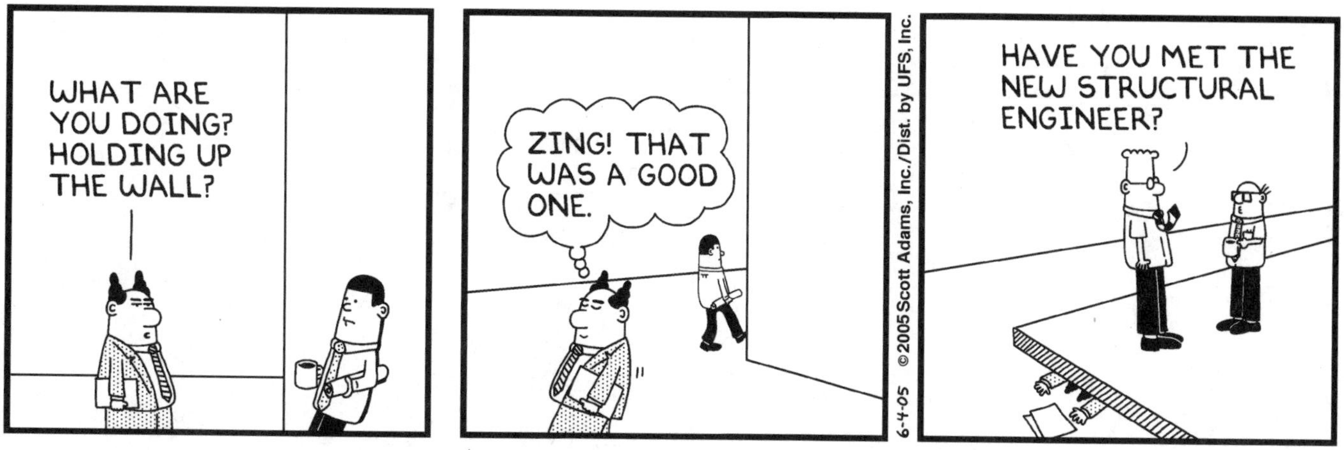
WHAT ARE YOU DOING? HOLDING UP THE WALL?
ZING! THAT WAS A GOOD ONE.
6-4-05 ©2005 Scott Adams, Inc./Dist. by UFS, Inc.
HAVE YOU MET THE NEW STRUCTURAL ENGINEER?

WALLY, THE STATUS REPORT THAT YOU E-MAILED ME IS BLANK.
THAT'S BECAUSE EAGLES CAN'T TYPE.
WHAT?
THE MOTIVATIONAL POSTER IN THE BREAK ROOM SAYS I SHOULD BE LIKE AN EAGLE.
THE POINT OF THAT POSTER IS THAT YOUR SPIRIT SHOULD SOAR LIKE AN EAGLE WHILE YOU CONTINUE TO DO MUNDANE WORK.
©2005 Scott Adams, Inc./Dist. by UFS, Inc.
WOULDN'T I DIE IF MY SPIRIT LEFT MY BODY TO GO SOAR?
YOU'RE CONFUSING YOUR SPIRIT WITH YOUR SOUL.
6-5-05
WHILE YOUR SPIRIT IS SOARING, YOUR SOUL SHOULD REMAIN TRAPPED IN YOUR BODY, SLOWLY DECAYING WHILE YOU CREATE YOUR STATUS REPORT.
WOULD IT CHANGE ANYTHING IF I GOT A POSTER THAT SAYS, "YOU WANT IT WHEN?!!"

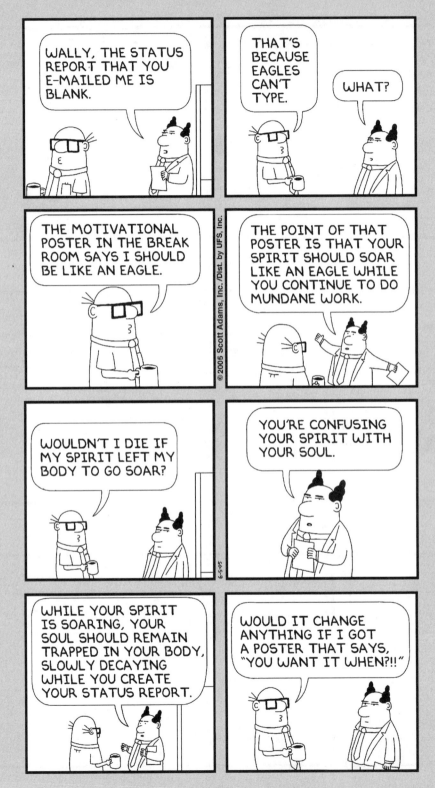

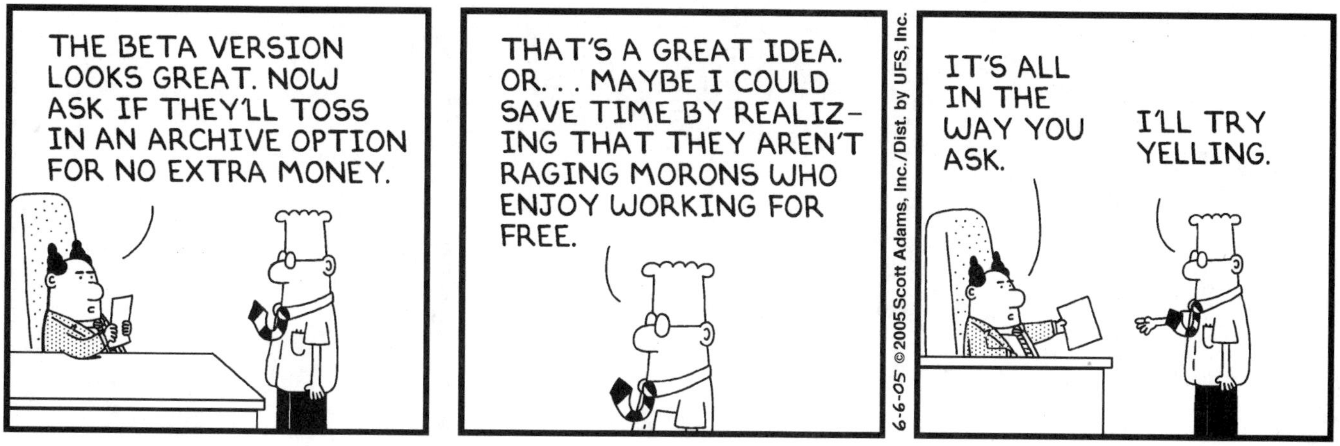
THE BETA VERSION LOOKS GREAT. NOW ASK IF THEY'LL TOSS IN AN ARCHIVE OPTION FOR NO EXTRA MONEY.
THAT'S A GREAT IDEA. OR. . . MAYBE I COULD SAVE TIME BY REALIZ-ING THAT THEY AREN'T RAGING MORONS WHO ENJOY WORKING FOR FREE.
6-6-05 © 2005 Scott Adams, Inc./Dist. by UFS, Inc.
IT'S ALL IN THE WAY YOU ASK.
I'LL TRY YELLING.

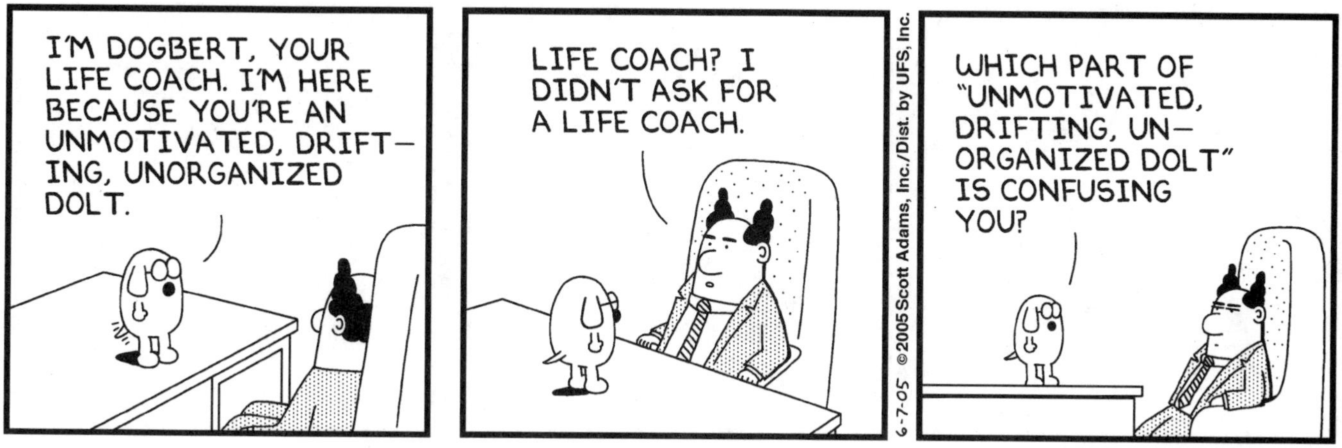
I'M DOGBERT, YOUR LIFE COACH. I'M HERE BECAUSE YOU'RE AN UNMOTIVATED, DRIFT-ING, UNORGANIZED DOLT.
LIFE COACH? I DIDN'T ASK FOR A LIFE COACH.
6-7-05 © 2005 Scott Adams, Inc./Dist. by UFS, Inc.
WHICH PART OF "UNMOTIVATED, DRIFTING, UN-ORGANIZED DOLT" IS CONFUSING YOU?

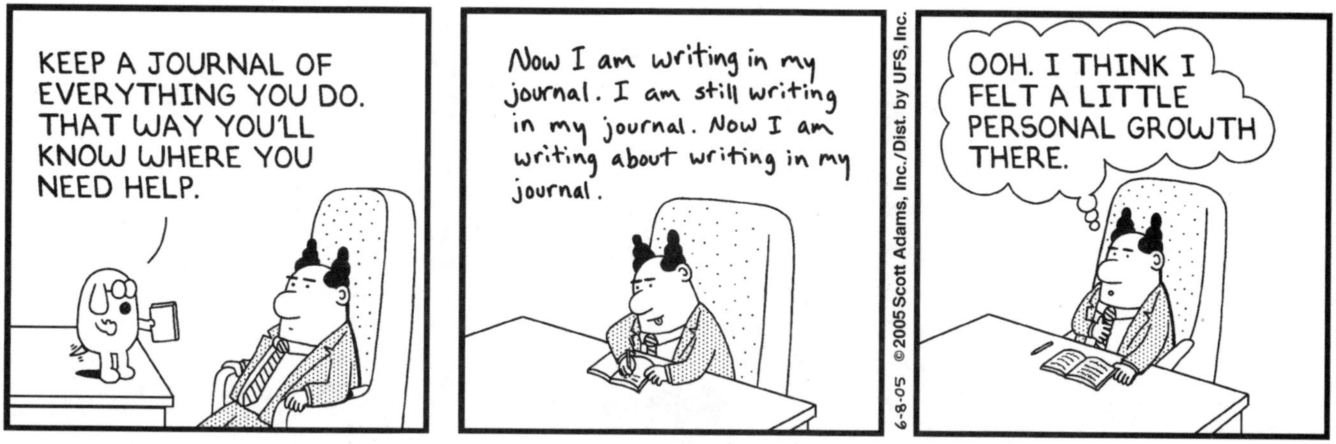
KEEP A JOURNAL OF EVERYTHING YOU DO. THAT WAY YOU'LL KNOW WHERE YOU NEED HELP.
Now I am writing in my journal. I am still writing in my journal. Now I am writing about writing in my journal.
6-8-05 © 2005 Scott Adams, Inc./Dist. by UFS, Inc.
OOH. I THINK I FELT A LITTLE PERSONAL GROWTH THERE.

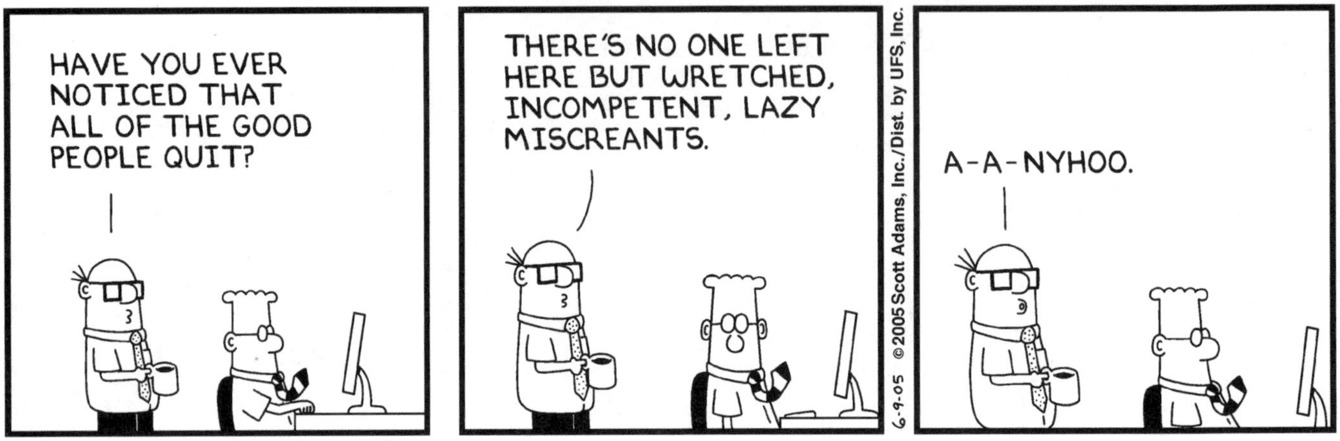
HAVE YOU EVER NOTICED THAT ALL OF THE GOOD PEOPLE QUIT?
THERE'S NO ONE LEFT HERE BUT WRETCHED, INCOMPETENT, LAZY MISCREANTS.
6-9-05 ©2005 Scott Adams, Inc./Dist. by UFS, Inc.
A-A-NYHOO.

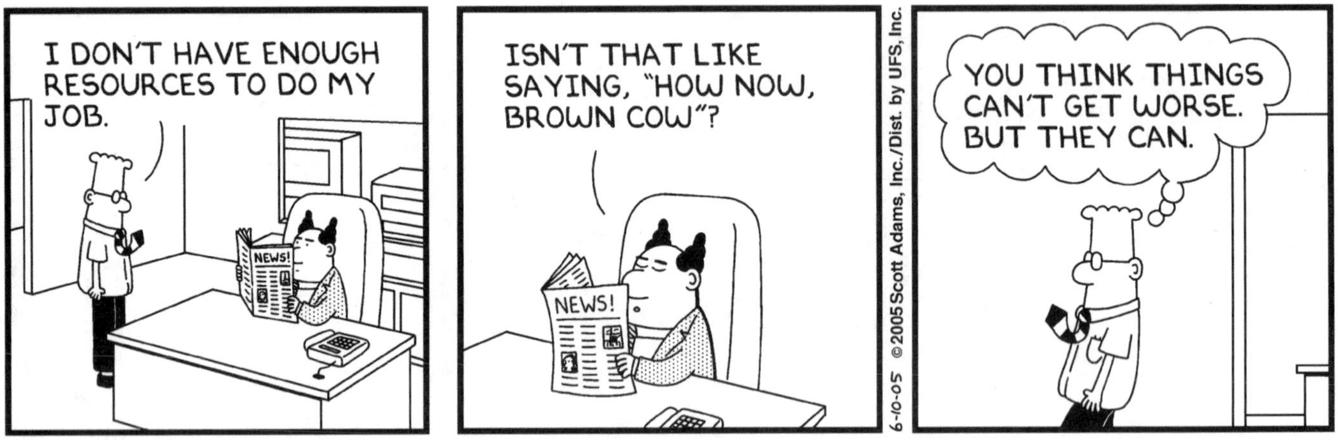
I DON'T HAVE ENOUGH RESOURCES TO DO MY JOB.
NEWS!
ISN'T THAT LIKE SAYING, "HOW NOW, BROWN COW"?
NEWS!
6-10-05 ©2005 Scott Adams, Inc./Dist. by UFS, Inc.
YOU THINK THINGS CAN'T GET WORSE. BUT THEY CAN.

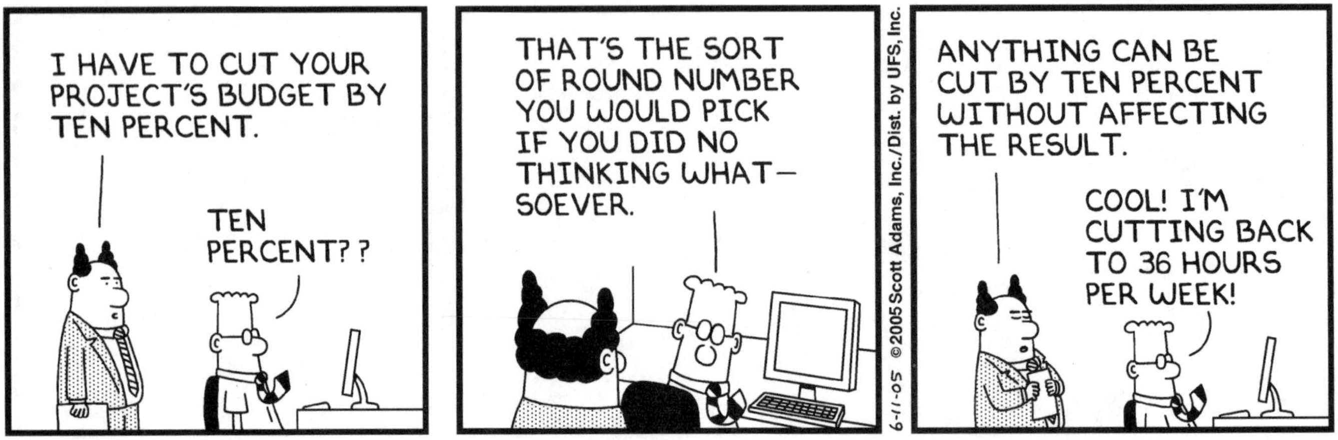
I HAVE TO CUT YOUR PROJECT'S BUDGET BY TEN PERCENT.
TEN PERCENT??
THAT'S THE SORT OF ROUND NUMBER YOU WOULD PICK IF YOU DID NO THINKING WHAT-SOEVER.
6-11-05 ©2005 Scott Adams, Inc./Dist. by UFS, Inc.
ANYTHING CAN BE CUT BY TEN PERCENT WITHOUT AFFECTING THE RESULT.
COOL! I'M CUTTING BACK TO 36 HOURS PER WEEK!

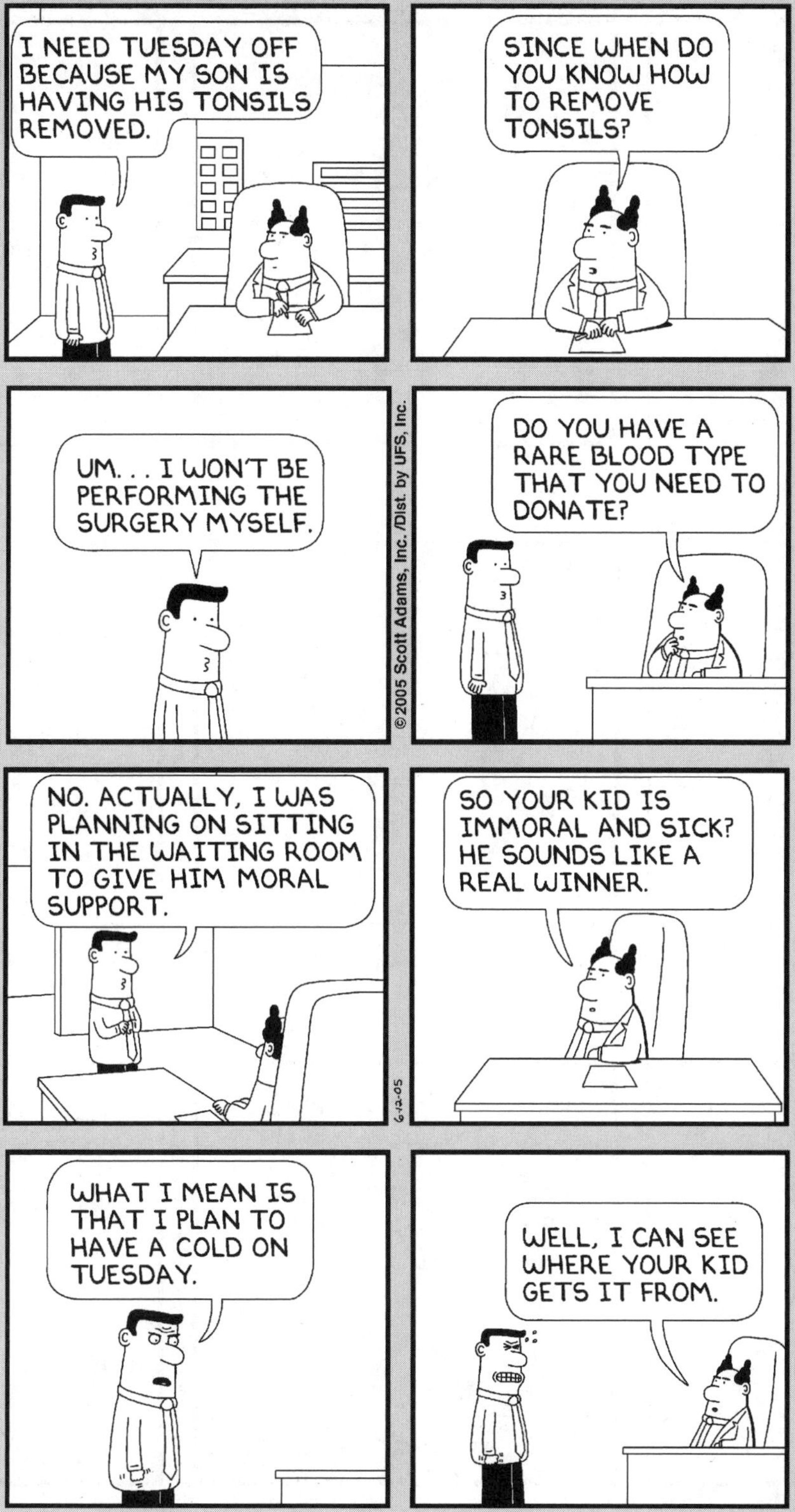
I NEED TUESDAY OFF BECAUSE MY SON IS HAVING HIS TONSILS REMOVED.
SINCE WHEN DO YOU KNOW HOW TO REMOVE TONSILS?
UM. . . I WON'T BE PERFORMING THE SURGERY MYSELF.
DO YOU HAVE A RARE BLOOD TYPE THAT YOU NEED TO DONATE?
NO. ACTUALLY, I WAS PLANNING ON SITTING IN THE WAITING ROOM TO GIVE HIM MORAL SUPPORT.
SO YOUR KID IS IMMORAL AND SICK? HE SOUNDS LIKE A REAL WINNER.
WHAT I MEAN IS THAT I PLAN TO HAVE A COLD ON TUESDAY.
WELL, I CAN SEE WHERE YOUR KID GETS IT FROM.
©2005 Scott Adams, Inc./Dist. by UFS, Inc.
6-12-05

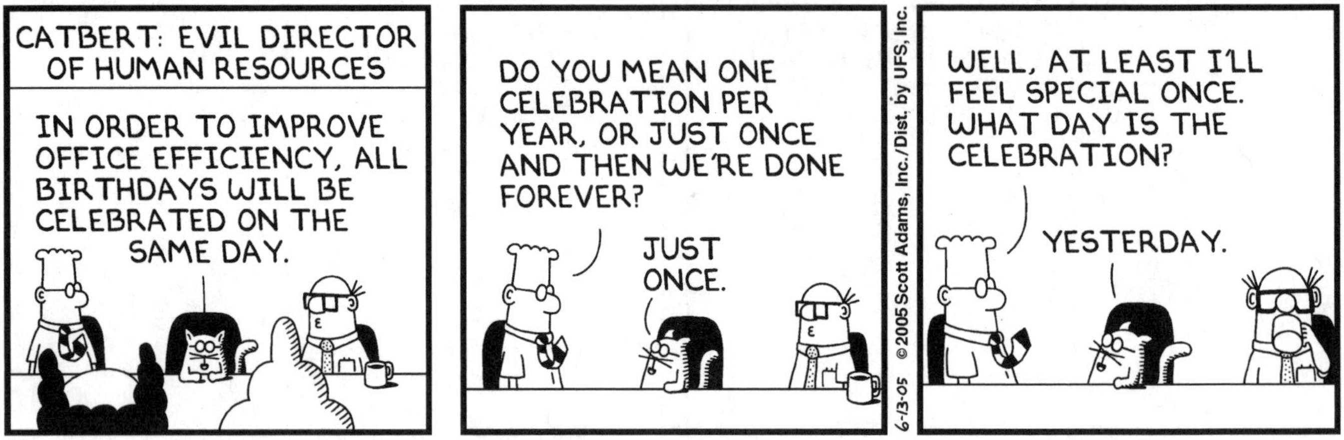
CATBERT: EVIL DIRECTOR OF HUMAN RESOURCES
IN ORDER TO IMPROVE OFFICE EFFICIENCY, ALL BIRTHDAYS WILL BE CELEBRATED ON THE SAME DAY.
DO YOU MEAN ONE CELEBRATION PER YEAR, OR JUST ONCE AND THEN WE'RE DONE FOREVER?
JUST ONCE.
6-13-05 © 2005 Scott Adams, Inc./Dist. by UFS, Inc.
WELL, AT LEAST I'LL FEEL SPECIAL ONCE. WHAT DAY IS THE CELEBRATION?
YESTERDAY.

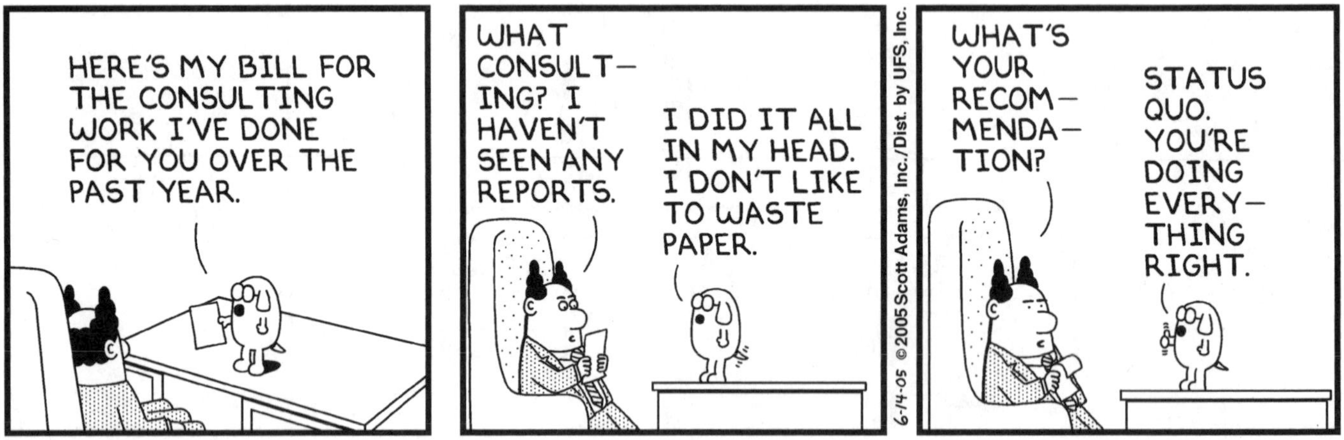
HERE'S MY BILL FOR THE CONSULTING WORK I'VE DONE FOR YOU OVER THE PAST YEAR.
WHAT CONSULT-ING? I HAVEN'T SEEN ANY REPORTS.
I DID IT ALL IN MY HEAD. I DON'T LIKE TO WASTE PAPER.
6-14-05 © 2005 Scott Adams, Inc./Dist. by UFS, Inc.
WHAT'S YOUR RECOM-MENDA-TION?
STATUS QUO. YOU'RE DOING EVERY-THING RIGHT.

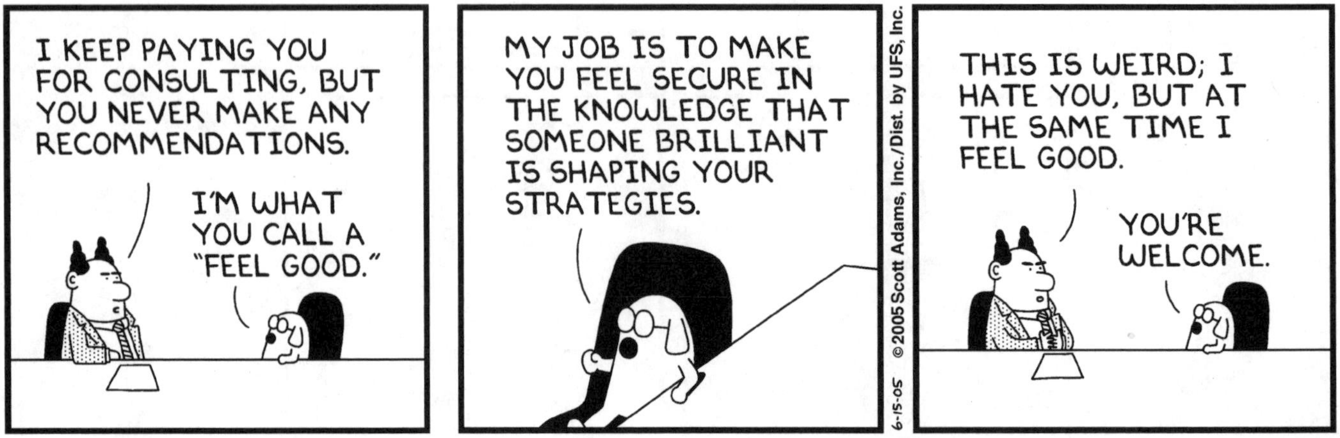
I KEEP PAYING YOU FOR CONSULTING, BUT YOU NEVER MAKE ANY RECOMMENDATIONS.
I'M WHAT YOU CALL A "FEEL GOOD."
MY JOB IS TO MAKE YOU FEEL SECURE IN THE KNOWLEDGE THAT SOMEONE BRILLIANT IS SHAPING YOUR STRATEGIES.
6-15-05 © 2005 Scott Adams, Inc./Dist. by UFS, Inc.
THIS IS WEIRD; I HATE YOU, BUT AT THE SAME TIME I FEEL GOOD.
YOU'RE WELCOME.

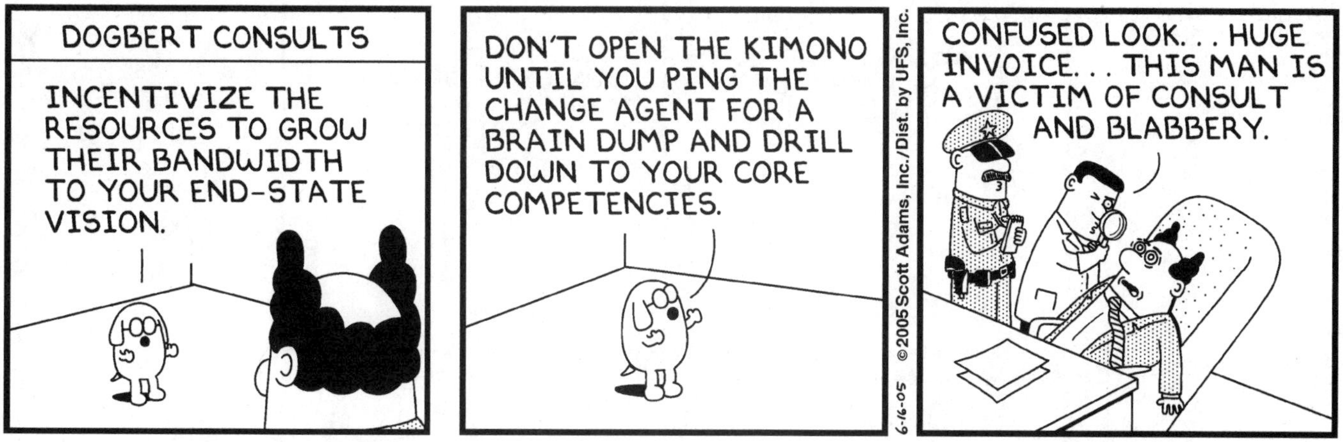
DOGBERT CONSULTS
INCENTIVIZE THE RESOURCES TO GROW THEIR BANDWIDTH TO YOUR END-STATE VISION.
DON'T OPEN THE KIMONO UNTIL YOU PING THE CHANGE AGENT FOR A BRAIN DUMP AND DRILL DOWN TO YOUR CORE COMPETENCIES.
6-16-05 © 2005 Scott Adams, Inc./Dist. by UFS, Inc.
CONFUSED LOOK. . . HUGE INVOICE. . . THIS MAN IS A VICTIM OF CONSULT AND BLABBERY.

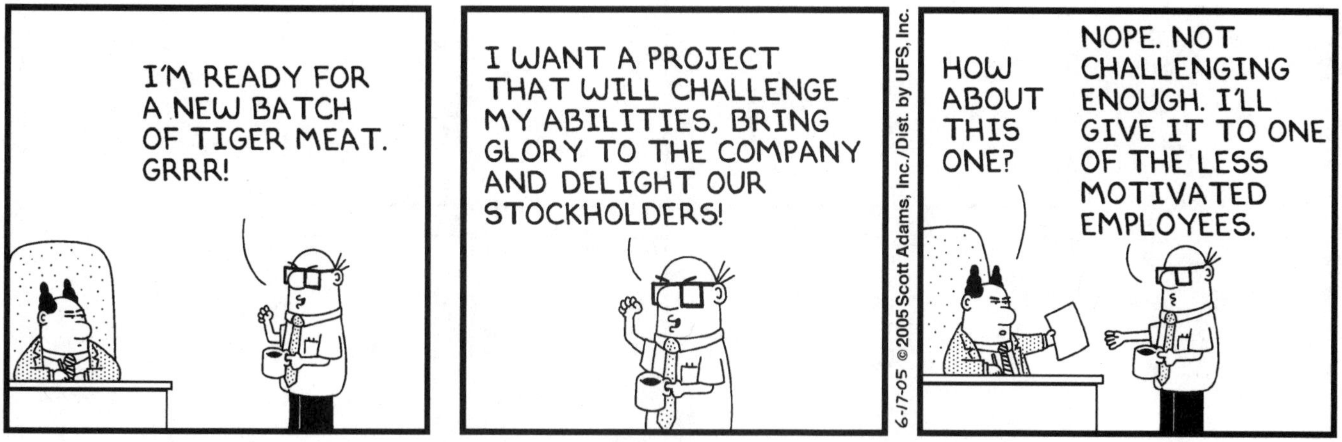
I'M READY FOR A NEW BATCH OF TIGER MEAT. GRRR!
I WANT A PROJECT THAT WILL CHALLENGE MY ABILITIES, BRING GLORY TO THE COMPANY AND DELIGHT OUR STOCKHOLDERS!
6-17-05 © 2005 Scott Adams, Inc./Dist. by UFS, Inc.
HOW ABOUT THIS ONE?
NOPE. NOT CHALLENGING ENOUGH. I'LL GIVE IT TO ONE OF THE LESS MOTIVATED EMPLOYEES.

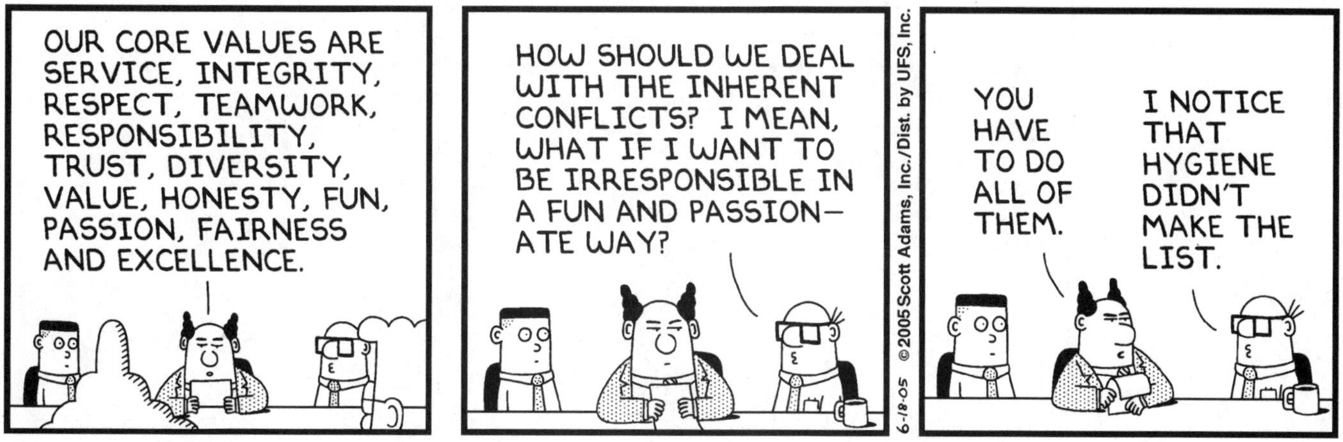
OUR CORE VALUES ARE SERVICE, INTEGRITY, RESPECT, TEAMWORK, RESPONSIBILITY, TRUST, DIVERSITY, VALUE, HONESTY, FUN, PASSION, FAIRNESS AND EXCELLENCE.
HOW SHOULD WE DEAL WITH THE INHERENT CONFLICTS? I MEAN, WHAT IF I WANT TO BE IRRESPONSIBLE IN A FUN AND PASSION-ATE WAY?
6-18-05 © 2005 Scott Adams, Inc./Dist. by UFS, Inc.
YOU HAVE TO DO ALL OF THEM.
I NOTICE THAT HYGIENE DIDN'T MAKE THE LIST.

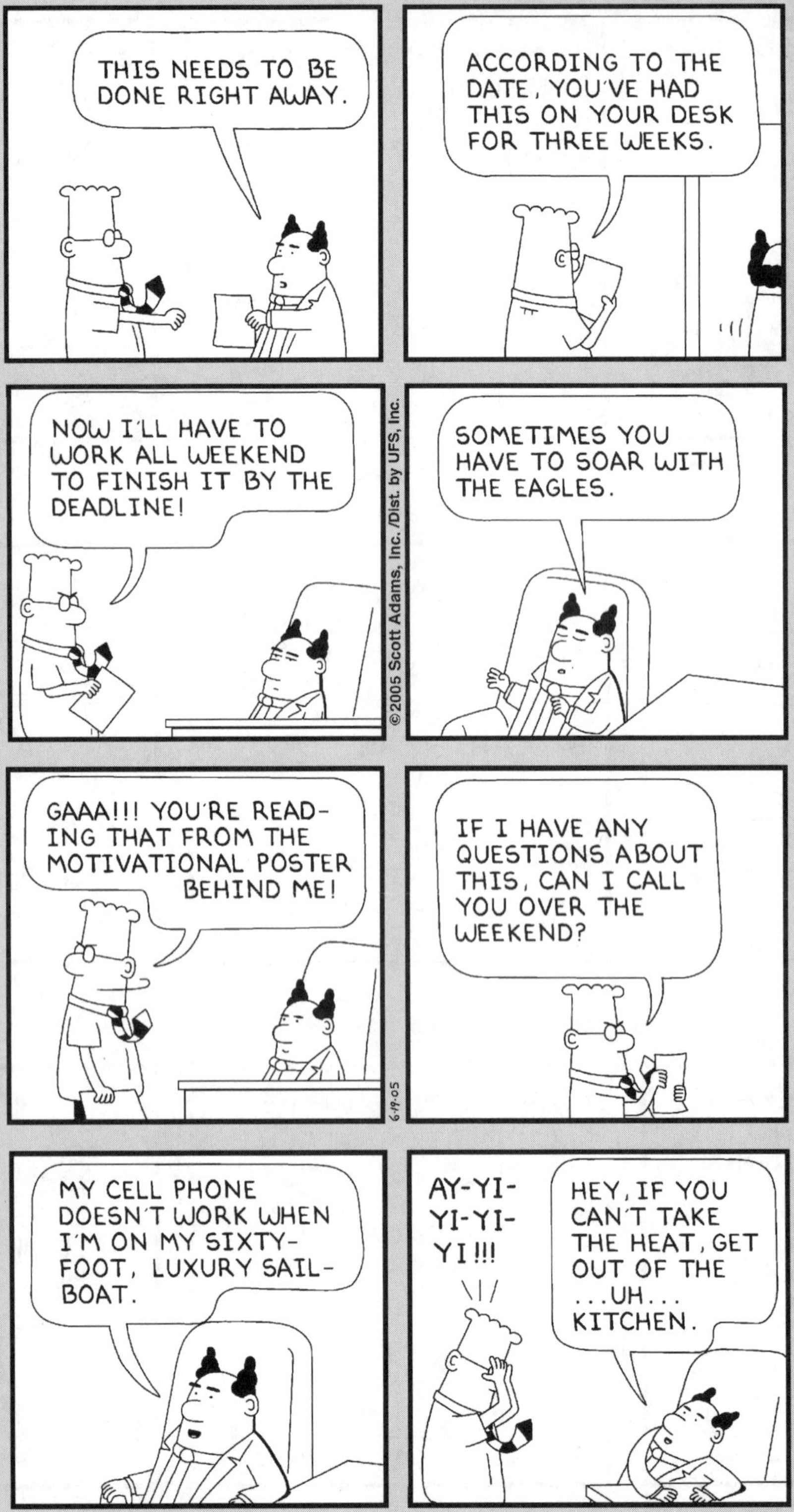
THIS NEEDS TO BE DONE RIGHT AWAY.
ACCORDING TO THE DATE, YOU'VE HAD THIS ON YOUR DESK FOR THREE WEEKS.
NOW I'LL HAVE TO WORK ALL WEEKEND TO FINISH IT BY THE DEADLINE!
SOMETIMES YOU HAVE TO SOAR WITH THE EAGLES.
GAAA!!! YOU'RE READING THAT FROM THE MOTIVATIONAL POSTER BEHIND ME!
IF I HAVE ANY QUESTIONS ABOUT THIS, CAN I CALL YOU OVER THE WEEKEND?
MY CELL PHONE DOESN'T WORK WHEN I'M ON MY SIXTY-FOOT, LUXURY SAILBOAT.
AY-YI-YI-YI-YI!!!
HEY, IF YOU CAN'T TAKE THE HEAT, GET OUT OF THE ...UH... KITCHEN.
©2005 Scott Adams, Inc. /Dist. by UFS, Inc.
6-19-05

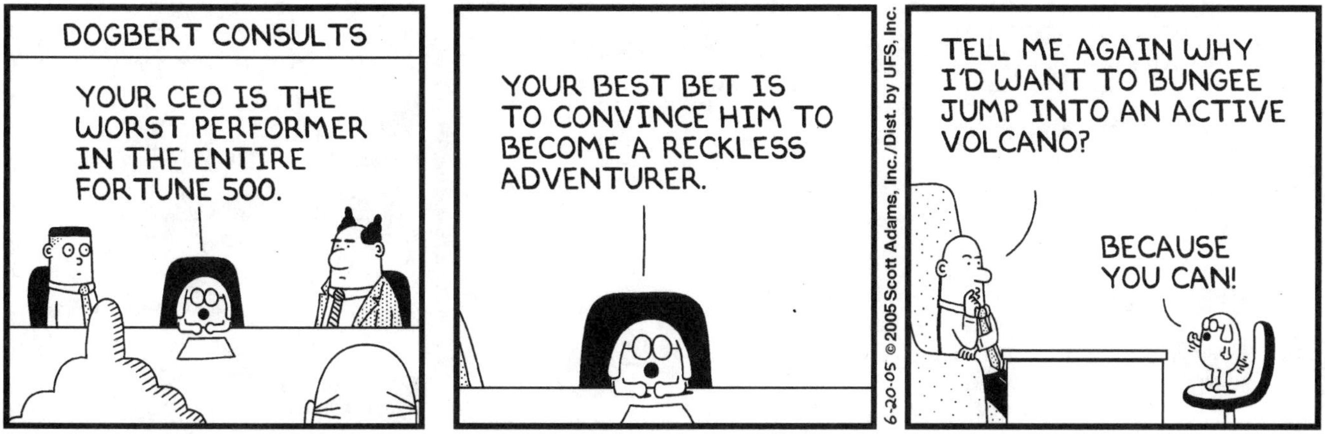
DOGBERT CONSULTS
YOUR CEO IS THE WORST PERFORMER IN THE ENTIRE FORTUNE 500.
YOUR BEST BET IS TO CONVINCE HIM TO BECOME A RECKLESS ADVENTURER.
6-20-05 ©2005 Scott Adams, Inc./Dist. by UFS, Inc.
TELL ME AGAIN WHY I'D WANT TO BUNGEE JUMP INTO AN ACTIVE VOLCANO?
BECAUSE YOU CAN!

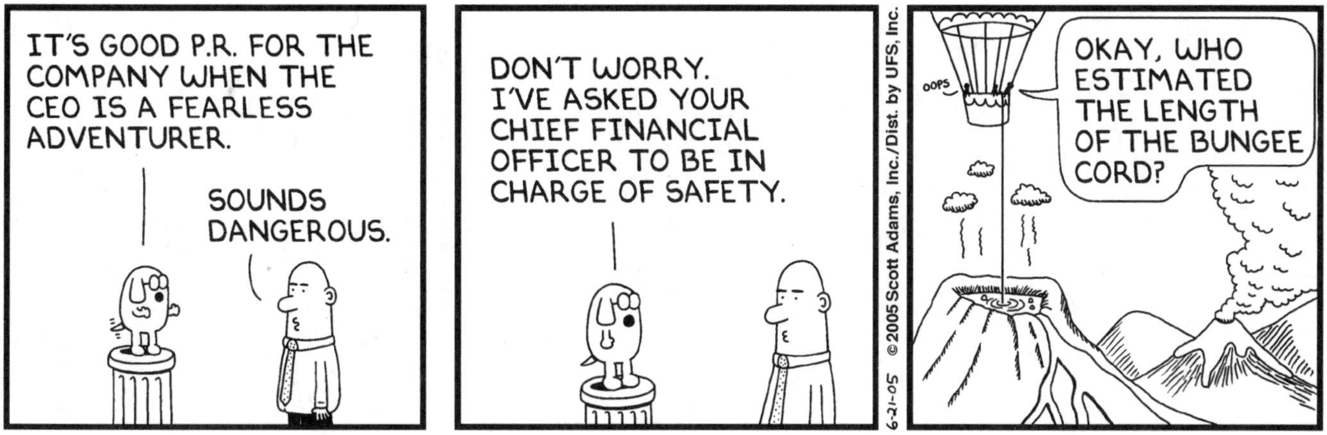
IT'S GOOD P.R. FOR THE COMPANY WHEN THE CEO IS A FEARLESS ADVENTURER.
SOUNDS DANGEROUS.
DON'T WORRY. I'VE ASKED YOUR CHIEF FINANCIAL OFFICER TO BE IN CHARGE OF SAFETY.
6-21-05 ©2005 Scott Adams, Inc./Dist. by UFS, Inc.
OOPS
OKAY, WHO ESTIMATED THE LENGTH OF THE BUNGEE CORD?

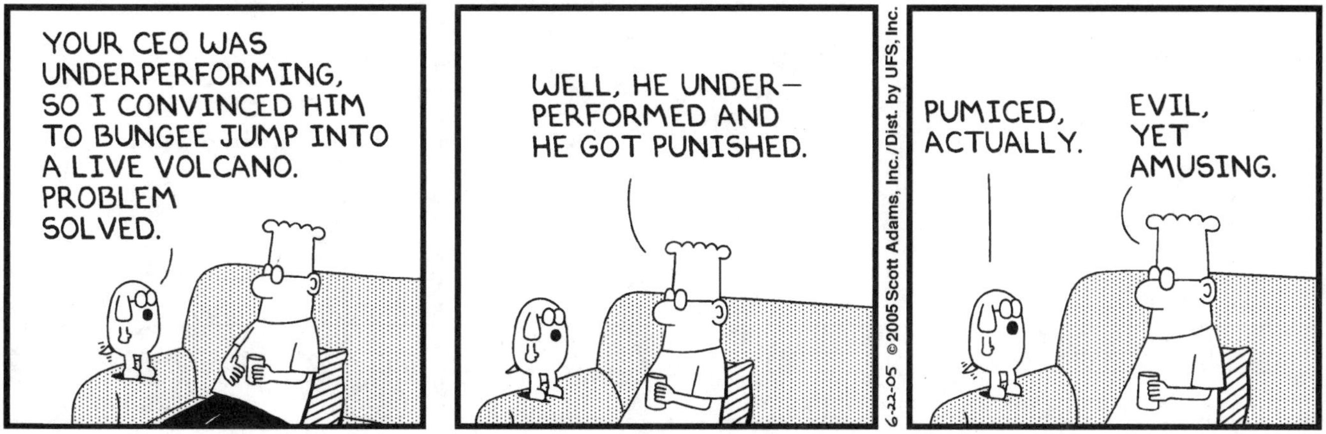
YOUR CEO WAS UNDERPERFORMING, SO I CONVINCED HIM TO BUNGEE JUMP INTO A LIVE VOLCANO. PROBLEM SOLVED.
WELL, HE UNDER-PERFORMED AND HE GOT PUNISHED.
6-22-05 ©2005 Scott Adams, Inc./Dist. by UFS, Inc.
PUMICED, ACTUALLY.
EVIL, YET AMUSING.

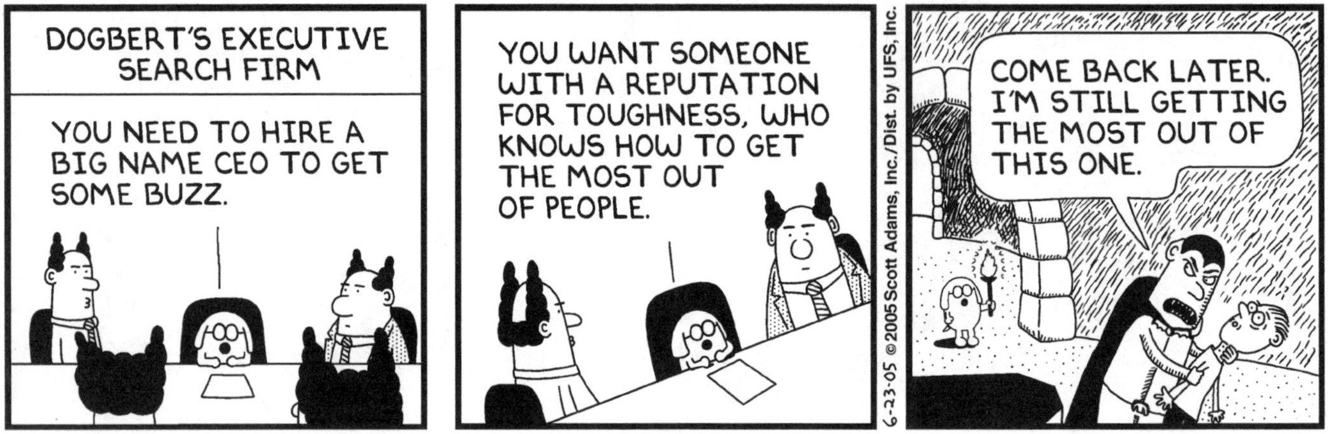
DOGBERT'S EXECUTIVE SEARCH FIRM
YOU NEED TO HIRE A BIG NAME CEO TO GET SOME BUZZ.
YOU WANT SOMEONE WITH A REPUTATION FOR TOUGHNESS, WHO KNOWS HOW TO GET THE MOST OUT OF PEOPLE.
6-23-05 © 2005 Scott Adams, Inc./Dist. by UFS, Inc.
COME BACK LATER. I'M STILL GETTING THE MOST OUT OF THIS ONE.

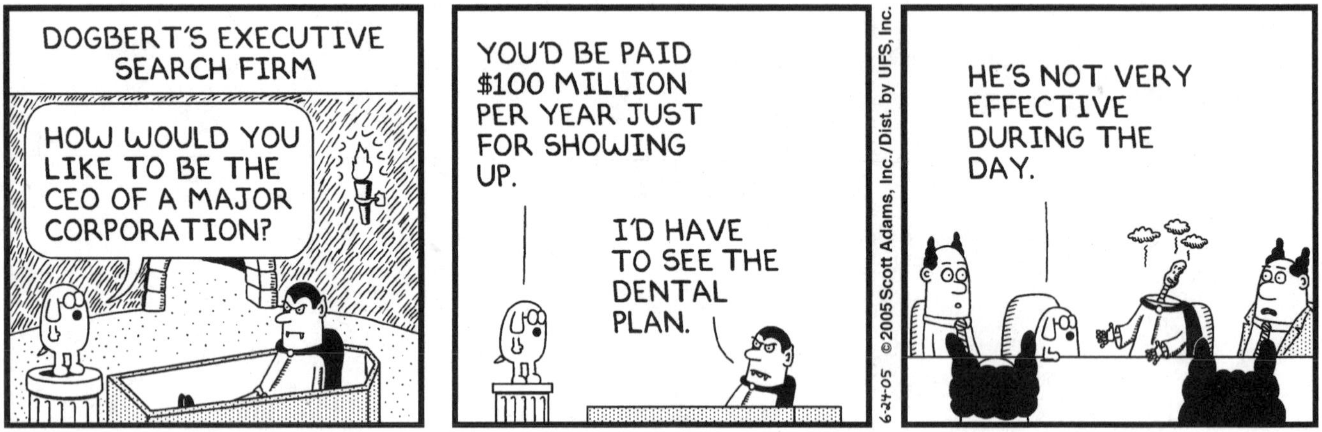
DOGBERT'S EXECUTIVE SEARCH FIRM
HOW WOULD YOU LIKE TO BE THE CEO OF A MAJOR CORPORATION?
YOU'D BE PAID $100 MILLION PER YEAR JUST FOR SHOWING UP.
I'D HAVE TO SEE THE DENTAL PLAN.
6-24-05 © 2005 Scott Adams, Inc./Dist. by UFS, Inc.
HE'S NOT VERY EFFECTIVE DURING THE DAY.

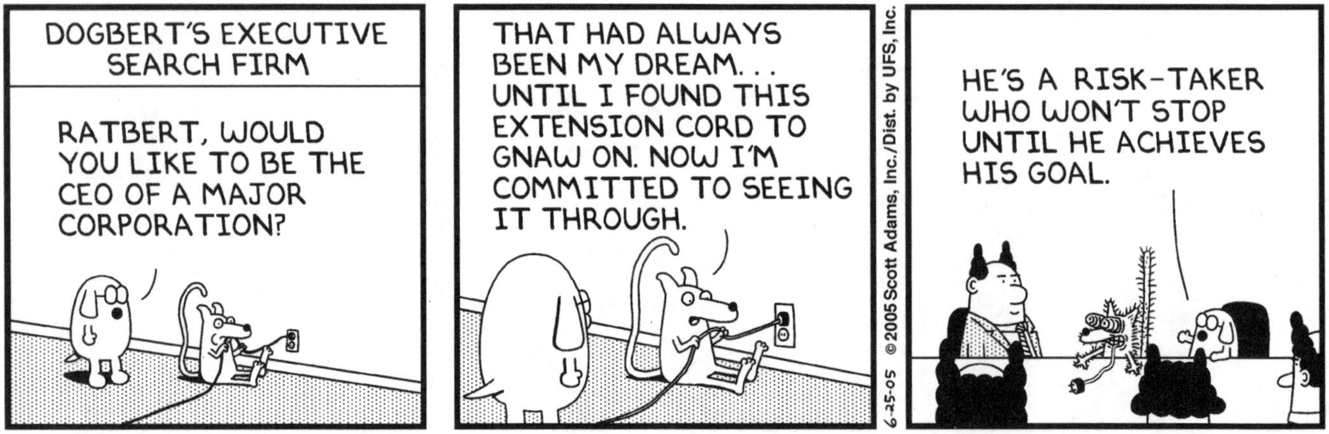
DOGBERT'S EXECUTIVE SEARCH FIRM
RATBERT, WOULD YOU LIKE TO BE THE CEO OF A MAJOR CORPORATION?
THAT HAD ALWAYS BEEN MY DREAM. . . UNTIL I FOUND THIS EXTENSION CORD TO GNAW ON. NOW I'M COMMITTED TO SEEING IT THROUGH.
6-25-05 © 2005 Scott Adams, Inc./Dist. by UFS, Inc.
HE'S A RISK-TAKER WHO WON'T STOP UNTIL HE ACHIEVES HIS GOAL.

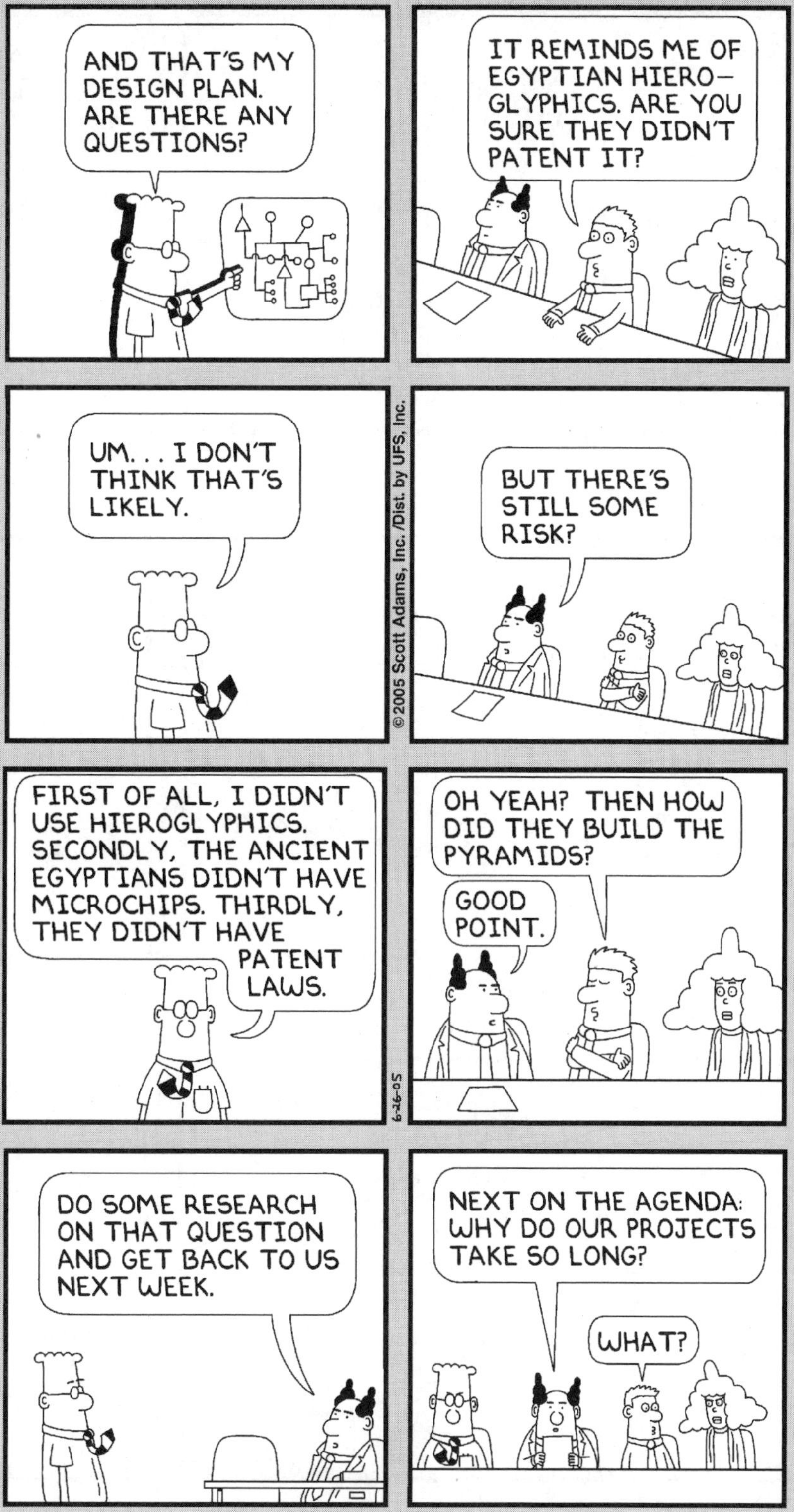
AND THAT'S MY DESIGN PLAN. ARE THERE ANY QUESTIONS?
IT REMINDS ME OF EGYPTIAN HIERO— GLYPHICS. ARE YOU SURE THEY DIDN'T PATENT IT?
UM. . . I DON'T THINK THAT'S LIKELY.
BUT THERE'S STILL SOME RISK?
FIRST OF ALL, I DIDN'T USE HIEROGLYPHICS. SECONDLY, THE ANCIENT EGYPTIANS DIDN'T HAVE MICROCHIPS. THIRDLY, THEY DIDN'T HAVE PATENT LAWS.
OH YEAH? THEN HOW DID THEY BUILD THE PYRAMIDS?
GOOD POINT.
DO SOME RESEARCH ON THAT QUESTION AND GET BACK TO US NEXT WEEK.
NEXT ON THE AGENDA: WHY DO OUR PROJECTS TAKE SO LONG?
WHAT?
6-26-05

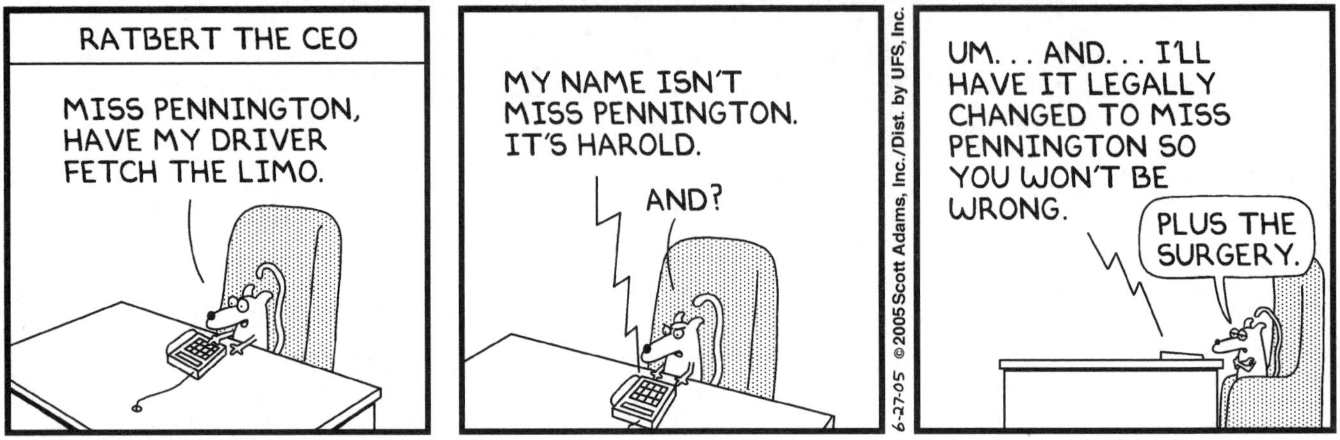
RATBERT THE CEO
MISS PENNINGTON, HAVE MY DRIVER FETCH THE LIMO.
MY NAME ISN'T MISS PENNINGTON. IT'S HAROLD.
AND?
UM. . . AND. . . I'LL HAVE IT LEGALLY CHANGED TO MISS PENNINGTON SO YOU WON'T BE WRONG.
PLUS THE SURGERY.
6-27-05 ©2005 Scott Adams, Inc./Dist. by UFS, Inc.

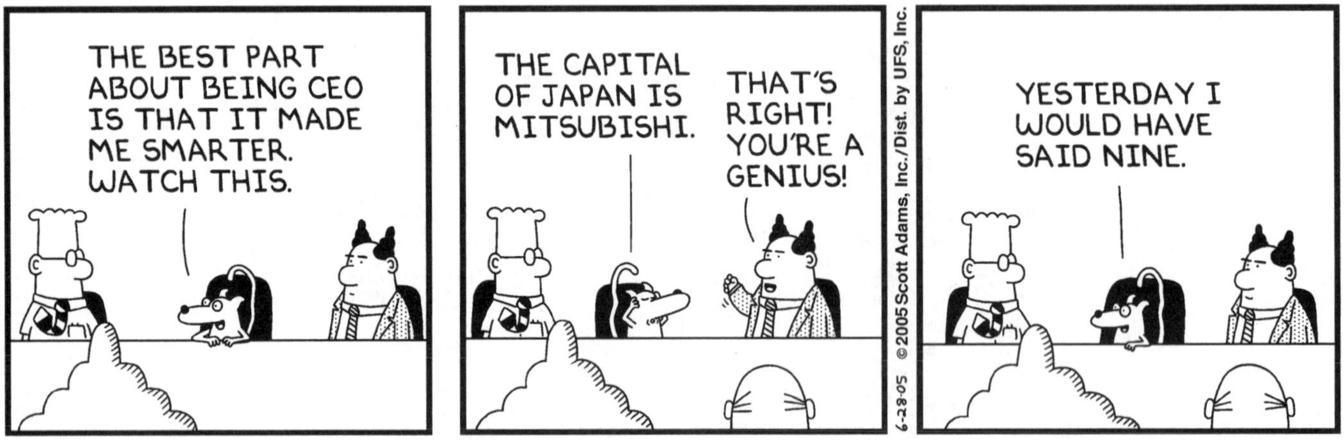
THE BEST PART ABOUT BEING CEO IS THAT IT MADE ME SMARTER. WATCH THIS.
THE CAPITAL OF JAPAN IS MITSUBISHI.
THAT'S RIGHT! YOU'RE A GENIUS!
YESTERDAY I WOULD HAVE SAID NINE.
6-28-05 ©2005 Scott Adams, Inc./Dist. by UFS, Inc.

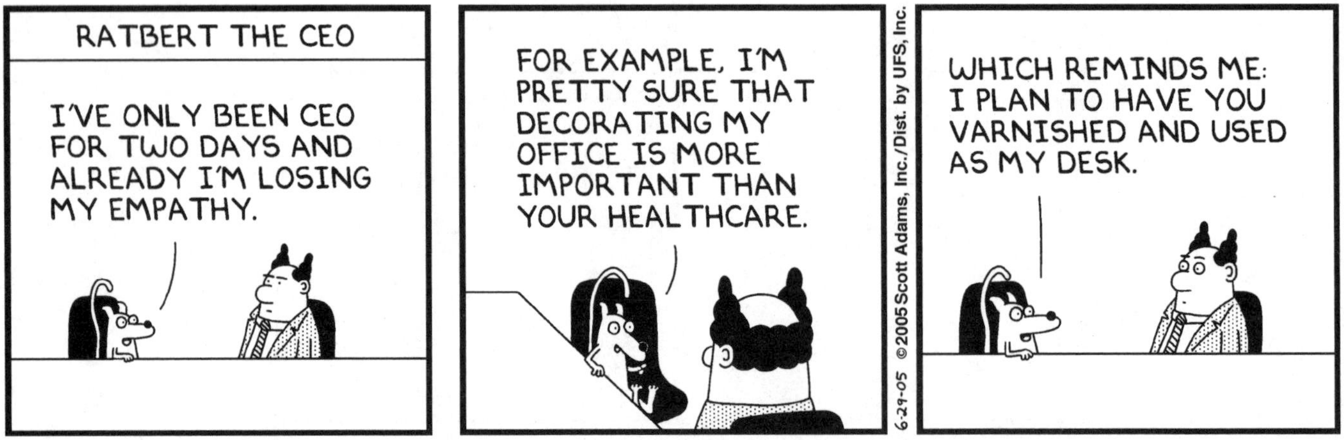
RATBERT THE CEO
I'VE ONLY BEEN CEO FOR TWO DAYS AND ALREADY I'M LOSING MY EMPATHY.
FOR EXAMPLE, I'M PRETTY SURE THAT DECORATING MY OFFICE IS MORE IMPORTANT THAN YOUR HEALTHCARE.
WHICH REMINDS ME: I PLAN TO HAVE YOU VARNISHED AND USED AS MY DESK.
6-29-05 ©2005 Scott Adams, Inc./Dist. by UFS, Inc.

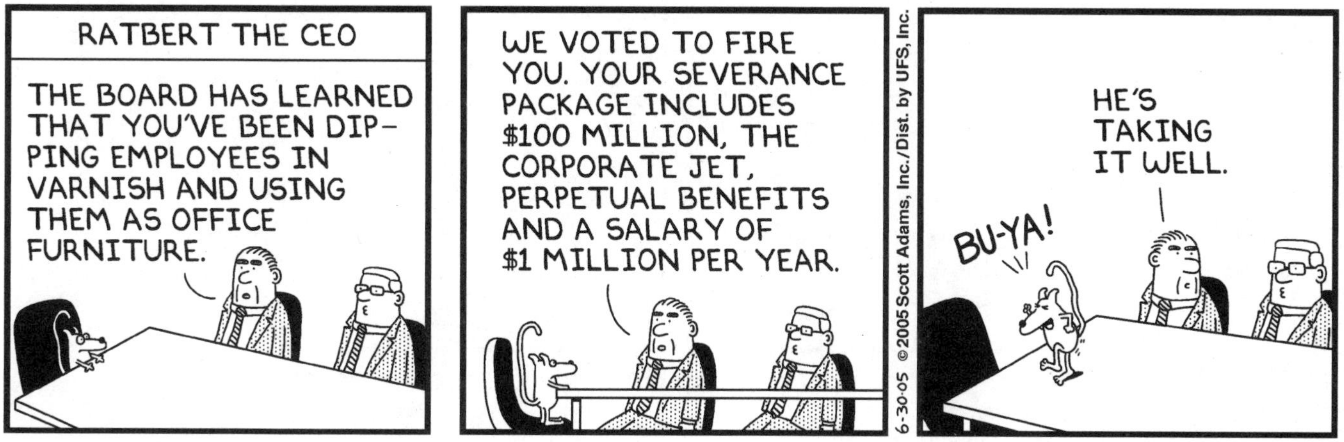
RATBERT THE CEO
THE BOARD HAS LEARNED THAT YOU'VE BEEN DIPPING EMPLOYEES IN VARNISH AND USING THEM AS OFFICE FURNITURE.
WE VOTED TO FIRE YOU. YOUR SEVERANCE PACKAGE INCLUDES $100 MILLION, THE CORPORATE JET, PERPETUAL BENEFITS AND A SALARY OF $1 MILLION PER YEAR.
6-30-05 ©2005 Scott Adams, Inc./Dist. by UFS, Inc.
BU-YA!
HE'S TAKING IT WELL.

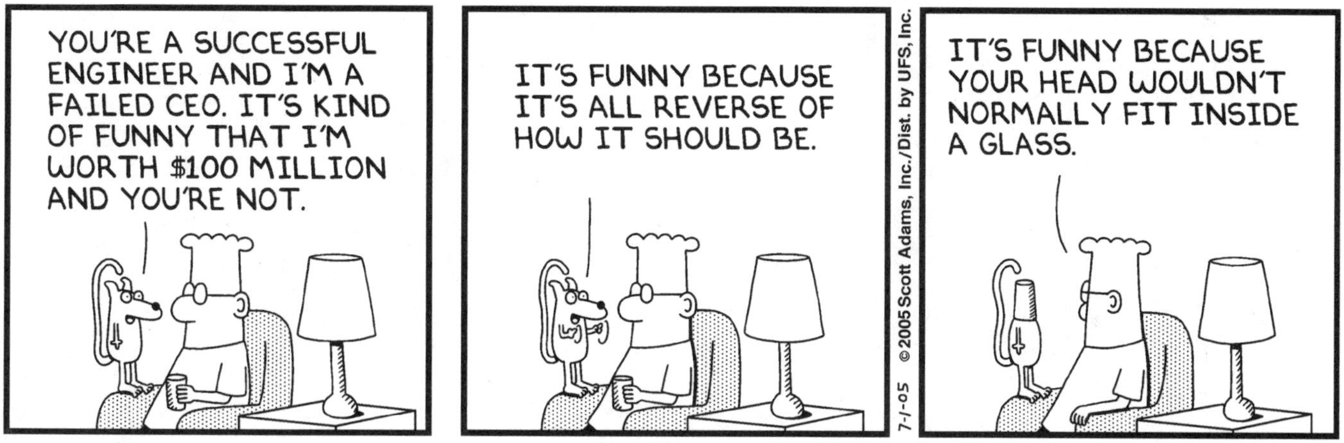
YOU'RE A SUCCESSFUL ENGINEER AND I'M A FAILED CEO. IT'S KIND OF FUNNY THAT I'M WORTH $100 MILLION AND YOU'RE NOT.
IT'S FUNNY BECAUSE IT'S ALL REVERSE OF HOW IT SHOULD BE.
7-1-05 ©2005 Scott Adams, Inc./Dist. by UFS, Inc.
IT'S FUNNY BECAUSE YOUR HEAD WOULDN'T NORMALLY FIT INSIDE A GLASS.

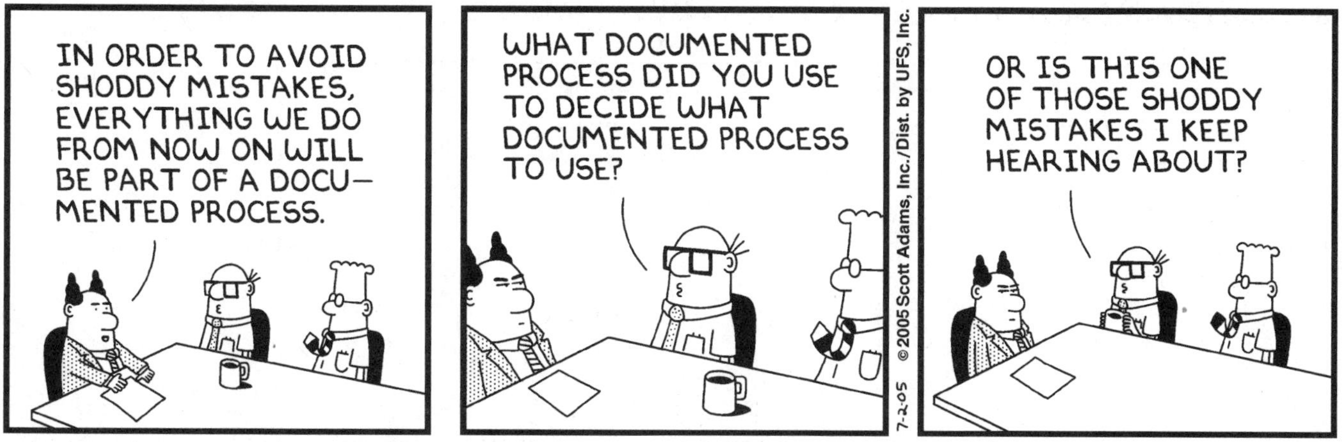
IN ORDER TO AVOID SHODDY MISTAKES, EVERYTHING WE DO FROM NOW ON WILL BE PART OF A DOCUMENTED PROCESS.
WHAT DOCUMENTED PROCESS DID YOU USE TO DECIDE WHAT DOCUMENTED PROCESS TO USE?
7-2-05 ©2005 Scott Adams, Inc./Dist. by UFS, Inc.
OR IS THIS ONE OF THOSE SHODDY MISTAKES I KEEP HEARING ABOUT?

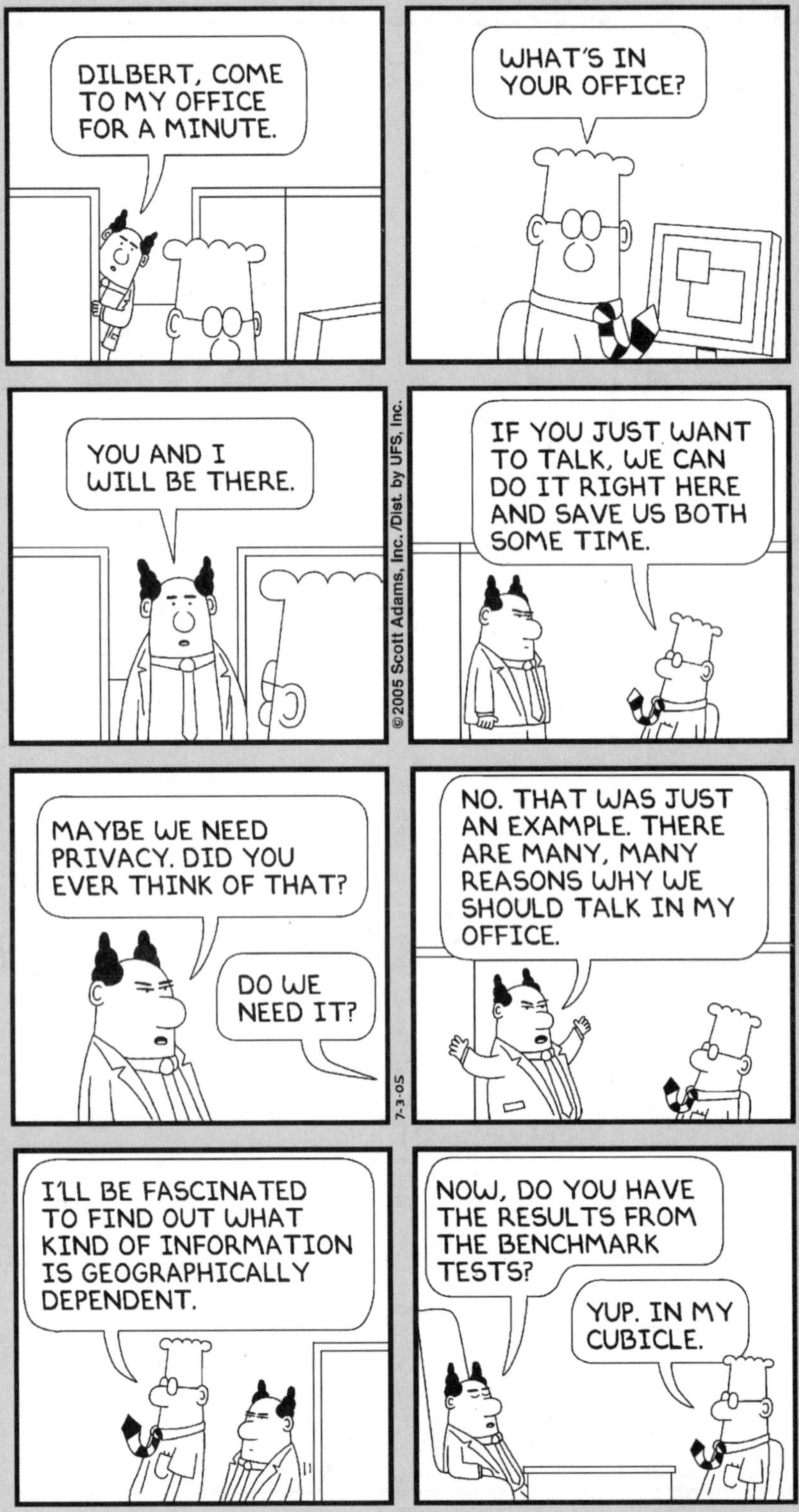
DILBERT, COME TO MY OFFICE FOR A MINUTE.
WHAT'S IN YOUR OFFICE?
YOU AND I WILL BE THERE.
IF YOU JUST WANT TO TALK, WE CAN DO IT RIGHT HERE AND SAVE US BOTH SOME TIME.
MAYBE WE NEED PRIVACY. DID YOU EVER THINK OF THAT?
DO WE NEED IT?
NO. THAT WAS JUST AN EXAMPLE. THERE ARE MANY, MANY REASONS WHY WE SHOULD TALK IN MY OFFICE.
I'LL BE FASCINATED TO FIND OUT WHAT KIND OF INFORMATION IS GEOGRAPHICALLY DEPENDENT.
NOW, DO YOU HAVE THE RESULTS FROM THE BENCHMARK TESTS?
YUP. IN MY CUBICLE.
©2005 Scott Adams, Inc./Dist. by UFS, Inc.
7-3-05

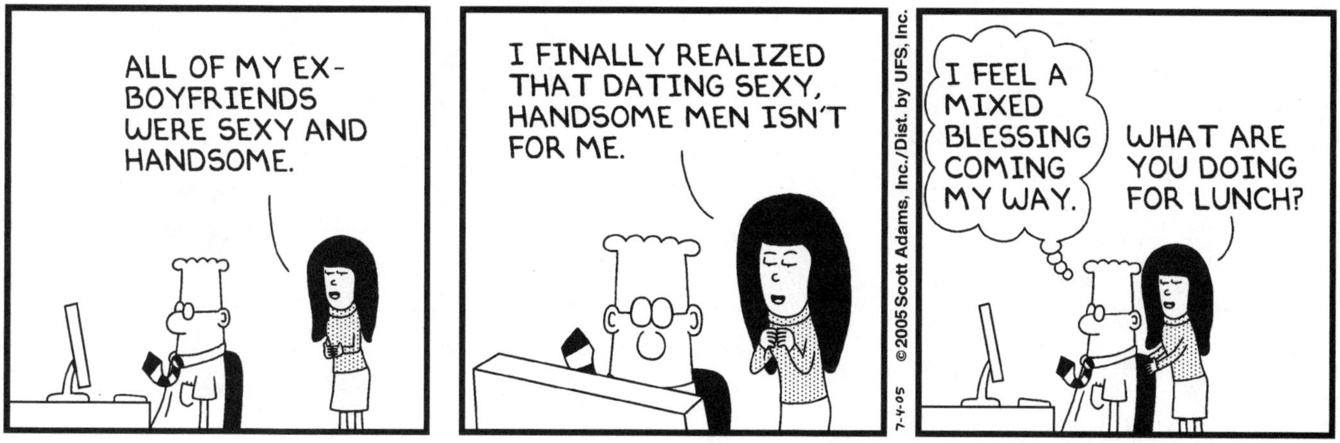
ALL OF MY EX-BOYFRIENDS WERE SEXY AND HANDSOME.
I FINALLY REALIZED THAT DATING SEXY, HANDSOME MEN ISN'T FOR ME.
7-4-05 © 2005 Scott Adams, Inc./Dist. by UFS, Inc.
I FEEL A MIXED BLESSING COMING MY WAY.
WHAT ARE YOU DOING FOR LUNCH?

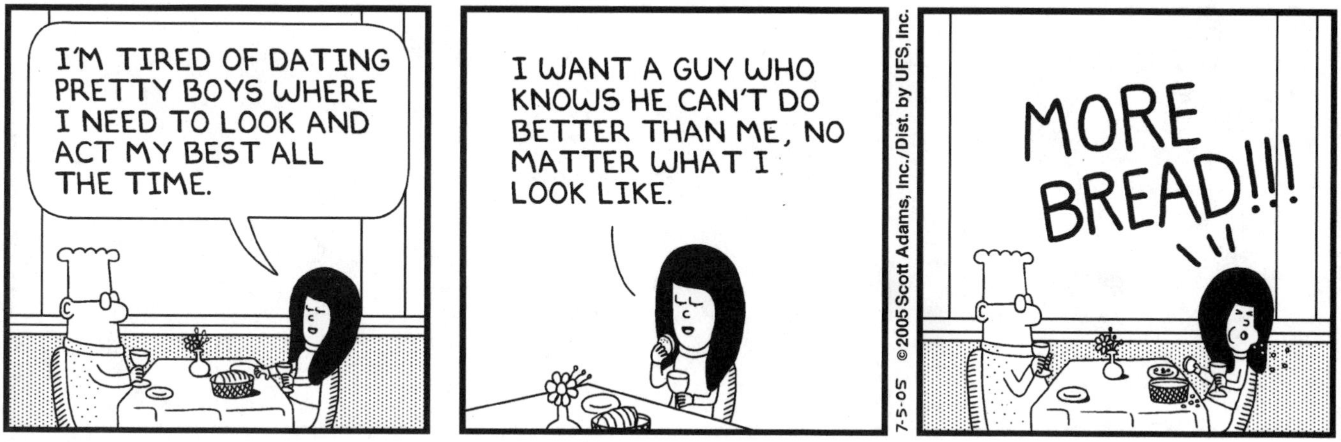
I'M TIRED OF DATING PRETTY BOYS WHERE I NEED TO LOOK AND ACT MY BEST ALL THE TIME.
I WANT A GUY WHO KNOWS HE CAN'T DO BETTER THAN ME, NO MATTER WHAT I LOOK LIKE.
7-5-05 © 2005 Scott Adams, Inc./Dist. by UFS, Inc.
MORE BREAD!!!

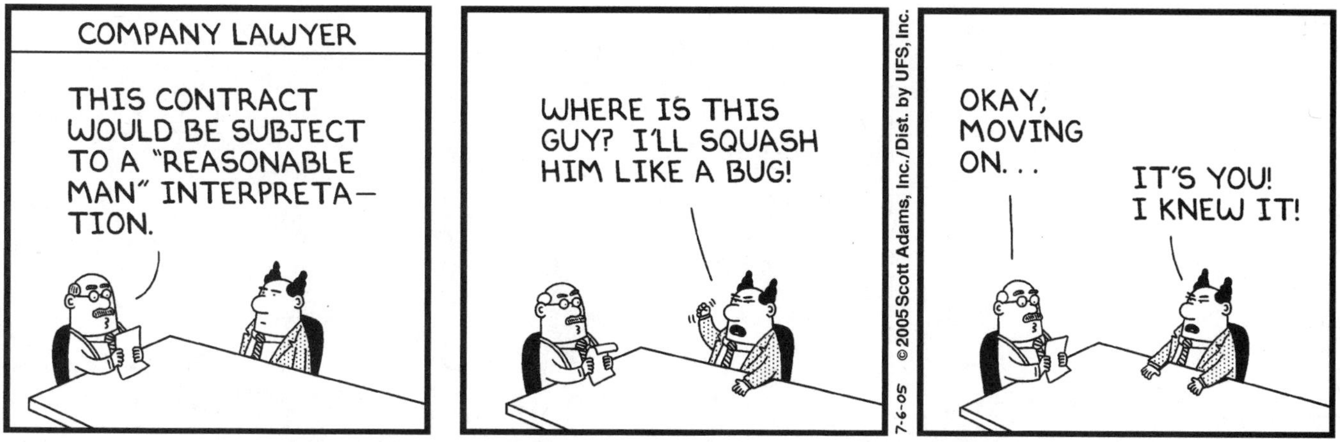
COMPANY LAWYER
THIS CONTRACT WOULD BE SUBJECT TO A "REASONABLE MAN" INTERPRETATION.
WHERE IS THIS GUY? I'LL SQUASH HIM LIKE A BUG!
7-6-05 © 2005 Scott Adams, Inc./Dist. by UFS, Inc.
OKAY, MOVING ON. . .
IT'S YOU! I KNEW IT!

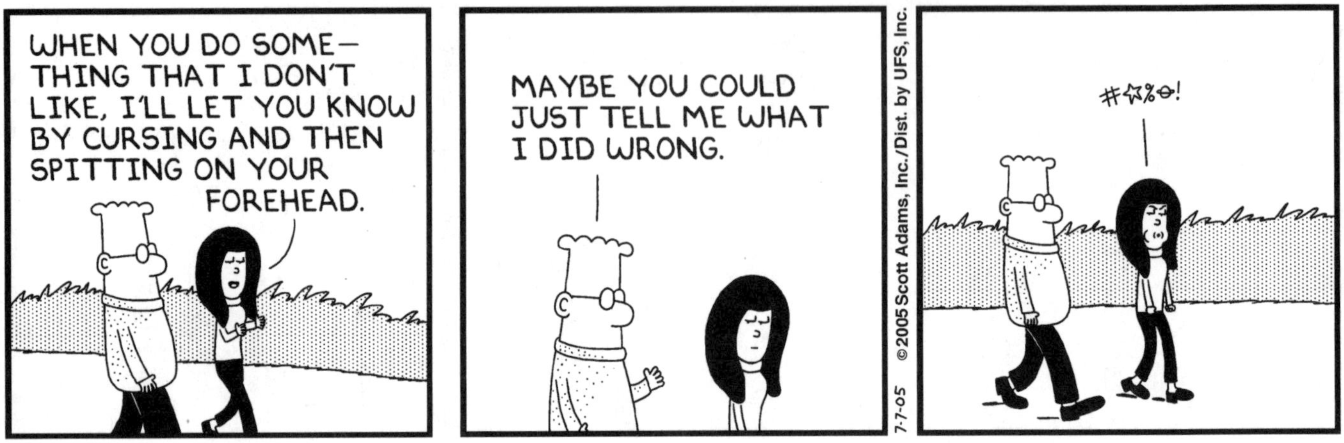
WHEN YOU DO SOME-THING THAT I DON'T LIKE, I'LL LET YOU KNOW BY CURSING AND THEN SPITTING ON YOUR FOREHEAD.
MAYBE YOU COULD JUST TELL ME WHAT I DID WRONG.
7-7-05 ©2005 Scott Adams, Inc./Dist. by UFS, Inc.

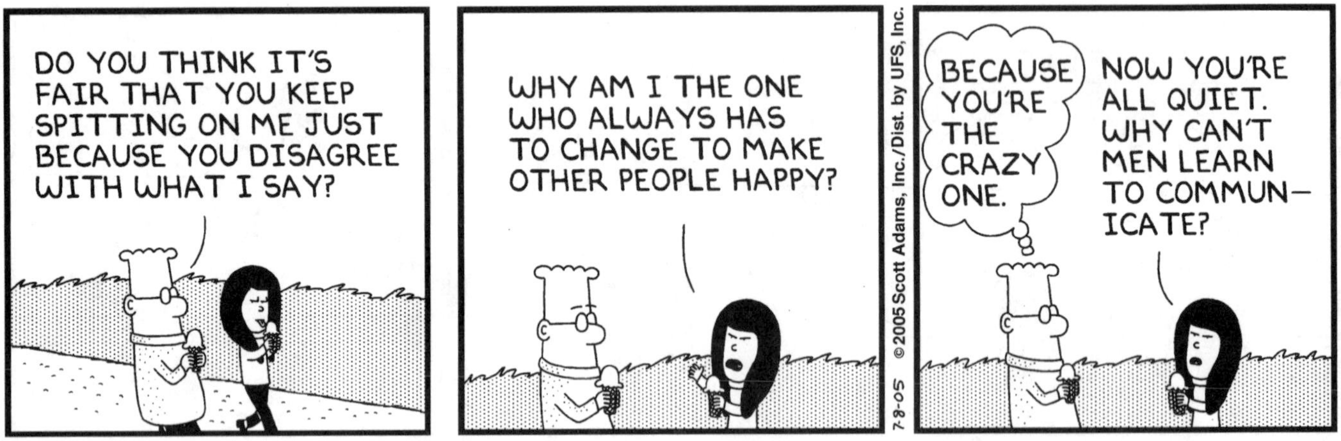
DO YOU THINK IT'S FAIR THAT YOU KEEP SPITTING ON ME JUST BECAUSE YOU DISAGREE WITH WHAT I SAY?
WHY AM I THE ONE WHO ALWAYS HAS TO CHANGE TO MAKE OTHER PEOPLE HAPPY?
BECAUSE YOU'RE THE CRAZY ONE.
NOW YOU'RE ALL QUIET. WHY CAN'T MEN LEARN TO COMMUN-ICATE?
7-8-05 ©2005 Scott Adams, Inc./Dist. by UFS, Inc.

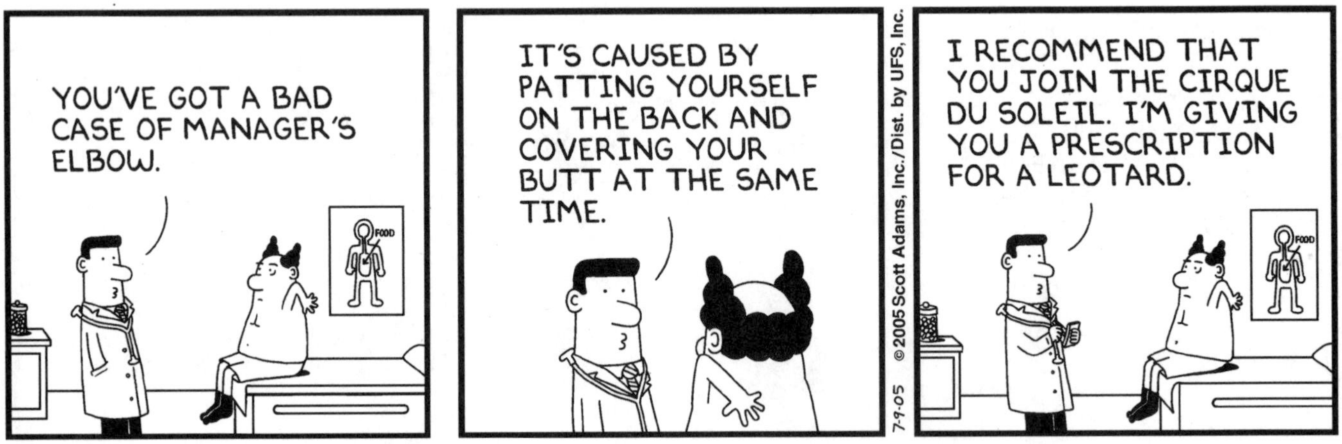
YOU'VE GOT A BAD CASE OF MANAGER'S ELBOW.
FOOD
IT'S CAUSED BY PATTING YOURSELF ON THE BACK AND COVERING YOUR BUTT AT THE SAME TIME.
I RECOMMEND THAT YOU JOIN THE CIRQUE DU SOLEIL. I'M GIVING YOU A PRESCRIPTION FOR A LEOTARD.
FOOD
7-9-05 ©2005 Scott Adams, Inc./Dist. by UFS, Inc.

ASOK, THE MOVE THAT I AM ABOUT TO TEACH YOU IS CALLED THE "WALLY REFLECTOR."
THROUGHOUT THE DAY, BAD PEOPLE WILL TRY TO MAKE YOU DO WORK FOR THEM.
AT FIRST, OFFER NO RESISTANCE, AS IF YOU ACTUALLY PLAN TO DO THE WORK.
THEN ASK THE OFFENDER TO DO A LITTLE BIT OF WORK HIMSELF.
ALLOW ME TO DEMONSTRATE.
© 2005 Scott Adams, Inc. /Dist. by UFS, Inc.
WALLY, I NEED YOU TO DESIGN A DATABASE FOR ALL OF OUR PRODUCT FEATURES AND SERVICES.
GLAD TO DO IT!
7-10-05
ALL I NEED FROM YOU IS A COMPREHENSIVE LIST OF THE DATA FIELDS YOU NEED INCLUDED.
OH. . . WOW. I'M REALLY BUSY. I'LL HAVE TO GET BACK TO YOU ON THAT.
AND I'LL NEVER SEE THAT IDIOT AGAIN.
YOU INSPIRE ME, IN A CREEPY KIND OF WAY.

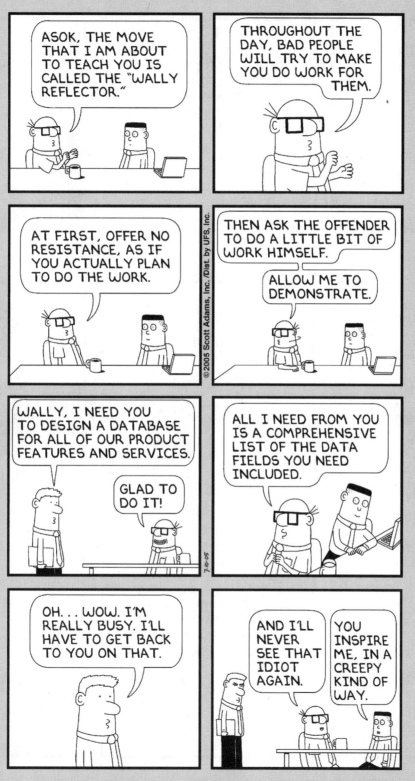

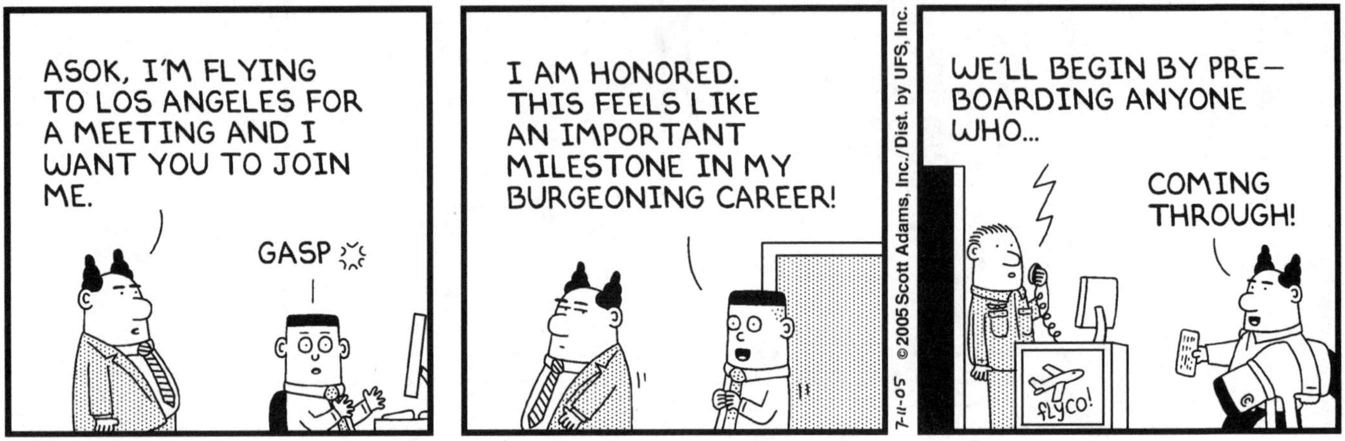
ASOK, I'M FLYING TO LOS ANGELES FOR A MEETING AND I WANT YOU TO JOIN ME.
GASP
I AM HONORED. THIS FEELS LIKE AN IMPORTANT MILESTONE IN MY BURGEONING CAREER!
7-11-05 © 2005 Scott Adams, Inc./Dist. by UFS, Inc.
WE'LL BEGIN BY PRE-BOARDING ANYONE WHO...
COMING THROUGH!
FLYCO!

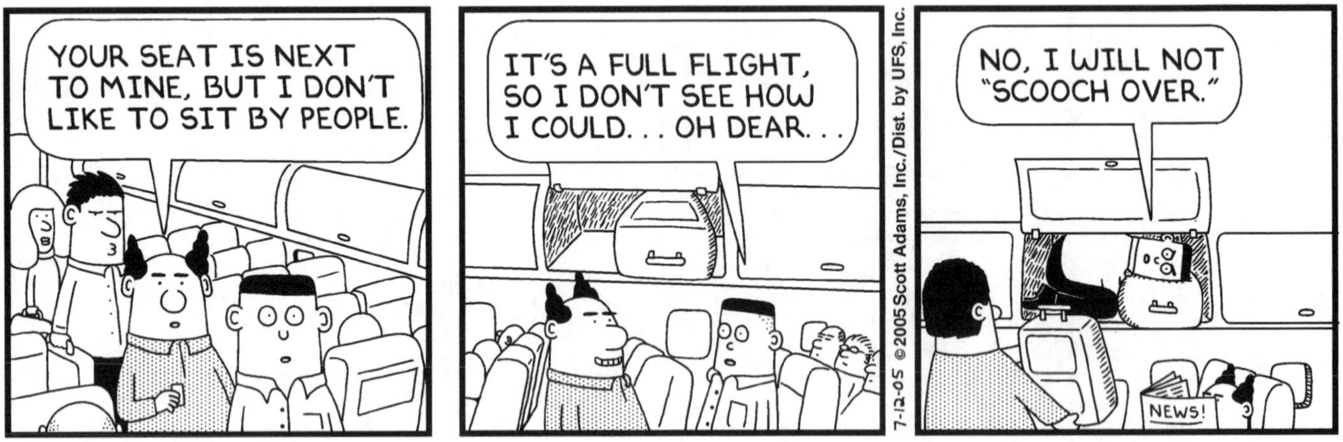
YOUR SEAT IS NEXT TO MINE, BUT I DON'T LIKE TO SIT BY PEOPLE.
IT'S A FULL FLIGHT, SO I DON'T SEE HOW I COULD. . . OH DEAR. . .
7-12-05 © 2005 Scott Adams, Inc./Dist. by UFS, Inc.
NO, I WILL NOT "SCOOCH OVER."
NEWS!

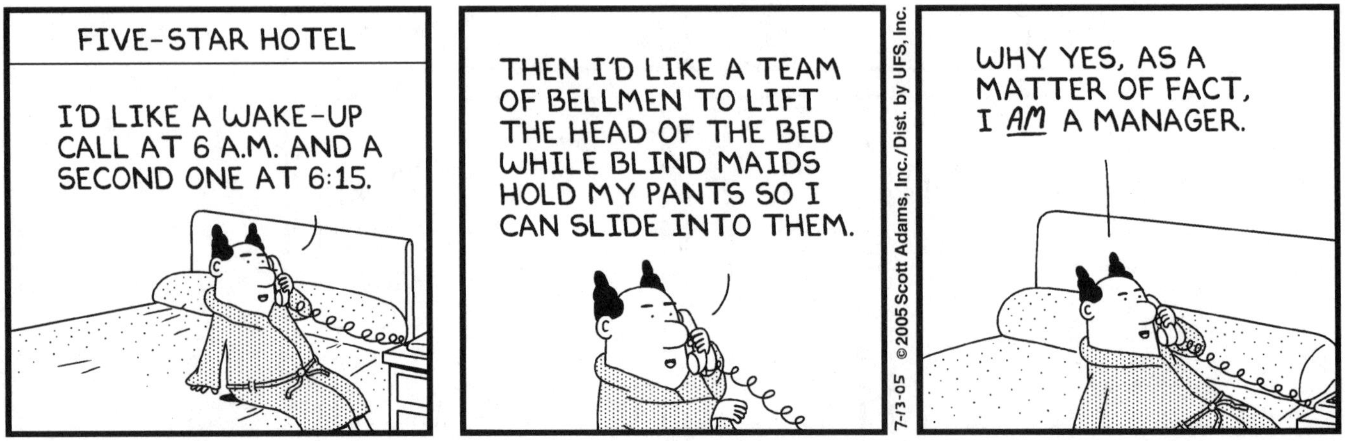
FIVE-STAR HOTEL
I'D LIKE A WAKE-UP CALL AT 6 A.M. AND A SECOND ONE AT 6:15.
THEN I'D LIKE A TEAM OF BELLMEN TO LIFT THE HEAD OF THE BED WHILE BLIND MAIDS HOLD MY PANTS SO I CAN SLIDE INTO THEM.
7-13-05 © 2005 Scott Adams, Inc./Dist. by UFS, Inc.
WHY YES, AS A MATTER OF FACT, I AM A MANAGER.

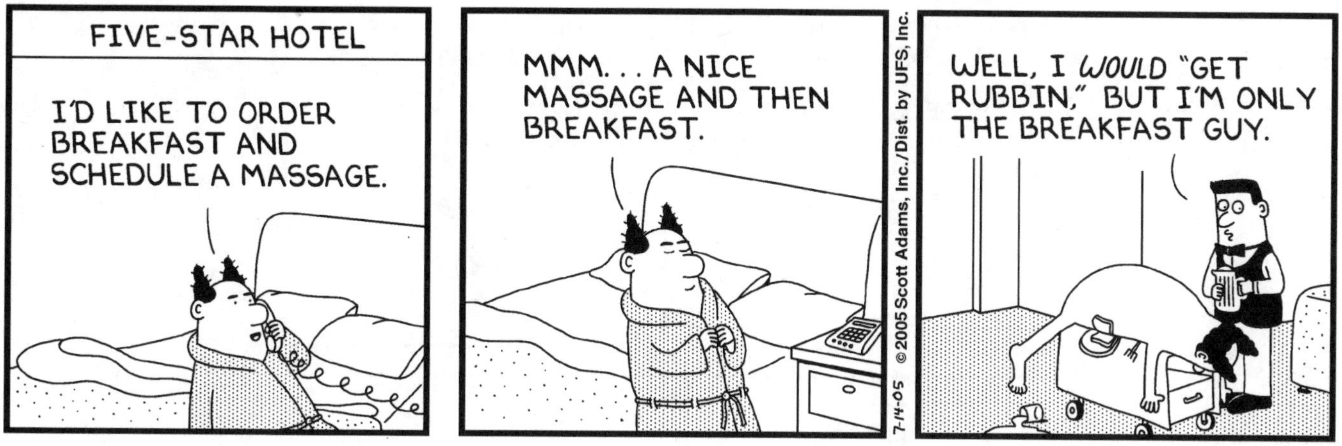
FIVE-STAR HOTEL
I'D LIKE TO ORDER BREAKFAST AND SCHEDULE A MASSAGE.
MMM. . . A NICE MASSAGE AND THEN BREAKFAST.
WELL, I *WOULD* "GET RUBBIN," BUT I'M ONLY THE BREAKFAST GUY.
7-14-05 © 2005 Scott Adams, Inc./Dist. by UFS, Inc.

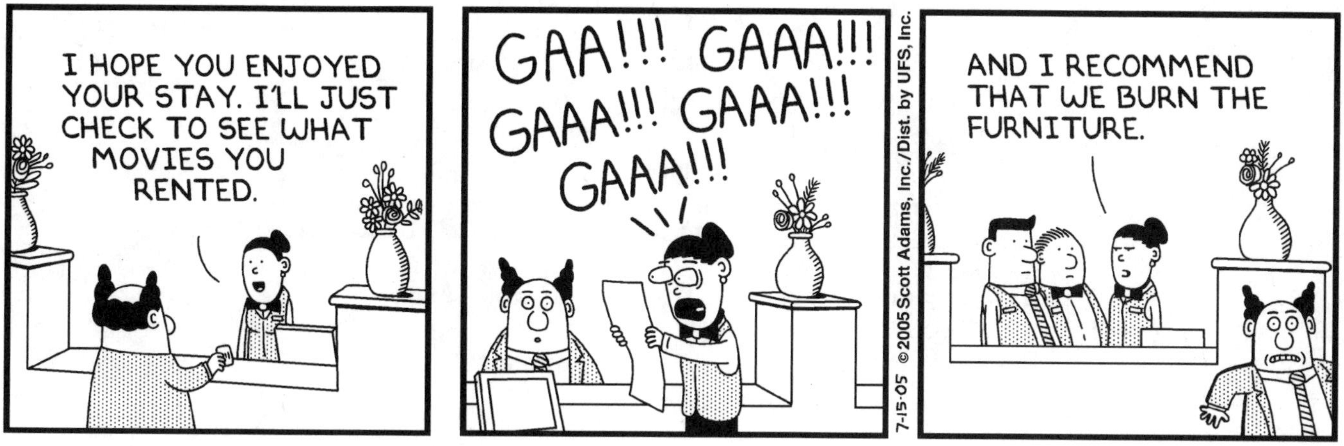
I HOPE YOU ENJOYED YOUR STAY. I'LL JUST CHECK TO SEE WHAT MOVIES YOU RENTED.
GAA!!! GAAA!!! GAAA!!! GAAA!!! GAAA!!!
AND I RECOMMEND THAT WE BURN THE FURNITURE.
7-15-05 © 2005 Scott Adams, Inc./Dist. by UFS, Inc.

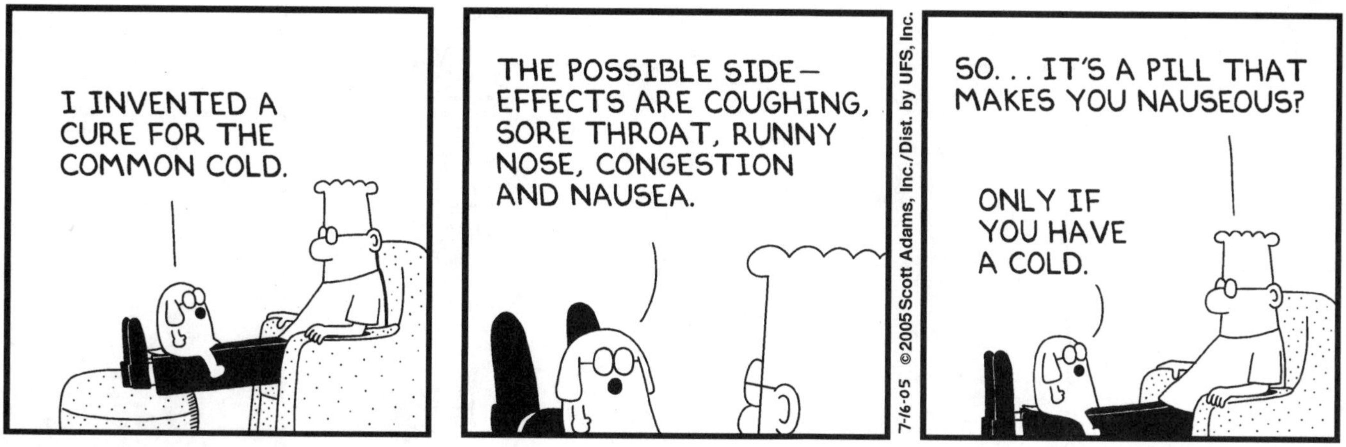
I INVENTED A CURE FOR THE COMMON COLD.
THE POSSIBLE SIDE–EFFECTS ARE COUGHING, SORE THROAT, RUNNY NOSE, CONGESTION AND NAUSEA.
SO. . . IT'S A PILL THAT MAKES YOU NAUSEOUS?
ONLY IF YOU HAVE A COLD.
7-16-05 © 2005 Scott Adams, Inc./Dist. by UFS, Inc.

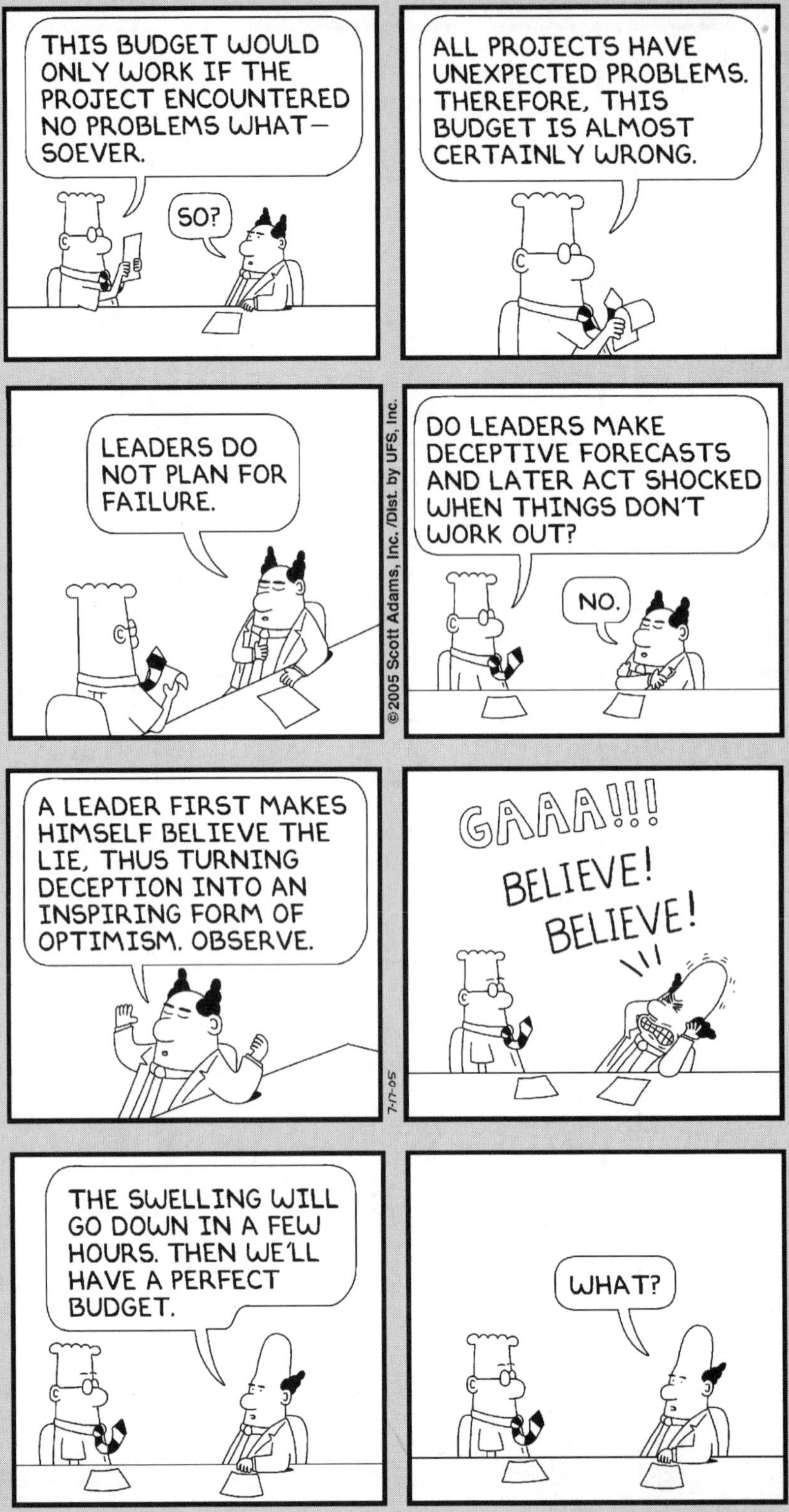
THIS BUDGET WOULD ONLY WORK IF THE PROJECT ENCOUNTERED NO PROBLEMS WHAT-SOEVER.
SO?
ALL PROJECTS HAVE UNEXPECTED PROBLEMS. THEREFORE, THIS BUDGET IS ALMOST CERTAINLY WRONG.
LEADERS DO NOT PLAN FOR FAILURE.
©2005 Scott Adams, Inc./Dist. by UFS, Inc.
DO LEADERS MAKE DECEPTIVE FORECASTS AND LATER ACT SHOCKED WHEN THINGS DON'T WORK OUT?
NO.
A LEADER FIRST MAKES HIMSELF BELIEVE THE LIE, THUS TURNING DECEPTION INTO AN INSPIRING FORM OF OPTIMISM. OBSERVE.
7-17-05
GAAA!!!
BELIEVE!
BELIEVE!
THE SWELLING WILL GO DOWN IN A FEW HOURS. THEN WE'LL HAVE A PERFECT BUDGET.
WHAT?

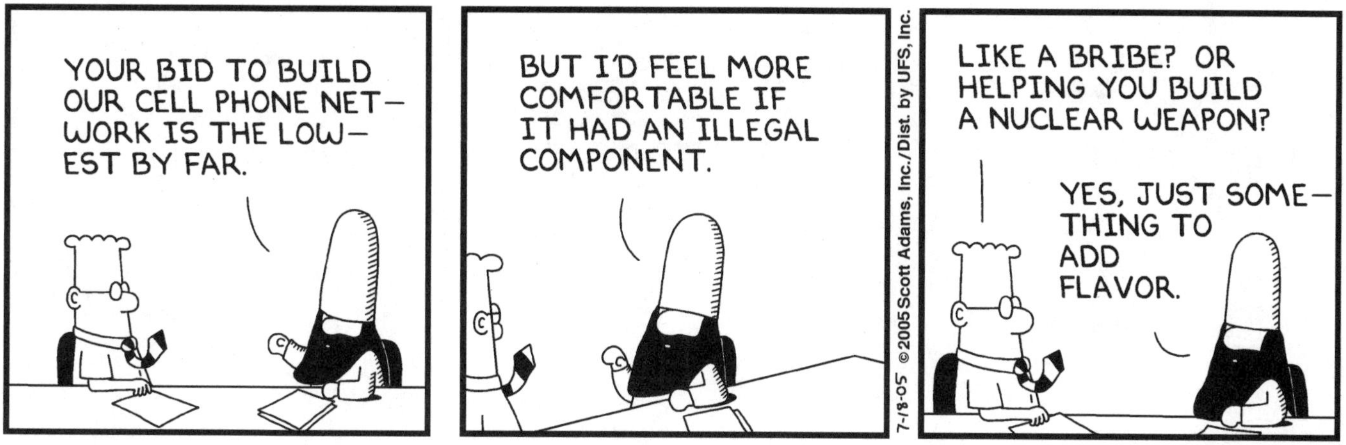
YOUR BID TO BUILD OUR CELL PHONE NET-WORK IS THE LOW-EST BY FAR.
BUT I'D FEEL MORE COMFORTABLE IF IT HAD AN ILLEGAL COMPONENT.
7-18-05 © 2005 Scott Adams, Inc./Dist. by UFS, Inc.
LIKE A BRIBE? OR HELPING YOU BUILD A NUCLEAR WEAPON?
YES, JUST SOME-THING TO ADD FLAVOR.

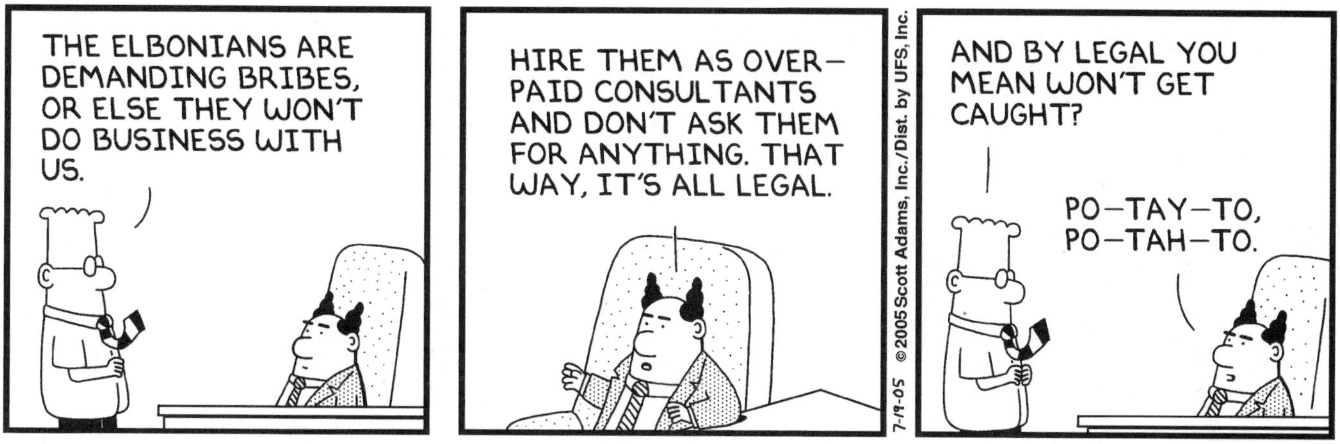
THE ELBONIANS ARE DEMANDING BRIBES, OR ELSE THEY WON'T DO BUSINESS WITH US.
HIRE THEM AS OVER-PAID CONSULTANTS AND DON'T ASK THEM FOR ANYTHING. THAT WAY, IT'S ALL LEGAL.
7-19-05 © 2005 Scott Adams, Inc./Dist. by UFS, Inc.
AND BY LEGAL YOU MEAN WON'T GET CAUGHT?
PO-TAY-TO, PO-TAH-TO.

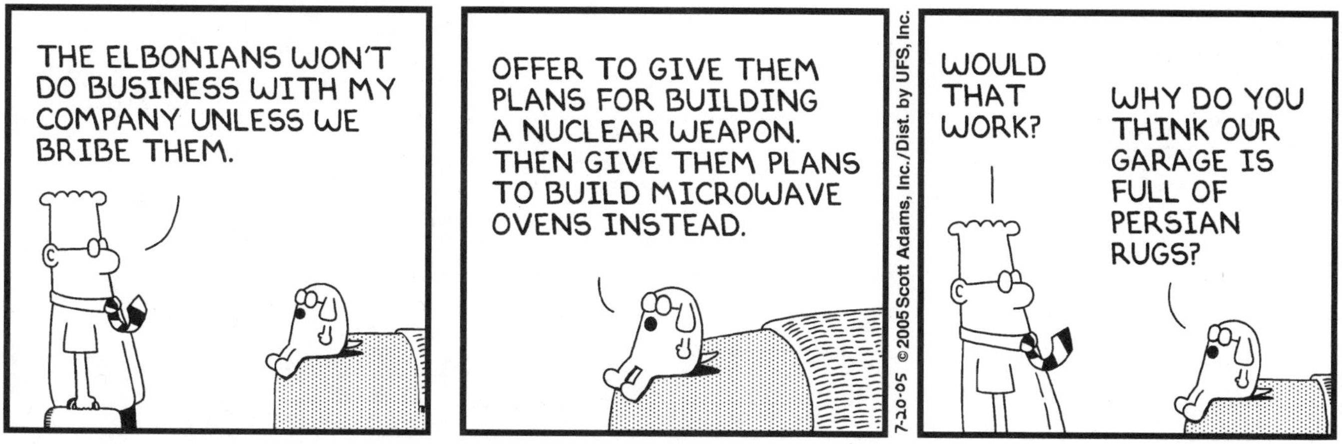
THE ELBONIANS WON'T DO BUSINESS WITH MY COMPANY UNLESS WE BRIBE THEM.
OFFER TO GIVE THEM PLANS FOR BUILDING A NUCLEAR WEAPON. THEN GIVE THEM PLANS TO BUILD MICROWAVE OVENS INSTEAD.
7-20-05 © 2005 Scott Adams, Inc./Dist. by UFS, Inc.
WOULD THAT WORK?
WHY DO YOU THINK OUR GARAGE IS FULL OF PERSIAN RUGS?

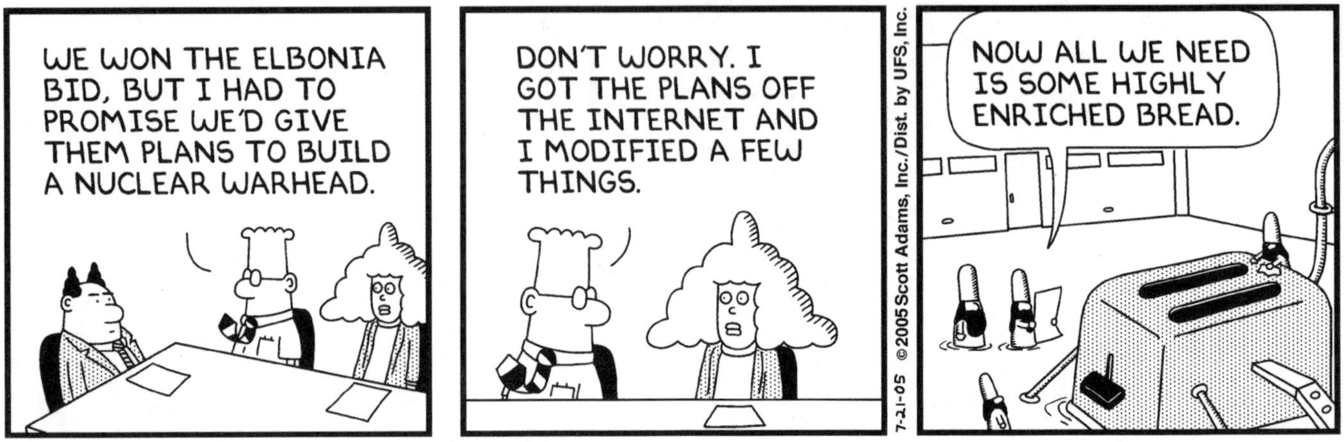
WE WON THE ELBONIA BID, BUT I HAD TO PROMISE WE'D GIVE THEM PLANS TO BUILD A NUCLEAR WARHEAD.
DON'T WORRY. I GOT THE PLANS OFF THE INTERNET AND I MODIFIED A FEW THINGS.
7-21-05 ©2005 Scott Adams, Inc./Dist. by UFS, Inc.
NOW ALL WE NEED IS SOME HIGHLY ENRICHED BREAD.

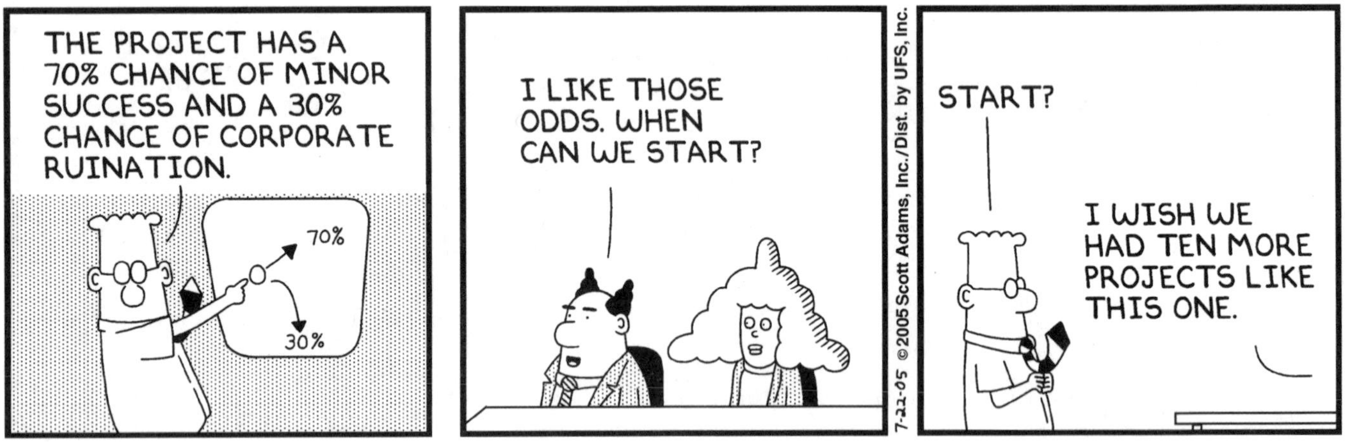
THE PROJECT HAS A 70% CHANCE OF MINOR SUCCESS AND A 30% CHANCE OF CORPORATE RUINATION.
70%
30%
I LIKE THOSE ODDS. WHEN CAN WE START?
7-22-05 ©2005 Scott Adams, Inc./Dist. by UFS, Inc.
START?
I WISH WE HAD TEN MORE PROJECTS LIKE THIS ONE.

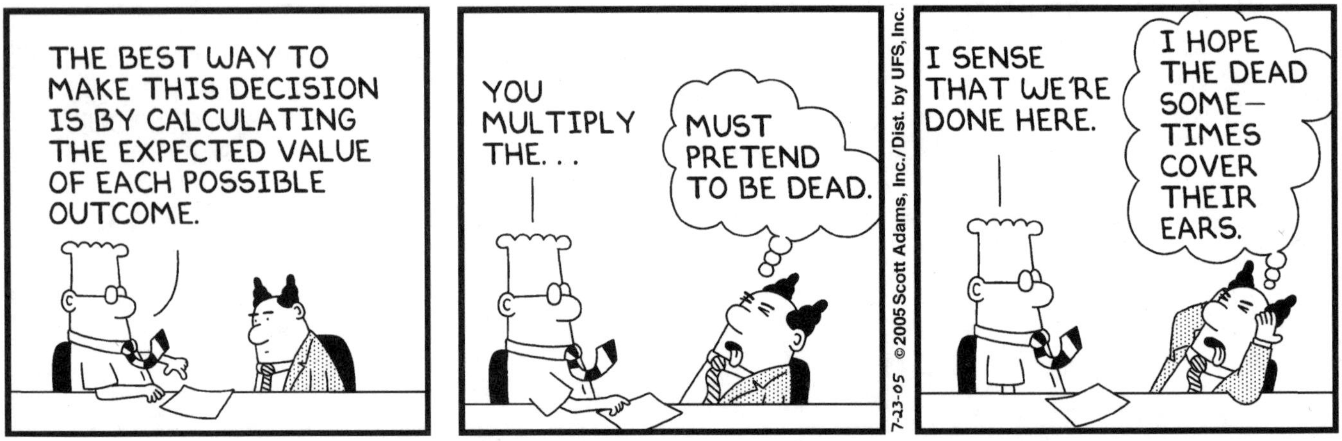
THE BEST WAY TO MAKE THIS DECISION IS BY CALCULATING THE EXPECTED VALUE OF EACH POSSIBLE OUTCOME.
YOU MULTIPLY THE...
MUST PRETEND TO BE DEAD.
7-23-05 ©2005 Scott Adams, Inc./Dist. by UFS, Inc.
I SENSE THAT WE'RE DONE HERE.
I HOPE THE DEAD SOME-TIMES COVER THEIR EARS.

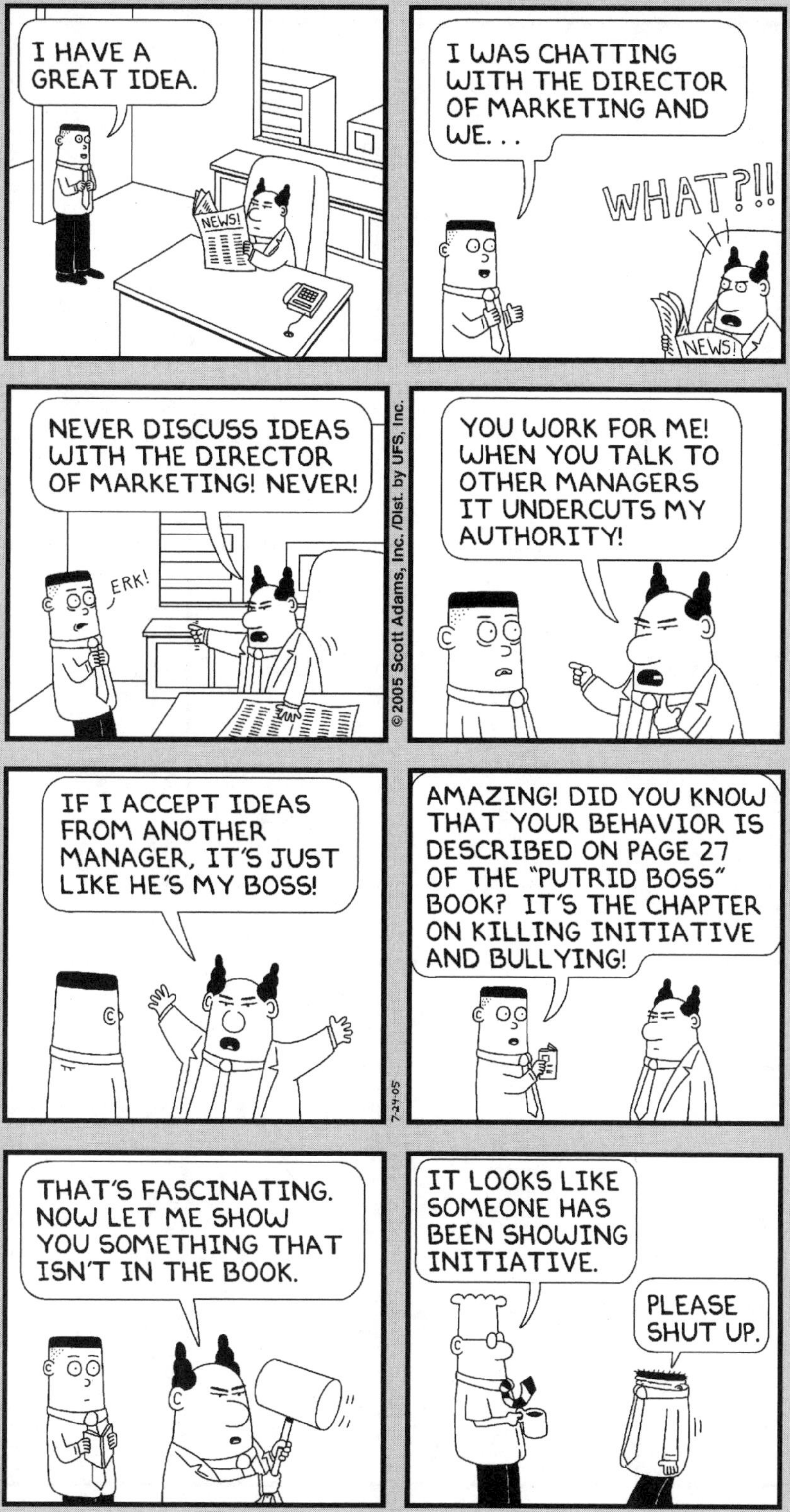
I HAVE A GREAT IDEA.
NEWS!
I WAS CHATTING WITH THE DIRECTOR OF MARKETING AND WE. . .
WHAT?!!
NEWS!
NEVER DISCUSS IDEAS WITH THE DIRECTOR OF MARKETING! NEVER!
ERK!
YOU WORK FOR ME! WHEN YOU TALK TO OTHER MANAGERS IT UNDERCUTS MY AUTHORITY!
IF I ACCEPT IDEAS FROM ANOTHER MANAGER, IT'S JUST LIKE HE'S MY BOSS!
AMAZING! DID YOU KNOW THAT YOUR BEHAVIOR IS DESCRIBED ON PAGE 27 OF THE "PUTRID BOSS" BOOK? IT'S THE CHAPTER ON KILLING INITIATIVE AND BULLYING!
THAT'S FASCINATING. NOW LET ME SHOW YOU SOMETHING THAT ISN'T IN THE BOOK.
IT LOOKS LIKE SOMEONE HAS BEEN SHOWING INITIATIVE.
PLEASE SHUT UP.
© 2005 Scott Adams, Inc./Dist. by UFS, Inc.
7-24-05

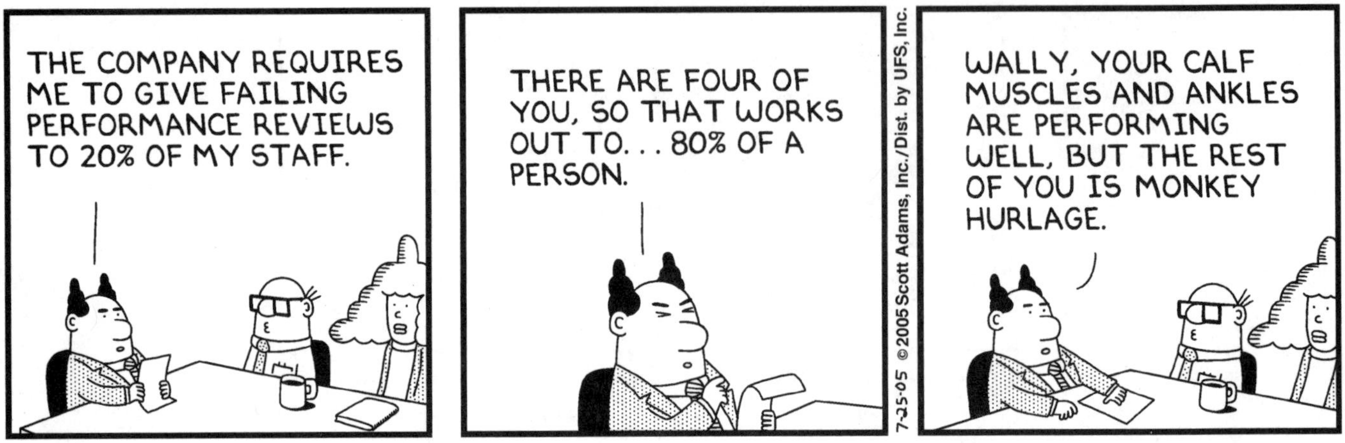
THE COMPANY REQUIRES ME TO GIVE FAILING PERFORMANCE REVIEWS TO 20% OF MY STAFF.
THERE ARE FOUR OF YOU, SO THAT WORKS OUT TO. . . 80% OF A PERSON.
7-25-05 © 2005 Scott Adams, Inc./Dist. by UFS, Inc.
WALLY, YOUR CALF MUSCLES AND ANKLES ARE PERFORMING WELL, BUT THE REST OF YOU IS MONKEY HURLAGE.

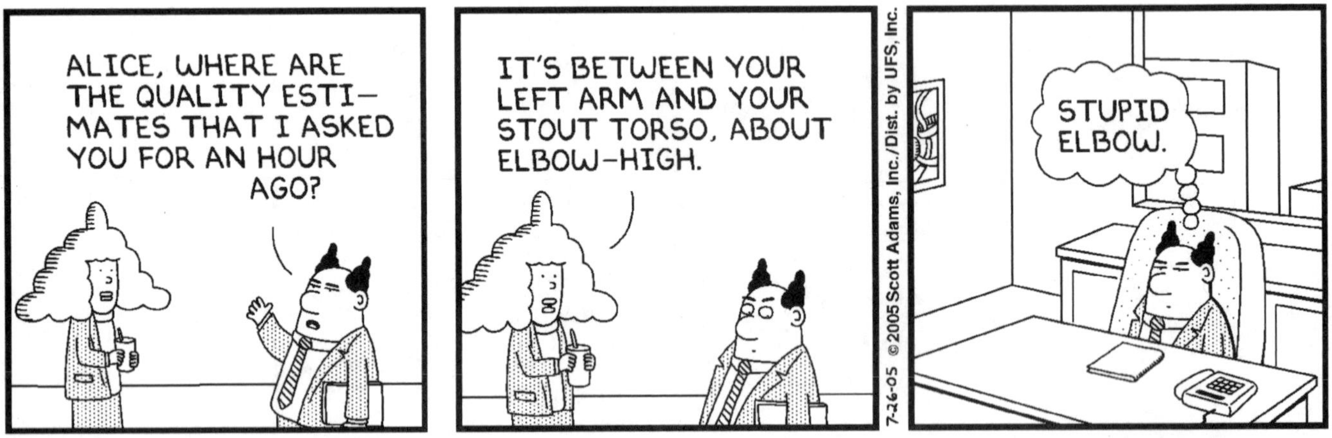
ALICE, WHERE ARE THE QUALITY ESTI–MATES THAT I ASKED YOU FOR AN HOUR AGO?
IT'S BETWEEN YOUR LEFT ARM AND YOUR STOUT TORSO, ABOUT ELBOW–HIGH.
7-26-05 © 2005 Scott Adams, Inc./Dist. by UFS, Inc.
STUPID ELBOW.

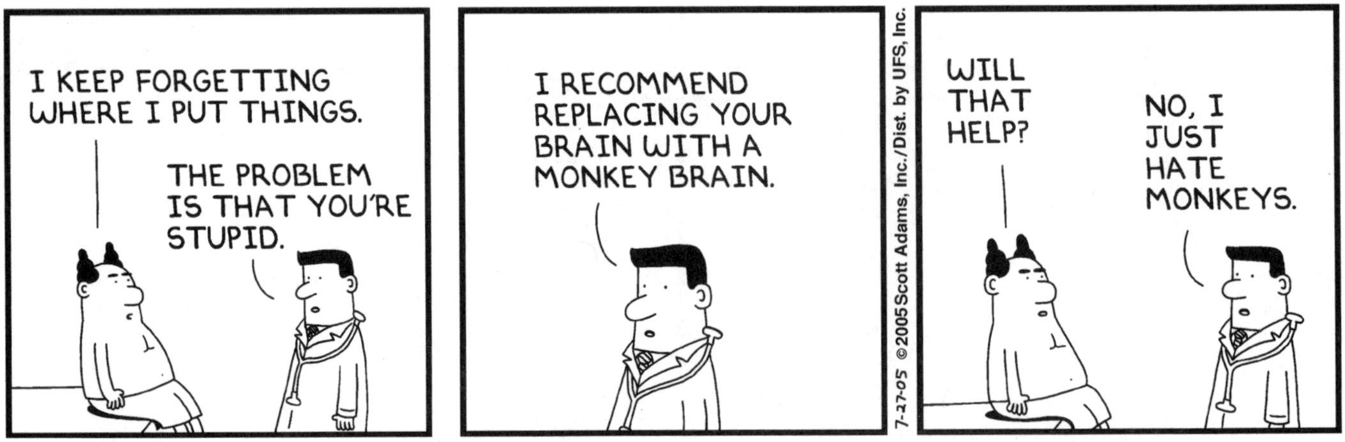
I KEEP FORGETTING WHERE I PUT THINGS.
THE PROBLEM IS THAT YOU'RE STUPID.
I RECOMMEND REPLACING YOUR BRAIN WITH A MONKEY BRAIN.
7-27-05 © 2005 Scott Adams, Inc./Dist. by UFS, Inc.
WILL THAT HELP?
NO, I JUST HATE MONKEYS.

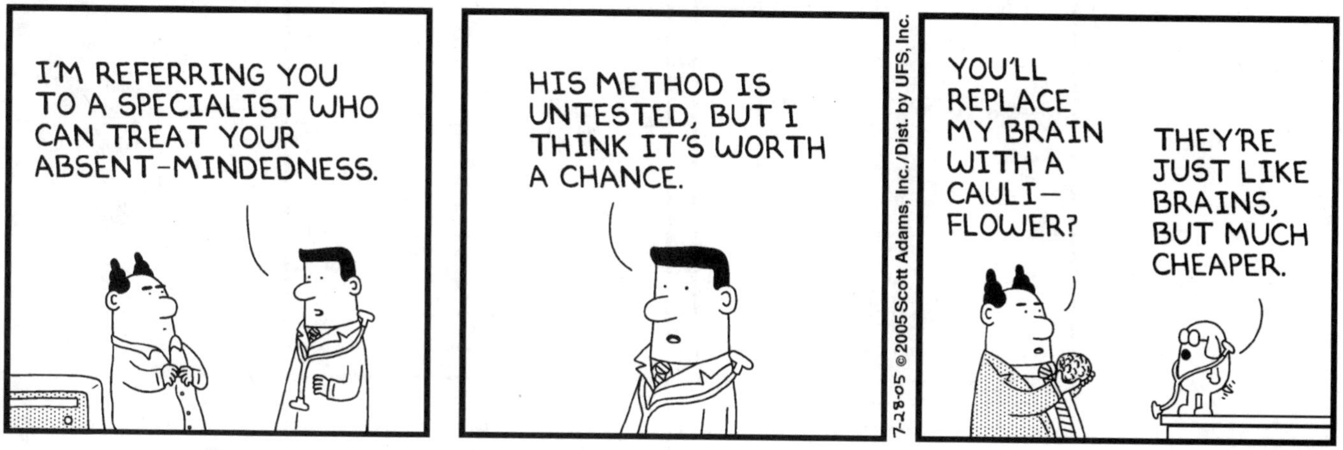
I'M REFERRING YOU TO A SPECIALIST WHO CAN TREAT YOUR ABSENT-MINDEDNESS.
HIS METHOD IS UNTESTED, BUT I THINK IT'S WORTH A CHANCE.
7-28-05 © 2005 Scott Adams, Inc./Dist. by UFS, Inc.
YOU'LL REPLACE MY BRAIN WITH A CAULI-FLOWER?
THEY'RE JUST LIKE BRAINS, BUT MUCH CHEAPER.

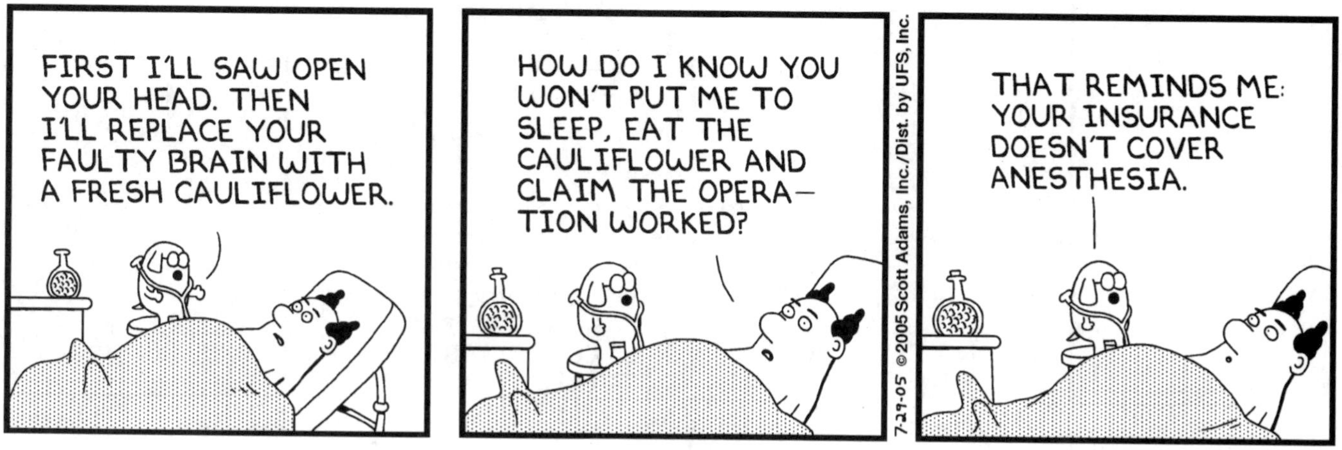
FIRST I'LL SAW OPEN YOUR HEAD. THEN I'LL REPLACE YOUR FAULTY BRAIN WITH A FRESH CAULIFLOWER.
HOW DO I KNOW YOU WON'T PUT ME TO SLEEP, EAT THE CAULIFLOWER AND CLAIM THE OPERA-TION WORKED?
7-29-05 © 2005 Scott Adams, Inc./Dist. by UFS, Inc.
THAT REMINDS ME: YOUR INSURANCE DOESN'T COVER ANESTHESIA.

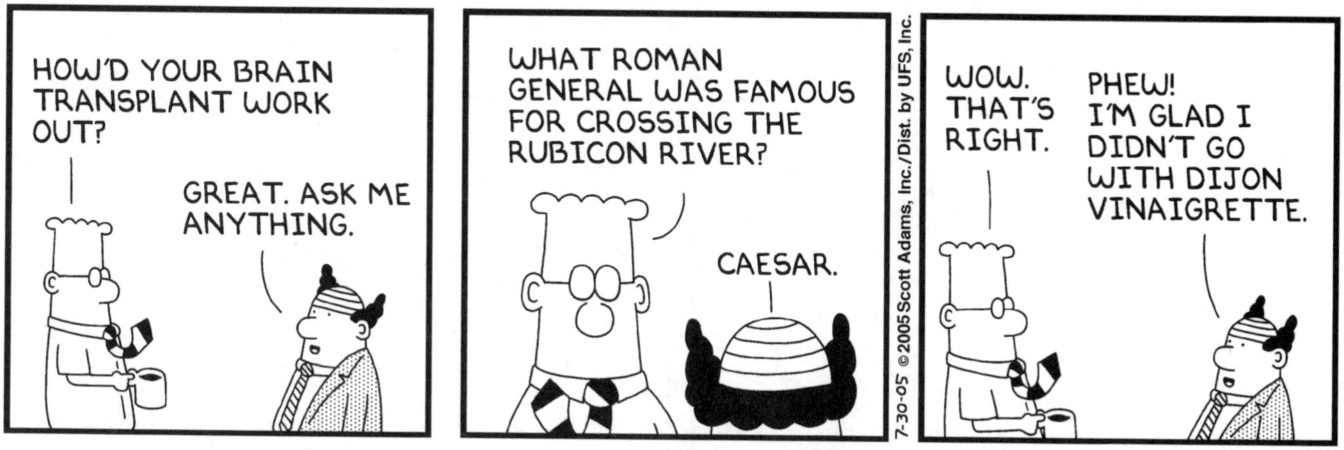
HOW'D YOUR BRAIN TRANSPLANT WORK OUT?
GREAT. ASK ME ANYTHING.
WHAT ROMAN GENERAL WAS FAMOUS FOR CROSSING THE RUBICON RIVER?
CAESAR.
7-30-05 © 2005 Scott Adams, Inc./Dist. by UFS, Inc.
WOW. THAT'S RIGHT.
PHEW! I'M GLAD I DIDN'T GO WITH DIJON VINAIGRETTE.

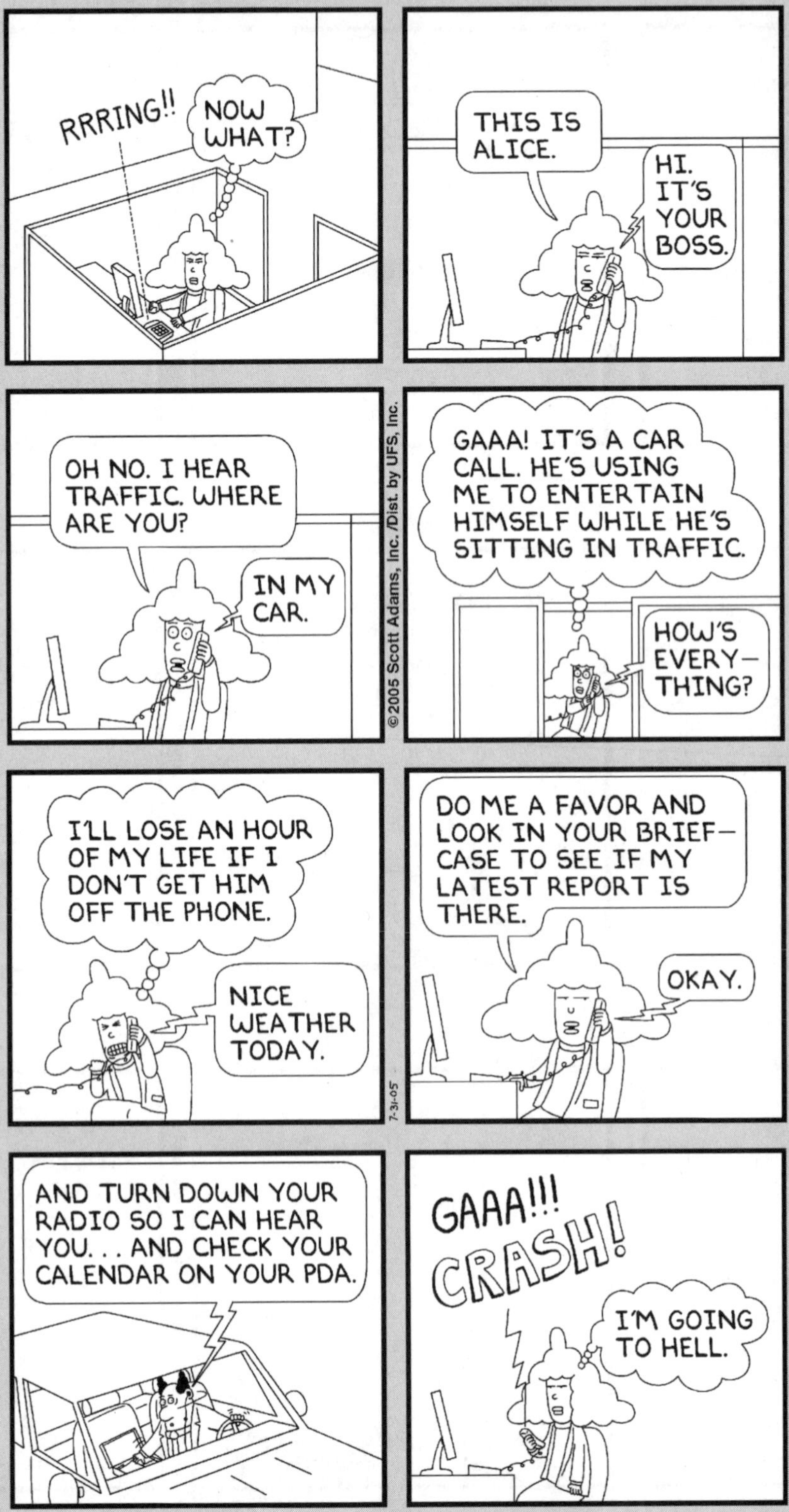
RRRING!!
NOW WHAT?
THIS IS ALICE.
HI. IT'S YOUR BOSS.
OH NO. I HEAR TRAFFIC. WHERE ARE YOU?
IN MY CAR.
GAAA! IT'S A CAR CALL. HE'S USING ME TO ENTERTAIN HIMSELF WHILE HE'S SITTING IN TRAFFIC.
HOW'S EVERY-THING?
I'LL LOSE AN HOUR OF MY LIFE IF I DON'T GET HIM OFF THE PHONE.
NICE WEATHER TODAY.
DO ME A FAVOR AND LOOK IN YOUR BRIEF-CASE TO SEE IF MY LATEST REPORT IS THERE.
OKAY.
AND TURN DOWN YOUR RADIO SO I CAN HEAR YOU. . . AND CHECK YOUR CALENDAR ON YOUR PDA.
GAAA!!!
CRASH!
I'M GOING TO HELL.
©2005 Scott Adams, Inc./Dist. by UFS, Inc.
7-31-05

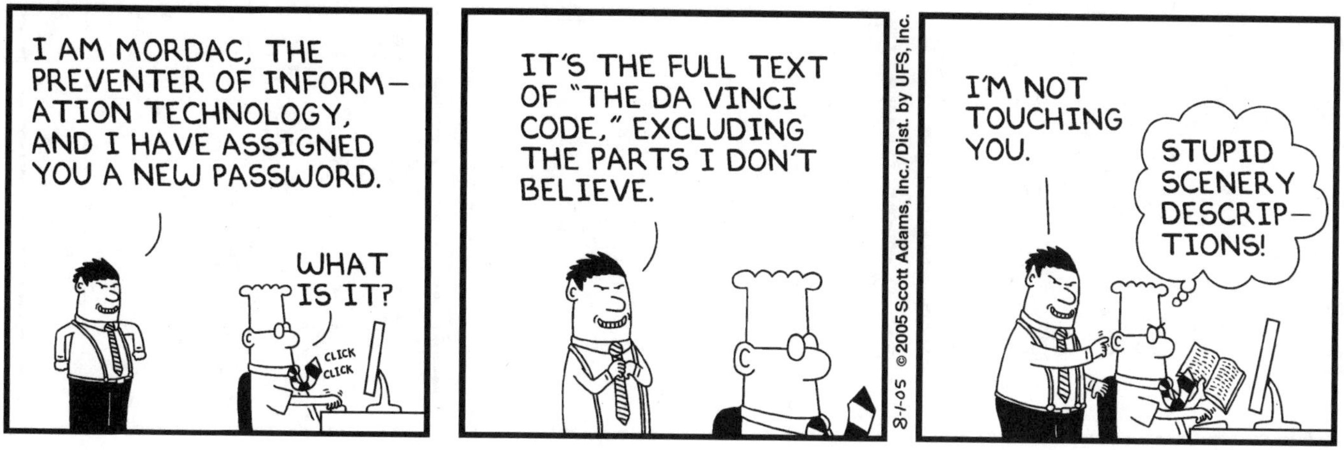
I AM MORDAC, THE PREVENTER OF INFORMATION TECHNOLOGY, AND I HAVE ASSIGNED YOU A NEW PASSWORD.
WHAT IS IT?
CLICK CLICK
IT'S THE FULL TEXT OF "THE DA VINCI CODE," EXCLUDING THE PARTS I DON'T BELIEVE.
8-1-05 © 2005 Scott Adams, Inc./Dist. by UFS, Inc.
I'M NOT TOUCHING YOU.
STUPID SCENERY DESCRIPTIONS!

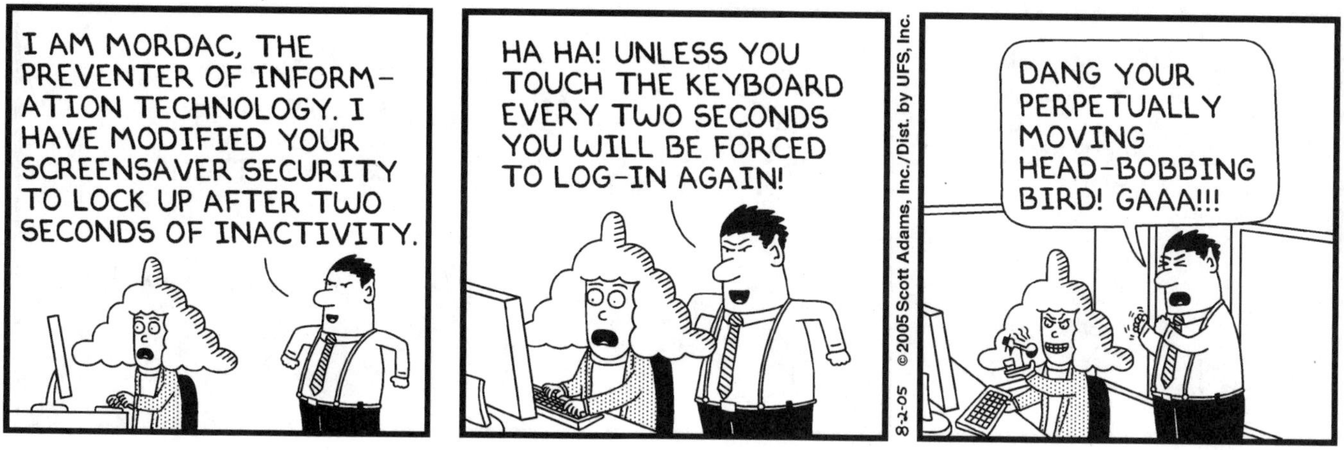
I AM MORDAC, THE PREVENTER OF INFORMATION TECHNOLOGY. I HAVE MODIFIED YOUR SCREENSAVER SECURITY TO LOCK UP AFTER TWO SECONDS OF INACTIVITY.
HA HA! UNLESS YOU TOUCH THE KEYBOARD EVERY TWO SECONDS YOU WILL BE FORCED TO LOG-IN AGAIN!
8-2-05 © 2005 Scott Adams, Inc./Dist. by UFS, Inc.
DANG YOUR PERPETUALLY MOVING HEAD-BOBBING BIRD! GAAA!!!

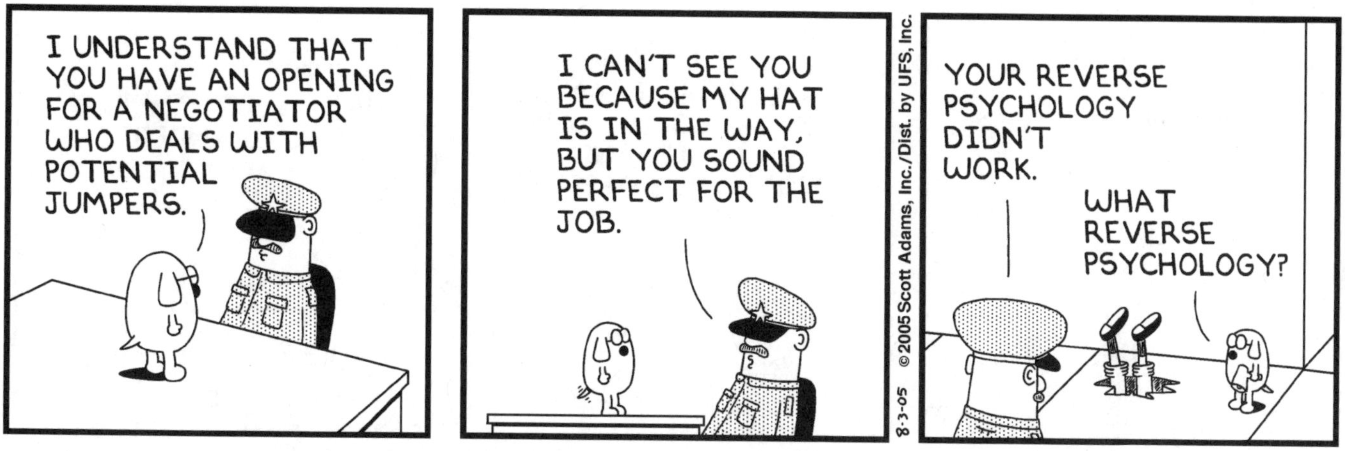
I UNDERSTAND THAT YOU HAVE AN OPENING FOR A NEGOTIATOR WHO DEALS WITH POTENTIAL JUMPERS.
I CAN'T SEE YOU BECAUSE MY HAT IS IN THE WAY, BUT YOU SOUND PERFECT FOR THE JOB.
8-3-05 © 2005 Scott Adams, Inc./Dist. by UFS, Inc.
YOUR REVERSE PSYCHOLOGY DIDN'T WORK.
WHAT REVERSE PSYCHOLOGY?

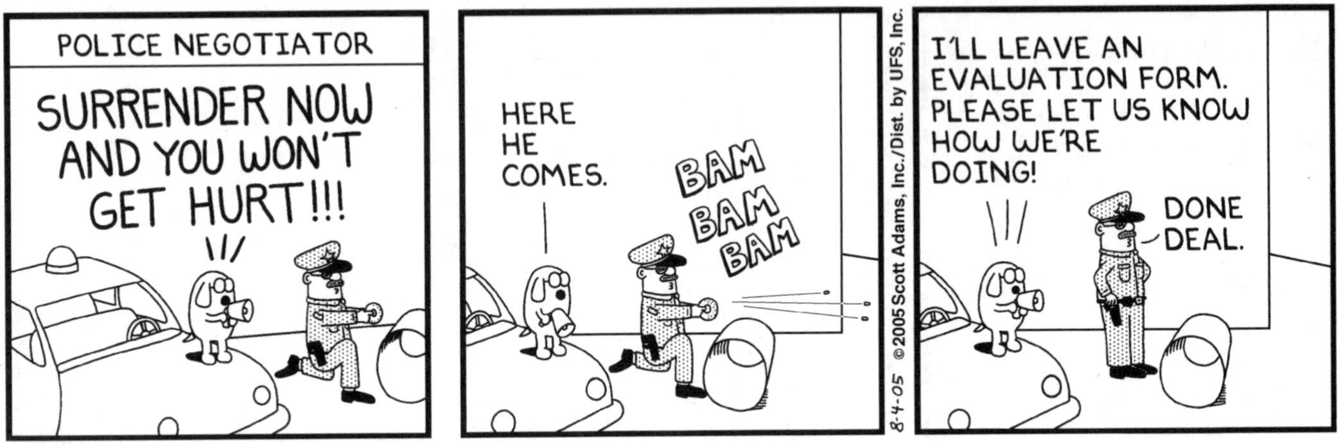
POLICE NEGOTIATOR
SURRENDER NOW AND YOU WON'T GET HURT!!!
HERE HE COMES.
BAM BAM BAM
I'LL LEAVE AN EVALUATION FORM. PLEASE LET US KNOW HOW WE'RE DOING!
DONE DEAL.
8-4-05 ©2005 Scott Adams, Inc./Dist. by UFS, Inc.

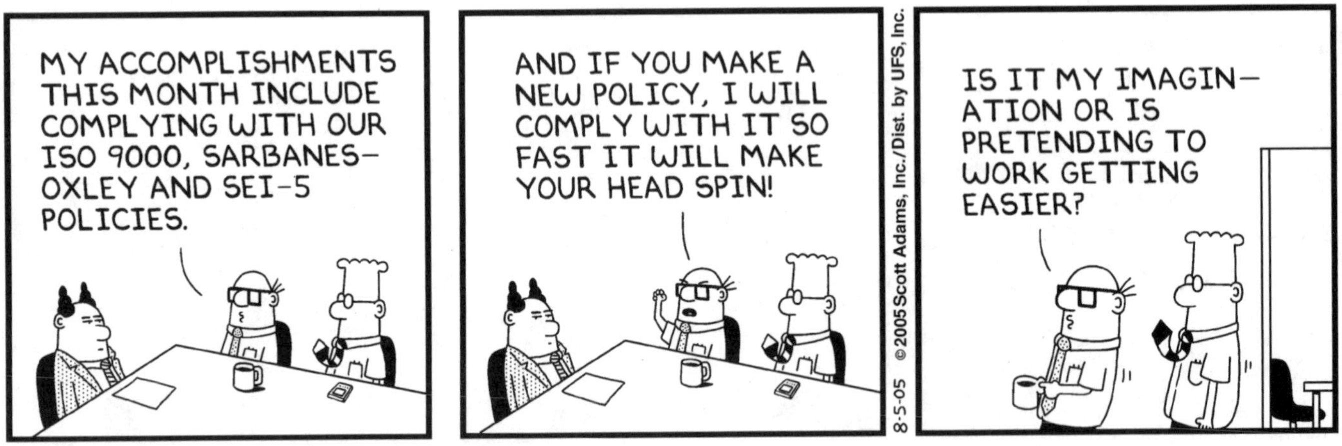
MY ACCOMPLISHMENTS THIS MONTH INCLUDE COMPLYING WITH OUR ISO 9000, SARBANES-OXLEY AND SEI-5 POLICIES.
AND IF YOU MAKE A NEW POLICY, I WILL COMPLY WITH IT SO FAST IT WILL MAKE YOUR HEAD SPIN!
IS IT MY IMAGIN-ATION OR IS PRETENDING TO WORK GETTING EASIER?
8-5-05 ©2005 Scott Adams, Inc./Dist. by UFS, Inc.

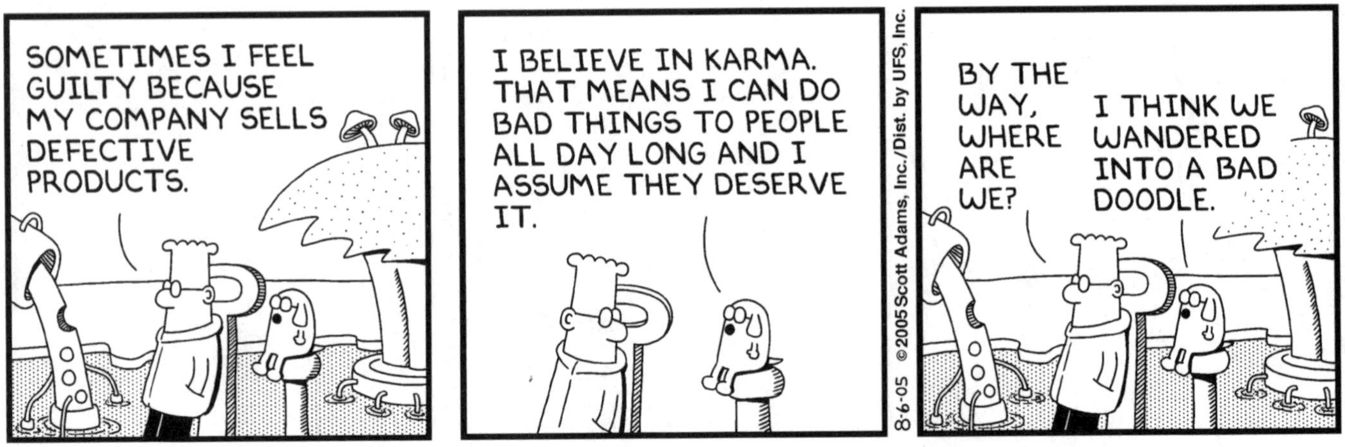
SOMETIMES I FEEL GUILTY BECAUSE MY COMPANY SELLS DEFECTIVE PRODUCTS.
I BELIEVE IN KARMA. THAT MEANS I CAN DO BAD THINGS TO PEOPLE ALL DAY LONG AND I ASSUME THEY DESERVE IT.
BY THE WAY, WHERE ARE WE?
I THINK WE WANDERED INTO A BAD DOODLE.
8-6-05 ©2005 Scott Adams, Inc./Dist. by UFS, Inc.

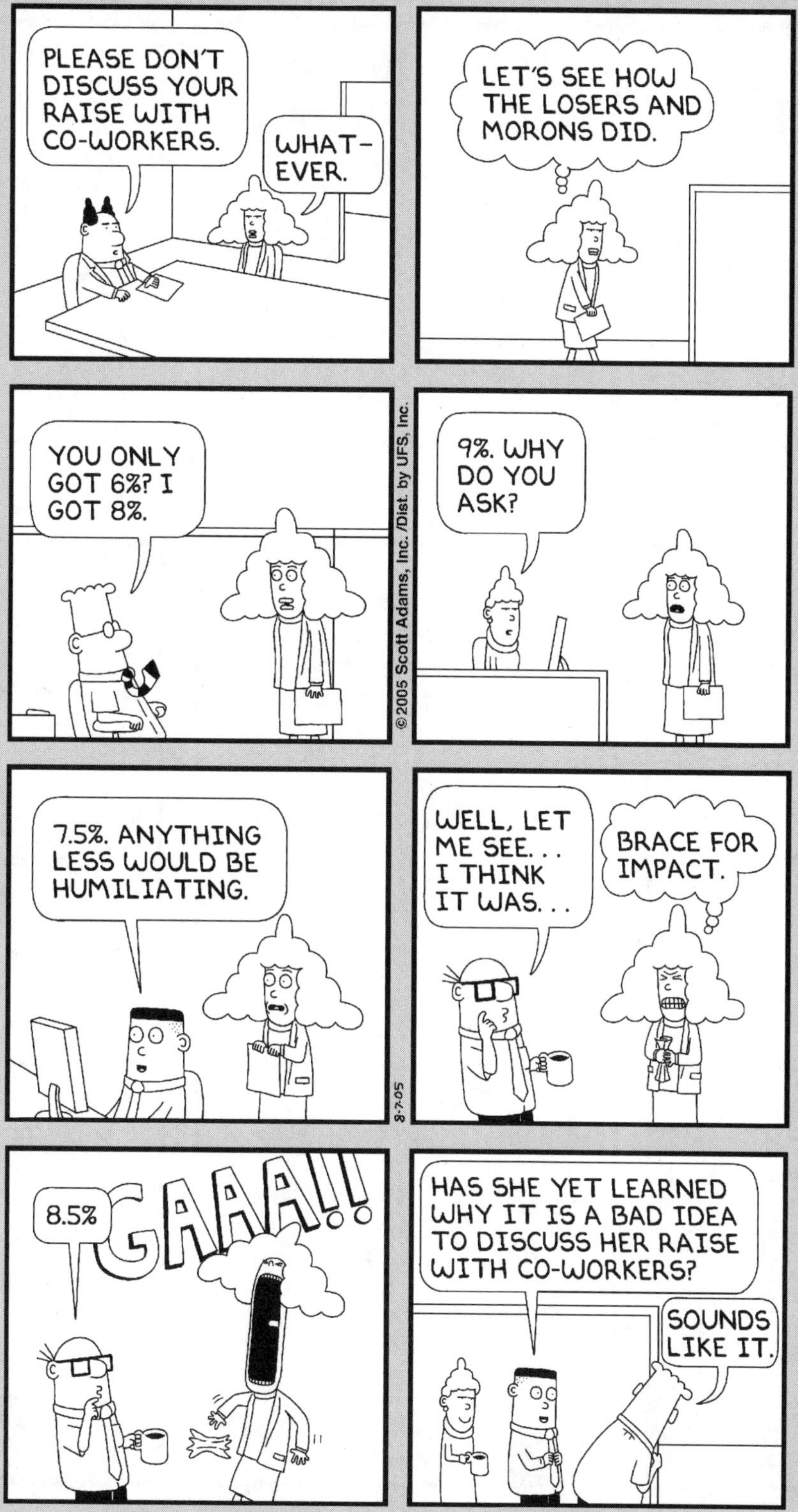
PLEASE DON'T DISCUSS YOUR RAISE WITH CO-WORKERS.
WHAT-EVER.
LET'S SEE HOW THE LOSERS AND MORONS DID.
YOU ONLY GOT 6%? I GOT 8%.
9%. WHY DO YOU ASK?
7.5%. ANYTHING LESS WOULD BE HUMILIATING.
WELL, LET ME SEE... I THINK IT WAS...
BRACE FOR IMPACT.
8.5%
GAAA!!
HAS SHE YET LEARNED WHY IT IS A BAD IDEA TO DISCUSS HER RAISE WITH CO-WORKERS?
SOUNDS LIKE IT.
©2005 Scott Adams, Inc. /Dist. by UFS, Inc.
8-7-05

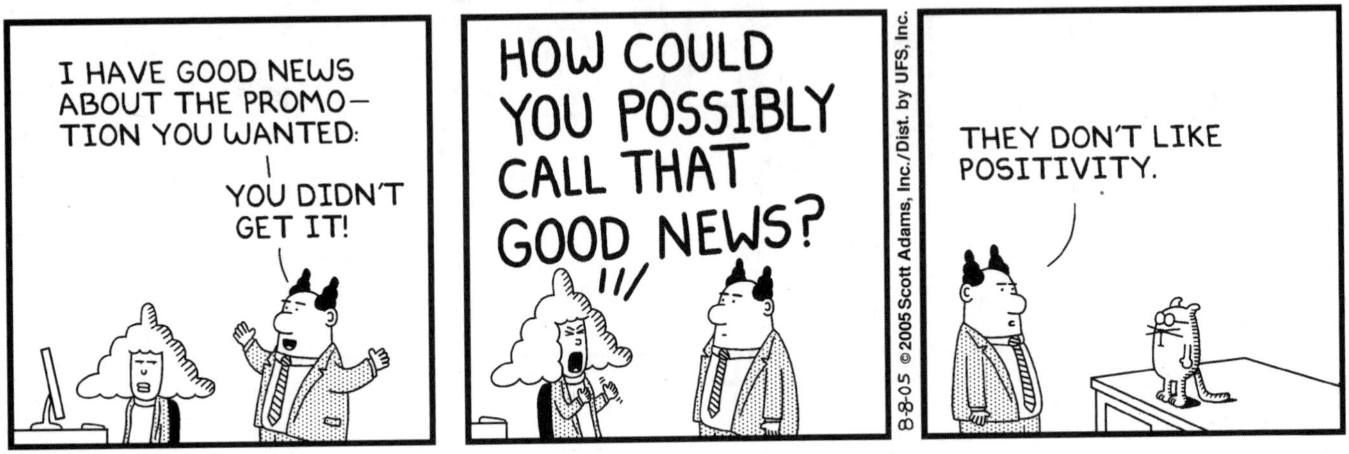
I HAVE GOOD NEWS ABOUT THE PROMOTION YOU WANTED:
YOU DIDN'T GET IT!
HOW COULD YOU POSSIBLY CALL THAT GOOD NEWS?
8-8-05 ©2005 Scott Adams, Inc./Dist. by UFS, Inc.
THEY DON'T LIKE POSITIVITY.

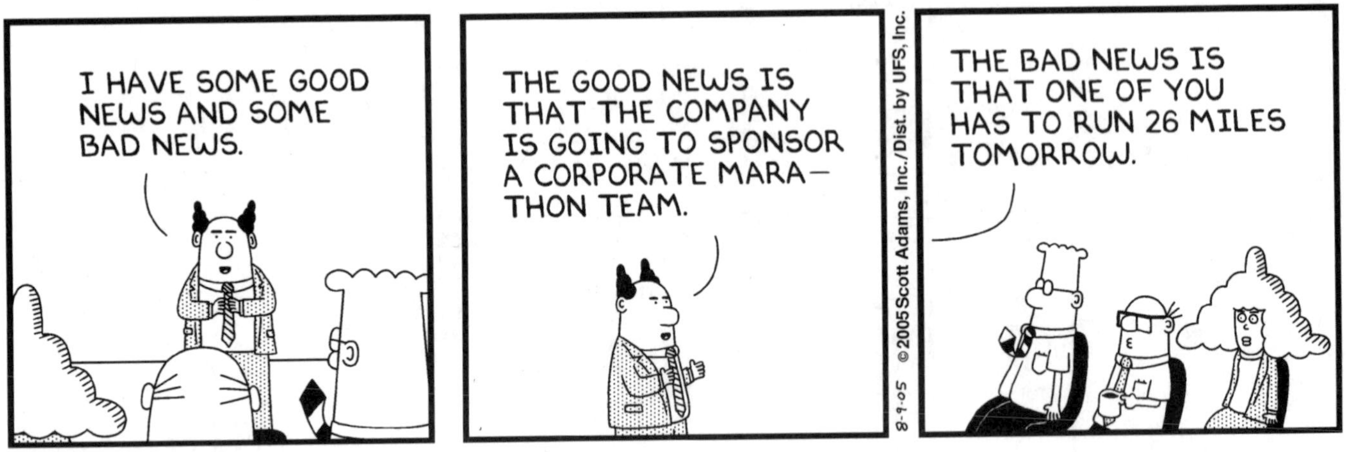
I HAVE SOME GOOD NEWS AND SOME BAD NEWS.
THE GOOD NEWS IS THAT THE COMPANY IS GOING TO SPONSOR A CORPORATE MARATHON TEAM.
8-9-05 ©2005 Scott Adams, Inc./Dist. by UFS, Inc.
THE BAD NEWS IS THAT ONE OF YOU HAS TO RUN 26 MILES TOMORROW.

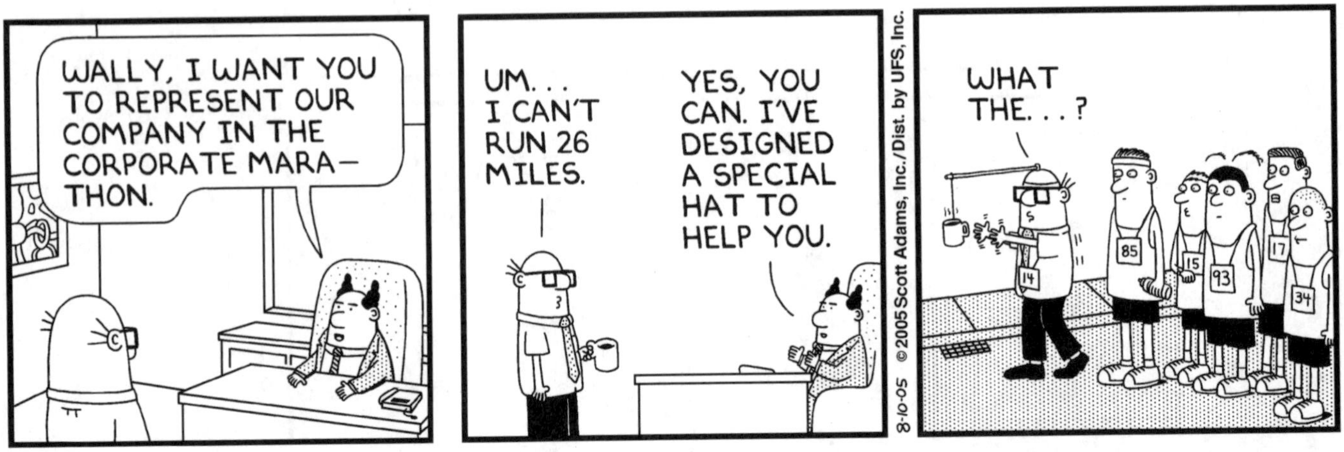
WALLY, I WANT YOU TO REPRESENT OUR COMPANY IN THE CORPORATE MARATHON.
UM... I CAN'T RUN 26 MILES.
YES, YOU CAN. I'VE DESIGNED A SPECIAL HAT TO HELP YOU.
8-10-05 ©2005 Scott Adams, Inc./Dist. by UFS, Inc.
WHAT THE...?
14
85
15
93
17
34

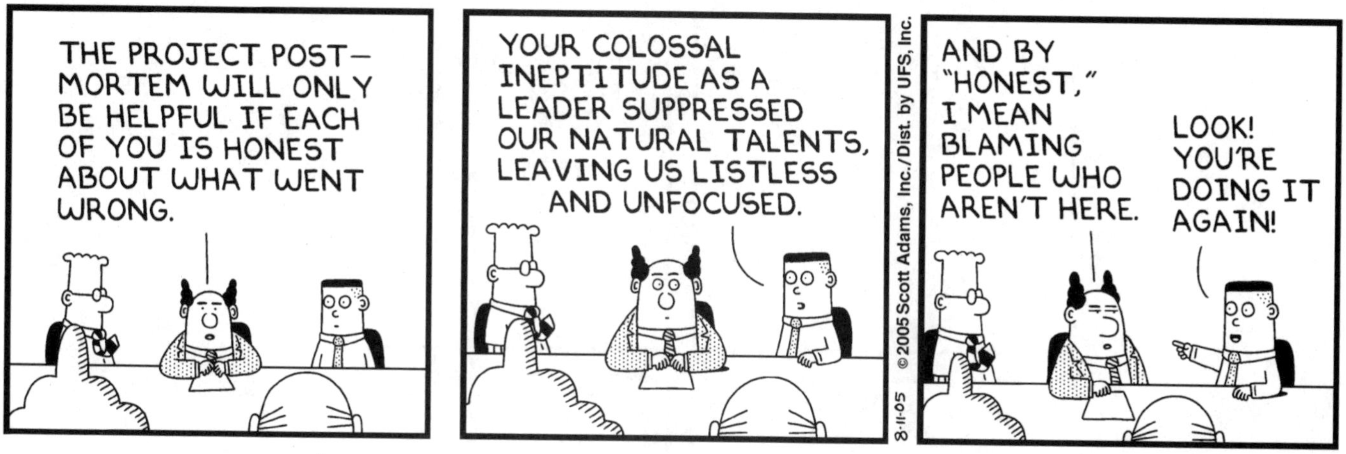
THE PROJECT POST-MORTEM WILL ONLY BE HELPFUL IF EACH OF YOU IS HONEST ABOUT WHAT WENT WRONG.
YOUR COLOSSAL INEPTITUDE AS A LEADER SUPPRESSED OUR NATURAL TALENTS, LEAVING US LISTLESS AND UNFOCUSED.
8-11-05 © 2005 Scott Adams, Inc./Dist. by UFS, Inc.
AND BY "HONEST," I MEAN BLAMING PEOPLE WHO AREN'T HERE.
LOOK! YOU'RE DOING IT AGAIN!

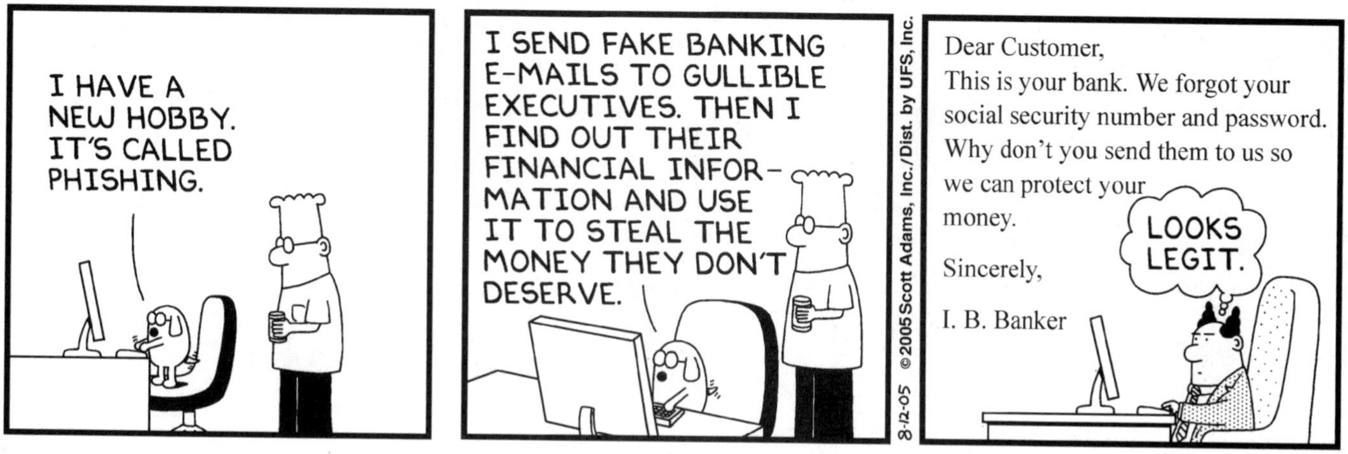
I HAVE A NEW HOBBY. IT'S CALLED PHISHING.
I SEND FAKE BANKING E-MAILS TO GULLIBLE EXECUTIVES. THEN I FIND OUT THEIR FINANCIAL INFORMATION AND USE IT TO STEAL THE MONEY THEY DON'T DESERVE.
8-12-05 © 2005 Scott Adams, Inc./Dist. by UFS, Inc.
Dear Customer,
This is your bank. We forgot your social security number and password. Why don't you send them to us so we can protect your money.
Sincerely,
I. B. Banker
LOOKS LEGIT.

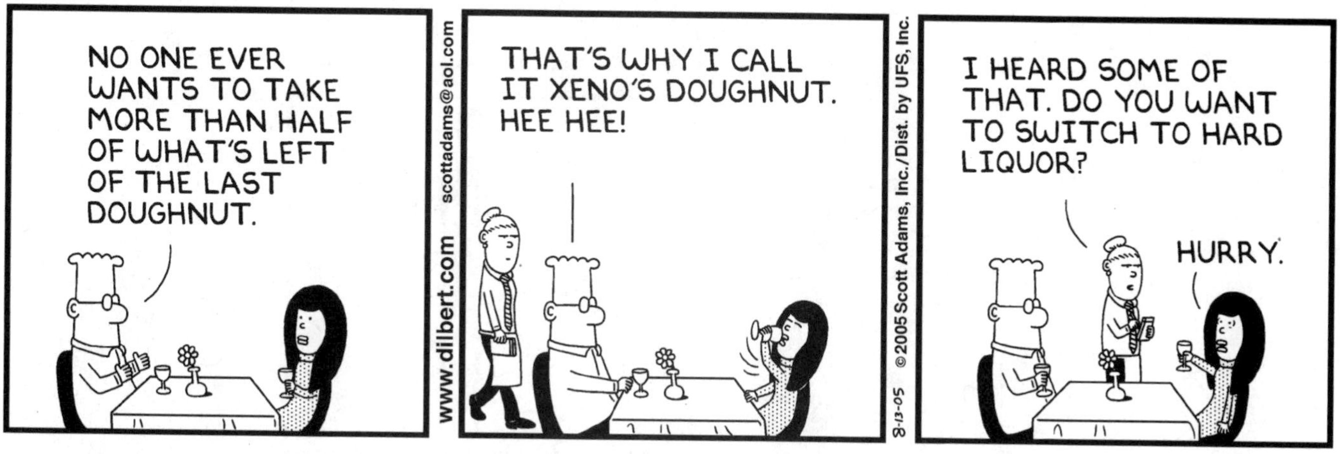
NO ONE EVER WANTS TO TAKE MORE THAN HALF OF WHAT'S LEFT OF THE LAST DOUGHNUT.
www.dilbert.com scottadams@aol.com
THAT'S WHY I CALL IT XENO'S DOUGHNUT. HEE HEE!
8-13-05 © 2005 Scott Adams, Inc./Dist. by UFS, Inc.
I HEARD SOME OF THAT. DO YOU WANT TO SWITCH TO HARD LIQUOR?
HURRY.

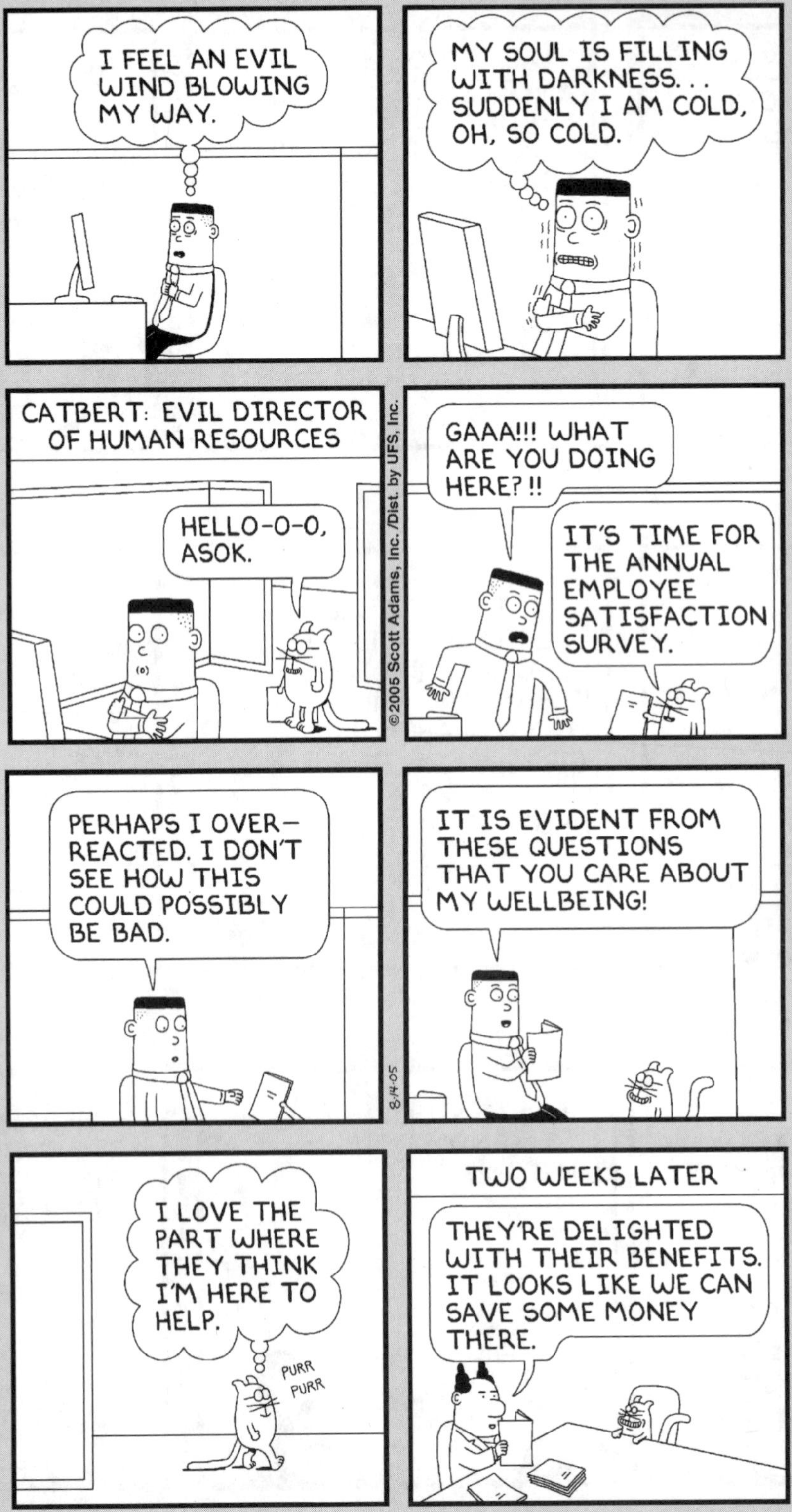
I FEEL AN EVIL WIND BLOWING MY WAY.
MY SOUL IS FILLING WITH DARKNESS. . . SUDDENLY I AM COLD, OH, SO COLD.
CATBERT: EVIL DIRECTOR OF HUMAN RESOURCES
HELLO-O-O, ASOK.
© 2005 Scott Adams, Inc./Dist. by UFS, Inc.
GAAA!!! WHAT ARE YOU DOING HERE? !!
IT'S TIME FOR THE ANNUAL EMPLOYEE SATISFACTION SURVEY.
PERHAPS I OVER-REACTED. I DON'T SEE HOW THIS COULD POSSIBLY BE BAD.
8-14-05
IT IS EVIDENT FROM THESE QUESTIONS THAT YOU CARE ABOUT MY WELLBEING!
I LOVE THE PART WHERE THEY THINK I'M HERE TO HELP.
PURR PURR
TWO WEEKS LATER
THEY'RE DELIGHTED WITH THEIR BENEFITS. IT LOOKS LIKE WE CAN SAVE SOME MONEY THERE.

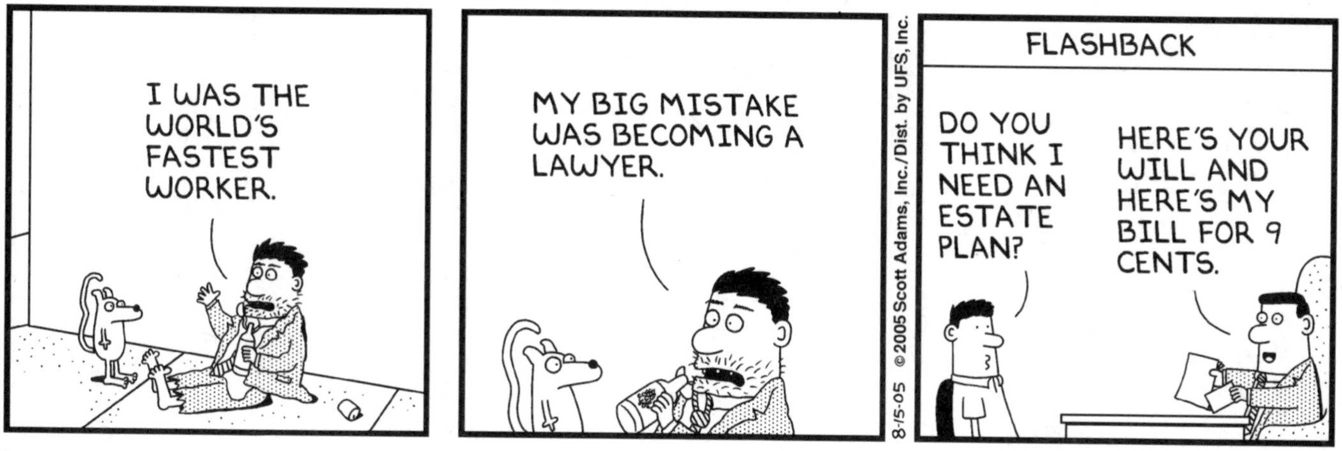
I WAS THE WORLD'S FASTEST WORKER.
MY BIG MISTAKE WAS BECOMING A LAWYER.
8-15-05 © 2005 Scott Adams, Inc./Dist. by UFS, Inc.
FLASHBACK
DO YOU THINK I NEED AN ESTATE PLAN?
HERE'S YOUR WILL AND HERE'S MY BILL FOR 9 CENTS.

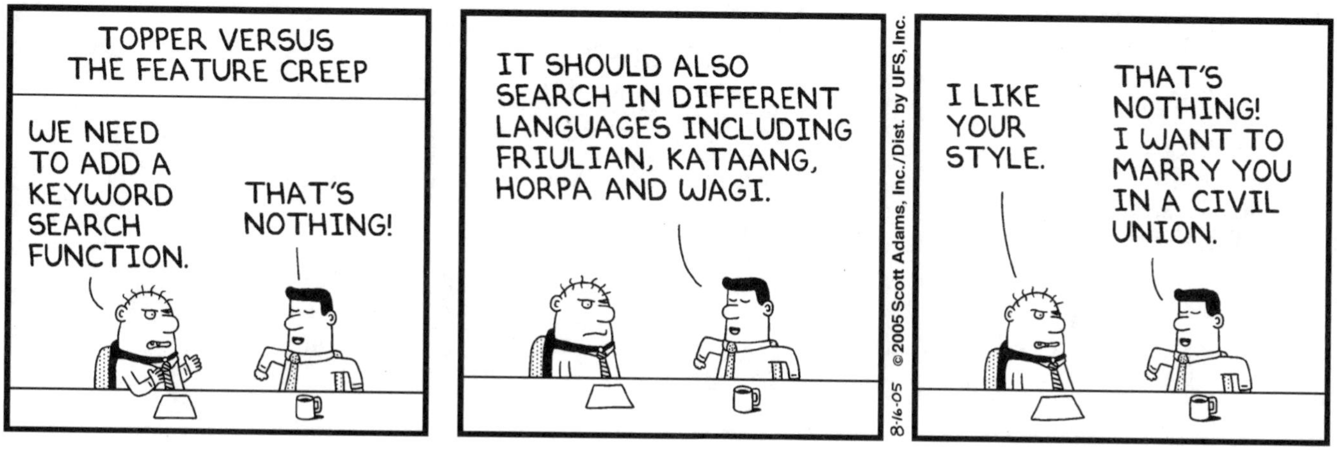
TOPPER VERSUS THE FEATURE CREEP
WE NEED TO ADD A KEYWORD SEARCH FUNCTION.
THAT'S NOTHING!
IT SHOULD ALSO SEARCH IN DIFFERENT LANGUAGES INCLUDING FRIULIAN, KATAANG, HORPA AND WAGI.
8-16-05 © 2005 Scott Adams, Inc./Dist. by UFS, Inc.
I LIKE YOUR STYLE.
THAT'S NOTHING! I WANT TO MARRY YOU IN A CIVIL UNION.

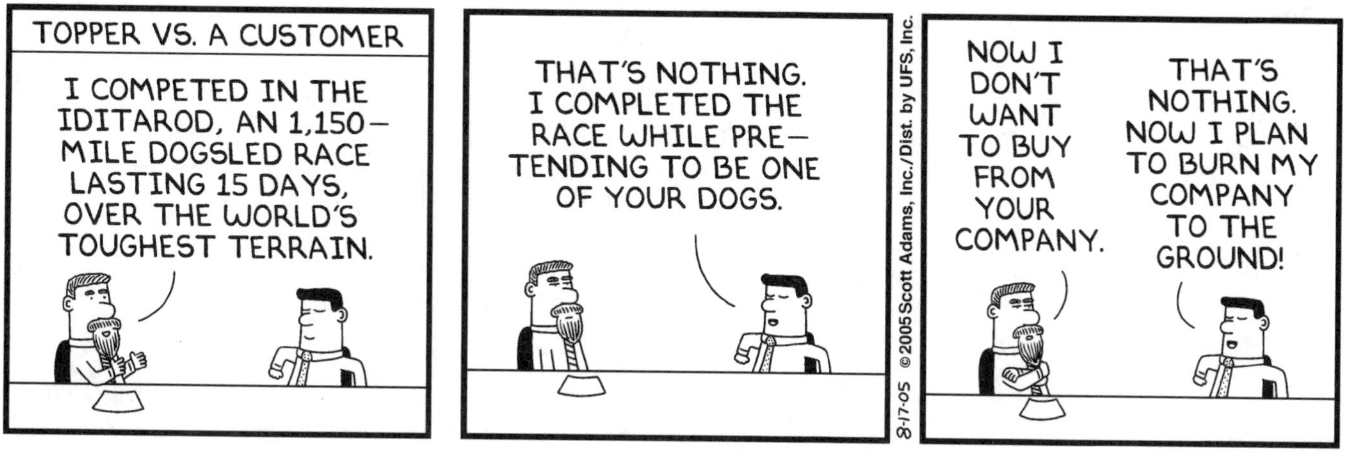
TOPPER VS. A CUSTOMER
I COMPETED IN THE IDITAROD, AN 1,150-MILE DOGSLED RACE LASTING 15 DAYS, OVER THE WORLD'S TOUGHEST TERRAIN.
THAT'S NOTHING. I COMPLETED THE RACE WHILE PRETENDING TO BE ONE OF YOUR DOGS.
8-17-05 © 2005 Scott Adams, Inc./Dist. by UFS, Inc.
NOW I DON'T WANT TO BUY FROM YOUR COMPANY.
THAT'S NOTHING. NOW I PLAN TO BURN MY COMPANY TO THE GROUND!

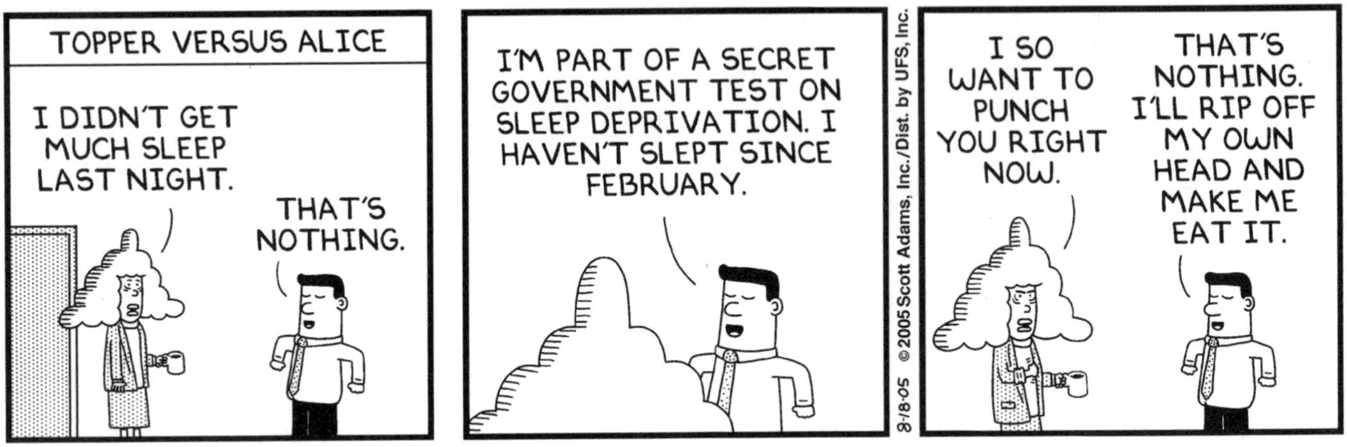
TOPPER VERSUS ALICE
I DIDN'T GET MUCH SLEEP LAST NIGHT.
THAT'S NOTHING.
I'M PART OF A SECRET GOVERNMENT TEST ON SLEEP DEPRIVATION. I HAVEN'T SLEPT SINCE FEBRUARY.
8-18-05 © 2005 Scott Adams, Inc./Dist. by UFS, Inc.
I SO WANT TO PUNCH YOU RIGHT NOW.
THAT'S NOTHING. I'LL RIP OFF MY OWN HEAD AND MAKE ME EAT IT.

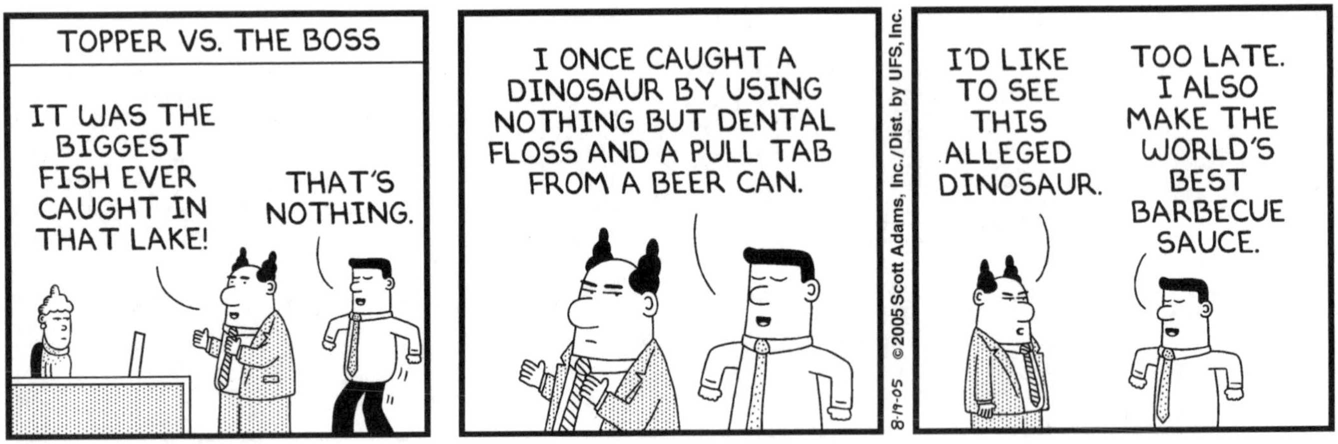
TOPPER VS. THE BOSS
IT WAS THE BIGGEST FISH EVER CAUGHT IN THAT LAKE!
THAT'S NOTHING.
I ONCE CAUGHT A DINOSAUR BY USING NOTHING BUT DENTAL FLOSS AND A PULL TAB FROM A BEER CAN.
8-19-05 © 2005 Scott Adams, Inc./Dist. by UFS, Inc.
I'D LIKE TO SEE THIS ALLEGED DINOSAUR.
TOO LATE. I ALSO MAKE THE WORLD'S BEST BARBECUE SAUCE.

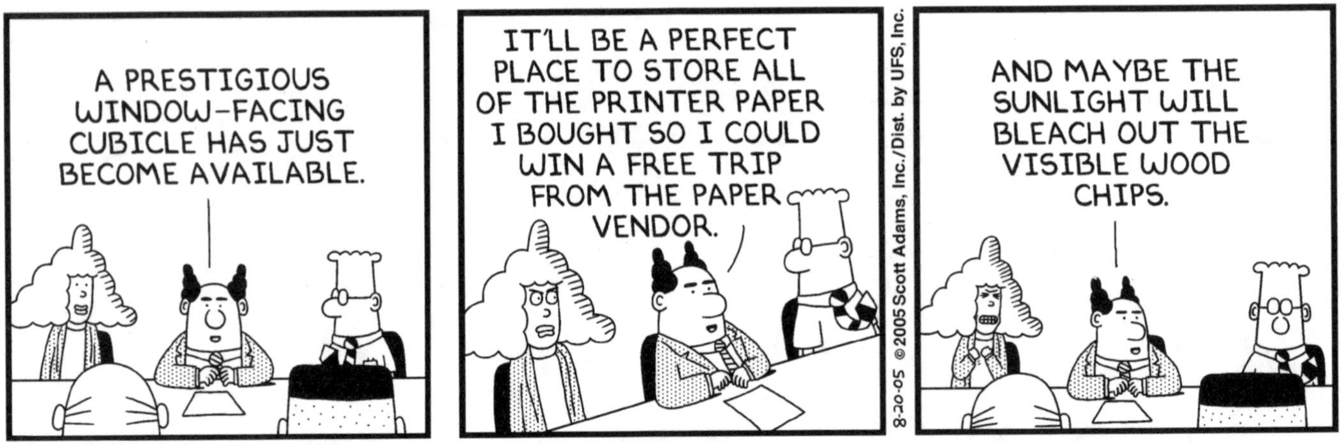
A PRESTIGIOUS WINDOW-FACING CUBICLE HAS JUST BECOME AVAILABLE.
IT'LL BE A PERFECT PLACE TO STORE ALL OF THE PRINTER PAPER I BOUGHT SO I COULD WIN A FREE TRIP FROM THE PAPER VENDOR.
8-20-05 © 2005 Scott Adams, Inc./Dist. by UFS, Inc.
AND MAYBE THE SUNLIGHT WILL BLEACH OUT THE VISIBLE WOOD CHIPS.

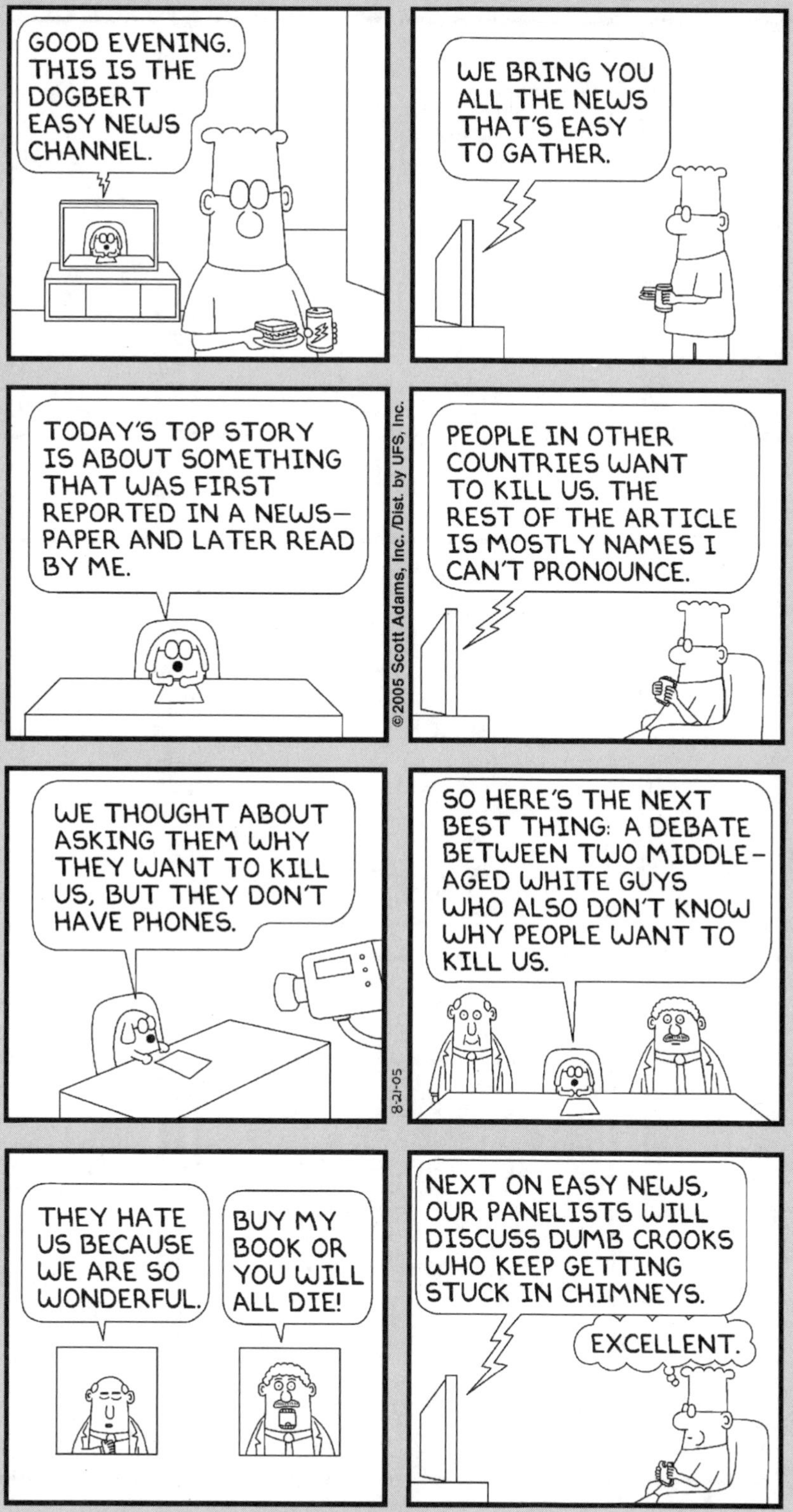
GOOD EVENING. THIS IS THE DOGBERT EASY NEWS CHANNEL.
WE BRING YOU ALL THE NEWS THAT'S EASY TO GATHER.
TODAY'S TOP STORY IS ABOUT SOMETHING THAT WAS FIRST REPORTED IN A NEWS-PAPER AND LATER READ BY ME.
PEOPLE IN OTHER COUNTRIES WANT TO KILL US. THE REST OF THE ARTICLE IS MOSTLY NAMES I CAN'T PRONOUNCE.
©2005 Scott Adams, Inc./Dist. by UFS, Inc.
WE THOUGHT ABOUT ASKING THEM WHY THEY WANT TO KILL US, BUT THEY DON'T HAVE PHONES.
SO HERE'S THE NEXT BEST THING: A DEBATE BETWEEN TWO MIDDLE-AGED WHITE GUYS WHO ALSO DON'T KNOW WHY PEOPLE WANT TO KILL US.
8-21-05
THEY HATE US BECAUSE WE ARE SO WONDERFUL.
BUY MY BOOK OR YOU WILL ALL DIE!
NEXT ON EASY NEWS, OUR PANELISTS WILL DISCUSS DUMB CROOKS WHO KEEP GETTING STUCK IN CHIMNEYS.
EXCELLENT.

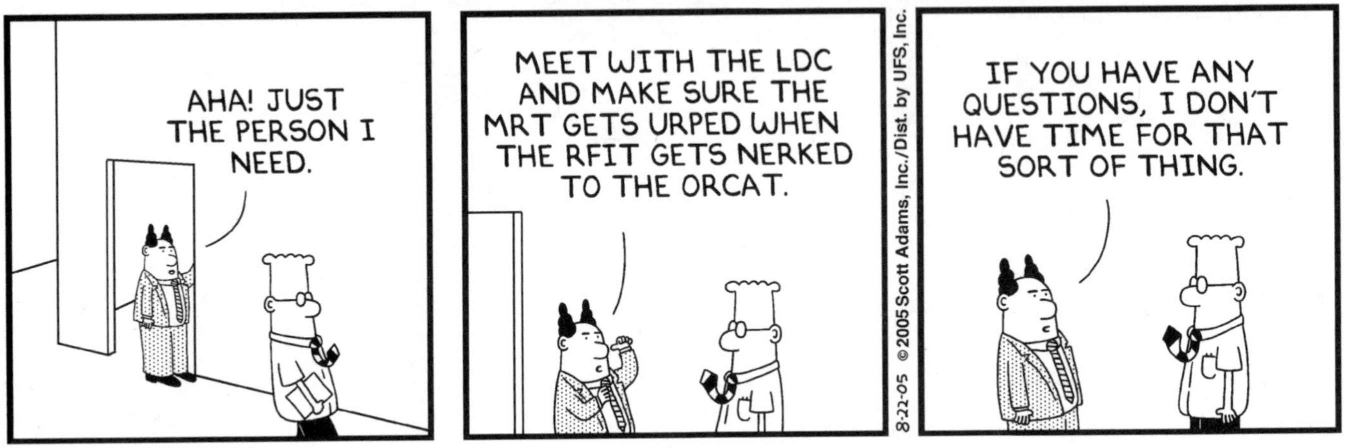
AHA! JUST THE PERSON I NEED.
MEET WITH THE LDC AND MAKE SURE THE MRT GETS URPED WHEN THE RFIT GETS NERKED TO THE ORCAT.
8-22-05 ©2005 Scott Adams, Inc./Dist. by UFS, Inc.
IF YOU HAVE ANY QUESTIONS, I DON'T HAVE TIME FOR THAT SORT OF THING.

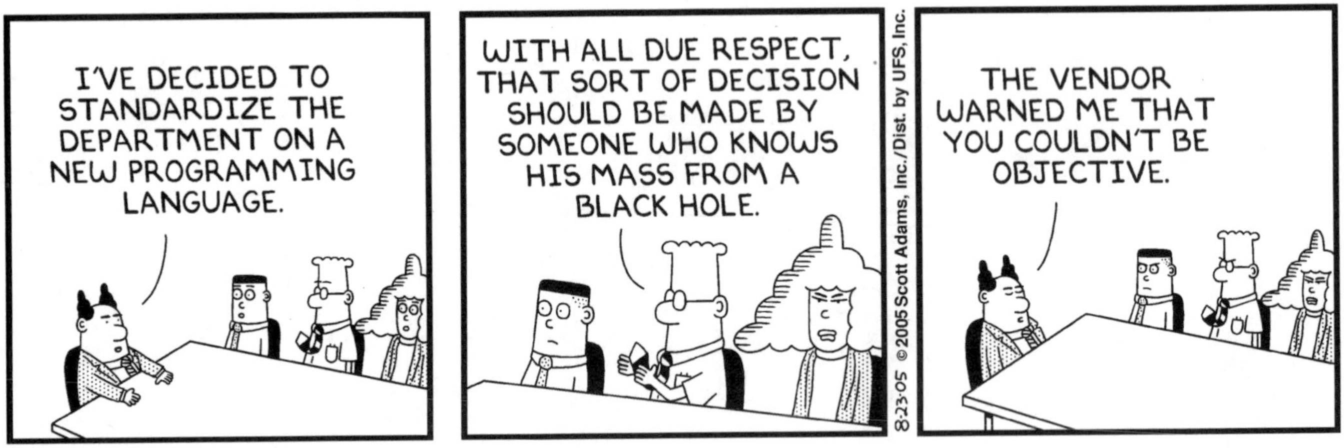
I'VE DECIDED TO STANDARDIZE THE DEPARTMENT ON A NEW PROGRAMMING LANGUAGE.
WITH ALL DUE RESPECT, THAT SORT OF DECISION SHOULD BE MADE BY SOMEONE WHO KNOWS HIS MASS FROM A BLACK HOLE.
8-23-05 ©2005 Scott Adams, Inc./Dist. by UFS, Inc.
THE VENDOR WARNED ME THAT YOU COULDN'T BE OBJECTIVE.

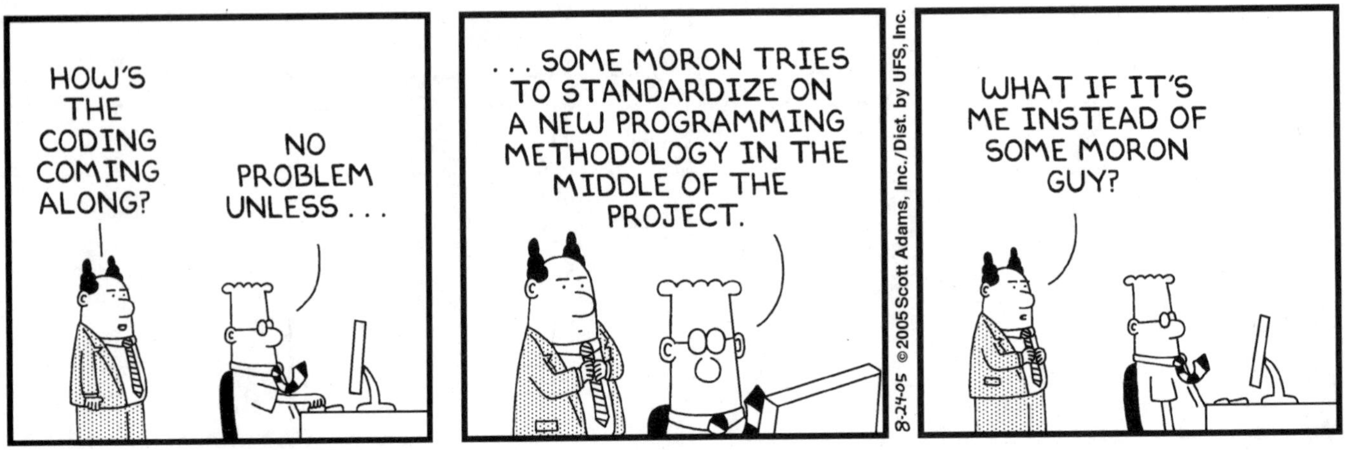
HOW'S THE CODING COMING ALONG?
NO PROBLEM UNLESS . . .
. . . SOME MORON TRIES TO STANDARDIZE ON A NEW PROGRAMMING METHODOLOGY IN THE MIDDLE OF THE PROJECT.
8-24-05 ©2005 Scott Adams, Inc./Dist. by UFS, Inc.
WHAT IF IT'S ME INSTEAD OF SOME MORON GUY?

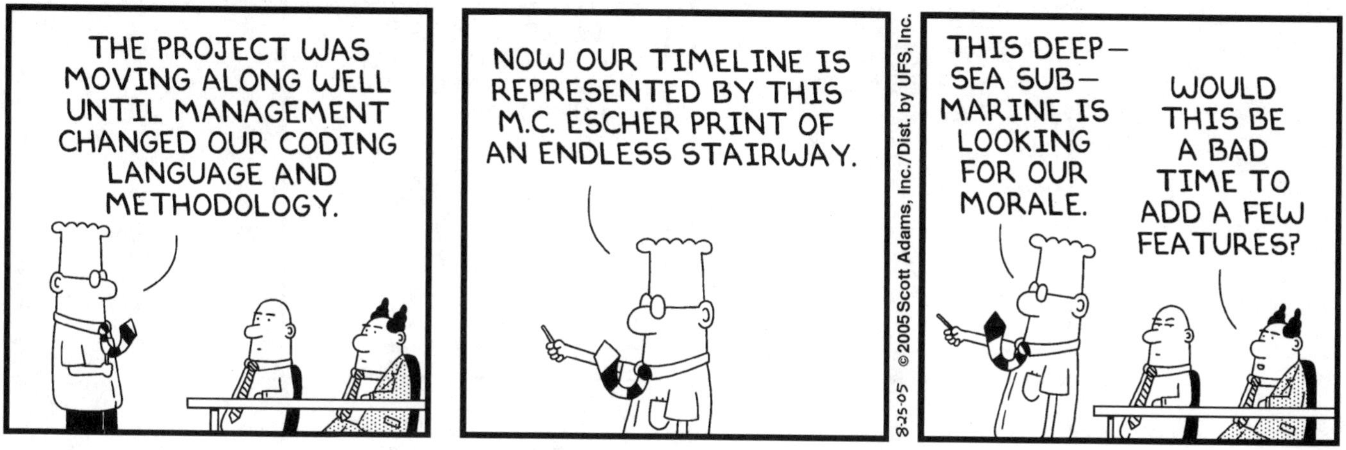
THE PROJECT WAS MOVING ALONG WELL UNTIL MANAGEMENT CHANGED OUR CODING LANGUAGE AND METHODOLOGY.
NOW OUR TIMELINE IS REPRESENTED BY THIS M.C. ESCHER PRINT OF AN ENDLESS STAIRWAY.
8-25-05 © 2005 Scott Adams, Inc./Dist. by UFS, Inc.
THIS DEEP-SEA SUB-MARINE IS LOOKING FOR OUR MORALE.
WOULD THIS BE A BAD TIME TO ADD A FEW FEATURES?

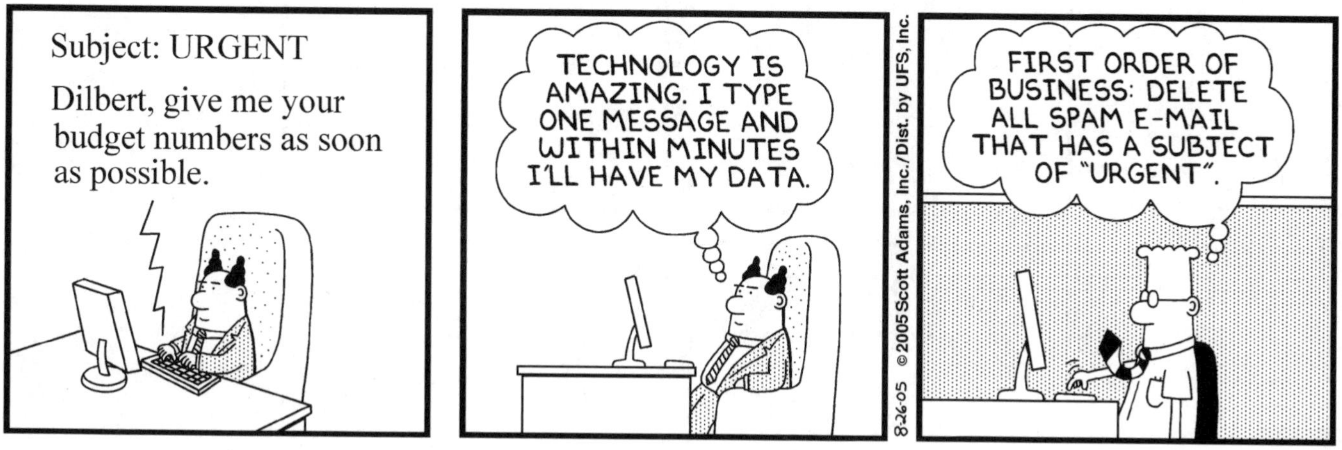
Subject: URGENT
Dilbert, give me your budget numbers as soon as possible.
TECHNOLOGY IS AMAZING. I TYPE ONE MESSAGE AND WITHIN MINUTES I'LL HAVE MY DATA.
8-26-05 © 2005 Scott Adams, Inc./Dist. by UFS, Inc.
FIRST ORDER OF BUSINESS: DELETE ALL SPAM E-MAIL THAT HAS A SUBJECT OF "URGENT".

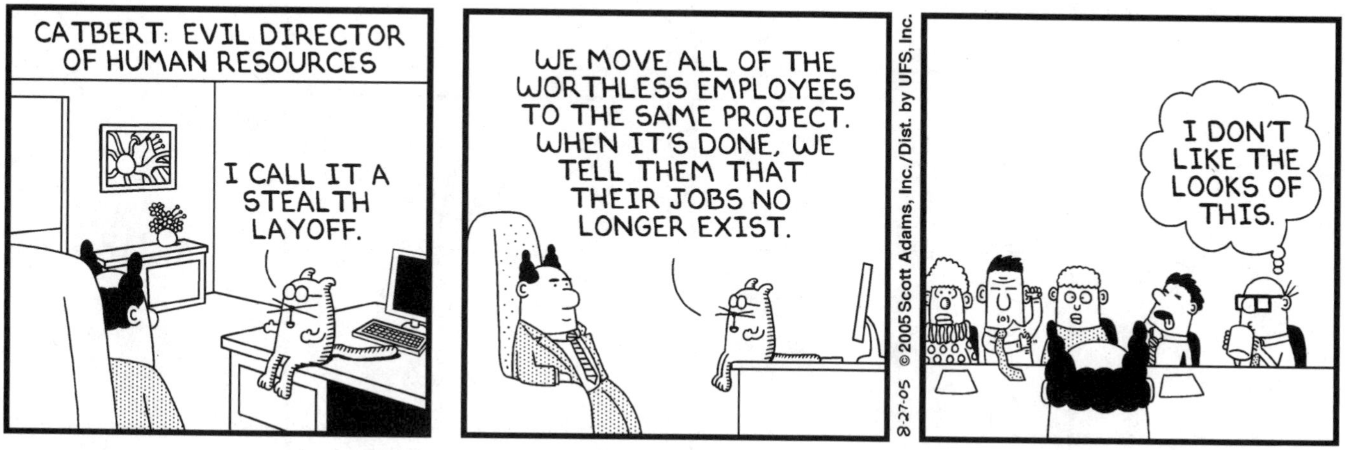
CATBERT: EVIL DIRECTOR OF HUMAN RESOURCES
I CALL IT A STEALTH LAYOFF.
WE MOVE ALL OF THE WORTHLESS EMPLOYEES TO THE SAME PROJECT. WHEN IT'S DONE, WE TELL THEM THAT THEIR JOBS NO LONGER EXIST.
8-27-05 © 2005 Scott Adams, Inc./Dist. by UFS, Inc.
I DON'T LIKE THE LOOKS OF THIS.

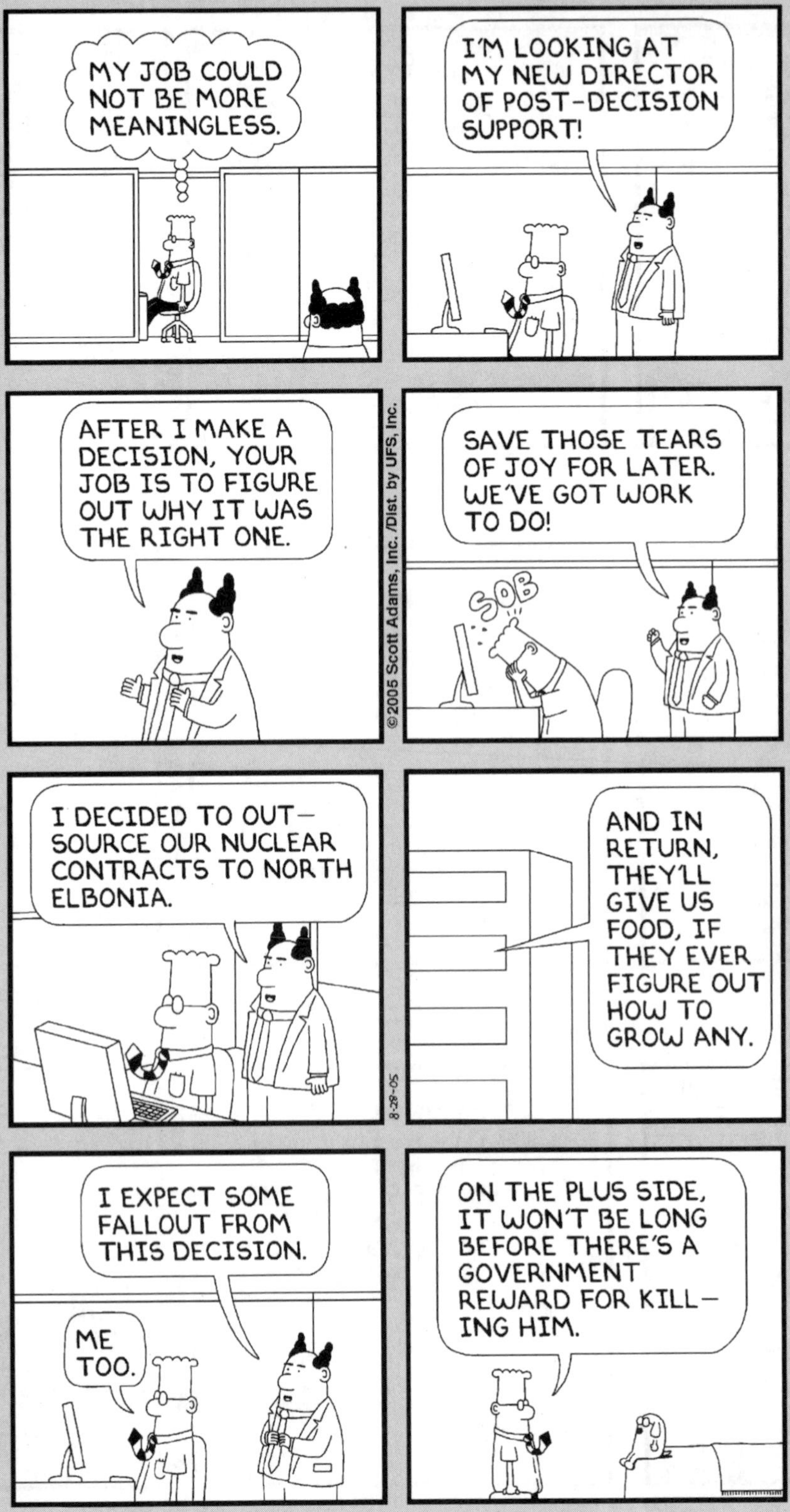
MY JOB COULD NOT BE MORE MEANINGLESS.
I'M LOOKING AT MY NEW DIRECTOR OF POST-DECISION SUPPORT!
AFTER I MAKE A DECISION, YOUR JOB IS TO FIGURE OUT WHY IT WAS THE RIGHT ONE.
SAVE THOSE TEARS OF JOY FOR LATER. WE'VE GOT WORK TO DO!
SOB
I DECIDED TO OUT-SOURCE OUR NUCLEAR CONTRACTS TO NORTH ELBONIA.
AND IN RETURN, THEY'LL GIVE US FOOD, IF THEY EVER FIGURE OUT HOW TO GROW ANY.
I EXPECT SOME FALLOUT FROM THIS DECISION.
ME TOO.
ON THE PLUS SIDE, IT WON'T BE LONG BEFORE THERE'S A GOVERNMENT REWARD FOR KILL-ING HIM.
©2005 Scott Adams, Inc./Dist. by UFS, Inc.
8-28-05

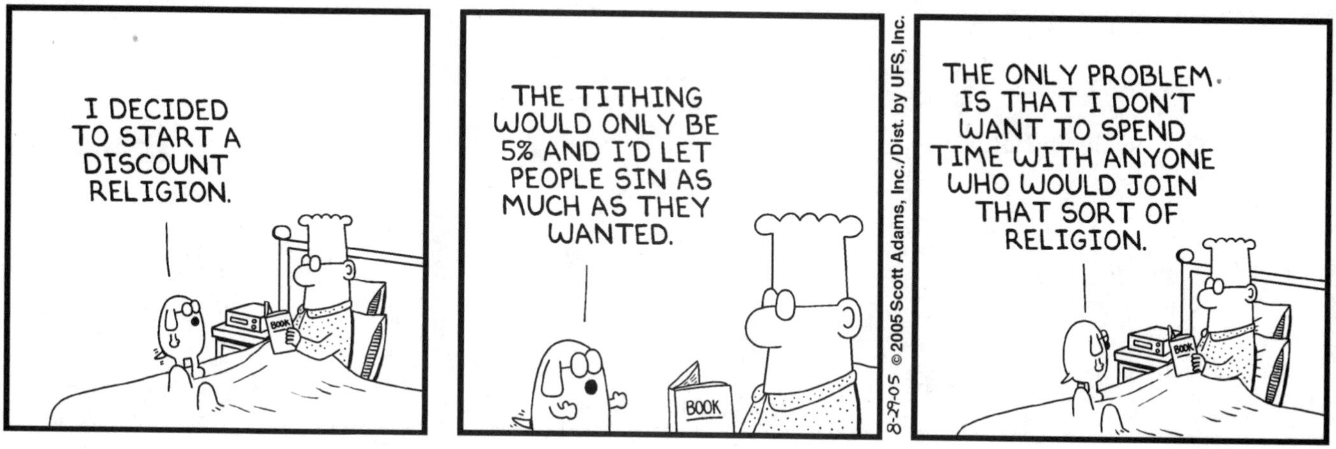
I DECIDED TO START A DISCOUNT RELIGION.
BOOK
THE TITHING WOULD ONLY BE 5% AND I'D LET PEOPLE SIN AS MUCH AS THEY WANTED.
BOOK
8-29-05 © 2005 Scott Adams, Inc./Dist. by UFS, Inc.
THE ONLY PROBLEM IS THAT I DON'T WANT TO SPEND TIME WITH ANYONE WHO WOULD JOIN THAT SORT OF RELIGION.
BOOK

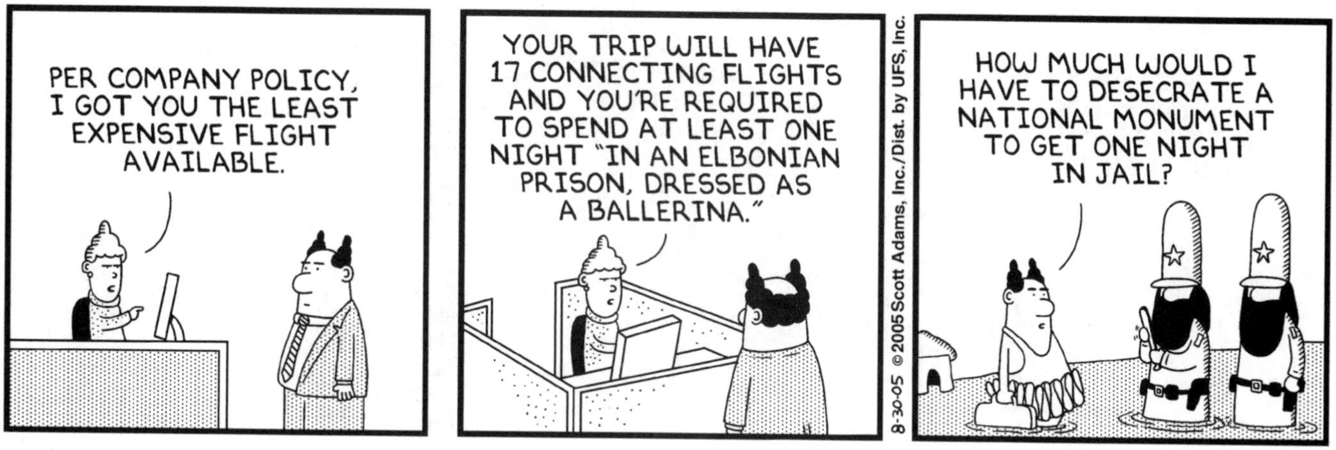
PER COMPANY POLICY, I GOT YOU THE LEAST EXPENSIVE FLIGHT AVAILABLE.
YOUR TRIP WILL HAVE 17 CONNECTING FLIGHTS AND YOU'RE REQUIRED TO SPEND AT LEAST ONE NIGHT "IN AN ELBONIAN PRISON, DRESSED AS A BALLERINA."
8-30-05 © 2005 Scott Adams, Inc./Dist. by UFS, Inc.
HOW MUCH WOULD I HAVE TO DESECRATE A NATIONAL MONUMENT TO GET ONE NIGHT IN JAIL?

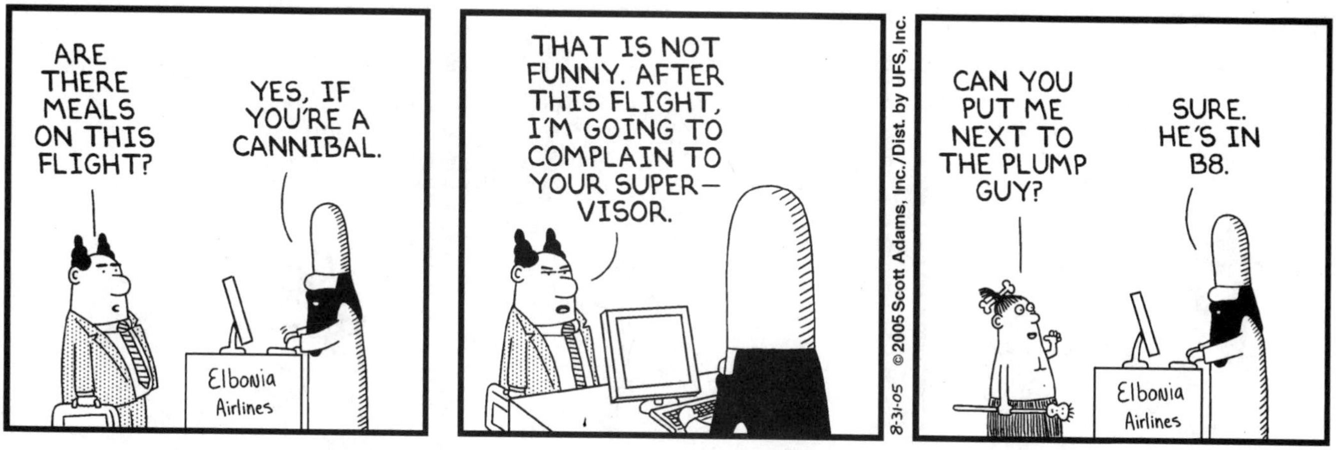
ARE THERE MEALS ON THIS FLIGHT?
YES, IF YOU'RE A CANNIBAL.
Elbonia Airlines
THAT IS NOT FUNNY. AFTER THIS FLIGHT, I'M GOING TO COMPLAIN TO YOUR SUPER-VISOR.
8-31-05 © 2005 Scott Adams, Inc./Dist. by UFS, Inc.
CAN YOU PUT ME NEXT TO THE PLUMP GUY?
SURE. HE'S IN B8.
Elbonia Airlines

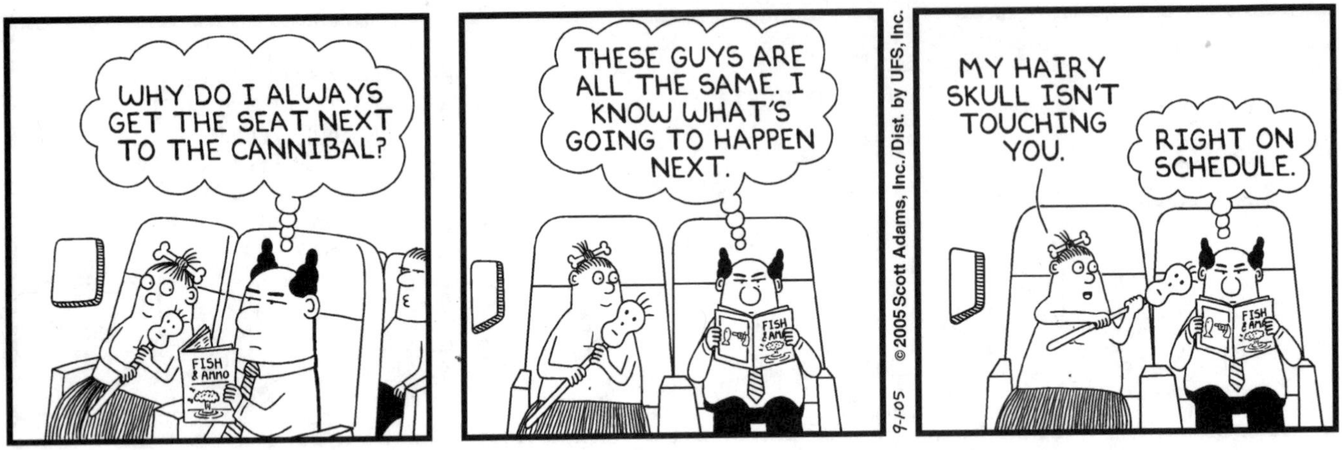
WHY DO I ALWAYS GET THE SEAT NEXT TO THE CANNIBAL?
FISH & AMMO
THESE GUYS ARE ALL THE SAME. I KNOW WHAT'S GOING TO HAPPEN NEXT.
9-1-05 © 2005 Scott Adams, Inc./Dist. by UFS, Inc.
MY HAIRY SKULL ISN'T TOUCHING YOU.
RIGHT ON SCHEDULE.

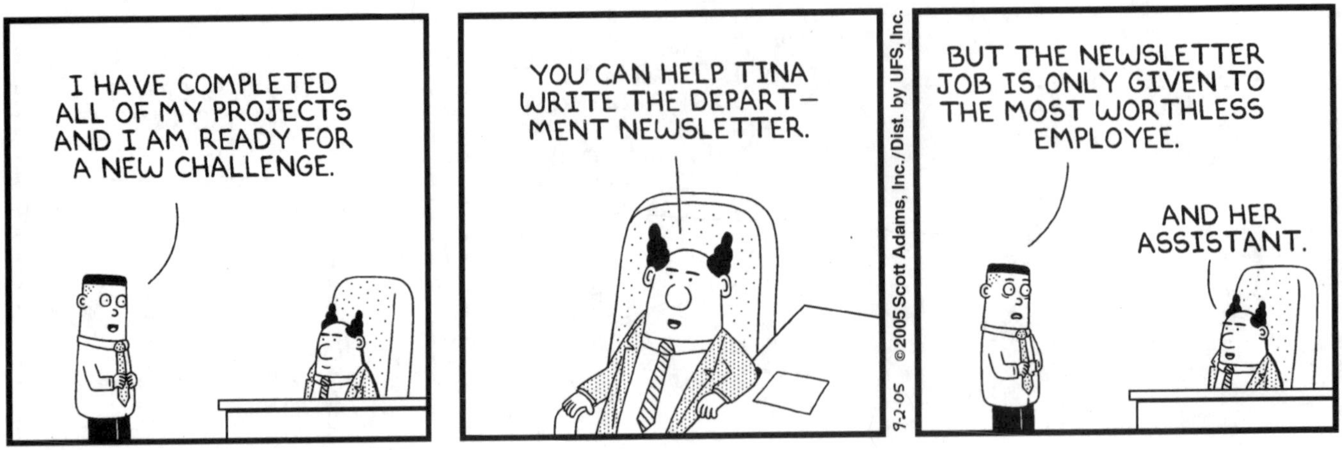
I HAVE COMPLETED ALL OF MY PROJECTS AND I AM READY FOR A NEW CHALLENGE.
YOU CAN HELP TINA WRITE THE DEPART- MENT NEWSLETTER.
9-2-05 © 2005 Scott Adams, Inc./Dist. by UFS, Inc.
BUT THE NEWSLETTER JOB IS ONLY GIVEN TO THE MOST WORTHLESS EMPLOYEE.
AND HER ASSISTANT.

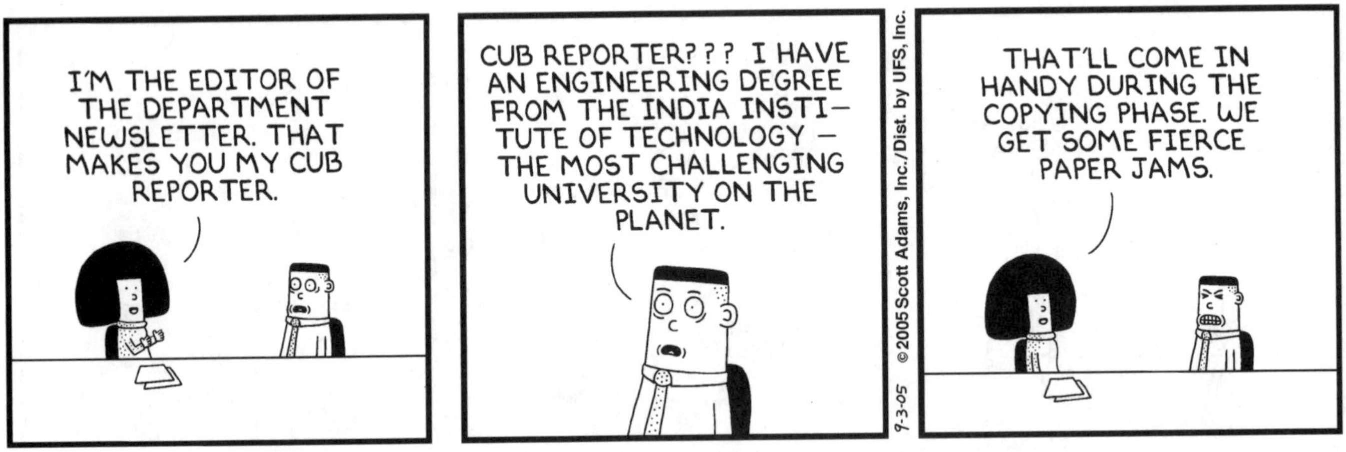
I'M THE EDITOR OF THE DEPARTMENT NEWSLETTER. THAT MAKES YOU MY CUB REPORTER.
CUB REPORTER??? I HAVE AN ENGINEERING DEGREE FROM THE INDIA INSTI- TUTE OF TECHNOLOGY – THE MOST CHALLENGING UNIVERSITY ON THE PLANET.
9-3-05 © 2005 Scott Adams, Inc./Dist. by UFS, Inc.
THAT'LL COME IN HANDY DURING THE COPYING PHASE. WE GET SOME FIERCE PAPER JAMS.

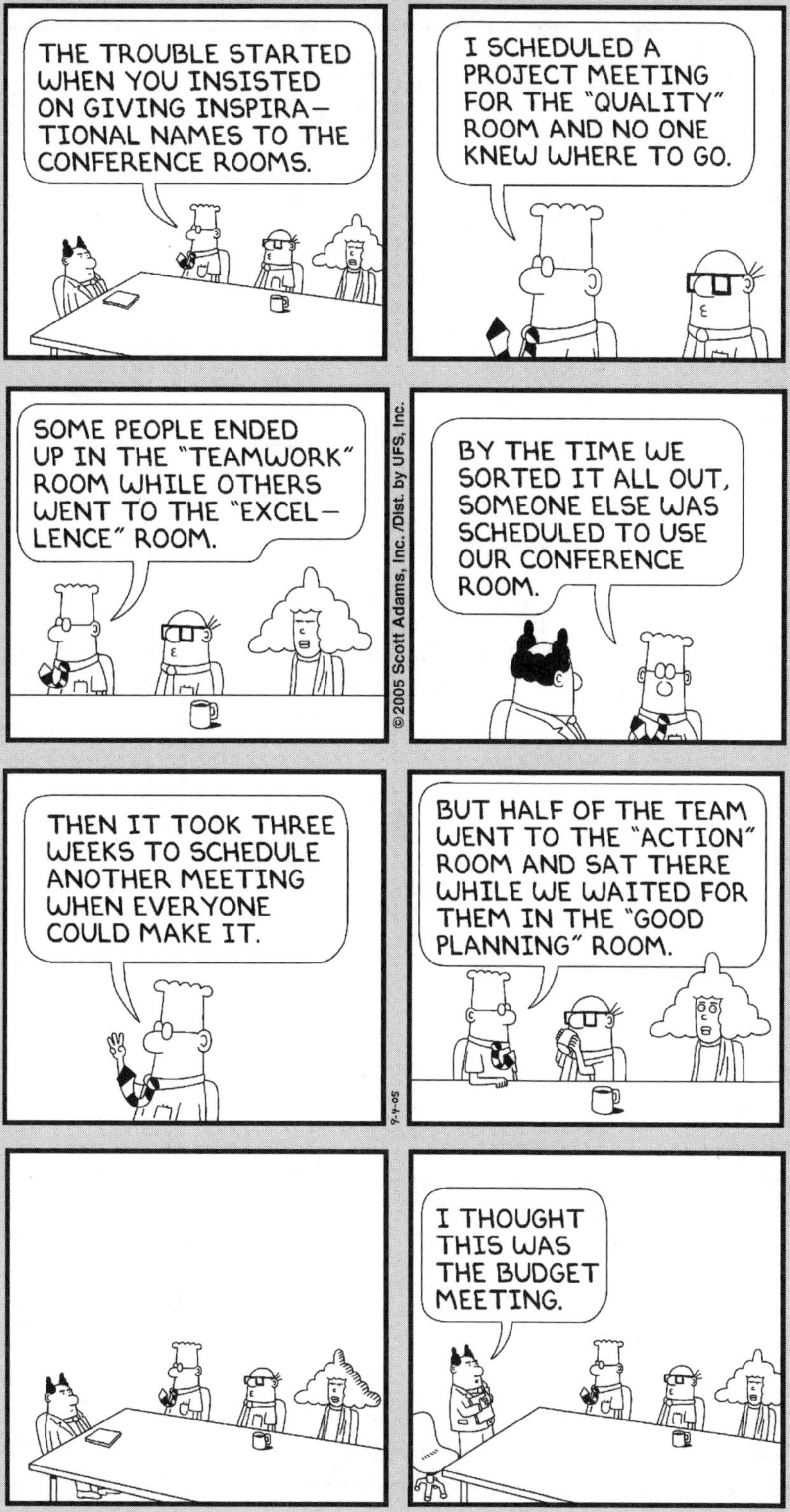
THE TROUBLE STARTED WHEN YOU INSISTED ON GIVING INSPIRA-TIONAL NAMES TO THE CONFERENCE ROOMS.
I SCHEDULED A PROJECT MEETING FOR THE "QUALITY" ROOM AND NO ONE KNEW WHERE TO GO.
SOME PEOPLE ENDED UP IN THE "TEAMWORK" ROOM WHILE OTHERS WENT TO THE "EXCEL-LENCE" ROOM.
BY THE TIME WE SORTED IT ALL OUT, SOMEONE ELSE WAS SCHEDULED TO USE OUR CONFERENCE ROOM.
THEN IT TOOK THREE WEEKS TO SCHEDULE ANOTHER MEETING WHEN EVERYONE COULD MAKE IT.
BUT HALF OF THE TEAM WENT TO THE "ACTION" ROOM AND SAT THERE WHILE WE WAITED FOR THEM IN THE "GOOD PLANNING" ROOM.
I THOUGHT THIS WAS THE BUDGET MEETING.
9-4-05

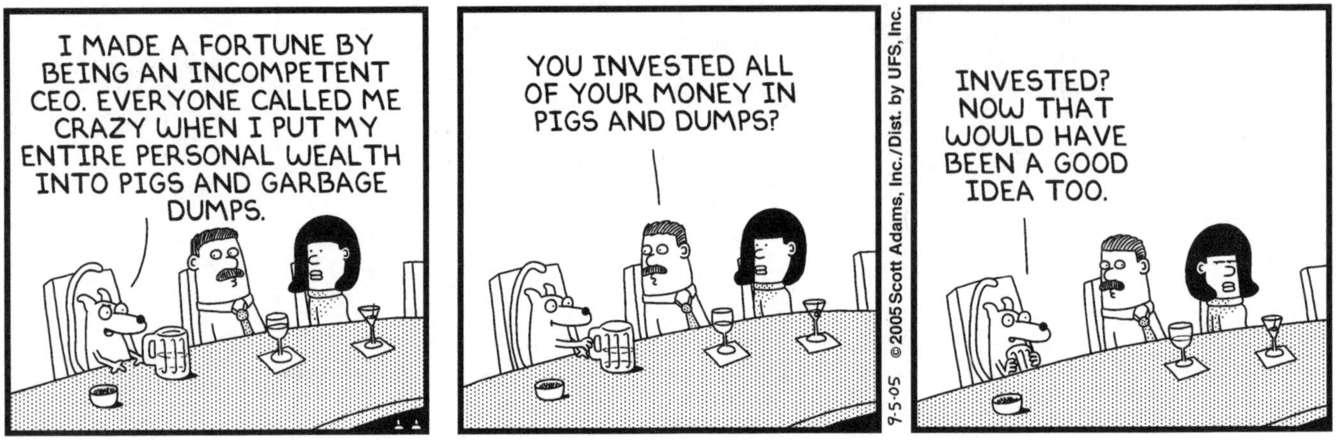
I MADE A FORTUNE BY BEING AN INCOMPETENT CEO. EVERYONE CALLED ME CRAZY WHEN I PUT MY ENTIRE PERSONAL WEALTH INTO PIGS AND GARBAGE DUMPS.
YOU INVESTED ALL OF YOUR MONEY IN PIGS AND DUMPS?
INVESTED? NOW THAT WOULD HAVE BEEN A GOOD IDEA TOO.
9-5-05 © 2005 Scott Adams, Inc./Dist. by UFS, Inc.

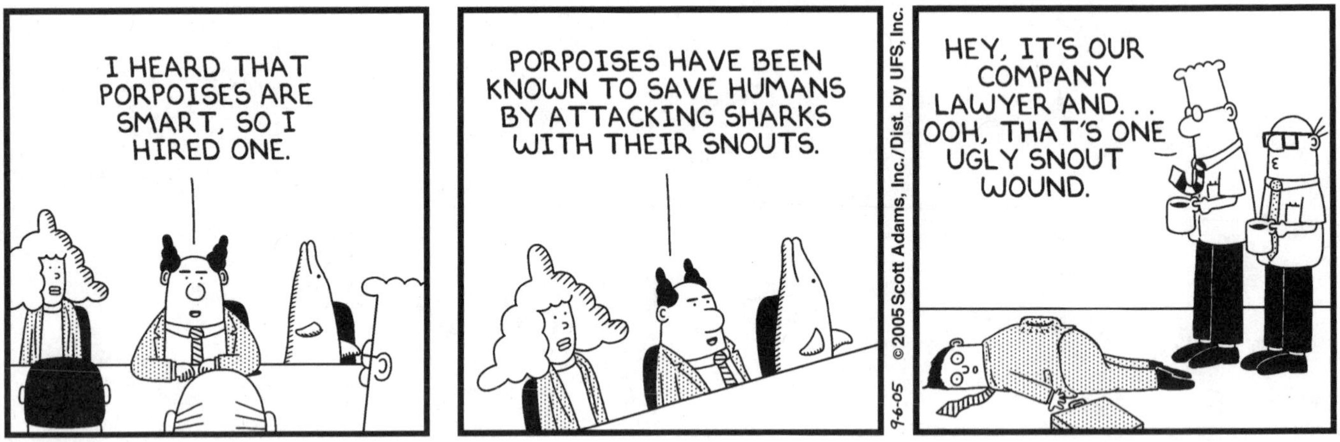
I HEARD THAT PORPOISES ARE SMART, SO I HIRED ONE.
PORPOISES HAVE BEEN KNOWN TO SAVE HUMANS BY ATTACKING SHARKS WITH THEIR SNOUTS.
HEY, IT'S OUR COMPANY LAWYER AND. . . OOH, THAT'S ONE UGLY SNOUT WOUND.
9-6-05 © 2005 Scott Adams, Inc./Dist. by UFS, Inc.

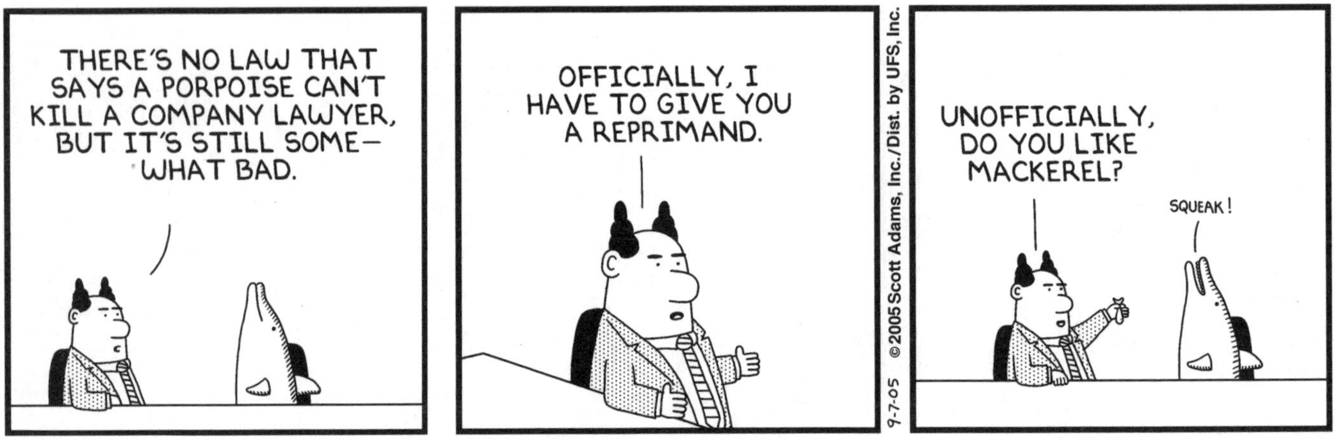
THERE'S NO LAW THAT SAYS A PORPOISE CAN'T KILL A COMPANY LAWYER, BUT IT'S STILL SOME-WHAT BAD.
OFFICIALLY, I HAVE TO GIVE YOU A REPRIMAND.
UNOFFICIALLY, DO YOU LIKE MACKEREL?
SQUEAK!
9-7-05 © 2005 Scott Adams, Inc./Dist. by UFS, Inc.

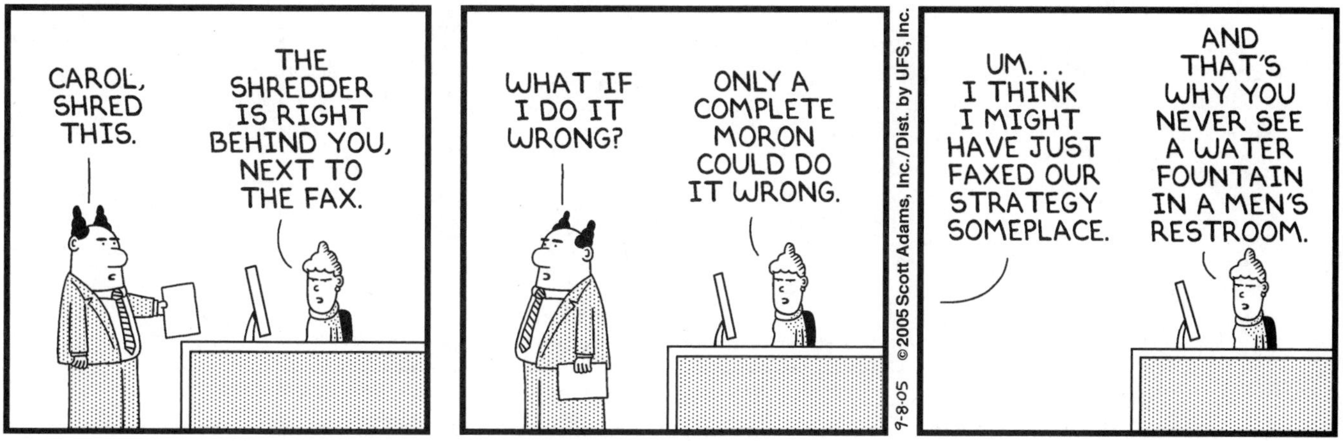
CAROL, SHRED THIS.
THE SHREDDER IS RIGHT BEHIND YOU, NEXT TO THE FAX.
WHAT IF I DO IT WRONG?
ONLY A COMPLETE MORON COULD DO IT WRONG.
9-8-05 ©2005 Scott Adams, Inc./Dist. by UFS, Inc.
UM. . . I THINK I MIGHT HAVE JUST FAXED OUR STRATEGY SOMEPLACE.
AND THAT'S WHY YOU NEVER SEE A WATER FOUNTAIN IN A MEN'S RESTROOM.

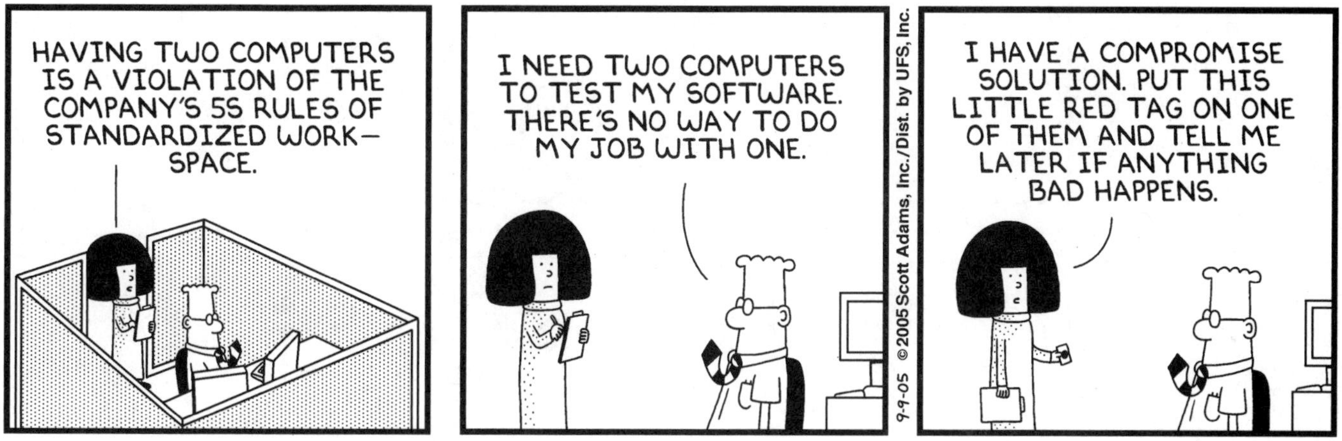
HAVING TWO COMPUTERS IS A VIOLATION OF THE COMPANY'S 5S RULES OF STANDARDIZED WORK-SPACE.
I NEED TWO COMPUTERS TO TEST MY SOFTWARE. THERE'S NO WAY TO DO MY JOB WITH ONE.
9-9-05 ©2005 Scott Adams, Inc./Dist. by UFS, Inc.
I HAVE A COMPROMISE SOLUTION. PUT THIS LITTLE RED TAG ON ONE OF THEM AND TELL ME LATER IF ANYTHING BAD HAPPENS.

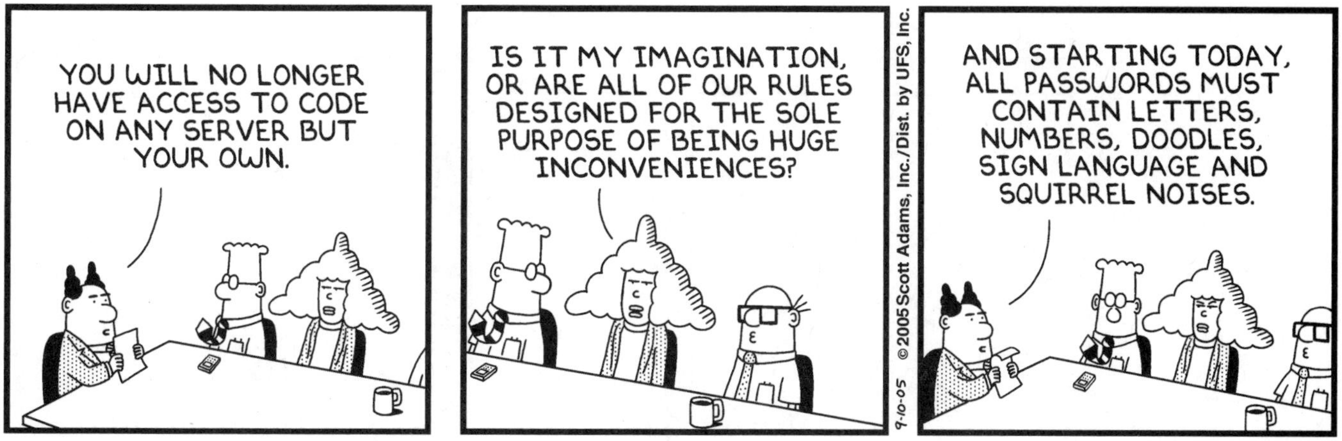
YOU WILL NO LONGER HAVE ACCESS TO CODE ON ANY SERVER BUT YOUR OWN.
IS IT MY IMAGINATION, OR ARE ALL OF OUR RULES DESIGNED FOR THE SOLE PURPOSE OF BEING HUGE INCONVENIENCES?
9-10-05 ©2005 Scott Adams, Inc./Dist. by UFS, Inc.
AND STARTING TODAY, ALL PASSWORDS MUST CONTAIN LETTERS, NUMBERS, DOODLES, SIGN LANGUAGE AND SQUIRREL NOISES.

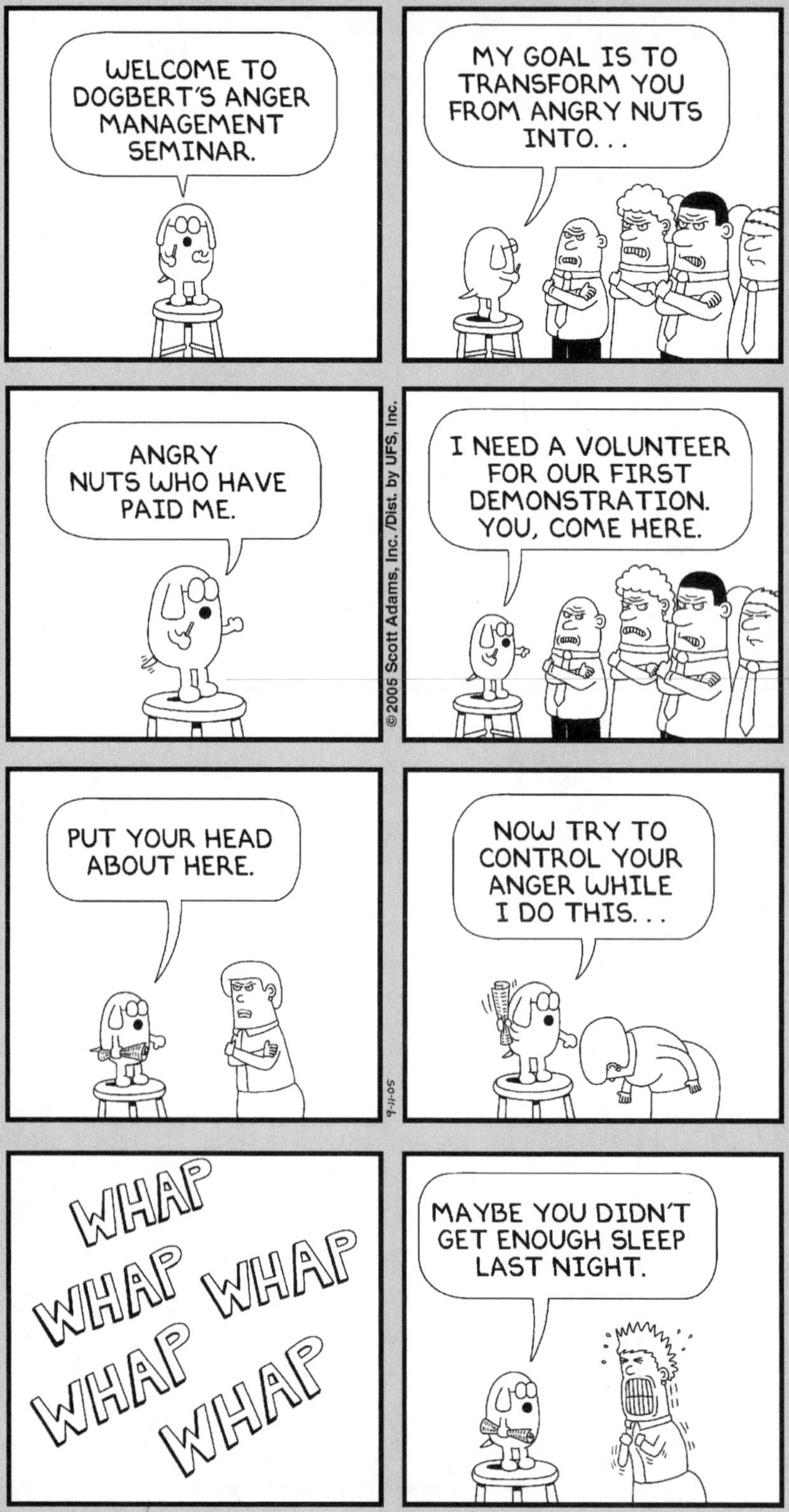
WELCOME TO DOGBERT'S ANGER MANAGEMENT SEMINAR.
MY GOAL IS TO TRANSFORM YOU FROM ANGRY NUTS INTO. . .
ANGRY NUTS WHO HAVE PAID ME.
I NEED A VOLUNTEER FOR OUR FIRST DEMONSTRATION. YOU, COME HERE.
PUT YOUR HEAD ABOUT HERE.
NOW TRY TO CONTROL YOUR ANGER WHILE I DO THIS. . .
WHAP WHAP WHAP WHAP WHAP
MAYBE YOU DIDN'T GET ENOUGH SLEEP LAST NIGHT.
9-11-05